TOPICS IN EXPERT SYSTEM DESIGN
Methodologies and Tools

STUDIES IN COMPUTER SCIENCE AND ARTIFICIAL INTELLIGENCE

5

NORTH-HOLLAND – AMSTERDAM • NEW YORK • OXFORD • TOKYO

TOPICS IN EXPERT SYSTEM DESIGN

Methodologies and Tools

edited by

Giovanni GUIDA
Carlo TASSO

Department of Mathematics
and Computer Science
University of Udine
Italy

N·H
P C

1989

NORTH-HOLLAND – AMSTERDAM • NEW YORK • OXFORD • TOKYO

ISBN: 0 444 87321 x

Publishers:

ELSEVIER SCIENCE PUBLISHERS B.V.
P.O. BOX 103
1000 AC AMSTERDAM
THE NETHERLANDS

Sole distributors for the U.S.A. and Canada:

ELSEVIER SCIENCE PUBLISHING COMPANY, INC.
655 AVENUE OF THE AMERICAS
NEW YORK, N.Y. 10010
U.S.A.

PRINTED IN THE NETHERLANDS

PREFACE

Expert systems have been, in the last decade, one of the most successful achievements of artificial intelligence research. The potential of this novel technology in developing innovative and challenging computer applications has been early realized by managers, technicians and users. Expert systems have in fact disclosed a new perspective on information processing, where the computer is considered not only as a tool to store information or to execute complex computations, but also as an intelligent aid to the human problem solving activity capable of contributing to high-level intellectual tasks such as decision making, planning, design, control, supervision, diagnosis, etc. These expectations have pushed the development of a number of projects devoted to experiment expert system technology in real-size applications of concrete interest in industry and business. Several of these projects have been very successful and have demonstrated the technical feasibility and the potential benefits of expert systems in a large number of application domains.

However, the establishment of expert system technology and its actual industrial impact are nowadays limited by the lack of a sound, general and reliable design and construction methodology. In fact, the development of expert systems does not follow the practice and methodologies established in the area of software engineering: expert system development is different from traditional software production and deserves specific methods, techniques and tools. Building expert systems still relies today on empirical approaches and it is more like handicraft than engineering. Methodologies and tools on which system designers and knowledge engineers can effectively rely in their job are widely recognized as a primary need for the progress of this emerging technology and its development towards a definitely viable and sound engineering practice.

The above issues led us to promote an International Summer School on "Expert System Design - Methodologies and Tools" held at CISM (International Center for Mechanical Sciences, Udine, Italy) during September 1986. The school turned out to be very successful, with many participants coming from several. countries, and confirmed the very high interest for the topic. For us, it has been a stimulating occasion for discussing several design issues with colleagues and leading experts in the filed. As an outcome of that event, it became apparent to us the need to stimulate a larger debate on the topic of expert system design and construction. Therefore, we decided to start the enterprise of editing a contributed volume, bringing together papers of outstanding researchers with concrete experience in the field.

The purpose of this book is twofold. From a concrete and focused point of view, it is devoted to provide actual indications and tools to expert system designers who like to keep up to date with the current state-of-the-art in the field. From a broader perspective, it is aimed at promoting basic and applied research on methodologies and tools for expert system development. So, the volume is primarily intended as an advanced tool for scholars and engineers, but it is also adequate as a textbook for a specific course in expert system design.

The main goal of the editorial work has been to collect contributions on the different aspects of expert system design and construction, paying particular attention to the most distinguishing techniques, especially with respect to traditional software engineering. Introductory aspects of expert system technology have been explicitly excluded from the coverage of the book, which therefore requires a good background in artificial intelligence. The book presents a coordinated collection of 16 papers, authored by 28 researchers from Europe and USA, on important and emerging topics in the field of expert system design, focusing both on methodological advances and on practical experience gained in specific application cases. Each paper focuses on one or more aspects of the design activity and includes a survey introduction to the specific topic dealt with, together with an illustration of original proposals and results obtained in research work. The volume is divided into parts, which closely mirror the main phases of the process of expert system building; namely: domain evaluation, design techniques, development tools, knowledge acquisition and modeling, validation and evaluation. Moreover, the first part of the book present an extensive discussion on the concept of expert system life cycle, and the last one a structured and comprehensive bibliography on expert system construction, which can serve as a guide for further reading.

As editors, it is our pleasure to thank all authors who have offered their creativity and valuable time to prepare the contributions for this volume.

Giovanni Guida and Carlo Tasso

CONTENTS

Part 5. Knowledge acquisition and modeling

Part 6. Validation and evaluation

Part 7. Further reading

PART 1

Life cycle

Topics in Expert System Design
G. Guida and C. Tasso (Editors)

BUILDING EXPERT SYSTEMS: FROM LIFE CYCLE TO DEVELOPMENT METHODOLOGY

Giovanni GUIDA and Carlo TASSO

Department of Mathematics and Computer Science
University of Udine
Udine, Italy

1. Introduction

An expert system is a software system which can provide expert problem solving performance in a specific competence domain by exploiting a knowledge base and a reasoning mechanism. Expert system technology has been developing very fast over the last decade and a huge amount of application projects has been started. However, while an impressive and rapidly growing number of expert system demonstrators and prototypes has been produced, the number of real operational applications in industry and business is still quite limited (Waterman, 1986; Buchanan, 1986). In fact, the development of expert systems largely relies today on empirical methods and is not supported by sound and general methodologies. It is more like handicraft than engineering, and it lacks several of the desirable features of an industrial process (reliability, repeatability, work-sharing, cost estimableness, quality assurance, etc.). It is widely recognized, indeed, that the availability of a sound methodology for the design and development of expert systems - possibly supported by suitable tools - could greatly help to overcome some of the major bottlenecks which presently hamper the large-scale application of expert system technology.

In recent years several proposals and research efforts have been reported in the literature, which more or less explicitly refer to the issue of expert system design and development (Guida and Tasso, 1988). However, the results so far obtained are scattered and partial, often lacking effective methodological support or sufficient practical experimentation, so as a clear and widely accepted concept of an expert system building methodology is still not yet available.

The purpose of this paper is to present a coherent framework which can serve as a basis towards the development of a methodology for design and construction of expert systems. The main standpoint in this work is that a methodology for developing expert systems, to be utilized in a real application environment, can not be defined in absolute terms, since it depends on the specific organization and application domain where the expert system is developed. On the contrary, the development process should be organized around a general, environment- and application-independent life cycle concept, whose structure and characteristics capture and take into account the peculiarities of expert system technology. We also claim that the design of a methodology should be based on the concept of life cycle, which, from this perspective, can be considered as the core and invariant part of any development methodology. Therefore, the main concern of the paper is twofold: proposing a life cycle adequate for expert systems and providing indications on how to develop a full methodology out of it.

In particular, the paper is organized as follows: section 2 surveys the main proposals presented in the literature and briefly comments on them. Section 3 discusses motivations and requirements for an expert system life cycle. In section 4 a life cycle for expert systems is proposed and its main features are discussed. Section 5 focuses on the issue of developing from the proposed life cycle a complete methodology for expert system development, and presents some guidelines for this purpose. Finally, section 6 proposes some conclusive remarks and discusses insights and forecasts about the future of methodologies and tools for building expert systems.

2. Literature proposals: a survey

In this section we review some of the most significant proposals that have been made in the literature on the subject of expert system development, outlining advantages and drawbacks of each approach.

The first proposal of a systematic approach to expert system construction appears in the seminal paper of Buchanan, Barstow, Bechtel, Bennett, Clancey, Kulikowski, Mitchell, and Waterman (1983), which derives from the first workshop on expert systems, held in San Diego in 1981. This work can not be considered a full methodology, since the proposed approach is presented only at a high level of abstraction: the development process is divided into stages, each one thoroughly described, but not further decomposed into specific operating activities. Furthermore, the proposal contains only a partial view of the development process, since it is limited only to the three aspects of problem identification, knowledge acquisition, and iterative development of the knowledge base. Moreover, important methodological topics such as project management, documentation, etc. are not mentioned at all. Nevertheless, this work has two evident merits: pointing out in a clear way that the development of expert systems should be inspired to a life cycle approach, and addressing the three most specific technical aspects of the expert system development process.

Also the two later proposals presented in (Harmon and King, 1985) and in (Waterman, 1986) can not again be considered detailed methodologies to be adopted for expert system development, as their level of generality is still rather high and do not define a specific operational practice. Anyhow, they take a larger perspective with respect to the proposal previously discussed, due to the substantial amount of experience made in the meantime (since the San Diego workshop) in practical applications. Harmon and King (1985), describe the process of building an expert system as a sequence of six phases (namely: selection of appropriate problem, development of prototype system, development of complete system, evaluation of system, and integration of system, maintenance) which cover rather completely all the aspects of the development. Each phase includes a specific set of activities to be executed, which are shortly outlined in the proposal. The authors do not describe in detail the activities related to the most specific aspects of expert system technology, but, on the other hand, they mention other important technical and organizational aspects, such as interface design, testing and evaluation, system integration, maintenance, cost/benefit analysis, resource planning, and technology transfer.

Waterman's (1986) work is inspired, especially for its focus on knowledge acquisition tasks, to (Buchanan, Barstow, Bechtel, Bennett, Clancey, Kulikowski, Mitchell, and Waterman, 1983), but it contains three major refinements. First, it provides more detailed criteria for problem analysis, which combine together different analysis perspectives, such as problem identification and system technical and organizational feasibility. Second, some aspects of expert system project management, such as identification and acquisition of the needed resources, organization of the interaction with the expert, temporal planning, user acceptance and system evaluation, are discussed, and their critical role is highlighted. Third, it proposes a clear classification of the stages of the expert system development process, in terms of sophistication and utility, namely: demonstration prototype, research prototype, field prototype, production model, and commercial system.

The three proposals described above can be considered as the milestones of the field, but, in recent years, several other authors have advocated the need for a more structured and systematic approach to expert system construction. Everybody agrees on the fact that the consideration of a development process divided into phases, each one described only at a very high level of abstraction, is not sufficient to guide design and implementation of real applications in a cost-effective way, within time and budget constraints, as it is the case with conventional software systems. These considerations motivate the appearance of specific methodological proposals, experimented in real application environments and partially supported by specific tools. The different proposals, which will be briefly commented upon in the following, are characterized by specific standpoints, scope, completeness, level of detail, specificity, and attention to organizational and managerial problems.

A first observable trend is to follow very closely traditional software engineering approaches. The European Space Agency (ESA) defines, very synthetically, a complete expert system life cycle to be followed in all ESA internal applications (ESA, 1986). For each phase, precise gaols, outputs, tasks, and operational activities are specified. Particular attention is given to project management and documentation: resources (both manpower and software tools) to be used and documents to be produced in each phase are illustrated. On the other hand, the proposal features a low level of specificity, since it does not pay much attention to several technical aspects typical of expert system technology, such as knowledge acquisition, validation, and refinement.

The work done at the National Archives and Records Administration and reported in (De Salvo, Glamm, and Liebowitz, 1987) goes even further in the direction of directly using standard techniques employed in software engineering: in this case, requirement analysis is performed utilizing data flow diagrams and system development is supported by standard structured programming techniques. Quite differently from the large majority of the authors, De Salvo, Glamm, and Liebowitz claim that an explorative approach is not adequate for business applications of expert systems, and according to this, they do not rely, for example, on rapid prototyping. On the other hand, the knowledge acquisition process is based on a systematic use of Clancey's (1984) knowledge level analysis. Little attention is devoted to project management and organization, but the philosophy which inspires the proposal suggests that these problems are approached by means of conventional techniques.

The work of Ebrahimi (1987) presents a systematic structured approach to the definition of a methodology for expert system construction. The level of the illustration is sufficient for effectively supporting the designer and knowledge engineer, however, the proposal concerns only some tasks of the development process, namely system design and knowledge acquisition. Details on validation criteria and organization of the development team are also given. Ebrahimi's work is clearly inspired by software engineering techniques, such as structured design and stepwise refinement.

Other proposals take more systematically into account the peculiarities of expert system technology. The projects carried on at Tektronix (Freiling, Alexander, Messick, Rehfuss, and Shulman, 1985) feature some interesting points along this line. Although restricted to some of the technical tasks and to documentation, the methodology developed appears both specific and effective. In more detail, it is centered around a systematic approach based on the use of semantic grammars for performing and documenting knowledge acquisition, knowledge representation, and prototype implementation. Specific automatic tools, well integrated with the methodology, are capable of supporting designer and knowledge engineer during the execution of the above mentioned activities. The proposal features two evident limitations: it is difficult to use (being based on the use of formal grammars, it requires a lot of training before it can be applied) and it is characterized by a low level of portability (both the grammar and the tools employed have been developed for the electronic troubleshooting domain and are largely domain dependent).

In the frame of the European Strategic Programme for Research and Development in Information Technology (ESPRIT) of the Commission of the European Communities, a specific project is devoted to the topic of expert system development methodology: "A methodology for the development of of knowledge based systems" (Project 1098). The project was started in September 1985 and has a duration of 60 months. It is carried on by Standard Telecommunications & Cables (UK), Polytechnic of the South Bank (UK), Scicon (UK), SCS (D), and the University of Amsterdam (NL), and it is specifically devoted to define a methodology, called KADS, to be utilized for expert system development (Breuker, Wielinga, and Hayward, 1986). The proposal appears, at the current moment, as the most engineered and tool-oriented one: it refers to a complete life cycle model and decomposes each phase into tasks and specific operative activities. Moreover, it is supported by automatic, general-purpose tools, devoted to specific aspects of expert system development, such as knowledge modeling, analysis, acquisition and documentation. KADS is not committed to any application domain neither to specific implementation techniques. The methodology is not yet completed since it covers only the initial phases of the life cycle and it does not deal with problem management aspects. Experimental work with KADS in several domains has proved its suitability even for rather inexperienced knowledge engineers.

In almost all the proposal presented so far, only limited attention, if any, has been given to another fundamental aspect of the development process, i.e. the issue of expert system project management. Although many authors recognize the need to approach expert system development also from this perspective, only a few works are specifically devoted to this topics. The very complete and extensive guide developed at Digital Equipment Corporation (DEC) illustrates a methodology consisting of precise guidelines that should be followed for managing the planning, design, and implementation of expert system applications (Wilkerson, 1985). It covers in detail all the stages of the development process from three points of view, namely: business/strategic, technical, and human resource/organizational. The guide does not contain any technical illustration of specific activities, such as knowledge acquisition or prototype implementation. Being the result of corporate projects carried on at DEC before 1985, the proposal is hardly transferable in a direct way outside DEC, but, nevertheless, it surely represents a good example of how a large organization can approach the management of expert system projects.

Also the two papers (Sargeant and Jardine, 1987) and (Cupello and Mishelevich,1988) specifically address the topic of managing expert system projects. Compared to DEC's methodology, however, they are far less systematic and structured, and they feature a much lower level of detail, and they can be considered only as survey accounts exploring some issues such as training, staffing, budgeting, scheduling, corporate politics, problem selection, and technology transfer.

Another topic pointed out by some authors and considered important for the successful application of expert systems is technology transfer. The scenario of literature proposals on this specific aspect appears fragmentary and heterogeneous since neither comprehensive work nor thorough analysis have been published on the subject. Some authors (Smith, 1984; Shri, Prerau, Lemmon, Gunderson, and Reinke, 1985) discuss the reasons that make expert system (and, more generally, artificial intelligence) technology transfer different from traditional technology transfer. As major motivation, they indicate the peculiarities of this new and unproved technology and its potential impacts on management, technical staff, and end users. Other problems of the application of artificial intelligence technology in industrial environment are the shortage of experienced professionals, and the use of design techniques not mastered by traditional software engineers, such as knowledge acquisition and rapid prototyping.

Polit (1985) describes DEC's experience in AI technology transfer. He emphasizes the critical role of training, aimed at teaching expert system design skills and at preparing personnell for maintaining an expert system in operation. He presents some specific training program, and, more generally, he discusses the role of liaison programs with academic environments, devoted to actual system development or to training.

Shri, Prerau, Lemmon, Gunderson, and Reinke (1985) illustrate motivations and peculiarities of expert system technology transfer and deal with the problem of moving the new expert system technology from a corporate research laboratory to the operating departments. They highlight the importance of defining, before actual transfer takes place, an action plan aimed at a smooth transition towards an application-oriented development.

Hazeltine (1987) shortly describes the experience developed at NCR Corporation with the specific problem of transferring expert system technology from researchers to developers and from developers to end users.

3. Expert system life cycle: motivations and requirements

This section is devoted to discuss two main points: why a life cycle for expert systems and, what should the concept of life cycle for an expert system be. To both these questions we will propose an answer that will serve as a background for the topics dealt with in the following sections.

In very general terms, a life cycle is associated to any industrial product, be it a mechanical part or a piece of software. By the term life cycle it is generally understood a way of organizing and distributing over the time the different activities needed to design, construct and maintain an artifact. The purpose of a life cycle is to allow the production process to be carried out in a rational, disciplined, effective, efficient, controlled, and uniform way, going beyond the peculiarities of individual skill and proficiency, ensuring high productive and qualitative standards specially in a large and varied production environment, and limiting possible risks. The definition of a life cycle is therefore a key point in the progress from craftsmanship to engineering. We claim that the specific case of expert systems is no exception to this general situation: if we aim at developing a full methodology for expert system design and construction we first must identify an appropriate life cycle which can serve as a reference and support.

Since the concept of life cycle is considered, in our approach, the basis for the development of a methodology, it seems appropriate, before we enter a more technical discussion, to analyze the concept of expert system development methodology and to identify a suitable set of requirements for it. We assume here the following definition for the term methodology: a methodology is an integrated set of methods (procedures) for carrying out a practical task, and of the rules needed for correctly and effectively applying them. An industrial methodology for expert system development should be designed to satisfy two sets of requirements. The first set is made up of general engineering requirements common to several technology fields (information system design and software production have been specifically taken into account) and deriving from the need of ensuring effectiveness, efficiency, quality, controllability and predictability of the production process. We assume here the following set of general engineering requirements to be taken into account for an expert system development methodology:

- It should be structured and modular, i.e. it should support as far as possible (hierarchical) work decomposition into elementary components.
- It should be complete, i.e., it should support the designer in all aspects and phases of expert system development process, from early problem analysis to maintenance, and it should offer both technical support, and project management features.
- It should be effective, i.e. it should support easy planning and control of project development for what concerns activities, resources, results and time.
- It should be efficient, i.e. easy to apply without a sensible overhead for the project.
- It should be practical, i.e. easy to teach, transfer, and use in a large variety of different contexts.
- It should be flexible, i.e. easily adaptable to projects of different size and complexity.

The second set of requirements is strictly specific to expert systems and derives from the need of taking into account the peculiar characteristics of expert system technology. We have identified the following set of specific requirements:

- It should be explorative, i.e. it should allow both system specification and design to proceed incrementally, experimenting alternative problem solving approaches. This implies a development paradigm based on the iteration of experiments, analysis of data, modeling, and validation.
- It should be focused, i.e. specially emphasizing those tasks which are typical of expert system development (domain and problem analysis,

knowledge modeling and acquisition, knowledge base verification and refinement, etc.);
- It should be open, i.e. it should support the use and integration of existing techniques and tools aimed at specific aspects or phases of the expert system development process (e.g., knowledge acquisition tools, project management tools, knowledge base verification and refinement techniques, etc.) and promote the development of new ones.

Turning now to the core problem of designing a life cycle for expert systems, the analysis of the current practice in expert system development can allow identification of a set of currently unsolved needs and exigencies, which motivate the main characteristics of our life cycle definition. These are shortly described below:
- In expert system development decisions about project feasibility and appropriateness of the technology are much more complex and critical than in a traditional software engineering environment. Thus, a clear separation between the preliminary study, devoted to problem identification and analysis, and the proper design and construction task is required.
- In current expert system development practice various definitions of the concepts of demonstrator, prototype, and target system and of the relationships among them can be found. Thus, a clear definition of such concepts and relationships is required.
- The main activities in the design of an expert system have usually been knowledge analysis, modeling and acquisition and knowledge base construction. Therefore, these activities deserve specific attention and a clear definition of their relationships to the life cycle is required.
- In expert system development validation and evaluation of the final target system, integration, user training and maintenance procedures are key points for the success of a project.
- In expert system development, evolutive and explorative design paradigms based on iterative refinement and step-wise design and construction have been proved particularly suitable to exploit the peculiar characteristics of the technology. A disciplined, structured approach is however also much needed specially for the development of large projects.
- Due to the limited practice and experience available in the area of expert system design, projects, specially those of large dimensions, are particularly difficult to plan and control during their development. The need for tools which can support effective planning and control of project advancements is widely recognized as a major exigency for an industrial applicability of expert system technology.

As an expert system is a kind of software product, it is natural that the first step towards the goal of proposing a life cycle for expert systems coping with the above listed needs and requirements is to explore whether the results obtained in the field of software engineering (Boehm, 1981; Myers, 1976; Yourdon and Constantine, 1978) can be transferred, to some extent, to the new area of expert system technology. However, while software engineering and expert system development methodology share some general goals such as project planning and monitoring, quality assurance, production standards, etc., they are based on essentially different standpoints. In fact, the key concepts underlying software engineering approaches are:

- Clear separation between requirements analysis and system design, assuming that it is possible to define in advance complete and correct system specification.
- Abstraction, step-wise refinement and modularization as the main techniques to cope with project complexity.
- Existence of several methods and techniques derived from a long practical experience in developing projects.
- View of computer systems as algorithms executors; software development is, thus, centered around the specification of how to let computers do what is stated in the requirements, favoring in such a way procedural, imperative programming.

Expert system technology is not a unitary discipline (as programming, largely speaking, is): in fact, it is actually the result of integration of several heterogeneous techniques which share however the following key concepts:

- A complete set of requirements for an expert system can not be stated in advance, since the problems usually approached are not algorithmic and the expected behaviors of the expert system are very numerous and it is not easy to exhaustively enumerate them in advance. This implies that it is impossible to fully separate requirement analysis from the other design issues. As a result, explorative programming, experimentation and extensive repeated prototyping become fundamental attitudes in expert system development which can not be completely discarded without sacrificing the very peculiar characteristics of expert system technology.
- It is hard to identify in an expert system the fundamental system components (the modules, in traditional software systems) which are the elementary objects of design and development activities: in complex systems even the conventional distinction between knowledge base and inference engine becomes fuzzy.
- Concrete experience with the design and development of real-size projects is still limited.
- View of computer systems as problem solvers; software products development is, thus, centered around the identification of what knowledge is needed to achieve a given behavior, favouring in such a way a declarative style of programming.

The features listed above show that expert systems are substantially different from traditional software systems and motivate the difficulty of directly adapting the traditional concept of software life cycle to expert system development. What need to be done consists in designing a novel life cycle explicitly oriented to expert system technology, in order to achieve the same desirable goals that proved so useful in the domain of conventional software.

4. A life cycle for expert systems

This section is devoted to illustrate the concept of expert system life cycle. As it has been already mentioned above, this represents a fundamental step towards the development of a full methodology. In fact, the concept of life cycle provides a basic framework around which the activities prescribed by a methodology can be organized. The design of a life cycle requires to take some fundamental decisions and to make them explicit through appropriate definitions, namely:

- Identification of a suitable decomposition of the production process into components, possibly at several levels of detail and abstraction.
- Precise definition of each component in terms of goals, and inputs and outputs, and activities involved.
- Definition of the logical relationships between components (precedences, preconditions, constraints, options, etc.).
- Definition of the temporal relationships between components (execution sequence, possible parallelisms, loops, entry and exit points, etc.).

Taking into account the requirements for an expert system life cycle stated in the previous section, we propose a life cycle concept with a typical waterfall structure. It comprises five phases, each one characterized by precise goals to be achieved and clear relationships with the other phases. Each phase is subdivided into a number of specific tasks, each one devoted to achieve a precise subgoal. Tasks can be can be performed by executing specific activities, which define at greater level of detail what to do and how.

In the following we will illustrate our life cycle proposal focusing on the level of phases, illustrating their goals, their role within the global development process, and their technical content. The detailed description of tasks and activities is not considered here, since it pertains more to the definition of a full development methodology, as it will be discussed in section 5. Moreover, the illustration of the proposed life cycle takes into account only technical activities and does not deal with such aspects as planning, project management, documentation, etc., that again will be approached in section 5.

The five phases of our life cycle are:

Phase 1 - Plausibility study
Phase 2 - Demonstration prototype construction
Phase 3 - Full prototype construction
Phase 4 - Target system implementation and installation
Phase 5 - Operation, maintenance, and extension.

The identification of the five phases listed above is the result of a comparative analysis of the numerous alternatives resulting from literature and professional practice. The proposed solution takes the requirements for the life cycle stated above specifically into account, and aims at maximizing the separation and independence between phases and their internal strength and level of aggregation.

Before describing each individual phase in detail, it is worth noting that before starting specific expert system projects in a given organization, it is generally appropriate to develop a preliminary, broad spectrum investigation, called opportunity analysis. This phase is devoted to identify, within a given application organization, the application areas which could benefit from the development of expert system projects, and to rank them according to their strategic value, tactic importance, expected benefits, technical complexity, suitability and readiness for expert system application, involved risk, logical and temporal precedence, etc. The result of this explorative activity provides a coarse reference framework which serves as a long-range master plan to guide the global effort in the area of expert system technology at corporate level. When a specific expert system project is initiated, the master plan is used to suggest the most appropriate application area to focus on, and thus it provides useful inputs to the first phase of the life cycle.

Each phase of the life cycle is defined and illustrated in detail in the following.

Phase 1 - Plausibility study

Phase 1 comprises three main goals:
- analyzing a given application area, identifying a promising domain, and selecting the specific problem to face;
- identifying the main functional and technical specifications of the expert system and assessing the plausibility of the application;
- taking the first technical decisions, developing a draft system design, and preparing a draft project plan.

The output of this phase is a technical document, called plausibility report, which illustrates the activities done and the obtained results, suggests choices and decisions about the expert system project, supporting them with appropriate motivations, and proposes a draft system design and project plan.

Phase 1 takes in input the results of the opportunity analysis and starts with the study of the selected problem area, focusing on a specific domain. This is centered on a preliminary knowledge acquisition activity, which aims at eliciting the types and size of knowledge involved in the application considered. Once the main features of problem domain have been precisely identified, its adequacy to expert system technology is verified. A precise identification of the problem to be tackled is then performed, the overall long-range goals of the project are formulated, and the main functional and technical specifications of the expert system to be developed are stated. Validation and (functional and technical) acceptance criteria are defined as well. A draft system design focusing on the major technical choices about architecture, knowledge representation methods and reasoning mechanisms is proposed, which serves as a basis for developing a draft project plan.

Plausibility, which is the main concern of Phase 1, comprises the following five main aspects:
- technical feasibility of the expert system application, taking into account the specific characteristics of the domain and problem

considered and the current state of the art in expert system technology;
- organizational impact, with reference both to the organizational interventions needed to prepare the insertion of the expert system in its target operational site and to the expected organizational transformations induced by the expert system in the operating environment;
- practical implementability, focusing on to the availability of the needed resources (personnel, hardware, software, knowledge sources, etc.);
- cost/benefit analysis, considering both direct and indirect costs and benefits and their distribution over time;
- environmental opportunity, with reference to the existence of adequate prerequisites and conditions for launching the project, such as involvement of top management, attitude towards technology innovation, funding opportunities, commercial and competition issues, global corporate trends, etc.

A positive evaluation of all the above five aspects allows to globally assess project plausibility.

Phase 2 - Demonstration prototype construction

The main goal of Phase 2 is to develop and demonstrate a first limited prototype of the complete expert system. The major output of this phase is therefore a running expert system, called demonstration prototype (or demonstrator), which can anticipate the type of performance the full system will be capable of on a limited part of the considered problem. The demonstrator may be developed with several different goals:
- obtaining a concrete insight on the complexity of the problem considered and validating, refining and, if necessary, revising some of the technical choices and preliminary design decisions proposed in Phase 1;
- collecting concrete reactions, suggestions, and critics from the users, so as to refine the identification of requirements and the definition of system specifications outlined in Phase 1;
- gaining involvement and commitment of the management and of the (potential) customer;
- gaining involvement of the experts and users in the project.

According to the ranking given to the above goals, several types of demonstrators may be identified, covering a full spectrum of possibilities ranging from explorative (first two goals above) to promotional (third and fourth goals above). In addition to the demonstrator, the outputs of this phase also include a revised and extended version of the plausibility report produced in Phase 1.

The construction of a demonstrator, although very common in most expert system projects, is not a mandatory step of the life cycle. In fact, if the goals of the demonstrator are considered as already achieved at the beginning of the project, the entire Phase 2 can be skipped, and the life cycle can directly proceed with Phase 3. It is one of the objectives of the plausibility study to suggest or discourage the development of a demonstrator.

Phase 2 takes in input the plausibility report produced in Phase 1, and starts with the identification of the goals and type of the demonstrator to bc developed. Then, from the whole problem to be solved, a limited subproblem is selected, on which the demonstrator will focus. Of course, the chosen subproblem must feature significant characteristics, adequate to the specific type of demonstrator. In order to analyze in more detail the selected subproblem, a limited initial knowledge acquisition activity is performed, which is devoted to identifying an appropriate conceptual model for the focused subproblem. The results of this activity provide important information to support the selection of the most suitable tool to be utilized for constructing the demonstrator. This choice is guided by the main objective of supporting as much as possible the effectiveness and efficiency of the development process, so as to keep costs and time within reasonable limits. So, generally an high-level and narrow tool (Harmon and King, 1985) is chosen which, after simple tailoring, can be directly used for the construction of the knowledge base. The knowledge base is developed in an incremental way through iterations over the following main steps:
- knowledge elicitation from the experts;
- knowledge coding and loading in the knowledge base;
- verification and refinement.

This cycle is repeated until the demonstrator reaches a satisfactory functional performance, with reference to its goals. Specific attention is devoted in the development of the demonstrator to the construction of the user interfaces, so as to ensure graceful interaction and full support in the use of the system.
At the end of the development process, one or more formal demonstrations take place so as to allow an extensive evaluation of the obtained results.

<u>Phase 3</u> - Full prototype construction

The main goal of Phase 3 is to develop a full expert system, called <u>full prototype</u> (or simply <u>prototype</u>), which can meet the functional specifications stated in the (revised) plausibility report. The prototype, although satisfying the functional acceptance criteria specified in Phase 1, is not the final output of the production process, since:
- it is not yet installed in the real operational environment, but it is operating in a laboratory environment (if necessary, connections with the external world are simulated);
- it has only been tested with realistic data samples prepared by the system designers with the support of domain experts and users;
- it is still embedded in the development environment and it is not engineered and optimized (it is generally not efficient and reliable as requested).

In addition to the prototype, the outputs of this phase also include a new version of the plausibility report produced in Phase 1, revised and extended for what concerns the construction of the target system (technical specifications, evaluation and validation criteria, project planning, etc.).

This phase is certainly one of the most fundamental of the entire development process, and includes several various tasks, devoted to the design and implementation of the complete prototype. Phase 3 takes in input the relevant parts of the revised and extended version of the plausibility report produced in Phase 2. At the beginning a wide knowledge acquisition activity is performed in order to identify an appropriate conceptual model for the entire problem considered. The technical choices concerning architecture, knowledge representation methods and reasoning mechanisms are then taken. On the basis of these results, the technical specifications of the empty system, i.e. the skeletal expert system with a still empty knowledge base, are defined, and the tools to be utilized in the development of the prototype are selected. Three main classes of possibilities exist here:

- adopting a low-level general purpose programming language;
- adopting a high-level expert system building environment;
- acquiring a narrow and specific expert system building tool.

In the former two cases extensive design and programming activities are needed for constructing the empty system, while in the latter the empty system can usually be obtained with a minor tailoring activity. The construction of the empty system includes, in addition to basic knowledge representation and reasoning modules, also development support tools, user and expert interfaces, external interfaces towards the outside world, a justification system, etc. according to the functional specifications. Once the empty system is fully developed and tested, the development of the prototype proceeds through the construction of the knowledge base. This basically follows the same iterative paradigm already mentioned in Phase 2, which, however, in this case involves a much larger and effort and an higher complexity. After completion of the knowledge base, formal testing is carried on. To this purpose, it may often be necessary to develop a simulator, which can simulate interaction of the prototype with the real operational environment. The prototype is tested with realistic data samples prepared by the system designers with the support of domain experts and users. The prototype is then evaluated with reference to the validation and acceptance criteria defined in Phase 1.

As outlined above, the prototype is generally a completely different system from the demonstrator. Only seldom the prototype may be obtained from the demonstrator through appropriate extension and refinement activities. In fact, the objectives, the design principles, and the development tools used for the two systems are so different that an incremental development of the prototype out of the demonstrator is generally not appropriate.

<u>Phase 4</u> - Target system implementation and installation

The goal of Phase 4 is to develop a complete expert system, with the same functional performance of the prototype, but installed in the real operational environment, fully tested with real data, engineered and optimized, and delivered to end users for routine use. Such a system, which is the final output of the production process, is called target system. The output of this phase also includes the complete set of manuals, including user, reference, and maintenance manuals, necessary for correct and effective system operation.

This phase takes in input the relevant parts of the plausibility report refined in Phase 3, and starts with a detailed technical analysis of the real operating environment, which often imposes severe constraints to hardware and software tools to be used for implementation of the target system. On the basis of this analysis, the final technical specifications of the target system are defined, and, taking into account the technical characteristics of the prototype already available, a specific production plan is developed. Three main approaches to the construction of the target system are generally considered:
- if the development and target environments are very similar or at least compatible from the hardware and software point of view, the target system can be obtained through incremental refinement of the prototype;
- if the development environment utilized for the construction of the prototype includes specific tools for the generation of a delivery version of the system which can run in the target environment, the target system can be obtained in a rather straightforward way using the available delivery tools;
- if the development and target environments are very different from the hardware and software point of view, the target system must be obtained through a complete re-implementation of the prototype.

Of course, the above three approaches imply different production plans, involving different cost and time, and also lead to different types of products featuring different technical characteristics. According to the choice taken, the target system is then developed and, as soon as it is completed, it is installed in the real operating environment. Extended field testing, system tuning, evaluation and validation are then carried on.

Phase 5 - Operation, maintenance, and extension

Phase 5 starts with the delivery of the target system to the end users for operational use. It comprises three main goals:
- supporting system use and operation;
- correcting possible bugs, faults, and lacks pointed out during system operation;
- monitoring system performance and collecting reactions, critics, suggestions, and needs from the users, in order to refine or extend system capabilities over time so as to keep it constantly fitting user requirement.

This phase, which lasts over the entire operational life of the expert system, has a fundamental importance for ensuring a long and effective use and for obtaining significant benefits from the whole project. Phase 5 takes in input the manuals produced in Phase 4 and the relevant parts of the documentation produced all during the expert system life cycle, and produces in output revisions, refinements and extensions to the target system and the manuals.

The concept of life cycle presented above is summarized and illustrated in Figure 1.

The five phases of the life cycle illustrated above are strictly sequential: after the goals of a phase have been completely accomplished and specific results have been produced, the development continues with the following phase and no return to previous phases is possible. Backtracking and iterations are possible only among tasks of a single phase and are to be precisely defined during the development of the full methodology. Parallel execution can be allowed also between (independent) tasks, but has to be carefully evaluated and defined during methodology construction.

Although the proposed life cycle is intended to cover the large majority of situations, some typical deviations from it are very common. We refer to cases where only the initial phases of the development process are carried on: consider, for example, a project specifically aimed at gaining management or client acquaintance with the expert system technology, which could be interrupted at the end of phase 2. We refer also to cases where some phases are considered optional, and are omitted: think, for example, to projects of limited complexity or, alternatively, projects carried on by an experienced development team for clients or users already acquainted with the technology, which may skip phase 2, devoted to the construction of the demonstrator.

5. From life cycle to development methodology

As already mentioned in section 3, the concept of life cycle is used, in our approach, as a framework for constructing a full development methodology for expert systems. Before proceeding further, two remarks seem important. First of all, while the concept of life cycle is very general and applies, at least in principle, to any kind of expert system project, the definition of a development methodology usually depends on several domain specific and company specific goals and constraints. Consider, for example, a methodology for the domain of real-time supervision and control which can not be the same as a methodology for the domain of financial advise giving, or think of the fact that an expert system development methodology should be homogeneous and well integrated with general corporate standards and procedures. Second, an expert system development methodology shares several issues and topics with other production methodologies and, therefore, its definition can benefit from a lot of already available results and inherit several general principles, approaches and also specific procedures from traditional engineering and management works. For these reasons, it seems appropriate to focus in this section only on general concepts, without going into more detailed and practical aspects which can be dealt with appropriately only in relation to specific application domains and organizations. Therefore, in this section we will concentrate on the way to be followed in deriving a development methodology from the above proposed life cycle, taking

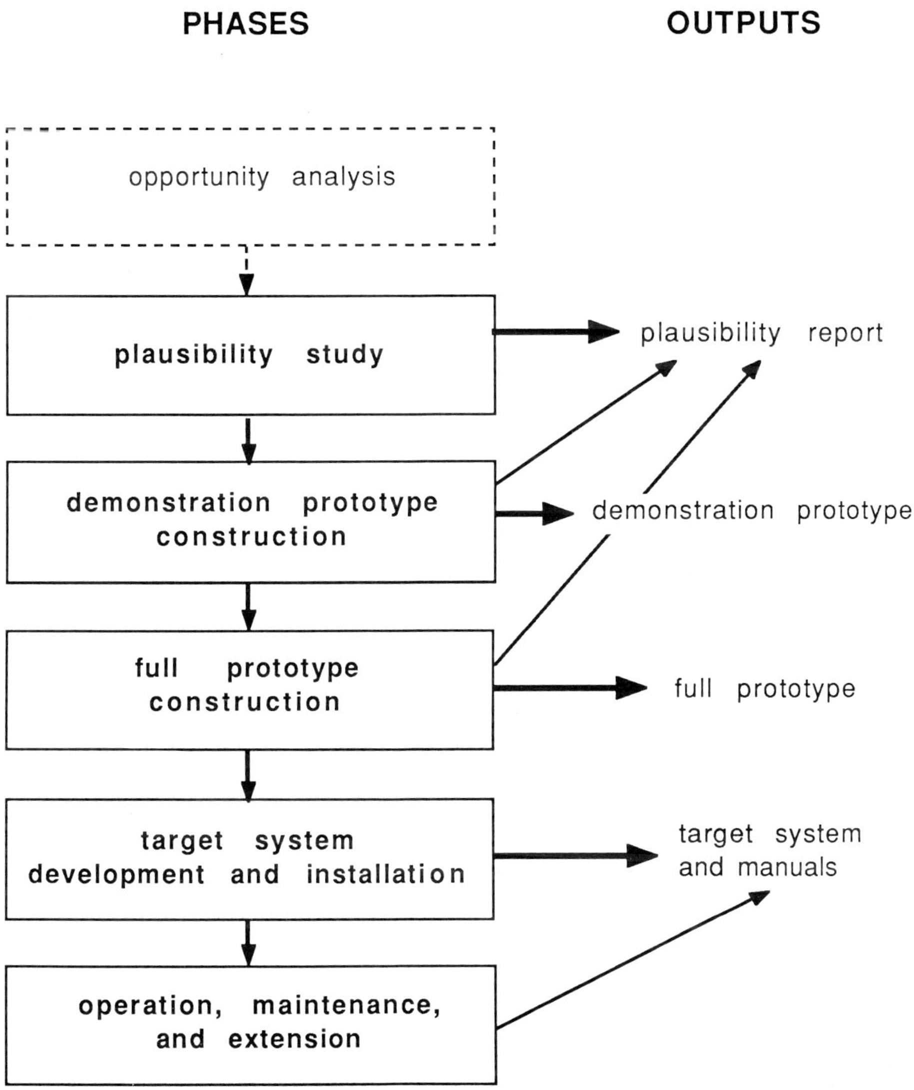

Figure 1 - Expert system life cycle.

specifically into account some of the peculiarities of the expert system technology, and restricting the illustration at a conceptual level, without going into specific details and without proposing a full specific methodology.

Designing a development methodology requires to complement the concept of life cycle with detailed knowledge concerning how it can be put in practice in an effective, efficient and controlled way. This involves three main aspects:

- refining the life cycle through the identification, for each phase, of appropriate tasks and activities (task and activity definition);
- specifying how to implement tasks and activities in practice, i.e. how to support expert system design and construction from a technical point of view (technique methods);
- specifying how to organize and manage people allocated to the project and their activities (management methods).

The reason why it is useful to organize methods in the two classes defined above is that while technique methods are largely technology and domain dependent, management methods are more or less the same for every kind of project and are strongly dependent on corporate standards. Figure 2 illustrates this concept.

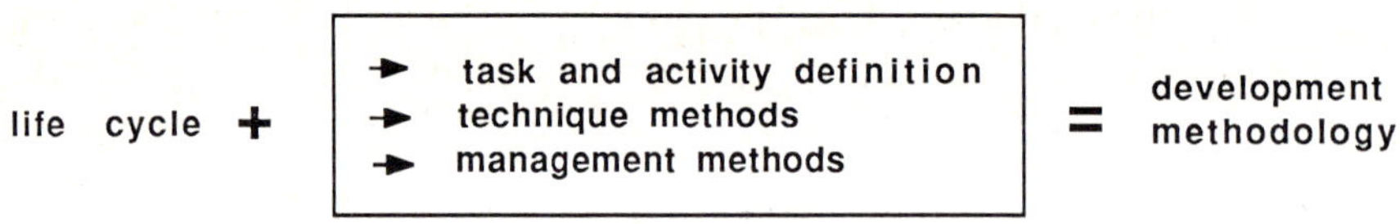

Figure 2 - From expert system life cycle to development methodology.

Going into more details, the main types of methods to be included in a development methodology should cover (at least) the following topics:

technique methods

- technology methods, which indicate for each task or activity prescribed in the life cycle the available techniques that can be used to execute it, and describe how such technologies should be implemented in practice;
- tools methods, which indicate for each task or activity prescribed in the life cycle and for each technology the available support tools, suggesting how they should be selected and used;
- role methods, which indicate for each task or activity prescribed in the life cycle the professional roles required for their execution, taking into account the use of specific technologies and tools;

- documentation methods, which specify for each task or activity prescribed in the life cycle and for each management method the type and form of the documents to be produced.

management methods
- project planning and control methods, which specify how to structure and compile project plans (both global and at phase level), how to monitor their execution, and how and when to revise them taking into account deviations and possible modifications of the goals;
- quality assurance methods, which deals with the procedures to be adopted to guarantee that the outputs of the production process show the desired quality standard;
- project team organization methods, which specifies the professional roles and organizational structure of the project team, in relation to the specific goals and technical features of a project;
- productivity evaluation methods, which prescribes how to evaluate the performance of the personnel involved in the project, taking into account the specific tools and techniques adopted;
- cost accounting and budget control methods, which prescribes procedures for budget formation, bookkeeping, cost accounting, and control;
- reporting methods, which defines how to keep the various components of the organization (top management, technical management, users, other departments, etc.) informed on the status, advancement and results of the project.

From the above description, it is apparent that the three components of a development methodology are not independent from each other but share a lot of common concepts, are bound to each other by input-output relationships, and are mutually constrained in several different ways. This requires that the refinement of the life cycle into tasks and activities and the definition of techniques and management methods is approached in a unitary way so as to ensure full coherence and integration.

6. Conclusion

In the paper we have discussed three major claims:
- Expert system technology is still largely relying today on empirical methods and is not supported by sound and general methodologies. It is therefore more like handicraft than engineering, and it lacks several of the desirable features of an industrial process (reliability, repeatability, work-sharing, cost estimableness, quality assurance, etc.).
- The transition of expert system technology from handicraft to engineering is widely recognized today as a much needed step aimed at overcoming some of the major bottlenecks which presently hamper the large-scale application of expert systems in business and industry.
- This transition may be grounded on a the concept of life cycle which can serve as a basis for designing full development methodologies specific to each individual organization and application domain.

According to these standpoints, we have proposed a possible life cycle for expert systems, and we have discussed how it can be used as a basis for building a full development methodology.

In our approach we have made one implicit assumption: expert systems are developed manually and their production process should be organized and disciplined according to a very detailed methodology based on a very specific life cycle concept. Of course, this does not exclude the use of dedicated support tools during the execution of some steps of the methodology. In fact, several tools are today going out of the research laboratories and some commercial products are already available on the market (for example, tools for the analysis, modeling and acquisition of knowledge, and tools for the construction, verification and refinement of the knowledge base). Nevertheless, in our methodological approach the impact of such tools is still supposed to be limited to well defined steps in the production process and, in any case, a potentially useful but not strictly necessary addition to the methodology. However, while this situation can reasonably be assumed today, it is not likely to last for a long time in the future. So it is worth sketching, as a conclusive remark, the possible scenario that, in the next years, will possibly characterize the expert system development process.

We believe that the quality of the results obtained so far by research in the expert system field and the consideration of the current trends in tool development allow to hypothesize that the type of expert system production environment outlined above will be, in fact, superseded by a major advancement in the technology. In the long run we may foresee that the production of expert systems will be deeply influenced by the more and more widespread use of tools. Tools will first cover a larger and larger number of the production steps, and later the trend towards integration will start. At last, we may imagine that expert system production will be fully supported by a pool of cooperating knowledge-based systems devoted to manage the whole life cycle, implementing some specific methodology and resorting to specialized tools for execution of the individual production steps, and this will also have, as a consequence, a very strong impact on resources (specially personnel), job organization, and project management.

Acknowledgments

We are indebted to Luca Majocchi and Marco Guida of Pirelli Informatica s.p.a. (Milano, Italy) for several stimulating discussions and suggestions on the topics of expert system life cycle and development methodology. In particular, some of the ideas reported in sections 3 and 4 stem from the experience gained in several expert system projects developed at Pirelli Informatica s.p.a. and are inspired to the first results of a common research effort.

References

B.W. Boehm, 1981. Software Engineering Economics. Prentice-Hall, Englewood Cliffs, NJ.

J.A. Breuker, B.J. Wielinga, and S.A. Hayward. 1986. Structuring of knowledge based systems development. In The Commission of the European Communities (Ed.), ESPRIT '85: Status Report of Continuing Work, North-Holland, Amsterdam, NL, 771-784.

B.G. Buchanan. 1986. Expert systems: Working systems and the research literature. Expert Systems 3(1), 32-51.

B.G. Buchanan, D. Barstow, R. Bechtel, J. Bennett, W. Clancey, C. Kulikowski, T. Mitchell, and D.A. Waterman. 1983. Constructing an expert system. In F. Hayes-Roth, D.A. Waterman, and D.B. Lenat. (Eds.) Building Expert Systems. Addison-Wesley, Reading, MA, 127-166.

W.J. Clancey. 1984. Knowledge acquisition for classification expert systems. Stanford University Heuristic Programming Project working paper HPP 84-18.

J.M. Cupello and D.J. Mishelevich. 1988. Managing prototype knowledge/expert system projects. Comm. of the ACM 31(5), 534-541.

D.A. De Salvo, A.E. Glamm, and J. Liebowitz. 1987. Structured design of an expert system prototype at the National Archives. In B.G. Silverman (Ed.), Expert Systems for Business, Addison-Wesley, Reading, MA, 40-77.

M. Ebrahimi. 1987. A structured approach to expert system design. Proc. WESTEX-87 Conf. on Expert Systems, Anaheim, CA, 18-24.

ESA, European Space Agency. 1986. Life-cycle for an expert system. TMS/86-091/MG/md, ESA, estec, Noordwijk, NL.

M. Freiling, J.H. Alexander, S.L. Messick, S. Rehfuss, and S.J. Shulman. 1985. Starting a knowledge engineering project: A step-by-step approach. AI Magazine 6(3), 150-164.

G. Guida and C. Tasso. 1989. Building expert systems: A structured bibliography. In G. Guida and C. Tasso (Eds.), Topics in Expert System Design - Methodologies and Tools, North-Holland, Amsterdam, NL, 419-435.

P. Harmon and D. King. 1985. Expert Systems - Artificial Intelligence in Business. John Wiley & Sons, New York, NY.

N. Hazeltine. 1987. Knowledge systems technology transfer. Proc. Annual Artificial Intelligence and Advanced Computer Technology Conf., Long Beach, CA, USA, April 22-24, 271-272.

G.J. Myers. 1976. Software Reliability. John Wiley, New York, NY.

S. Polit. 1985. R1 and beyond: AI technology transfer at DEC. AI Magazine 5(4), 76-78.

R.A.E. Sargeant, A. Jardine. 1987. Expert systems project management. Proc. Offshore Computer Conference, Aberdeen, UK, 1500-1520.

K. Shri, D.S. Prerau, A.V. Lemmon, A.S. Gunderson, and R.E. Reinke. 1985. COMPASS: An expert system for telephone switch maintenance. Expert systems 2(3), 112-126.

R.G. Smith. 1984. On the development of commercial expert systems. AI Magazine 5(3), 61-73.

D.A. Waterman. 1986. A Guide to Expert Systems. Addison-Wesley, Reading, MA.

W.S. Wilkerson. 1985. Guide to expert systems program management. Artificial Intelligence Guide Series, Intelligent Systems Technologies Group, Digital Equipment Corporation, Merrimack, NH.

E. Yourdon and L.L. Constantine. 1978. Structured Design. 2nd Ed. Prentice-Hall, Englewood Cliffs, NJ.

PART 2

Domain evaluation

Topics in Expert System Design
G. Guida and C. Tasso (Editors)
Elsevier Science Publishers B.V. (North-Holland), 1989

CHOOSING AN EXPERT SYSTEM DOMAIN

David S. PRERAU

Computer and Intelligent Systems Laboratory
GTE Laboratories Inc.
Waltham, MA, USA

1. INTRODUCTION

In this paper, we will discuss techniques by which the knowledge engineering team working on an expert system development project can investigate possible application domains to determine the best available application for the expert system. To accomplish this task, they must identify potential application domains, evaluate the potential domains, and select the most appropriate domain for the project.

The choice of the domain is a critical task in the development of an expert system. The ultimate success of the development project may well depend the effectiveness of the domain selection process—a well-selected domain will facilitate expert system development, while a poorly-selected domain may put major obstacles in the way of project success. Because domain selection is so important, the project should devote a a significant amount of effort to this task.

For some expert system development projects, there is a very specific application, chosen by management, for which an expert system is to be developed. In such a situation, it is often true that the people who selected the application area had little or no technical knowledge of artificial intelligence or expert systems. If so, then even if the project team is given no other choice of application, a decision should be made on whether the selected application is one that is best suited to solution by present expert system technology, or whether there might be a better way (or, possibly, no way) to attack the problem. If expert system technology is not the best solution to the given problem, then the project team should inform management and attempt to redirect the project.

In other cases, the project team is asked to select one of several given corporate problems or to survey corporate concerns to find a good application of expert system technology. Here, the project team must not only decide if an application is suited to present expert system technology but must also evaluate and rank potential domains to select the best available application.

This paper will examine the process of domain selection for an expert system and will detail a set of attributes that are desired in a good expert system domain. The selection process and the set of desirable attributes were developed at GTE Laboratories, where they were used to select the application domain for two large expert system development projects, *COMPASS* and *PROPHET*. They have also been used for domain selection elsewhere in GTE and in several other companies.

In the next section, we will examine the process of domain selection. The following section will discuss the *COMPASS* and *PROPHET* expert system projects and how the domain selection process worked in those developments. Finally, we will present the set of desired expert system domain attributes.

2. THE PROCESS OF DOMAIN EVALUATION AND SELECTION

If there is a broad choice of application areas available to the expert system, then the selection process might proceed as follows:

- A list is compiled of initial candidate domains to investigate. This list contains business areas of high impact or major problems.

- Meetings with domain personnel in these areas are set up.

- If the domain personnel at these meetings are not familiar with artificial intelligence and expert system technology, then a short introduction to these fields is given at the meetings. A discussion of the set of desired expert system attributes is an excellent way to give the meeting attendees a quick idea of the kinds of application areas that are being sought.

- Domain personnel are asked to describe problems that might be solvable by expert systems. As each potential application surfaces, a brief check through the desired attribute list can be used to identify possible problems related to the candidate area and thus focus further questions.

- Expert system project personnel select to investigate those suggested applications that seem to be most ameniable to expert system technology. This selection can be based, in large part, on an examination of each candidate application using a set of desirable attributes for an expert system domain such as that of section 4 of this paper. The attribute set makes it relatively easy to highlight the good and bad points of each potential application.

- During the investigation process, the list of candidate applications is continually narrowed. This narrowing is accomplished, as more information is found out about each application, by using the attribute list to identify applications that may present problems in development. The list may prove very useful to justify the dropping of politically-favored application areas.

- As the process continues, new potential applications that surface are added to the list of candidates.

- When the candidate list is narrowed to a small number, each application remaining is analyzed in great detail.

- Finally, the best application domain is selected. The attribute list can used to to justify the decision.

Although the above methodology pertains to the situation where domain selectors are given a wide choice of domains, the same techniques can be used when the application area must be chosen from a limited list.

If there is a single assigned domain, much of the above methodology does not apply, but it is still very important to investigate the given domain in detail. By analyzing the domain using the set of desirable domain attributes, potential problems in the expert system development might be identified. This identification would allow the expert system project to take steps to minimize or eliminate the potential problems, if possible, or to reformulate the task accordingly.

3. DESIRED PROPERTIES OF AN EXPERT SYSTEM DOMAIN

To evaluate the potential of a possible application, it has proven very useful to have a set of the desired attributes of a good expert system domain. This section presents such a set of attributes. The set includes technical attributes as well as attributes related to non-technical issues.

The set of attributes was developed to determine the domain of an expert system for a corporate application, as we shall discuss in Section 4. Although many of these attributes are applicable to all expert systems, there are some that are specific to the development of an expert system in a corporate environment. These involve, for example, the likelihood of corporate acceptance of a system, the support for the system development by corporate management, and so on. For most of these points, there are analogous points that apply to an academic or other environment.

The attribute set was developed from the perspective of providing a real working expert system to solve a corporate problem, using state-of-the-art expert system techniques. The discovery of new or better methods for expert system development was not an objective—in fact, a domain that requires a major breakthough in expert system methodology is probably not a good domain to choose if the goal is to maximize the likelihood of success. Yet, any project that is the first to attack a particular domain is likely to find some unique properties of the domain that may require new approaches.

Very few of these desired attributes are absolute, and it is unlikely that any domain will meet all of them completely. Furthermore, in each different situation, the weighting of the factors will be different, and additional factors may apply. This set does provide, however, a fairly extensive list of aspects to consider in domain selection. There may be a degree of commonality between some of the attributes listed in this section. However, to encourage consideration of the different aspects of domain selection, these commonalities were not eliminated.

3.1 Fundamental Features

- The use of expert knowledge, judgment and experience is the key element in the performance of the domain task being considered.

  The expert system development project has as its primary objective the acquisition and implementation in a computer program of a portion of the knowledge, judgment and experience that an expert uses in the performance of a domain task.

- There is a need for a non-conventional approach.

  Consider using expert system technology when conventional programming (algorithmic) approaches to the task are not satisfactory. If a conventional approach will work well, then there is usually less technical risk to using it rather than an expert system approach. Note, however, that expert system methodology may offer some additional advantages over conventional techniques, such as the expected ease of updating and maintaining a knowledge base and the ability to explain results.

- Experts exist in the domain today.

  The domain must be established to the extent that there are recognized experts that solve the problem. The domain experts must be provably better than amateurs in performing the task. If an area is too new or too quickly changing, there may be no real experts. However, such areas are often suggested for expert system developments.

- There is a need to "capture" the expertise from an expert.

  If domain expertise is easily available and inexpensive, there may be no need for an expert system development. However, if the expertise is not or will not be available on a reliable and continuing basis, then there is a need to capture it. Some examples: Expertise may scarce, or it may be expensive. The need for expertise may be growing. There may be a strong dependence on overworked experts. Expertise available today may be expected to be unavailable, or less available, in the future.

- Limited success is acceptable.

  It is likely that the completed expert system will be no better than a limited version of an expert. This must be enough.

- The completed system is expected to have a significant payoff.

  The payoff must be able to justify the development effort. However, the payoff can be of several forms. It might be direct, in money made or expenses saved. It might be more indirect, such as improved product quality, improved corporate image, higher levels of customer loyalty, etc. It might be the result of the system development itself, such as introduction of expert system technology into the company. Many systems will produce payoff from more than one of these sources.

- Among possible application domains, the domain selected best meets overall project goals regarding the tradeoff of project payoff versus risk of failure.

  A conservative approach would be to attempt to develop a system that would meet some criterion for minimum payoff if successful, and that seems to offer the best chance of success. A more aggressive approach would attempt a high payoff application even if there are clear obstacles to success.

3.2 Task Definition

- The task primarily requires symbolic reasoning.

  Although expert systems certainly can handle numerical calculations, if a task primarily involves numerical computation, then consideration should be given to the use of other programming approaches.

- The task requires the use of heuristics. It may require consideration of an extremely large number of possibilities, or it may require decisions to be based upon incomplete or uncertain information.

  A strength of expert systems is their ability to handle heuristics—domain experts' rules-of-thumb and strategies. In addition, problems with very large numbers of possibilities or with incomplete or uncertain information are difficult to attack by conventional approaches, but may be amenable to expert system methodologies.

- The task does not require knowledge from a very large number of areas, and it does not involve common sense reasoning.

  If the task required detailed knowledge in a large number of areas, then the amount of knowledge needed for the expert system would probably be beyond the practical limits of state-of-the-art expert systems. Common sense reasoning can be thought of as utilizing a very large accumulation of small chunks of knowledge from a very large number of areas, and thus also would require amounts of knowledge in an expert system that are beyond present practical limits. Furthermore, in both cases there would be difficulties in combining very heterogeneous knowledge.

- The system development has as its goal either to develop a system for actual use or to make major advances in the state-of-the-art of expert system technology.

  An expert system project should not attempt to achieve both of these goals at the same time. Doing both simultaneously is laudable, but more difficult.

- The system development is not driven by a particular technology within expert systems.

  A practical system development should be free to select the best of all available technologies. Thus, the choice of approach should be problem-driven, and not driven by a desire to make use of a particular expert system technology.

- The task is defined as clearly as possible.

  This is a good attribute of any task. At the project outset, the task to be performed and the inputs and outputs of the system to be developed should be defined. However, it is not necessary that the task definition be fixed for all time. As the system evolves and as situations change, it should be possible to change the task definition accordingly.

- The inputs needed to perform the task are available to the system.

  If an expert uses inputs that are not documented or not "computerized", such as local knowledge or informal knowledge, then ways must be identified to allow the expert system to have access to such knowledge. For an expert system to make decisions the way an expert does, it needs the same input information. If such information cannot be made available, then the effect of the missing information on the performance of the expert system must be considered.

- The required outputs for the domain task can reasonably be produced in the manner desired and delivered to the location desired.

  If the output is required to be in a form that may be difficult or very expensive for the expert system to produce or to deliver to the appropriate location, then this problem must be considered when evaluating the domain.

3.3 Experts and Expertise

- A top domain expert is available to work on the expert system project.

  It must be very likely that a leading domain expert will be available to the project. The domain expert is the source of expertise for the expert system. If the system is to perform at or near expert level, the project should get its expertise from one of the very best experts in the domain.

- The expert's knowledge and reputation is such that the expert system's output will have credibility and authority.

  The credibility of the expert lends authority to the decisions of the expert system. If the expert system is able to capture a reasonable portion of the expert's expertise, the system's output should have credibility and authority. However, in a domain where an accepted test for "goodness" of result exists, this credibility may be less of an issue since it should be possible to demonstrate the expert system's expertise on an absolute basis.

- The expert has built up expertise over a long period of task performance.

  Thus, the expert has had the amount of experience necessary to be able to develop the insights into the area that result in heuristics.

- The expert will commit a substantial amount of time to the development of the system.

  Obtaining the full commitment of an expert is often a problem. Experts may not want to or be able to take the time away from their regular job to devote the time needed to work on an expert system project.

- There is strong managerial support from the domain area regarding the large commitment by an expert.

  The best experts, in the most vital areas, are usually the ones that can be least spared from their usual position. Therefore, if possible, the commitment of one or more top experts (including their possible travel or temporary relocation, if required) should be agreed upon with their management as soon as possible in the expert system development process.

- The expert has good communication skills.

  It is important to find an expert that has not only domain expertise, but also the ability to impart it to the project team, whose members probably know little or nothing about the subject area. The expert should be capable of communicating his knowledge, judgment, and experience, and the methods he uses to apply these to the particular task. The expert should be able to introspect, analyzing his reasoning process, and then should be able to describe the reasoning process clearly to the project team, and to discuss it with them.

- The expert is cooperative.

  The expert should be eager to work on the project or, at worst, non-antagonistic. If the expert considers working on the project a bother or a distraction from his primary job, then he may not put in the large effort required of the expert to make the development of a major expert system a success.

- The expert is easy to work with.

  The project team and the expert will be spending a lot of time together. It is clearly important for the group to be able to get along with each other.

- The expertise for the system, at least that pertaining to one particular sub-domain, is to be obtained primarily from one expert.

  It is advantageous to select a domain where it is possible to acquire the expertise for the system (or at least for each sub-domain) principally from a single expert. This avoids the problem of dealing with multiple experts whose conclusions or problem-solving techniques do not agree. However, there may be some advantages to using multiple experts, e.g., strength of authority and breadth of expertise in sub-domains.

- If multiple experts contribute in a particular sub-domain, one of them should be the primary expert with final authority.

  This allows all the expertise to be filtered through a single person's reasoning process. (Note that some techniques have been developed, in disciplines such as economic modeling and technological forecasting, to allow combining inputs from multiple experts.)

3.4 Bounds on the Task

- The task is neither too easy nor too difficult.

  If the task is too easy (e.g., taking a human expert less than a few minutes), then the development of the system may not warrant the effort. If the task is too difficult (e.g., requiring more than a few hours for an expert), then the amount of knowledge needed may be beyond the state of the art in knowledge base size.

- The amount of knowledge required by the task is large enough to be non-trivial.

  If it is too small, the task may be more amenable to another approach, such as a decision tree.

- The amount of knowledge required by the task is small enough to make the system development practical.

  If the estimated number of important concepts required is bounded to several hundreds or a few thousands, then that is a reasonable size for an expert system in the current state of the art. However, estimating this number is very difficult, especially before knowledge acquisition has begun.

- The task is sufficiently narrow and self-contained.

  The aim should be not for a system that is expert in an entire domain, but for a system that is an expert in a limited task within the domain. This more tightly bounds the task, which should help keep the size of knowledge base bounded.

3.5 Domain Area Personnel

- Personnel in the domain area are realistic regarding their expectations for the expert system.

  Domain personnel—the expected recipients, users, and beneficiaries of the expert system—should be realistic, understanding the potential of an expert system for their domain, but also realizing that thus far only a limited (though growing) number of expert systems have resulted in production programs with major industrial payoff. The expert system project team may have to educate them to understand what are reasonable expectations, so that they are neither overly optimistic nor overly pessimistic.

- Domain area personnel understand that even a successful system will likely be limited.

  As has been mentioned, the expert system can not be expected to be better than a limited version of the expert. It probably will be limited in scope and, just as a human expert, it may not produce optimal or correct results 100% of the time.

- The specific task within the domain is jointly agreed upon by the system developers and the domain area personnel.

  This agreement helps insure that the system, if successful, will be useful and will be used.

- Managers in the domain area have previously identified the need to solve the problem that the system attacks.

  If the problem has been previously identified by domain managers, than this provides strong evidence that the system is needed. It makes managerial support of the expert system more likely.

- The project is strongly supported by a senior manager.

  A senior manager as the sponsor of the expert system project can provide the project access, protection, support, and follow-up.

- Potential users would welcome the completed system.

  If users do not want the expert system, the system may never be used. Potential users may fear, for example, that the expert system threatens their job security or disrupts their comfortable methods of doing things. The project team should consider how to make the system unthreatening to the users and welcome by them.

3.6 System Introduction and Domain Area Politics

- The system can be introduced into the working environment with minimal disturbance of the current practice.

  This will make the users' acceptance of the system more likely. As has been mentioned, if system use requires a radical change in working procedures, there is more potential for problems.

- The potential user group is cooperative and patient.

  If they are likely to be uncooperative with the project or impatient regarding the planned deployment of the system, then these potential problems should be considered.

- The introduction of the system will not be politically sensitive or controversial.

  Political problems related to putting the system into use might damage possibilities for system success. Such potential problems should be considered in advance. One typical problem: the control or use of the system goes across existing organizational boundaries, and more than one group wants control of it.

- The knowledge contained by the system will not be politically sensitive or controversial.

  For example, there may be certain practices, embodied in heuristics, that may prove embarrassing if written down. For example, unwritten rules concerning how certain customers are treated relative to other customers. But if an expert system is to be developed, such practices will either have to be recorded, which would cause embarrassment (or worse) if discovered, or will have to be left out of the system, which would weaken (possibly severely) the performance of the expert system.

- The system's results will not be politically sensitive or controversial.

  If there will be corporate parties who will challenge the system if its results do not favor them politically (for example, on appropriation of funds), then these challenges may make it much harder to gain system acceptance.

3.7 The Task

- The task is such that the expert system can be phased into use gracefully.

  Some percentage of incomplete coverage for the task should be tolerable (at least initially). Also, the determination of whether a sub-problem is covered by the present system should not be difficult. If the system does not have to do everything in order to do something, it can be put in place much sooner. The more difficult problems can be solved later, if at all.

- The task, and preferably every subtask, is decomposable.

  The task should allow relatively rapid prototyping for a closed small subset of the complete task, and then expansion to the complete task. This will make development much easier. Furthermore, decomposability allows the implementation to be modularized in a meaningful form.

- The task does not require perfect results.

  The task definition should allow for some percentage of incorrect or non-optimal results. The more toleration for incorrect results, the faster the system can be deployed and the easier it will be to win system acceptance. For example, in a domain where even the best experts are often wrong, system users may not be surprised or upset by an incorrect result from the system.

- The task's payoff is measurable.

  If the payoffs of the expert system can be measured, it is easier to demonstrate success of the system, especially to skeptics.

3.8 Additional Features

- The skill required by the task is taught to novices.

  If this is so, then the task is not "unteachable", and there is some experience with teaching the domain knowledge to neophytes, such as the project team (and, ultimately, the system). Furthermore, if the skill has been taught, then this usually means that there is an organization to the knowledge which can prove useful (at least initially) in building the system.

- There are books or other written materials discussing the domain.

  If this is true, then an expert has already extracted and organized some of the domain expertise. As in the previous point, this organized knowledge might prove useful (at least initially) in building the system. Note, however, that one benefit of capturing an expert's domain knowledge might be to make a step towards formalizing a domain that has not been treated in a formal manner before.

- Experts would agree on whether the system's results are correct (or, when there is no single correct result, acceptable).

  If experts cannot agree on whether the system's results are correct or acceptible, the system's results are open to challenge, even if the system accurately embodies a leading expert's knowledge.

- Test cases are available.

  The development of an expert system is greatly facilitated by the availability of test cases.

- The need for the task is projected to continue for several years.

  The need must exist enough beyond the period of system development to generate the payoff.

- The domain is fairly stable or, at least, slowly changing.

  Expected changes should be such that they utilize the strengths of expert systems (such as the ease of updating or revising specific rules in a knowledge base), but will not require major changes in reasoning processes. An unstable domain may yield a situation where a large number of previously developed knowledge structures (e.g., rules) are no longer valid but cannot easily be changed without redoing the entire development process.

- The effects of developments that will significantly change the definition of the task can be foreseen and taken into account.

  If the domain situation is expected to change in a way that will affect the potential expert system task, then these potential changes should be investigated and considered during domain selection.

- No alternative solution to the problem is being pursued or is expected to be pursued.

  If the project's goal does not duplicate the goal of other existing efforts, then the chances of the expert system providing an important payoff are increased. However, if a project goal is to compare expert system technology to other technologies, this duplication may be just what is desired.

- The project is not on the critical path for any other development, and has loose milestones for completion.

  The use of expert system technology for real corporate applications is still relatively new, and so any development has some risk. Thus, the less dependent other activities are on the success of the expert system development, the better. Also, the amount of knowledge necessary to perform a task at a specified skill level and the time it would take to acquire that knowledge from an expert are both very difficult to estimate. Therefore, accurately estimating the time required for the development of an expert system is not an easy task.

- The task is similar to that of a successful existing expert system.

  Although no guarantee, this is a positive indication of the likelihood of project success.

- Any requirement for system performance will not involve extensive effort.

    Although it is certainly possible to develop a system for a problem with a strong performance requirement, such as real-time system, the considerations involved may substantially divert effort from the primary tasks of knowledge acquisition and implementation. This may prove critical in a project with limited resources, However, if other factors (such as the expectation of a very large payoff) are present, then such a domain may well be the best one to select.

- The user interfaces and data communications of the system will not require extensive effort.

    As with a performance requirement, a large requirement for work on an elaborate user interface or on extensive complex data communications could divert effort from knowledge acquisition and implementation in a project with fixed resources. The additional efforts required should therefore be considered in domain selection, and if the domain is selected, appropriate additions to project resources should be sought.

4. UTILIZING THE DOMAIN SELECTION PROCESS

The methodology for domain selection presented in this paper was initially developed and used in the selection of the domain for the GTE Laboratories project that eventually produced the *COMPASS* expert system. The set of desired expert system attributes was used recurrently (and modified and expanded continually) throughout an extensive application domain evaluation and selection process. Over fifty corporate managers and experts were interviewed, and over thirty extremely diverse possible expert system applications areas were considered. This list was narrowed to eight major possibilities, and these were further analyzed and ranked. Two primary candidates areas were studied in great detail. Finally, the *COMPASS* application area was chosen.

GTE's *COMPASS* (*C*entral *O*ffice *M*aintenance *P*rintout *A*nalysis and *S*uggestion *S*ystem) is an expert system that aids in the maintenance of large telephone switching systems [1,7,8,11,12]. *COMPASS* accepts maintenance printouts from telephone company central office switching equipment and suggests maintenance actions to be performed.

In particular, *COMPASS* accepts maintenance printout information from a GTE Number 2 Electronic Automatic Exchange (No. 2 EAX). A No. 2 EAX is a large, complex telephone call switching system ("switch") that can interconnect up to 40,000 telephone lines. Such a switch generates hundreds or thousands of maintenance messages daily. The manual procedure for analyzing these messages to determine appropriate maintenance actions takes a significant amount of time and requires a high level of expertise. *COMPASS* uses expert techniques to analyze these messages and produce a prioritized list of recommended maintenance actions for a switch maintenance technician.

The *COMPASS* implementation utilizes multiple AI paradigms: rules, frame hierarchies, demon mechanisms, object-oriented programming facilities, and Lisp code [4]. The *COMPASS* program was designed to be transferred out of GTE Laboratories to other organizations for operation and maintenance, and therefore techniques to support program maintainability were developed and employed [2,10]. *COMPASS* is a large expert system: The *COMPASS* "knowledge document", which contains a succinct English language record of the *COMPASS* expert knowledge, is approximately 200 pages long. In field uses, *COMPASS* has displayed performance comparable to (and, in some cases, better than) that of domain experts, and significantly better than that of average No. 2 EAX maintenance personnel.

The domain selection methodology was again used at GTE Laboratories in the selection of the domain for the project that is presently developing the *PROPHET* expert system.

In the domain selection process that resulted in the selection of the *PROPHET* domain, we again used the set of desired expert system attributes—modified and upgraded—throughout an extensive application domain evaluation and selection process. Here over thirty corporate managers and experts were interviewed, and about ten diverse possible expert system applications areas were considered. This list included several of the applications that had scored high in the *COMPASS* domain selection (but, of course, not as high at that time as *COMPASS*). Again, the list was narrowed, and the remaining major possibilities further analyzed and ranked. Finally, the *PROPHET* application area was chosen.

PROPHET (*P*roactive *R*ehabilitation of *O*utside *P*lant using *H*euristic *E*xpert *T*echniques) is expert at detecting problems in deteriorating telephone company outside plant before any customer reports are received, and in prioritizing dispatching for repair and rehabilitation [9]. "Outside plant" refers to the physical media used to connect a telephone subscriber to a central office telephone switch, including buried or aerial cabling, terminals, cross-connection boxes, drop wires, and other related hardware.

Telephone companies spend very substantial amounts on outside plant maintenance, but even with this expenditure, the maintenance must be prioritized to allow rehabilitation or replacement of the outside plant most in need of maintenance. Typically, problems in outside plant are handled by telephone companies on a first-reported, first-repaired basis, based on trouble reports from customers. However, experts can analyze large sets of test measurement data and recognize problems that can be repaired before the outside plant deteriorates to the point that the customer's service is affected. This approach, known as proactive maintenance, produces several benefits for telephone companies, including higher quality service, lower costs, and increased customer satisfaction. However, to perform proactive maintenance analysis at an expert level, large amounts of telephone company data are required. The *PROPHET* expert system uses the techniques and knowledge of a top telephone company outside plant maintenance expert to determine outside plant problems proactively and to prioritize the dispatching of these problems for repair and rehabilitation.

The effort put into the domain selection process that resulted in the selection of the *COMPASS* and *PROPHET* domains proved to be very worthwhile. Many times during the development processes for these expert systems, it was evident that a potential problem did not exist or was minimized because the domain possessed one or more of the attributes on the desired attributes list. It frequently seemed clear that such a potential problem would have been a major obstacle in another domain that we had considered– a domain that we had rated lower than the *COMPASS* or *PROPHET* domains specifically because we had identified the potential problem by use of the attribute list.

ACKNOWLEDGMENT

I would like to thank the management and members of the Knowledge Based Systems Department at GTE Laboratories for their continuing support in this work. Especially, I would like to thank Ralph Worrest and Mark Adler of the Department for their work with me on the application evaluation and selection phases of the *COMPASS* and *PROPHET* projects, respectively. Also, I would like to acknowledge Shri Goyal, Alan Gunderson, Alan Lemmon, Sam Levine, Robert Reinke, and Roland Van der Meer of the Department, Charles Rich of M.I.T., Rick Johnson of GTE Southwest, and Lonnie Lewis of GTE Florida for their support and suggestions throughout the course of the work that led to this paper and Marie Goslin of the Department for her editorial assistance. A portion of this paper is revised and updated from a paper that appeared in *AI Magazine* [6].

REFERENCES

[1] Goyal, S., Prerau, D., Lemmon, A., Gunderson, A. and Reinke, R., "*COMPASS*: An Expert System for Telephone Switch Maintenance," *Expert Systems*, Vol. 2, No. 3, pp. 112-126, 1985.

[2] Gunderson, A., "A Meta-level Utility For Configuration Control of Expert System Development," *Proceedings of the 2nd ACM Northeast Regional Conference*, pp. 20-29, 1985.

[3] Hayes-Roth F, Waterman D., and Lenat, D., *Building Expert Systems*, Addison-Wesley, Reading MA, 1983.

[4] Kunz, J., Kehler, T. and Williams, M., "Applications Development Using a Hybrid AI Development System," *AI Magazine*, pp. 41-54, Fall 1984.

[5] McDermott, J., "R1 Revisited: Four Years in the Trenches," *AI Magazine* Vol. 5, No. 3, pp. 21-32, Fall 1984.

[6] Prerau, D., "Selection of an Appropriate Domain for an Expert System," *AI Magazine*, Vol. 6, No. 2, pp. 26-30, Summer 1985.

[7] Prerau, D., "Knowledge Acquisition in the Development of a Large Expert System," *AI Magazine*, Vol. 8, No. 2, pp. 43-51, Summer 1987.

[8] Prerau, D., *Developing a Major Expert System*, Addison-Wesley, Reading MA. In publication.

[9] Prerau, D., Gunderson. A., and Levine, S., "The *PROPHET* Expert System: Proactive Maintenance of Telephone Company Outside Plant," *Proceedings of the Fourth Annual Artifical Intelligence and Advanced Computer Technology Conference (AI'88)*, Long Beach CA, May 1988.

[10] Prerau, D., Gunderson. A., Reinke, R., and Adler, M., "Maintainability Techniques in Developing Large Expert Systems," *IEEE Expert*, in publication.

[11] Prerau, D., Gunderson, A., Reinke, R.,and Goyal, S., "The *COMPASS* Expert System: Verification, Technology Transfer, and Expansion," *Proceedings of the Second IEEE Conference on Artificial Intelligence Applications*, pp. 597-602, Miami, FL, December 1985.
[12] Prerau, D., Lemmon, A., Gunderson, A., and Reinke, R., "A Multi-Paradigm Expert System for Maintenance of an Electronic Telephone Exchange," *Proc. Ninth IEEE Computer Software and Applications Conference* (COMPSAC-85), pp. 280-286, Chicago IL, October 1985.
[13] Smith, R., "On the Development of Commercial Expert Systems," *AI Magazine*, Vol. 5, No. 3, pp. 61-73, Fall 1984.

PART 3

Design techniques

Topics in Expert System Design
G. Guida and C. Tasso (Editors)

PROTOTYPING: TOOLS AND MOTIVATIONS

Gary S. KAHN and Mike BAUER

Carnegie Group Inc.
Pittsburgh, PA, USA

1. INTRODUCTION

Developers of knowledge-based systems rely heavily on prototypes. Prototypes are critical to several phases of the software lifecycle. Engineers develop prototypes in the course of producing functional requirements, design specifications, and incremental implementations. Consequently, there is often confusion about the purposes of prototypes. Questions like, "How much time should go into a prototype?"; "Should prototypes solve "real" or toy problems?", and "Should prototypes evolve into production quality systems or be thrown away?" are often answered quite differently by equally well-qualified practitioners of the art. Our contention is that answers differ because the purpose of prototyping differs across developmental phases.

Thus, this paper, as its primary purpose, provides an inquiry into the complexity of goals developers pursue with prototypes. To a large extent, prototyping is motivated by sophisticated development environments which enable the rapid development of code. Specialized editors, incremental compilation, and the simultaneous display of I/O and editing windows encourage hands-on design and incremental implementation. Nevertheless, the motivation behind prototyping is deeper and more varied than this.

Section 2 of this paper provides a discussion of prototyping goals across development phases and identifies phase-dependent requirements for prototyping tools. By discussing how Knowledge Craft^{tm} meets these requirements, Section 3 gives concrete meaning to a rather open, and ill-defined, set of terms. While it would be interesting to examine how other tools realize these requirements, that is beyond the scope of this paper.

While Knowledge Craft provides developers with a powerful toolkit for building knowledge-based systems, it does have limitations. Section 4 discusses a prototyping methodology and shows how toolkits can be enhanced by the addition of shells specifically structured to support prototyping. Finally, as illustration of our points, Section 5 provides an example application.[1]

---

[1]This paper assumes a large systems perspective; and thus, many issues discussed may not be directly relevant to developers of small rule-based systems or application shells.

In order to understand the many uses of prototyping, familiarity with some standard terminology is helpful. Knowledge-based systems are typically composed of three architectural units: the *problem solver*, the *knowledge base*, and the *interface*. The problem solver, or inference engine, typically provides an approach to interpreting or using the contents of a knowledge base. Applications differ widely in the degree to which the problem solver contains domain specific information. In this paper, we use "knowledge base" to refer to a domain model of factual or process information. We assume that the problem solver embodies procedural and inferential know-how, which may or may not be domain specific.

The *interface* provides for transactions with a user of an application. The task of acquiring human expertise from a particular domain and codifying it into a knowledge base is called *knowledge engineering* or *knowledge acquisition*.

2. WHY PROTOTYPE

2.1. Prototyping as Functional Specification

Prototypes enable developers to convey to their management, customers, and end users the look, feel, and capability of a proposed system with more success than that permitted by a paper-based requirements document. Given the complexity of knowledge-based systems, such documents would run to hundreds or thousands of pages -- and consequently, fail to convey a cohesive understanding of a system to critical decision makers.

The complexity of functional requirements for knowledge-based systems comes from several sources. For one, the desired problem-solving capabilities are often ill-specified; and the methods for achieving the desired functional results are ill-structured or non-algorithmic. In other words, a precise description of what a program is expected to do under a variety of conditions cannot be provided except in terms of examples. Furthermore, even where behavioral descriptions of problem-solving behavior are simple, control and interface requirements add dimensions of complexity. Functionality is often evoked under both goal- and data-driven conditions that occur outside of any exact procedural description. Finally, interfaces are designed for flexibility, resulting in a set of displays that cannot be easily enumerated because of their heavy use of multiple user-defined windows and modeless access to menus.

While functional prototypes typically emphasize the external look and feel of a system, requirements cannot be understood apart from the knowledge a system will require in order to perform correctly.

In eliciting functional requirements, developers must determine, among other things,

1. **The scope and granularity of knowledge.** What knowledge is required to solve a problem; and to what level of detail? In a diagnostic application, for example<, is it necessary for a system to understand how experts generate an ordered list of hypothesis to pursue or only that they do? How explicit a representation of order should there be?

2. **The degree of procedural regularity in the use of knowledge.** Is a diagnostic solution always achieved in the same way, or are there alternative technique for the different failures that occur?

3. **The need for and availability of data at run time.** What can be considered permanent knowledge vs. what must be acquired at run time? What are reasonable default assumptions? Is it reasonable, for example, to assume the possibility of extreme temperatures in Arizona in the summer, or should temperature factors be elicited at run time.

4. **The degree of accuracy acceptable in a resulting recommendation or situation assessment.** Is it acceptable to terminate an analysis of a diagnostic problem with the identification of a likely cause or should all possibilities be considered and evaluated?

2.1.1. Tool Requirements

Given the importance and complexity of eliciting knowledge-base requirements as part of the functional requirements, externally-oriented prototyping methods and tools [3] are insufficient in themselves. Developers need tools which not only enable rapid interface development but which allow rapid modeling of knowledge bases and problem-solving procedures. The speed of development is important as the specification of requirements tends to be a highly iterative activity making use of scarce human resources for both developer and client.

In order to support rapid iteration on functional prototypes, tools need to be modular, expressive, flexible, and varied. Modularity is desirable in several respects. First, decomposition into modular functional units reduces the likelihood that modifications will have unforeseen consequences elsewhere in the system. Second, modularity between the domain representation and problem solver enables a preliminary capture of knowledge whose use can be explored from alternative problem-solving perspectives. And finally, modularity between the interface and the underlying knowledge and problem-solving components, enables either an outside-in or inside-out design strategy. In the first case, designers focus on a blackbox implementation where the transactional interfaces are well defined and prototyped prior to working out internal representations and problem-solving capabilities. In the latter case, designers focus on knowledge requirements and problem-solving capabilities prior to conceiving a successful user interface.

Tools need to be expressive relative to the task. As the gap between the human expression of knowledge and the programming concepts in which prototypes are implemented is narrowed, both knowledge acquisition and system design tasks can be accomplished in less time. This gap can be most effectively narrowed by application-specific shells [5]. However, general purpose tools can be more or less effective depending on the extent to which developers are given the flexibility required to create a "natural representation". In addition, the tool must be flexible enough to enable designers to frequently revise knowledge-bases without sitting through long compilation cycles.

A functional prototype emphasizes a demonstration of capability rather than a design that is sufficient to achieve function, coverage, performance, and maintainability objectives. Consequently, it is desirable to have a rich collection of tools, or design options, each of which can minimize the time it takes to produce a component or resolve an issue within the prototype. It is better not to force a particular design paradigm to be used throughout. For this reason, hybrid tools that combine objects (frames, schemata) and rules (with forward and backward chaining) are preferred, even though performance and maintainability objectives may be better met within a single paradigm.

2.2. Design Specification

It is important to distinguish between functional prototypes whose purpose is to elicit requirements, and design prototypes whose purpose is to explore solutions. Prototypes developed as functional specifications typically focus on capturing the requirements of a system, not the design. In order to achieve desired functionality, a design exploration is required.

Prototypes prove useful to this enterprise primarily because they

- Provide an effective tool for managing design complexity; and
- Allow iterative evaluation with respect to function and coverage.

The complexity of functional requirements discussed in the previous section carries forward into the design phase. Without an algorithmic core to provide simplification, a knowledge-based system frequently evolves through the introduction of interacting entities (objects, relations, rules, messages, and functions) that co-adapt as the designer's attention turns from one issue to another. Prototyping provides a means of managing this development process by providing a "live" mechanism that will either adapt or break as the design progresses.

Interestingly, as with any evolutionary process, this one too will result in incongruities and unsuccessful spinoffs. For this reason, the design prototype should usually be discarded and reimplemented in order to achieve a maintainable production quality release.

The need for iterative evaluation provides a second motivation for prototyping. As a design evolves, functional goals shift. There are three reasons for this. First, the design process will both identify limitations and new opportunities. Some functionality is too difficult to implement given time and budget constraints; other functionality, particularly more powerful generalizations, will be best realized as part of the current design effort. Second, as designers test their proposed solutions against a greater number of cases, the need for additional functionality may become apparent. Finally, client or management objectives evolve as greater familiarity with technical possibilities and realities is achieved. Iterative prototyping during the design phase offers an opportunity to recalibrate project goals all around.

2.2.1. Inapplicability of conventional techniques

A final reason for reliance on prototypes is that conventional design specification techniques are not typically useful. Design languages and techniques, such as flow charts, pseudo-code, PDL (program design languages) and data flow, were developed to deal with structured programming languages that assume sequential control and use a small number of subroutines and data structures [7]. The non-sequential programming styles [Lisp, Ops, Prolog] that are associated with knowledge-based programming differ in all these respects. Control is very dynamic and is either event-driven or search-oriented. Rather than a small number of subroutines, one finds an overwhelming number of small interacting functional units. These languages offer the capability of defining new, specialized data structures. All these factors lead to programs that exceed the ability of humans to comprehend them from static descriptions.

In addition, factors which encouraged the development of formal techniques are in less evidence. These techniques evolved to avoid the high cost of iterative coding within the impoverished software development environments characteristic of time-shared systems a decade or more ago. With more sophisticated computer-based software environments, the tradeoff between iterative coding and more formal techniques has shifted toward a prototyping methodology. Secondly, the sociology of the workplace differs substantially between conventional and knowledge-based system programming projects. In particular, the distinction between system analysts and coders has all but disappeared. Knowledge-based systems are developed by highly educated professionals who can move gracefully between issues of conceptual design and implementation. Thus, the need to use non-ambiguous design specifications to communicate between work units is greatly diminished.

2.2.2. Tool Requirements

In the design phase, prototyping tools should allow developers to effectively explore and evaluate alternative solutions. As with functional prototypes, tools which are modular, expressive, flexible, and varied will help for similar reasons. In addition, tools need to address issues unique to the design phase and as a consequence require power, coherence, and openess.

During design, the capability of a system will expand at the same time as care is taken to assure parsimony in the architecture, and to lay foundations for future lines of development and deployment. Thus, a tool should provide not only a range of representational and problem-solving options, but the options should be sufficiently powerful to capture the functional breadth of a system in a context within which elaborations and refinements appear natural. While one expects functional prototypes to draw on an assortment of representational and problem-solving devices in order to rapidly demonstrate functionality, design prototypes are expected to narrow in on a parsimonious and coherent design philosophy.

Finally, a general purpose prototyping tool needs to support an open architecture which provides call-outs to other languages and enables call-ins to its capabilities. No tool can adequately predict the needs of a specific application. Thus, the flexibility to call-out to a more general purpose, though more primitive language is desirable. Similarly, no tool can afford to assume that applications are complete stand-alone systems.

2.3. Implementation Prototypes

Once a design is articulated, implementation can begin. While a design may change during the implementation phase, it is desirable to distinguish between design prototypes that serve exploratory purposes and implementation prototypes that milestone partially complete systems. Design prototypes tend to be exploratory, undisciplined, and generally messy. Implementation prototypes must incrementally realize a maintainable production quality system.

Implementation prototypes serve two purposes. First, they demonstrate progress to project managers and clients. Second, and in strong comparison to conventional methods, they serve as knowledge-acquisition tools. Knowledge acquisition occurs throughout the project lifecycle. Prior to implementation, knowledge acquisition supports a design goal, namely that of arriving at a knowledge-base definition sufficiently robust to accommodate whatever knowledge is required to meet the performance goals of the system. It is during implementation, however, that knowledge-base expansion or "knowledge-stuffing" occurs, that is the fleshing out of the knowledge base under the constraints imposed by its design. Iterative prototyping, at this point, aims not at strengthening the design but at ensuring knowledge-base completeness and accuracy.

The concept of rapid and iterative prototyping, in fact, achieved greatest currency after being introduced as a methodology for knowledge acquisition rather than a design technique [4]. The accuracy and completeness of an expert's account cannot be fully assessed outside a context of demonstrated use. As a result, it is necessary to engineer expertise into a system (knowledge engineering), and then run test cases to get an expert's assessment of performance and an explanation for errors. After tests of this kind, the knowledge engineer can tune confidence factors, correct errors, and incorporate knowledge found to be missing. Prototyping, in this sense, need not ever terminate, as the scope of an expert system's capability evolves overtime and its sensitivity to critical detail increases with experience.

Like experts, a true expert system continues to acquire and refine knowledge indefinitely. While valid, this point has often been misinterpreted by developers to legitimize the internal reworking of a core design. This unfortunate practice results in projects which get stalled in the design phase and never get realized as maintainable implementations.

2.3.1. Tool Requirements

In order to support "knowledge stuffing", tools need to provide representations that enable successive refinements. The terms in which new knowledge may be added must be precisely presented to the knowledge engineer. And specialization of existing representations must be possible in an incremental fashion that does not throw into question the overall reliability of the system. If it did, development would be overwhelmed by recurring cycles of regression testing. Furthermore, it must be possible to rapidly move between editors through which changes are made, and execution environments within which the dynamic consequences may be examined.

3. KNOWLEDGE CRAFT

As discussed, prototyping tools need to meet a very broad set of requirements. Although these requirements can be met in many ways, it is instructive to consider one prototyping tool in some depth. Knowledge Craft provides an example that both shows how our prototyping requirements may be realized and reveals some additional needs.

3.1. Overview

Knowledge Craft^{tm} meets many of the tool requirements stated above: it includes a representation language (CRL), problem-solving languages (CRL-OPS and CRL-PROLOG), interface tools to assist in the development of user applications, and programming workbenches.[2] Many applications, primarily in engineering, manufacturing, and field support, have used Knowledge Craft across all development phases.

CRL (Carnegie Representation Language) provides a tool for building object-oriented

---

[2]A full description of Knowledge Craft goes beyond the scope of this paper. Further description is available from Carnegie Group Inc., 5 PPG Place, Pittsburgh, Pa. 15222 and [6].

knowledge bases or domain models. Objects (called schemata) may be given attribute values and put into relations with other objects. A **machine**, for instance, might have an attribute of *criticality* with value *high* and a relation of *has-alarm* to an object which represents an alarm at a monitoring station. As is typical with such languages, inheritance down a classification hierarchy is supported. Less typical, and perhaps unique, is that CRL enables inheritance (or value access) over arbitrary relations between objects. For instance, the *condition* attribute of **machine**, for example, might returns its value by inheriting it across the *has-alarm* relation from the *status* slot of the machine's alarm. In other words, CRL generalizes the concept of inheritance to enable dynamic access across any relation, or relational pathway, of a semantic network.

CRL-OPS provides an implementation and extension of OPS-5 [2]. OPS programs consist of large numbers of IF-THEN rules, each of which can execute whenever the conditions defined in the "IF" portion of the rule are satisfied. If more than one rule satisfies its preconditions, OPS uses a conflict resolution strategy to select the one rule that will fire during a given cycle. CRL-PROLOG is an implementation and extension of PROLOG [1], a logic programming language based on a Horn clause representation. Such clauses may be procedurally interpreted as rules, or in the minimal case, as facts.

Knowledge Craft interface tools include the Window and Command Systems. The Window System provides high-level functions for creating windows and supports the display of graphical objects such as lines, rectangles, circles, splines, and text objects of different font size, style and orientation. The Command System allows the system developer to define input devices and commands; and it provides mechanisms for maintaining state and preserving data integrity within multi-tasking applications.

Knowledge Craft includes software engineering workbenches for both system design and knowledge-base expansion. Workbenches, called workcenters, are tailored to the use of CRL, CRL-OPS, and CRL-PROLOG. As Window and Command system behavior is defined though instantiating CRL objects, the CRL Workcenter may be used to develop interfaces. The CRL-PROLOG and CRL-OPS Workcenters trace and modify rule-based program modules.

3.2. Using KC for Functional Prototypes

Functional prototypes require tools that enable the rapid development of interfaces and the building of domain models and problem-solving procedures. Knowledge Craft's interface tools provide a library of functions that cover many standard interface options and allow customization for special requirements. Knowledge Craft has characteristics that support the rapid development of models and problem-solving procedures. These were identified above as expressiveness, flexibility, modularity, and variety.

The CRL-languages are expressive relative to knowledge-based systems applications. CRL provides for arbitrary semantic networks, allowing developers to define representations which closely correspond to the terms with which experts describe their domains -- it is not necessary to force all relational concepts into a classificatory hierarchy as with many frame-based systems. CRL-PROLOG and CRL-OPS are variants of languages that have been used successfully to design expert systems that depend heavily on capturing and expressing IF-THEN knowledge as rules.

While expressive with respect to problem-solving behavior, standard implementations of OPS and PROLOG have proved to be of limited use in domain modeling. This is corrected in the CRL-variants which provide strong integration with CRL. The syntax of OPS and Prolog is extended by introducing special forms which enable explicit pattern matching against CRL schemata rather than the simple clauses and vectors which constitute facts in conventional PROLOG and OPS programs. Apart from simple pattern matching, CRL-PROLOG supports special forms for backtracking through slots with multiple values and matching against lists which represent the range or domain of specified CRL relations.

Knowledge Craft provides for flexibility by supporting interpretive execution. This enables developers to modify programs without needing to recompile large knowledge bases or program modules. Knowledge Craft is implemented in Common Lisp, and consequently, preserves the ability to execute either interpretatively or as a compiled image. In an interpretive mode, schemata (both types and instances), relations, rules, and auxiliary lisp functions may be defined freely and incrementally. This leads to an increase in productivity when compared to alternative tools, including databases, that force time consuming recompilations when definitions change.

The elicitation of functional requirements demands modularity to enable both problem decomposition ("divide and conquer" strategies), and rapid incremental refinement. Knowledge Craft provides several kinds of modularity. First, the CRL-languages are based on modular concepts. In particular, rules enable the capture and refinement of small chunks of conditional knowledge; and objects enable data structures to be appropriately segmented across different levels of abstraction.

Knowledge Craft's interface tools are designed to allow modularity between tasks, and between the knowledge base and the user interfaces. Based on an object-oriented methodology, the interface tools allow programmers to segment functional units as perceived by system users (separate tasks or task groups). Similarly, problem-solving capabilities may be isolated from the interface by this approach. By sending messages which evoke methods located in the interface objects, (e.g. display-result), the problem solver can remain immune from interface design changes.

Domain models and problem-solving procedures can be distinguished as semi-autonomous modules. CRL domain models can often be elaborated without modifying the way in which the problem solvers work, and vice-versa. Finally, object-oriented programming is provided as a variant interpretation of CRL object attributes. That is, under a programming interpretation, object slots may be interpreted as pointers to methods, represented as lisp functions, rather than as attributes or relations. Object-oriented programming proves invaluable for modular architectures which enable localized refinement.

Effective prototyping depends most on the fit between tool and problem. Thus, variety, the remaining characteristic, is required. Developers are most productive if provided an assortment of tools, each of which can minimize the time it takes to prototype a particular component or requirement. To address this need, Knowledge Craft provides a hybrid approach to program development. Not only are developers given a palette of tools, but the tools may be easily integrated into a single application. In the context of a diagnostic application, for instance, the data-driven characteristic of OPS might be exploited to generate hypotheses on the basis of observed symptoms. The goal-driven, or proof-oriented, approach to problem solving offered by PROLOG could then be used to find and evaluate further evidence associated with each hypothesis. Both languages may share data and results as they have access to the same CRL schemata. Knowledge Craft also supports an agenda mechanism that is especially suited to scheduling or other event-driven applications. Support for event queues and user defined evaluation metrics enables blackboard architectures to be easily implemented. CRL-OPS and CRL-PROLOG modules may be evoked as actions associated with events or as evaluation procedures for assessing event preference.

3.3. Using KC for Design Prototypes

In the design phase, developers use prototyping tools to explore and evaluate alternative solutions. As with functional prototypes, tools which are modular, expressive, flexible, and varied will help for similar reasons. In addition, tools need to address design phase requirements for power, coherence, and openess.

Functional prototypes typically demonstrate possibilities but lack a coherent design philosophy that can be readily understood by implementation and maintenance teams. Thus, the Knowledge Craft strategy is to provide tools that enable the designer to achieve complex behavior from simple but powerful architectures. In well-designed KC applications, the skeletal core of a program, i.e. the overall control strategy, exploits a single paradigm (e.g., OPS, PROLOG, Agenda Scheduling, or Blackboard) as a simplification which helps program comprehensibility, and consequently, maintenance.

Special purpose modules, however, might well be implemented with other tools. Consequently, each tool must be powerful enough to enable an interesting range of functional modules. For this reason, OPS and PROLOG are both supported, rather than a single combined forward and backward chaining language. Much more power and coherence can be realized within the bounds of these languages than has been realized so far within languages that combine forward and backward chaining.

A second consideration during design is that the prototyping tool support an open architecture with call-outs to other languages and call-ins to its capabilities. While CRL-OPS and CRL-PROLOG provide built-in inferencing methods, a more general-purpose programming language is required to accomplish some design goals. Common Lisp is most typically used, as it is the most easily accessed from Knowledge Craft, and strongly supports symbol manipulation.

Call-in is provided from Common Lisp to CRL. CRL includes a lisp library of functions for creating, modifying, and deleting schemata, and for defining relations. CRL-PROLOG and -OPS may be evoked from Common Lisp. More generally, Knowledge Craft can be seen as thoroughly embedded in Common Lisp. Access to any Knowledge Craft module is possible from arbitrary Common Lisp functions.

3.4. Using KC for Implementation Prototypes

In order to support knowledge-base expansion, Knowledge Craft provides representations that enable successive refinements. Furthermore, Knowledge Craft workcenters allow developers to move rapidly between editors and execution environments.

As a frame-based system in which data types can be arbitrarily defined, CRL permits rapid expansion by enabling architectures in which growth can be entirely supported through the specification of instances of known types. CRL provides the capability of defining restrictions on acceptable slot values for each type of object. When used, the integrity of the knowledge base can be preserved during rapid expansion as the restrictions will provide the constraints necessary to ensure the proper instantiation of new instances.

Because of the complex structure of many knowledge bases, the expansion of a knowledge base requires special-purpose tools for displaying and browsing the knowledge base. Knowledge Craft provides an Interactive Schema Editor. This editor can be customized to acquire knowledge through prompts to domain experts or knowledge engineers whose task it is to expand systems by instantiating types of schemata. Prompts, restriction tests, help messages, and error messages can be associated with each slot of a schema type. When a knowledge engineer instantiates or fills in a schema of a particular type, the interaction is managed by the Interactive Schema Editor in accordance with the schematic type specification.

In more complex cases, developers rely on a a tree-editor to display connectivity within the knowledge-base. The developer can request that the entire connectivity be shown; or that only connectivity over a specified set of relations be displayed. A schema editor provides access to the slot values associated with each object.

3.5. Knowledge Craft limitations

Although the Knowledge Craft toolkit is a rich one that supports many prototyping needs, function and design prototypes took longer to build with Knowledge Craft than its users typically found desirable. On examination, this was traced to two causes. First, while the necessary tools and function libraries were available, building a system in which they could be used was a time-consuming first step. For instance, identifying files and creating load functions, specifying skeletal control mechanisms, and defining cleanup routines, were basic operations left to the KC user. Developers, however, wanted an initial system configuration within which customized prototypes could be developed. Secondly, novice developers were floundering without stronger guidance on how to use KC tools effectively. Less-experienced developers simply did not architect their systems to enable local refinement in a manner that did not disrupt the system as a whole.

The Rapid Prototyping Methodology^{tm} (RPM), discussed in the following section, addresses these problems. RPM enhances Knowledge Craft with a structured prototyping environment and an explicit programming methodology.

4. RAPID PROTOTYPING METHODOLOGY

The Rapid Prototyping Methodology expands Knowledge Craft capabilities and addresses its limits. RPM is realized in terms of a Rapid Prototyping Shell (RPS). The shell is a partially complete, but functional, knowledge-based system. It provides both a default system architecture and a library of system management, control, and user interface functions. The key idea is for developers to use RPS as a core or seed architecture for application-specific prototypes. Within RPS, developers unfold prototypes using or customizing modular pre-packaged options. The default system provides a testbed, allowing functional specification and design efforts to focus on critical modules. Thus, using an inside-out strategy, a designer could articulate the domain model and problem solver, while relying on RPS to provide default interfaces and basic system management functions. Alternatives are explored quickly, while basic system engineering issues are kept at bay.

RPS provides novice developers with a system design that facilitates iterative modification and the effective use of Knowledge Craft tools. Based on a knowledge-based architecture, RPS provides an example of effective design. RPS is extended using an explicit methodology of program devclopmont. As a roadmap to the system and its use, users receive modular, well-documented code.

4.1. Architecture

The RPS architecture relies on a model of a generalized knowledge-based system, (figure 4-1). The model is composed of five key objects, each of which is represented as a CRL schema: the System, Knowledge-Base, Problem-Solver, Interface, and Environment. Each of these objects has important attributes, relations, and methods associated with it.

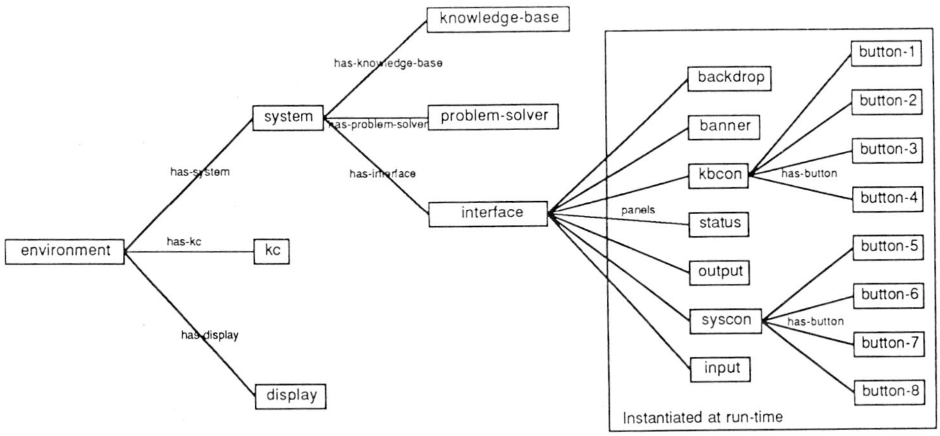

Figure 4-1: RPS Architecture

The **System** represents an application in its entirety. A system is defined by instantiating the relational slots -- *has-problem-solver, has-knowledge-base* and *has-interface*. In addition, the System object identifies a working directory and source file. Developers build customized applications by substituting or modifying system components and identifying appropriate files and system management information.

The three system components each define appropriate default behavior and include a backpointer (relation) to the system to which they belong. The **Knowledge-Base** represents the domain model. Methods for managing the entire knowledge-base (load, initialize, modify, display, and destroy) are associated here. The **Problem-Solver** represents the application's problem solver. Necessary methods for execution,

```
{{ SYSTEM
   INSTANCE:               ENTITY
   NAME:                   "RPM PROTOTYPING SHELL"
   WORKING-DIRECTORY:      "[BAUER.RPM.32.EG]"
   SOURCE-FILES:           "KERNEL" "ENVIRONMENT" "SYSTEM"
                           "PANELS" "BUTTONS" "INTERFACE"
                           "KNOWLEDGE-BASE" "PROBLEM-SOLVER"
   HAS-KNOWLEDGE-BASE:     KNOWLEDGE-BASE
   HAS-PROBLEM-SOLVER:     OPS-PROBLEM-SOLVER
   HAS-INTERFACE:          INTERFACE
}}
```

Figure 4-2: The System Schema

initialization and state display, among others are instantiated here. The **Interface** includes basic methods for input and output, as well as screen management and clean-up. The **Interface** is a composite object, defined in terms of more primitive objects, such as windows (panels) and mouseable buttons. Different interface options are available as schema instances which may be optionally referenced by the composite **Interface**.

Finally, the **Environment** extends the **System** concept to include information of global relevance to a development effort with multiple versions, or systems. The machine platform, software versions, user ID, and site conventions on file names, are stored here.

In addition to the specialized methods identified above, each of the system components has a set of methods that RPS requires for any programming object, or **Entity**, within it. These are

- **Instantiate** creates an instance of an entity.
- **Input** changes its state.
- **Execute** runs the entity (a noop by default).
- **Output** acquires the entity's state.
- **Initialize** returns the entity to its created state.
- **Eradicate** destroys the entity.

Something can be created, modified, and executed; it can be displayed, reset, and destroyed. Other behaviors can be defined, but these few are basic to clean system design. Prior to the availability of RPS, such behaviors were often implemented in a time consuming, haphazard method. By having a core set of names that cover the engineering basics, fewer methods proliferate making programming easier.

Each type of entity has default methods defined in a manner appropriate to its functional role. For instance, "Instantiate the Knowledge-Base" means load the application specific domain model; "Initialize the Interface" clears the screen by default; "Execute the Problem-Solver" runs the application-specific problem solver. RPS includes over sixty default methods.

4.2. Customizing RPS

RPS may be customized or extended in the small or in the large. By *in the small*, we refer to the modification of existing methods or objects. When developers modify default methods, for instance, adjusting the screen location of an input window, they are making local or "in the small" refinements. By *in the large* we refer to the substitution or addition of new objects and methods. When developers substitute knowledge bases or add new objects, such as a simulation engine, they are making modifications "in the large". The addition of new methods to existing objects, for instance, associating record and playback methods with the **Interface** object, may be classified as major modifications.

RPS facilitates extensions of both kinds. By providing default methods which exemplify and document syntax and functionality, small modifications which follow RPS conventions are unlikely to disrupt system integrity. With over sixty defaults, considerable customizations can be achieved through the modification of default methods.

"In the large" modifications are supported by example and explicit constraints. For instance, the substitution of a new interface for one which is hindering communication with a client can be done as long as the developer makes sure that all the attributes, relations, and methods associated with an **Interface** object are either properly inherited (from the Entity or Interface object) or specified in the new instance.

When new object types are added, RPS provides an example of effective programming. For instance, where a problem solver is designed to assess alternatives proposed by a simulation engine, the RPS approach would urge creating a *has-simulation-engine* relation from the problem solver to the simulation engine. Following RPS examples, the developer would access methods in the simulation engine indirectly by sending messages to the value of the *has-simulation-engine* relation. Consequently, modularity is preserved, as the developer can substitute one simulation engine for another without changing problem-solver code, as long as the messages remain the same.

4.3. Experience with RPS

RPS has been introduced recently to developers at Carnegie Group as well as to clients attending a knowledge engineering course. While we have no formal data on RPS's impact on prototype development, informal reports are encouraging. The benefit of starting with a minimal, but functional, system has been widely appreciated. The categorization and documentation of default methods has greatly facilitated customization. Finally, though premature, there is the expectation that the modular methodology inherent in RPS will reduce the effort to develop production quality code following a design exploration. Rather than continuously altering a module, developers are encouraged to substitute alternative options across the many small modules that are brought together in the system model.

5. EXAMPLE

The following provides an example of RPS and Knowledge Craft in use. It illustrates many of the concepts discussed above by walking through the construction of a simplified functional prototype. The application is an expert system for monitoring alarm conditions associated with factory floor machines. The requirements are to 1) filter out redundancy in multiple alarm conditions associated with the same event; 2) present the operator with alarms in order of importance; and 3) help the operator select a corrective action for the most pressing alarm.

As background, consider a temperature sensitive process isolated at a single machine. Deviations from the thermal set point are monitored and distinct alarms are triggered under three conditions: 1-5, 5 - 10, and 10 degrees above the set point. The alarms may cascade, such that when the temperature deviates more than 10 degrees all the alarms become active.

When the alarms activate, the operator's attention must be drawn to the most critical, or primary, alarm. Associated with each alarm is a corrective action. In order of seriousness, these are to open vents, add coolant, and shut down with a call to the line supervisor.

Starting with RPS, the developer has an operational system in hand. The system can be started; an interface comes up; and default buttons can be mouse selected (see figure 5-1). RPS provides a robust mock-up of the future system -- the default actions don't do a whole lot, but they keep the system integral and crash-proof. Starting with a robust, functioning system, the developer can turn quickly to address issues of application customization. Customization is achieved by modifying default methods, copy and editing system objects, such as buttons, and creating application-specific knowledge bases and problem solvers.

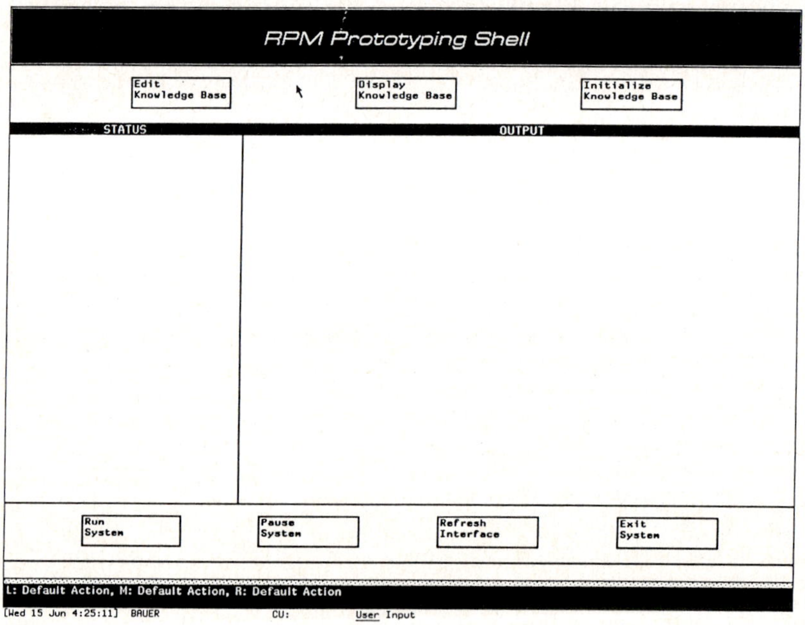

Figure 5-1: RPS Default Interface

5.1. Building the Prototype

5.1.1. Restructuring the Interface

We begin by replacing RPS's two default windows with an application-specific interface composed of three panels. These will display the primary alarm, carry on a dialogue with the user, and display status messages. In order to do this, the default behavior of the the *instantiate* method for the **Interface** object must be changed.

Figure 5-1 shows the default calls. Each method is expressed using the RPS send function (->). The function is followed by arguments for the receiving object, the method, an ID for the panel, a label, coordinates, and an association to an interface object.

```
(-> 'text-panel   'instantiate 'status    "STATUS"
    :xl 0.00 :xr 0.40 :yt 0.20 :yb 0.86 :panel-of interface)

(-> 'text-panel   'instantiate 'output    "OUTPUT"
    :xl 0.40 :xr 1.00 :yt 0.20 :yb 0.86 :panel-of interface)
```

Figure 5-2: Default Methods

Using these methods as examples, the developer can make simple changes with respect to the number of panels, labels, and position. These changes are shown in figure 5-3. In the first of the new methods, for example, notice that there is a new internal name (e.g. 'output), a new label, "DIALOGUE", and new coordinates.

```
(-> 'text-panel   'instantiate 'output    "DIALOGUE"
    :xl 0.00 :xr 0.40 :yt 0.20 :yb 0.50 :panel-of interface)

(-> 'text-panel   'instantiate 'primary   "PRIMARY ALARM"
    :xl 0.40 :xr 1.00 :yt 0.20 :yb 0.50 :panel-of interface)

(-> 'text-panel   'instantiate 'status    "STATUS"
    :xl 0.00 :xr 1.00 :yt 0.50 :yb 0.86 :panel-of interface)
```

Figure 5-3: Application Specific Methods

The system name and the buttons that are part of the two control panels are also redefined. Changing the value in the name slot of the **System** object from "Prototyping Shell" to "Alarm Management Assistant", results in the display of an an appropriate nameplate. The top control panel's three generic buttons (see figure 5-1) are replaced with application-specific ones: "Show State", "Test Alarm", "Give Help", and "Take Action". This is done by copying and editing example buttons. Exiting the Shell and starting it up again results in the application-specific interface, as in figure 5-4.

Control in the program is through the user interface. When "Test Alarm" is selected, temperature sensors are read and alarms activated as appropriate. Users can ask for corrective actions to be recommended and executed through the help and action buttons. Thus, the basic programming strategy is to associate an application-specific *execute* method with each button.

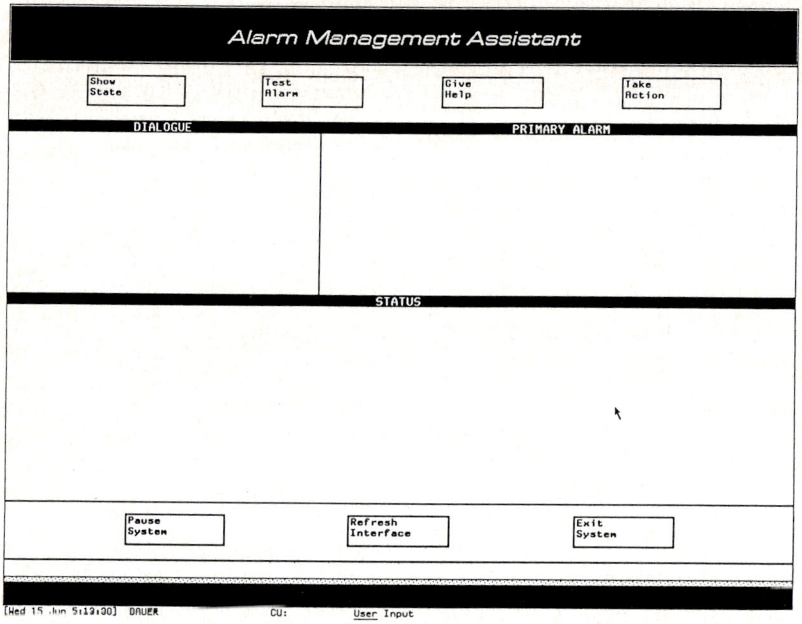

Figure 5-4: Application Specific Interface

5.1.2. Creating the Knowledge Base

The next step in this application is to build the domain model. A simple model composed of machines and alarms is sufficient. The Knowledge Craft Network Editor can be entered from RPS in order to create the necessary schemata, see figure 5-5.

Each of the alarms is represented as an instance of **alarm**; and each of the corrective actions as an instance of **corrective-action**. By RPS convention, all objects are members of the class **domain-entity**. This is an RPS schema that defines default behavior for all domain entities, as opposed to entities which are system objects, like the **Interface** or **Problem Solver**.

Relations between objects in the domain model are also created in the Network Editor. In order to represent the cascading alarm sequence, we use the relation *follows*. A relation between alarms and corrective actions is shown with the relation *corrects*, and its inverse *corrected-by* (not shown). Once the knowledge base is created, the RPS default for "Show State" will display the **domain-entities** created in the Network Editor. Application-specific display of domain knowledge can be realized by simply modifying the default method. The domain model is completed when alarm conditions are associated with each alarm.

5.1.3. Defining the Problem Solver

The problem-solving or inferential goal is to filter the alarms by recognizing which is the most critical, or primary, alarm; and to display its status to the operator. After a "TEST ALARM" selection determines the status of all alarms, a CRL-OPS knowledge source is activated.

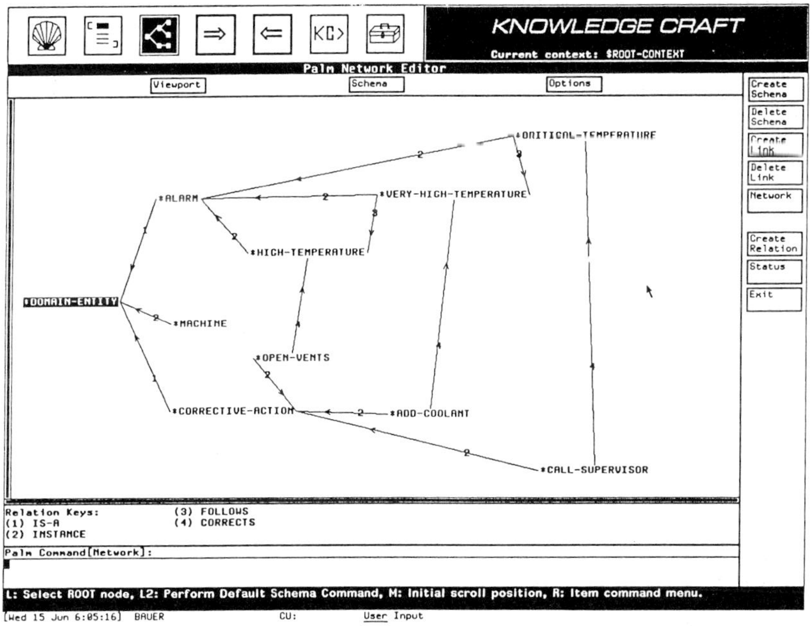

Figure 5-5: KC Network Editor

Three CRL-OPS rules are used to match different patterns across the alarms, (figure 5-6). The first condition of each determines that the rule's knowledge source is active. The additional conditions look for relations between activated alarms. The right hand actions of each rule can both modify the domain model and send messages that affect system behavior.

The **handle-primary-alarm** rule is matched when there is an active alarm that is not followed by another active alarm. In this case, the active alarm reflects the highest temperature in the current sampling. When this rule fires, the applications's **interface** object is indirectly referenced, in line with RPM programming style. Attribute and relational fields of the **machine** object are updated. And finally, the occurrence of a primary alarm is brought to the operator's attention by sending an *output* message to the appropriate panel.

The **handle-secondary-alarm** rule matches an active alarm that is followed by another, more critical, active alarm. Secondary alarms of this kind are noted, but not reported to the operator. Finally, the **notify-nominal** rule just lets the operator know that there are no current alarm conditions.

In larger applications, developing a rule-based component would require use of the Knowledge Craft CRL-OPS Workcenter for testing and debugging (figure 5-7). Effective use of the Workcenter requires a suspension of the normal application interface, as the Workcenter takes over the screen. However, it is also desirable to direct application I/O to a window appropriately superimposed within the Workcenter. If this were not done, application window manipulation would compete with the Workcenter. In most programming environments, this situation must be addressed by modifying application code during a debug cycle.

```
(p handle-primary-alarm
   (knowledge-source
     ^status active)
   (alarm
     ^status active
     ^schema-name <alarm>
     )
  -(alarm
     ^status active
     ^follows <alarm>
     )
   -->
   (let ((interface
          (get-value *current-system* 'has-interface))
         )
     (-> interface 'initialize :panel 'primary)
     (new-value 'machine 'status 'in-trouble)
     (new-value 'machine 'primary-alarm <alarm>)
     (-> <alarm> 'output :panel 'primary)
     )
   )

(p handle-secondary-alarm
   (knowledge-source
     ^status active)
   (alarm
     ^status active
     ^schema-name <alarm>
     )
   (alarm
     ^status active
     ^follows <alarm>
     )
   -->
   (add-value 'machine 'secondary-alarm <alarm>)
   )

(p notify-nominal
   (knowledge-source
     ^status active)
  -(alarm
     ^status active
     )
   -->
   (let ((interface
          (get-value *current-system* 'has-interface))
         )
     (-> interface 'initialize :panel 'primary)
     (new-value 'machine 'status 'ok)
     (-> 'machine 'output :panel 'status)
     )
   )
```

Figure 5-6: CRL-OPS Rules

RPM provides a better approach. Since RPS has an entity [the Interface object] that defines I/O, and supports indirect access [e.g., (get-value *current-system* 'has-interface)], another interface instance that maps application I/O to a panel within the CRL-OPS Workcenter can be swapped into the current-system *has-interface* relation. Aftor the rules are debugged, the full screen application interface may be swapped back in. No modification of code is needed in order to design variant interfaces appropriate to the development task; nor has it been necessary to lose control over the application interface while in the CRL-OPS Workcenter.

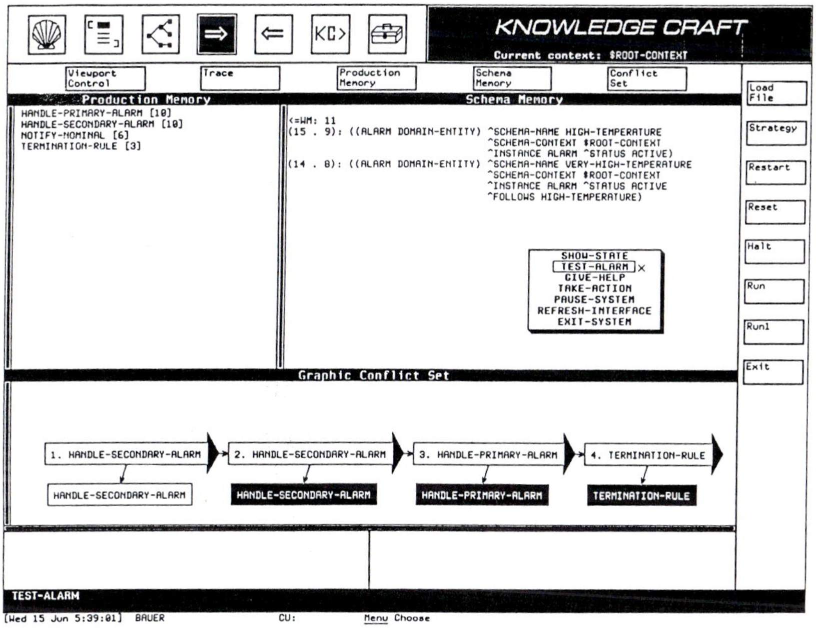

Figure 5-7: CRL-OPS Workcenter

5.1.4. Completing the Functional Prototype

Finally, the corrective action for the primary alarm condition must be displayable. An *output* method is defined for the "GET HELP" button. Taking advantage of the domain model, this method accesses the **corrected-by** relation of machine. Since the correction depends on which alarm is the primary alarm for the machine, this value is implicit -- i.e., the domain model is used to inherit the action from the *corrected-by* slot of the alarm.

Next, it is necessary to evolve the behavior of the "Show State" button from displaying all domain entities (for development purposes) to displaying the status of all alarms (for application purposes). The **"Show State" button** has an *execute* method that sends a message to the *output* method of the **knowledge base**. Modifying this method to send a message to each alarm's *output* method - a method, that is already designed to print out status - will achieve the desired result.

Finally, in order to print active alarms ahead of inactive one, CRL-PROLOG is used to determine the class of alarms of a particular status. The axiom (figure 5-8) provides a general mechanism for finding schemata with a specific status in a specific relation to another schema. The head of of the axiom is matched by a term in which Find-Object is followed by instantiations for all variables (?A) except for ?Some-Object, to which an answer is bound. The tail has two terms. The :Related operator is used to test or access CRL relations. The :Schema operator tests or accesses the value of a slot.

```
((FIND-OBJECT ?RELATION ?SOME-OBJECT ?THIS-OBJECT ?STATUS)
 <
 (:RELATED ?THIS-OBJECT <RELATION> <SOME-OBJECT>)
 (:SCHEMA <THIS-OBJECT> (STATUS ?STATUS))
 ))
```

Figure 5-8: CRL-PROLOG Axiom

A properly formulated query will match this axiom in determining all the alarms which are active; and a similar query will find the inactive ones. In more complex CRL-PROLOG applications, developers make use of the CRL-PROLOG workcenter shown in figure 5-9.

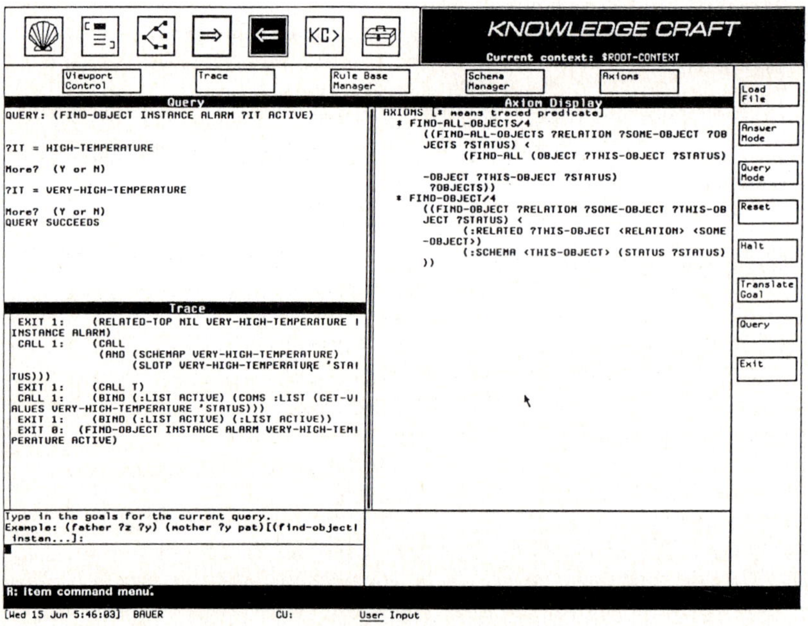

Figure 5-9: CRL-PROLOG Workcenter

5.1.5. Conclusion

Although superficial, the above example illustrates many RPM concepts, as well as specific features of Knowledge Craft and RPS. Both "in the small" and "in the large" modifications have been shown. Starting with the RPS shell, the developer can rapidly modify interfaces through the refinement of default methods. "In the large" modifications are evident in the creation of a domain-specific knowledge base and problem solver. Module substitution illustrates a technique for easily moving between a Workcenter development environment and application-specific interfaces.

Knowledge Craft Workcenters and capabilities appear throughout the example. Both CRL-OPS and CRL-PROLOG were shown to match easily against the domain model expressed in terms of CRL schemata. Object-oriented programming is integrated with CRL-OPS and RPS.

6. CONCLUSION

Developers of knowledge-based systems rely heavily on prototypes across several phases of the software lifecycle. Prototyping goals naturally differ across these phases. Functional prototypes elicit requirements; design prototypes explore solutions; and implementation prototypes mark milestones as partially complete systems. While design prototypes may be exploratory and undisciplined, implementation prototypes must incrementally realize a maintainable production quality system.

Across all phases, tools need to be modular, expressive, flexible, and varied. In addition, tools need to address issues unique to the different phases. For design, this means power, coherence, and openess. During implementation, it means support for successive refinements that do not throw the overall reliability of a system into question.

In discussing Knowledge Craft, we illustrated one approach to fulfilling this very broad set of requirements. Knowledge Craft's toolkit strategy, however, has limits. It does not provide developers an initial system configuration within which customized prototypes may be built without time-consuming attention to system management functions. Secondly, it does not provide novice developers adequate guidance in the effective use of Knowledge Craft tools.

The Rapid Prototyping Methodology and Shell address these problems by extending Knowledge Craft with a structured prototyping environment. RPS is a partially complete, but functional, knowledge-based system. It provides both a default system architecture and a library of system management, control, and user-interface functions. Based on a knowledge-based architecture, RPS provides an example of effective design to novice developers.

References

1. Clocksin, W.F., Mellish, C.S.. *Programming in Prolog.* Springer-Verlag, Berlin, 1981.

2. Forgy, C.L. The OPS5 Users Manual. Carnegie-Mellon University, 1981.

3. Gomaa, H., and Scott, D..B. Prototyping As a Tool in the Specification of User Interfaces. Proceedings of ICSE 5, San Diego, 1981.

4. Hayes-Roth, F., Waterman, D.A., Lenat, D.B.. *Building Expert Systems.* Addison-Wesley, Reading, Mass., 1983.

5. Kahn, G.S. TEST: A Model-Driven Application Shell. Proceedings AAAI-87, Los Altos, Ca., 1987, pp. 814-818.

6. Pepper, J. and Kahn, G. Knowledge Craft: An Environment for Rapid Prototyping of Expert Systems. Proceedings of Artificial Intelligence for the Automotive Industry, 1986.

7. Zelkowitz, M., Shaw, A., Gannon, J.. *Principles of Software Engineering and Design.* Prentice Hall, Englewood Cliffs, New Jersey, 1979.

Topics in Expert System Design
G. Guida and C. Tasso (Editors)

FAST PROTOTYPING OF EXPERT SYSTEMS USING PROLOG

Ivan BRATKO

**E. Kardelj University and J. Stefan Institute
Ljubljana, Yugoslavia**

1. INTRODUCTION

Rapid prototyping is one of important recent paradigms of software development, offering at least a partial alternative to the traditional software life-cycle. According to the review in Agresti (1986), the objective of prototyping is to clarify the characteristics and operation of a product or a system by constructing a version that can be exercised. Prototyping is specially important when the user's requirements for a system are not well understood. A prototype eases the discussion between developers and users by allowing their discussion to focus on real behaviour in exercising the prototype.

In expert systems, the need for creating behaviour, although in prototype form, is clearly even more obvious than in traditional software development because uncertainty in development of expert systems is much higher than in traditional software. This uncertainty comes from the user's lack of understanding of his or her own needs, lack of understanding how expert knowledge can be represented in the system, transferred to the system, and made operational in the system. It is also often

(b) there is no syntactic distinction between the knowledge base and the rest of the program.

3. PROGRAMMING BASIC MECHANISMS OF RULE-BASED EXPERT SYSTEMS IN PROLOG

3.1 Prolog's own backward chaining

Basic mechanisms of rule-based programming are easily implemented in Prolog. For example, consider a small knowledge base in Figure 1, comprised of four rules. This can be, for a start, written as a Prolog program directly:

```
a  :-  b.
a  :-  c.
b  :-  d, e.
c  :-  e.
```

Now suppose the user knows that **e** is true. Then this can also be added to the program as the fact:

```
e.
```

The Prolog interpreter can now be asked directly whether **a** is true:

```
?-  a.
yes
```

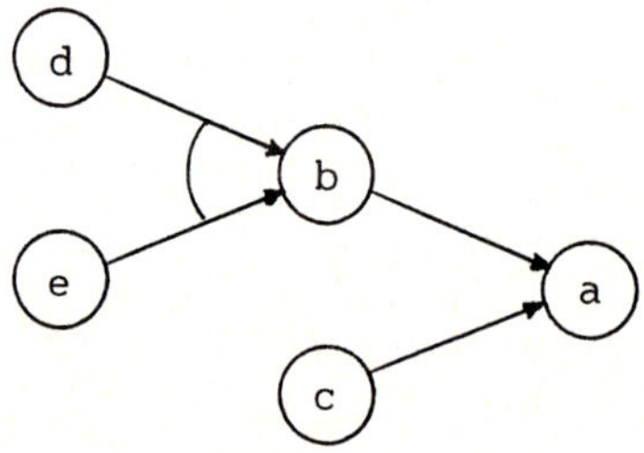

FIGURE 1 A small knowledge base. The arc connecting two links indicates conjunctive connection between the links.

Even this very basic level of using Prolog for an expert system, although too simplistic for a more ambitious application, is often used. For example, Allen and Saxon (1988) developed a legal expert system in which direct application of Prolog as a reasoning shell in the style essentially as above was quite sufficient. To make this Prolog part work with the rest of their program, which is written in Pascal, they even extended their Pascal part to transform legal rules into the syntax of Prolog clauses.

In the foregoing example, Prolog's own reasoning strategy was used as an inference mechanism. Prolog's strategy is backward chaining in the depth-first fashion. Accordingly, in our example the reasoning started with the goal **a**, and ended when the fact **e** was encountered. As Prolog is a general programming language, other types of reasoning can be implemented. The only difference is that to implement depth-first backward chaining no programming is needed at all, whereas other strategies have to be programmed.

3.2 Tailoring the syntax of rules

Before we discuss other strategies let us consider the syntax for rules. Up till now we have simply been using Prolog's own syntax for rules. This has disadvantages:

(1) this syntax may not be the most suitable for a user unfamiliar with Prolog, for example the domain expert who should be able to read the rules, specify new rules and modify them;

(2) the knowledge base is thus not syntactically distinguishable from the rest of the program; a more explicit distinction between the knowledge base and the rest of the program may be desirable.

It is easiest to tailor the syntax of expert rules to our needs by using Prolog operator notation. For example, we can choose to use 'if', 'then' and 'and' as infix operators, which can be appropriately declared by:

```
:- op( 800, fx, if).
:- op( 700, xfx, then).
:- op( 200, xfy, and).
```

This suffices to write our example rules as:

```
if b then a.
if c then a.
if d and e then b.
if e then c.
```

Of course we now need a new interpreter. This is easily defined as in Figure 2. This interpreter still does depth-first backward chaining.

```
% Backward chaining interpreter

is_true( P)  :-
  fact( P).

is_true( P)  :-
  if Cond then P,
  is_true( P).

is_true( P1 and P2)  :-
  is_true( P1),
  is_true( P2).
```

FIGURE 2 A simple backward chaining interpreter.

3.3 Implementing forward chaining

Figure 3 shows a forward chaining interpreter. This starts with the known facts, represented as the **fact** relation, and adds to this relation all the facts that follow from the current facts and rules. For simplicity this program assumes that the generated facts do not contain variables. **bagof** is a Prolog built-in predicate that generates all solutions. That is, in Figure 3, all new facts that can be derived in one step. If there is no such new fact then **bagof** fails.

```
% Forward chaining interpreter

forward :-
  bagof( Fact, new_fact( Fact), NewFacts),     % Infer new facts
  forward.


new_fact( Concl) :-
  if Cond then Concl,          % A rule
  not fact( Concl),            % Rule's conclusion not yet a fact
  composed_fact( Cond),        % Condition true?
  asserta( fact( Concl)).      % Assert Concl as new fact

composed_fact( Cond) :-
  fact( Cond).                 % Simple fact

composed_fact( Cond1 and Cond2) :-
  composed_fact( Cond1),
  composed_fact( Cond2).             % Both conjuncts true
```

FIGURE 3 A forward chaining interpreter.

3.4 Adding uncertainty

The foregoing example can be easily extended to handle uncertainty. Each assertion is simply added a certainty qualification, usually as a number between, say, 0 and 1. We can choose to represent this as a pair of the form:

Assertion / CertaintyFactor

Rules with uncertainty can be similarly extended with degree of certainty to which the rule is valid:

if Condition then Conclusion / Certainty.

Figure 4 shows simple interpreter for rules with uncertainty. This interpreter uses the following simple rules for combining certainties (complicated discussion on what is the best way of combining certainties is clearly beyond the scope of this paper). Let P1 and P2 be assertions, and c(P1) and c(P2) denote

```
% Rule interpreter with certainties

certainty( P, Cert)  :-
  given( P, Cert).

certainty( P, Cert)  :-
  follows_from_rule( P, Cert),     % Cert follows from a rule
  not ( follows_from_rule( P, Cert1),
        Cert1 > Cert).             % No higher certainty
                                   % follows from any other rule

certainty( Cond1 and Cond2, Cert)  :-
  certainty( Cond1, Cert1),
  certainty( Cond2, Cert2),
  minimum( Cert1, Cert2, Cert).

follows_from_rule( P, Cert)  :-
  if Cond then P/C1,
  certainty( Cond, C2),
  Cert is C1*C2.

% A sample rule-base

if b then a/0.7.
if c then a/0.8.
if d and e then b/1.
if e then c/1.

given( d, 0.1).
given( e, 0.9).
```

FIGURE 4 An interpreter for rules with certainties.

the certainties of P1 and P2 respectively. Then:

c(P1 and P2) = min(c(P1), c(P2))

c(P1 or P2) = max(c(P1), c(P2))

If there is a rule

if P1 then P2 / C

then

c(P2) = c(P1) * C

If there are two rules bearing on the same assertion, then they are interpreted as disjunction.

3.5 Explanation and querying the user

Interaction with the user involves explanation of the system's decisions, and querying the user about information that is currently needed during the reasoning process. There are two standard types of explanation: how-type and why-type. They are generated in response to the user's questions of the forms: How did you derive this answer? Why do you need this particular information?

These features can be implementing as a more general predicate:

solve(CurrentQuestion, Trace, ProofTree)

Figure 5 illustrates the meaning of the three arguments: **CurrentQuestion** is the question the system is currently trying to answer. This can be a subquestion of some initial, more complex question, denoted by **TopQuestion** in Figure 5. **TopQuestion** and **CurrentQuestion** are connected by a chain of rules and intermediate questions. This chain is here called **Trace. ProofTree** is a proof of the answer to **CurrentQuestion.**

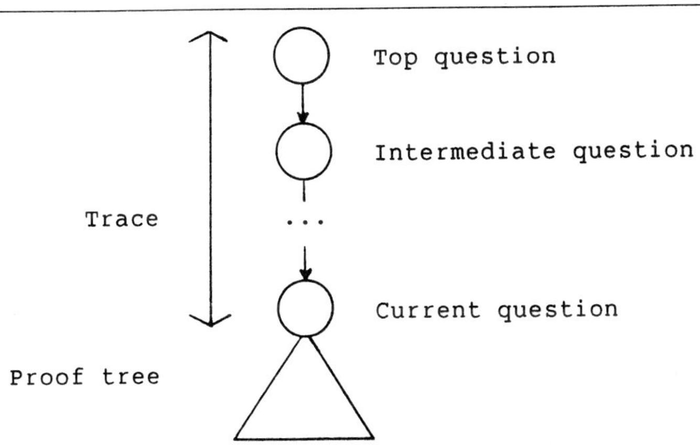

FIGURE 5 Objects for explanation.

The predicate **solve** can answer the current question by one of the three main alternative ways:

(1) If the current question can be found as a fact in the knowledge base then the answer is immediately known and the proof tree (trivial in this case) contains the answer.

(2) If the current question can be asked of the user then query the user (for example, in the case of medical diagnosis the user is asked about external manifestations). The user may now ask 'Why?'. If so, present the user with **Trace** as the why-explanation.

(3) If there is a rule in the knowledge-base bearing on the current question, then apply the rule and solve the thus created subquestions, inserting all these into the proof tree.

A complete expert system shell in Prolog that implements these principles is given in (Bratko 1986). It should be noted that querying the user is one thing that cannot be programmed nearly as elegantly as the rest of the program. The reason for this is that querying the user requires precise statement of the interaction procedure with the user. In this case it is not sufficient to merely produce the right logical conclusions, but also to produce them in a sequence that appears natural from the point of view of the user who is interacting with the system.

4. IMPLEMENTING KNOWLEDGE REPRESENTATION FORMALISMS IN PROLOG

A computational formalism for representing knowledge consists of:

(1) a description language that has some syntax and formal meaning, and

(2) an interpreter, i.e. a procedure that realises the formal meaning of a description written in the description language.

Prolog itself is a computational formalism for representing knowledge. Prolog's description language is predicate logic limited to Horn clauses. Prolog's interpretation procedure is SLD resolution (this is a simplification, of course, disregarding Prolog's built-in predicates). Logic itself is a good knowledge representation formalism.

Other known knowledge representation formalisms include semantic networks, frames, and object-oriented programming. Prolog, being based on predicate logic, is more general of all these. As Malpas (1986) points out, the 'conceptual overhead' of predicate logic as a representation formalism is limited to two ontological assumptions:

(1) entities exist, and
(2) relations between entities exist.

Other formalisms come with additional built-in concepts, such as objects, hierarchical relations, inheritance, and default values. These concepts are often useful in representing knowledge, but they also impose constraints on the way of representing knowledge. Representing knowledge in Prolog is in this respect more general as none of these additional concepts is necessarily imposed. On the other hand, each of them can be easily implemented in Prolog. Doing any of them in Prolog then more or less amounts to a particular style of representing knowledge in Prolog.

Implementing semantic networks in Prolog is obviously straightforward as it mainly requires handling binary relations. Implementing frames and mechanisms of object-oriented programming is slightly more interesting, and we outline the principles in the next paragraphs. Other paradigms, such as blackboard architecture, are easily done in Prolog as well. Bratko (1986) gives an interpreter in Prolog for pattern-directed systems which are closely related to blackboard systems.

4.1 Implementing frames

A frame can be viewed as a data structure, consisting of a number of slots. Each frame has a name, and each slot has a name. A slot can be filled by a value. There are relations between frames, the most important relation being 'a kind of'. This relation enables the frame system to infer values for unfilled slots by means of inheritance. If frame F1 is 'a kind of' frame F2, and a slot in F1 is not filled, then the slot's value can be obtained (inherited) from F2. Let us outline one possible implementation of this in Prolog.

The value of a filled slot can be, for example, stated as a Prolog fact of the form:

```
FrameName( SlotName, Value)
```

Further, the relation

```
a_kind_of( Frame1, Frame2)
```

says that **Frame1** is a kind of **Frame2**. Let the relation

```
value( Frame, Slot, Value)
```

be: **Value** is the value of slot **Slot** in frame **Frame**. If this slot is filled then this is the value; otherwise the value is obtained by climbing the **a_kind_of** relation thus obtaining the parent frame and inheriting the relevant value from it. Notice that the parent's frame value can also be obtained through inheritance. Here is the Prolog code:

```
value( Frame, Slot, Value)  :-
  Query =.. [Frame, Slot, Value],
  call( Query), !;
  value( Frame, a_kind_of, ParentFrame),
  value( ParentFrame, Slot, Value)
```

The Prolog built-in predicate '=..', used above, constructs a term **Query** of the form:

```
Query = Frame( Slot, Value)
```

The cut above prevents Prolog from further finding slot values from upper frames once a value has already been extracted.

Handling other concepts of frame representation, such as qualifying slots or the extension relation can be done in Prolog as easily. Rowe (1988) gives more examples.

4.2 Mechanisms of object-oriented programming

In object-oriented programming paradigm we have objects. Each object has a number of associated methods. Methods are nothing but procedures. Objects can send messages to other objects. Objects respond to messages by executing appropriate methods. Thus a message is in effect a procedure call.

As in frame representation, there are relations between objects: an object can be a kind of another object. For example, a rectangle is a kind of a polygon. Methods can be inherited. Suppose an object P1 receives a message mentioning method M, and P1 does not have method M. Then an object P2 can be found such that P1 is a kind of P2, and method M can be inherited from P2. P2 could have inherited M in turn from an upper object.

To implement these concepts we have to handle these essential mechanisms:

- adding new objects
- message passing
- inheritance

Figure 6 shows a simple Prolog program that does all this. Objects are represented by the relation

```
object( ObjectName, ObjectMethods)
```

where the methods are collected into a list:

```
ObjectMethods = [Method1, Method2, ...]
```

Each method here is in fact a Prolog term representing a call to a Prolog procedure. Each corresponding procedure is then stated separately in the rest of the program. A more sophisticated implementation, which introduces compilation of objects into Prolog, is given by Stabler (1986).

```
add( Object, Methods)  :-
  assert( object( Object, Methods)).

send( Message, Object)  :-
  find_method( Message, Object, Method),
  call( Method).

find_method( Message, Object,Message)  :-
  object( Object, Methods),
  member( Message, Methods), !.                  %Private method

find_method( Message, Object, Method)  :-
  a_kind_of( Object, ParentObject),
  find_method( Message, ParentObject, Method).   %Inherited
```

FIGURE 6 Outline interpreter for object-oriented programming

5. CONCLUSIONS

Prolog is a powerful language for expert systems programming. Its power comes mainly from its data structuring mechanism, built-in pattern matching, and other symbolic programming features.

The practical limitation of Prolog can turn out to be its relative computational inefficiency, relative compared with procedural languages such as Pascal and C. Also, not many existing Prolog implementations convincingly provide sophisticated user interaction facilities, graphics, and links for smooth and easy connection to other programming languages. As efficiency and these additional features are less important in prototyping in general, they are less critical in prototyping of expert systems as well. On the other hand, the expressive power of Prolog is such that developing a prototype in Prolog typically progresses simultaneously with the general development of ideas and decisions regarding knowledge representation and inference mechanisms.

Prolog itself can be used as a knowledge representation formalism, but other popular knowledge representation paradigms can be easily implemented in Prolog as well.

Lisp has in respect to expert systems similar advantages as Prolog, although structured objects are handled less naturally. The logical variable of Prolog is a very useful device, lacking in Lisp. To Lisp's advantage, Lisp environments and special purpose hardware are more advanced than their Prolog counterparts. Sophisticated Lisp environments contain large numbers of built-in functions which is a point for discussion. Although these functions are powerful programming means, since they are so many they take long time to learn which is an additional burden on the programmer, and can thus turn to Lisp's disadvantage.

In addition to computational inefficiency, another possible limitation of using Prolog could be that it requires the knowledge of programming in Prolog. In this respect, other tools for implementing expert systems may be advantageous. Some expert systems shells are much easier to learn to use than Prolog. If such a shell has a better user interface than Prolog then an impressive feasibility demonstration can be developed easier than in Prolog. Shells have, however, other disadvantages compared to Prolog: they are limited to a particular knowledge representation formalism, a particular inference mechanism and control strategy, and they do not

contain a general programming language.
Comparison between Prolog and sophisticated knowledge engineering environments is also many sided. Although powerful, sophisticated knowledge engineering environments typically take long time to learn to use, are more expensive and can be computationally inefficient. A significant and often overlooked drawback of such environments is simply the fact that there is less 'programming culture' built around each particular environment than around general programming languages such as Prolog. Each new environment is in effect a new programming language and it takes a lot of time and experience before programming in a new language is really understood by its users community and before appropriate textbooks appear. Also in comparison with shells and other environments, Prolog has a more sophisticated formal basis so that its syntax is clearer and semantics much better understood.

REFERENCES

Agresti, W.W. (1986, editor) New Paradigms for Software Development. IEEE Computer Society Press.

Allen, L.E., Saxon, C.S. (1988) Automatic generation of legal expert system of Article 12 of the Inheritance Act of Serbia. Proc. Int. Symp. Computer at University, Cavtat, Yugoslavia, June 1988.

Bratko, I. (1986) Prolog Programming for Artificial Intelligence, Addison-Wesley.

Bratko, I., Mozetic, I., Lavrac, N. (1988) KARDIO - a Study in Deep and Qulitative Knowledge for Expert Systems. MIT Press (to appear).

Malpas, J. (1987) Prolog: a Relational Language and its Applications. Prentice-Hall.

Mozetic, I., Bratko, I., Lavrac, N. (1986) Automatic synthesis and compression of electrocardiological knowledge. Expert Systems: Automating Knowledge Acquisition (D.Michie, I.Bratko) Addison-Wesley. Also to appear in Machine Intelligence 11 (eds. J. Hayes, D. Michie, J. Richards) Oxford Univ. Press.

Rowe, N.C. (1988) Artificial Intelligence through Prolog. Prentice-Hall.

Stabler, E.P. (1986) Object-oriented programming in Prolog. AI Expert, Oct. 1986, pp. 46-57.

Sterling, L., Shapiro, E. (1986) The Art of Prolog. MIT Press.

Taylor, T., Standish, T.A. (1982) Software Eng. Notes, December 1982, pp. 160-166. Also reprinted in Agresti 1986.

Topics in Expert System Design
G. Guida and C. Tasso (Editors)

FROM CLASSIC EXPERT SYSTEMS TO MODELS: INTRODUCTION TO A METHODOLOGY FOR BUILDING MODEL-BASED SYSTEMS

John C. KUNZ, Marilyn J. STELZNER, and Michael D. WILLIAMS

Intellicorp
Mountain View, CA, USA

1. Abstract

Classical expert systems have been built by representing empirical associations as described by experienced human experts. This paper presents examples of knowledge systems which are model-based: they represent and manipulate descriptions of the structure of a domain and the principles which characterize its behavior. Model-based systems have been developed as a way both to exploit existing knowledge of the principles of a domain and to extend the limited flexibility which is often found in classical expert systems. The model-based approach emphasizes representation of the structure and function of the modeled system and reasoning with respect to that structure and function. We discuss the methodology which has been used to develop such model-based systems and a number of important design issues. We particularly emphasize the model-based representation and reasoning and the interactive interfaces required to support these models. Examples are first presented of two different models, of different kinds of reasoning and interfaces which were used with those models. Following discussion of models, model-based reasoning and interactive interfaces, there is a discussion of the way that model-based reasoning and its supportive interfaces extend traditional expert systems and the engineering discipline of modeling.

2. Introduction

The model-based reasoning methodology described in this paper has been used extensively in diverse knowledge systems applications, including computer integrated manufacturing (CIM) applications [Kunz 88]. In this paper, examples are first presented of different models and of different kinds of reasoning which was done using those models. Then models and model-based reasoning are defined, and finally there is a discussion of the way that model-based reasoning extends and relates traditional expert systems and the engineering discipline of modeling. This model-based reasoning methodology has now been applied in more than a score of applications.

The model-based systems place significant new demands on user interfaces [Stelzner 88]. First, the models represent the structural and functional representation of a domain, so the interface must communicate those representations to users. The model-based systems tend to be built using a highly cooperative relation between the user and system in which users define the generic model, may specialize the model for a particular applications, and often participate actively in analysis of the model. Thus, the models can be characterized as expert advisory systems, rather than classical expert systems. This participatory style of interface for expert advisory systems suggests the metaphor of the *interface as model world* in which the user can define, analyze and manipulate a model. The concurrent increase in size and complexity of models with demand for support of modeling have led to methodologies for interface building which we discuss in this paper and to development of new technology for interface building.

Consider control, fault diagnosis, fault repair, and simulation of a spacecraft subsystem which is being designed for the space station of the 1990's. Operational versions of the proposed subsystem have not yet been built, although the system has been modeled mathematically and initial hardware prototypes have been created in the laboratory. Thus, its operational characteristics are not well understood, yet its operation will be complex enough that there is very high value in developing effective operational support systems which can be placed in service at the start of operations. In addition, because both system design and operations will inevitably change significantly, flexibility to modify and extend the operational systems will have great benefit.

Formal symbolic model-based reasoning provides a methodology which can be used effectively to develop knowledge systems in multiple related areas in which applications expertise may be lacking. In addition, because symbolic modeling is an extension of classical engineering modeling, the methodology of formal symbolic modeling provides the usual benefits of engineering modeling including the ability to create consistent related applications, testability, and effective explanation.

This paper introduces concepts of symbolic modeling and model based reasoning. Symbolic models describe the structure and function of modeled systems, and model based reasoning attempts to solve problems by analyzing the structure and function which is described in a model. A model is usually built with multiple purposes including investigating and solving some set of related problems and providing a framework for continuing to solve problems even as the modeled system changes. Interfaces then make the structure and function of the model available to the user for inspection, extension and modification.

The interface for these systems must support both the developers and the multiple users with their multiple intended uses. Thus, the interfaces must provide for descriptions and support for manipulation of:

- Symbolic models of a domain. The symbolic model is built of objects, relations among those objects and attributes of those objects. Graphs showing objects and their relations and displays of the detailed definition of objects are useful functions in support of symbolic description of models.

- Natural descriptions of the structure of domains, where natural is from the perspective of users. The users' model is often graphical, such as an electromechanical circuit diagram, layout of a complex system, or chart indicating design of some system. We have called these representations the "*natural metaphors*" of a domain. Graphical circuit diagrams which can be examined, modified and created are useful function in support of natural description of models.

- Natural descriptions of the behavior of domains, where natural is again from the perspective of users. Sometimes behavior can be shown by rule traces or, more usefully, rule graphs. We find that animation of circuit diagrams and layouts is often more effective, however, in showing the behavior of models.

3. Motivation

There is now a large literature on expert systems. Classical expert systems, as represented for example in [Buchanan 84], are designed to provide expert-level analysis of complex problems; to be understandable by their designers and their users; and to be flexible enough to accommodate new knowledge and change in the knowledge which is represented in them [Duda 83]. The wide discussion of these systems and their frequent use in business and science provide a measure of their intellectual interest and their practical value.

The methodology of building classical expert systems has focused on extracting the heuristic knowledge of experts and then representing that knowledge in the computer. For example, Buchanan and Shortliffe relate that an original goal of the MYCIN system was "computer acquisition of judgemental knowledge" [Buchanan 84]. They continue to say "...this work seeks to permit experts in the field of infectious disease therapy to teach the MYCIN system the therapeutic decision rules that they find useful in their clinical practice." The clinical practice of medicine appears to be based strongly on a systematic analysis of the data about a case in light of broad experiential knowledge [Eddy 82]. This early strong influence of the domain of clinical medicine led to experience-based judgemental knowledge as the fundamental knowledge content of expert systems.

There is an irony that experential knowledge became the knowledge of expert systems because there is an enormous and a rapidly expanding medical scientific literature in areas such as biochemistry, biomechanics and physiology. The classical expert systems do not explicitly represent this knowledge of the scientifically-founded principles of the domain. One of the motivations of the model-based approach is to use this principled knowledge when it is available and useful. This paper discusses the way that model-based systems include structure and functional principles of the domain in the content of the systems.

The early strong influence of the domain of clinical medicine led to another important characteristic of classical expert systems. In clinical medicine, therapeutic knowledge is expressed as rules relatively naturally. For example, a MYCIN rule is

```
IF:  1) The site of the culture is blood, and
     2) The gram stain of the organism is gramneg, and
     ...
THEN: There is suggestive evidence (.6) that the identity
of the organism is e.coli
```

The IF-THEN rule formalism is natural for expressing heuristic associations such as this relation between a set of observations and a conclusion. These associations indeed are often expressed by humans as rules. The IF-THEN rule formalism was then used as a formalism for representation of knowledge in the computer, and rule-based knowledge representation became associated with classical expert systems.

The knowledge representation formalisms which are appropriate for models, specifically for representing domain structure and functional principles, is often different than the representation which is appropriate for associations. This paper also discusses the use of frames and algorithms as AI knowledge representation formalisms which are useful, in addition to rules, for representing domain knowledge in model-based systems. The way in which frames, algorithms, rules and graphics complement each other in a "hybrid" AI system is discussed in [Kunz 84].

4. Examples

Model based reasoning can be used to analyze systems which are concrete, such as the built system described below in Section 4.1, or conceptual systems such as the theory of project management, as discussed later in Section 4.2[1]. An application system might include models of several concrete and several conceptual systems.

4.1. Fault Diagnosis in a System to Remove CO_2 from a Manned Spacecraft

NASA engineers wanted to test their ability to diagnose operational faults in an electrochemical system which is being designed to remove CO_2 from a new generation of manned spacecraft [Malin 85], [Malin 87]. The software developers chose to build their diagnostic system using an explicit symbolic model of the electromechanical design of the CO_2 removal system as shown in Figure 4-1. The knowledge based application system was developed from system design information, rather than description of empirical operational knowledge of an expert. When implemented on a graphics workstation, formal symbolic models can exploit natural graphical metaphors such as those implicit in this engineering diagram.

There is a crucial distinction in modeling methodology between the model and the modeled system: a formal symbolic model is a description, in a knowledge system, of some portions of the structure and function of a system which exists and is used independently of the model. The modeled system in this example is a piece of hardware, a fuel cell which removes CO_2 from air circulating in a spacecraft. Hardware engineers were designing, testing and building the prototype modeled system concurrently with the model development by the knowledge system development team. There were several purposes in creating the model-based reasoning system. In the example of the CO_2 removal system, the model includes the structure, function and purposes shown in Figure 4-2. This figure lists part of the structure and function of the modeled system diagrammed in Figure 4-1 which is represented in a knowledge system. In addition, this figure lists some of the purposes of the developers in creating their model-based reasoning system.

This application runs on AI workstations with graphics. The user can set

[1]The examples of this paper were implemented in KEE™, the Knowledge Engineering Environment. The KEE system is a product of IntelliCorp.

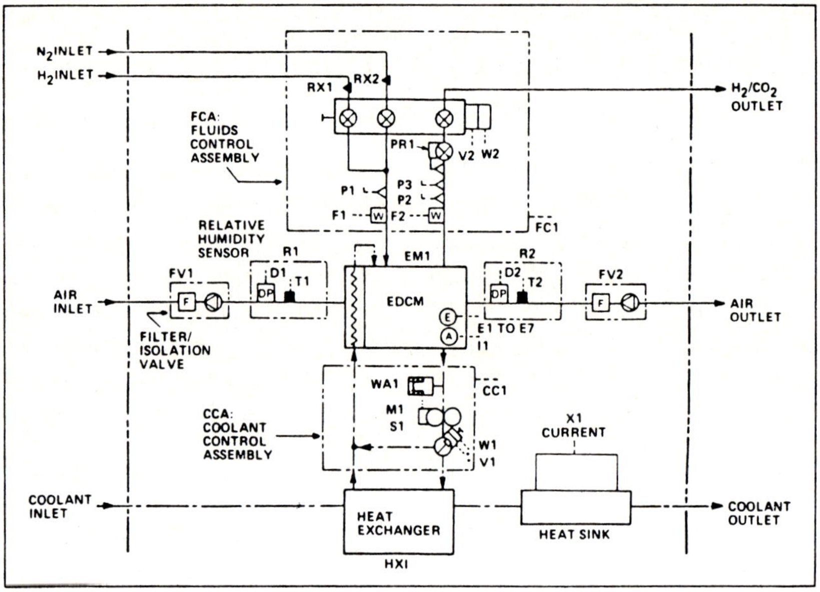

Figure 4-1: Schematic diagram of a system which is used by NASA design engineers.

parameter values by adjusting dials and gauges shown in Figure 4-3 and by selecting model components with the mouse and inspecting or changing component parameter values. Each of the icons in this diagram is active: using the mouse, a user can change the structure of the model by adding or deleting model components; examine and change component parameters; and introduce or remove faults. In addition, the user can ask the system or a component to perform particular functions. Model components highlight to show the changing focus of attention of the reasoning process, and various rule traces and invocation graphs can be displayed under user command. The interactive graphical workstation implementation facilitates browsing by allowing the user to view and modify the underlying symbolic structure of model components.

An "active rule graph", as shown in Figure 4-4, animates the invocation of rules, assisting the developer in debugging rules, and the end user in understanding the reasoning strategies the system is taking. This graph shows the successful and unsuccessful invocation of rules in a graphic form, helping both developers and users to understand the rule invocation process in a particular application.

This example model represents the structure of a modeled system both graphically and symbolically, and complementary use of both graphical and symbolic models is a recurring theme of model-based reasoning. Figure 4-3 shows the graphical description of the CO_2 removal system as included in the

- Structure of the CO_2 removal system, including:
  - o Concepts, including fluids circulating in the spacecraft, subsystems, and components;
  - o Concrete objects, including fluids such as coolant and CO_2, subsystems such as the air and coolant subsystems, and parts such as valves and pipes;
  - o Attributes of objects, including pressure, voltage;
  - o Relations among objects, including connections for gas flow, electrical connectivity.
- Function of the CO_2 removal system, including:
  - o Fluid transport through the system;
  - o CO_2 removal from the circulating air;
  - o Power generation, a byproduct of the fuel cell operation.
- Purposes of the developers in creating the model-based system, including to:
  - o Demonstrate the functions of the modeled system when operating normally;
  - o Identify all likely single faults in the modeled system and characterize modeled system functions when operating with any such fault;
  - o Develop diagnostic data collection, fault detection, isolation, compensation, correction and reporting procedures for the CO_2 removal system;
  - o Changing system operation mode in event of a detected fault to protect it and its environment from further damage or failure;
  - o Test diagnostic procedures, including procedures to make the system safe while preserving ability to collect diagnostic data;
  - o Introduce faults into the model and fix faults in the model;
  - o Explore heuristics for design and diagnosis.

Figure 4-2: Structure and function represented in a model-based system.

knowledge system, and Figure 4-5 shows a small subset of the knowledge base (KB) representing concepts and concrete objects in the model. Each object in this knowledge base (KB) is a frame which describes a concept, or object in the

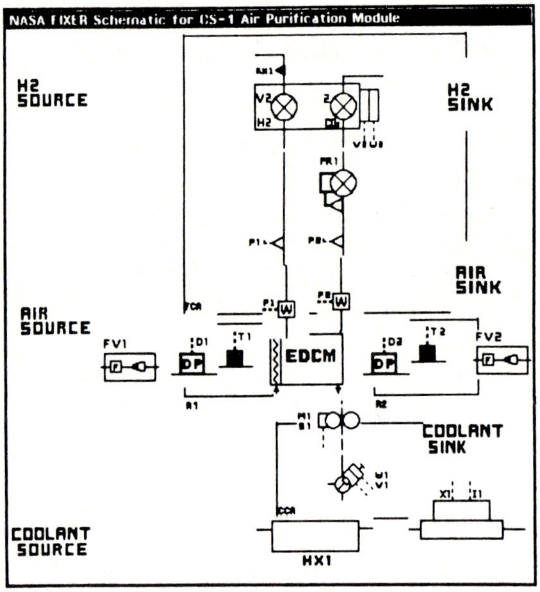

Figure 4-3:

Schematic diagram of the example system of Figure 4-1, as shown on the screen of the knowledge system.

model. Some KB objects have corresponding icons in the graphical model shown in Figure 4-3. Each graphical icon in Figure 4-3 has an underlying symbolic description in the application knowledge base. A KB is composed of a set of frames or "units" which describe related concepts and concrete objects. In a frame-based representation system, there is a frame for each concept and graphical object in a model. Thus, the KB for the CO_2 system has units describing structural elements of the modeled system, associated icons contained in the graphical model, and rules for analyzing the model.

A model also represents the behavior of a modeled system. Frame-based representation systems use "object-oriented" representation in which objects have attributes which may be either descriptive or behavioral. A descriptive attribute might be the color or voltage of some device, and a behavioral attribute might be a procedure to display an object graphically or to diagnose a problem. In general, behavior can be represented either as rules or as computer code.

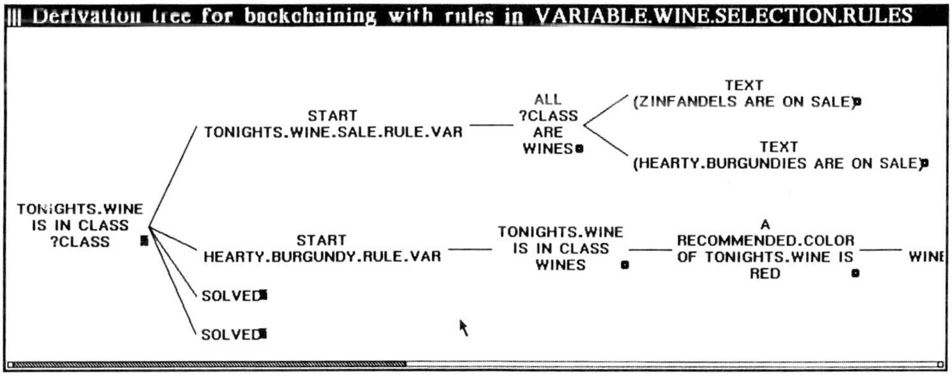

Figure 4-4: An example of the active rule graph.

4.2. Project Management

This section describes an example of modeling the abstract discipline of project management. While the example of Section 4.1 discussed a model of a built artifact, this section introduces modeling of and model-based reasoning using an abstract conceptual system. The discipline of project management has standard texts, such as [Barrie 84], university training programs, industrial practitioners, and scores of computer programs designed to facilitate its use [Gido 86]. This work is discussed in greater detail in [Levitt 85].

The discipline of project management provides a methodology, or a normative theory, describing its use. Practitioners are taught that the discipline is appropriate for managing projects which can be organized as a number of activities which together produce one or more major deliverable results. In addition, the methodology prescribes that problems are to be addressed in particular ways, namely identifying the activities and resources of individual projects and performing the functional operations of the discipline.

As in the previous example, the knowledge system explicitly describes the structure and function of the modeled system, where in this example the modeled

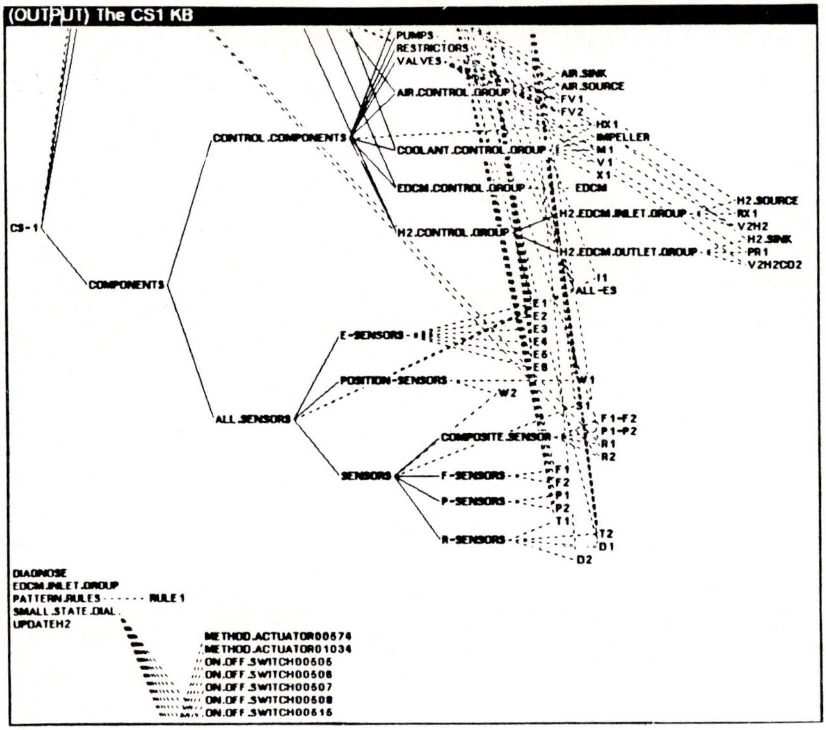

Figure 4-5:

Part of the symbolic representation of the modeled system which is represented graphically in Figure 4-3.

system is the abstract theory of project management. In this example of the theory of project management, the model includes the descriptions shown in Figure 4-6. The figure also lists some purposes for which the application was designed.

The builders of this example model had several purposes in building their system, including performing traditional functions of the theory of project management for particular projects, identifying favorable and unfavorable risk factors which might cause particular activities to be completed in less or more time than initially projected, and allowing the developers to explore new heuristic methods for analyzing projects.

As in the case of built systems, disciplines such as project management use graphical metaphors to describe problems which are to be analyzed. Figure 4-7 shows two example diagrams taken from the workstation screen of the application described in [Levitt 85]. This figure shows some of the diagrams

- Structure of theory of project management, including:
    - Concepts, including activities, milestones, risk factors;
    - Concrete objects, including descriptions of particular activities, milestones and risk factors for particular projects;
    - Attributes of objects, including activity duration, start time, end time and utilization of particular resources;
    - Relations among objects, including activity predecessors and successors.

- Function defined in the theory of project management, including:
    - Determine critical path and its duration;
    - Identify resource utilization;
    - Show activities and milestones in time;

- Purposes of the developers in creating the model-based system, including:
    - Identify risk factors which have been favorable or unfavorable in completed activities and project their effects on uncompleted activities;
    - Perform traditional project management functions;
    - Explore heuristics to find better ways of analyzing risk factors.

Figure 4-6:

Part of the structure and function described in a model of the abstract theory of the discipline of project management.

which are used in the practice of project management as they are seen on the screen of the workstation. The left figure is a "Gantt chart" which shows activity start and end times, and the right diagram shows the precedence relations among activities.

A knowledge base is associated with the model, such as that shown in Figure 4-5.

There is a detailed description of each KB object, such as that shown in Figure 4-8. Concepts and concrete objects have detailed descriptions, such as the description of an example activity shown in this figure. The detailed object description specifies both the descriptive attributes and behavior of the particular object. In this example, **ACTIVITY.DURATION**[2] is a descriptive attribute of the particular activity, and **ADD.RESOURCE.TO.ACTIVITY** is a possible behavior of the activity, or an action which the activity can perform.

[2] The bold face in the text indicates names which appear in bold on the workstation screen image and which are mouse-sensitive.

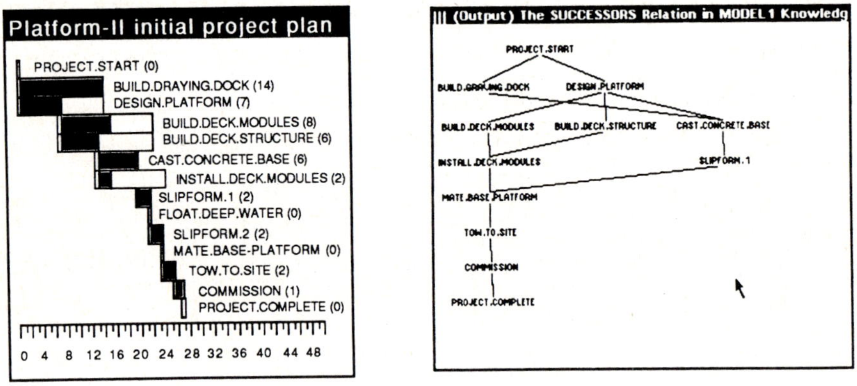

Figure 4-7:
Diagrams used in a model-based reasoning application.

5. Models and Model-Based Reasoning

"A model is a representation of a system." [Fegley 84]

"Model" is a term with different meanings in different technical communities, including physical models, informal symbolic models, diagrams, mathematical models, and formal symbolic models. The source of these differences seems to lie in *what* is represented in a model, rather than *how* it is represented: different kinds of models represent different characteristics of systems. This section considers these different perspectives on models and then discusses model-based reasoning using symbolic models.

```
(Output) The DESIGN.PLATFORM Unit in MODEL1 Knowledge Base
Unit: DESIGN.PLATFORM in knowledge base MODEL1
Created by KUNZ on 1-7-88 15:01:08
Modified by KUNZ on 1-7-88 15:06:12
  Superclasses: ACTIVITIES
  Member Of: CLASSES in GENERICUNITS

  Activity to design the platform

Member slot: ACTIVITY.DURATION from DESIGN.PLATFORM
   Inheritance: OVERRIDE.VALUES
   ValueClass: NUMBER
   Cardinality.Max: 1
   Cardinality.Min: 1
   Comment: "Planned activity duration.  This value is assigned to duration.expected during initialization."
   Values: 7

Member slot: ACTIVITY.FINISH.TIME from DESIGN.PLATFORM
   Inheritance: OVERRIDE.VALUES
   ValueClass: NUMBER
   Cardinality.Max: 1
   Cardinality.Min: 1
   Comment: "Scheduled (or actual) finish time."
   Values: 15

Member slot: ACTIVITY.START.TIME from DESIGN.PLATFORM
   Inheritance: OVERRIDE.VALUES
   ValueClass: NUMBER
   Cardinality.Max: 1
   Cardinality.Min: 1
   Comment: "Scheduled (or actual) start time."
   Values: 8
```

Figure 4-8:
Partial example of the description of an activity.

5.1. Models

Physical models are physical representations of physical systems, such as scale models or "breadboard models" of physical systems. Physical models, such as the astrolabe, have been developed since antiquity, and pilot or prototype physical models continue to be developed and tested routinely when time permits or when the application is complex and valuable. Physical models describe parts, some of their attributes and some of their relations. Such models can be used as tools for anticipating the structure and for predicting the behavior of modeled systems.

Informal symbolic models are the way people describe systems. Models are system descriptions based largely on public knowledge about systems, where public knowledge includes the way that users describe systems to peers, to novices in analysis of the systems, and to executive users. Public structural and functional knowledge in models may be complemented by more arcane private knowledge of experts in how to use models to analyze and predict behavior of modeled systems.

The symbolic model is used by the knowledge system for its processing. The power of the model lies in the combination of the active natural metaphor with the symbolic model. The one could be implemented as a drawing on a paper and the other as an uncomprehensible computer program; the combination of the two is far more useful than either individually.

The symbolic model should be presented to users and manipulated by users at the

- Object description level, as shown in Figure 4-8, showing the detailed description of an object;

- Object-object relations, such as shown in Figure 4-7, showing user-defined relations among objects;

- Object hierarchies, such as such as shown in Figure 4-5, showing various standard relations among objects such as class-subclass, part/part- of, etc.

- Collections of object classes and collections of related sets of objects, i.e., libraries of generic and specific models.

6. Discussion: Model-Based Reasoning and Interfaces as an Extensions of Expert Systems

There have been several motivations for developing model-based reasoning systems. Several investigators have attempted to represent minimal amounts of knowledge of physical principles and have investigated inferring detailed behavior of simple digital electronic circuits by analyzing circuit structure and generic description of function [Davis 84], [deKleer 84], [Genesereth 84]. These investigations have analyzed both normal and faulty circuit operation. The work reported in this paper generalizes and extends the work reported in [Kunz 83]. That work describes use of a model-based approach to represent and exploit knowledge of principles of scientific domains in which at least some of the principles have been elucidated. In that application, the structure was that of the human kidney and circulation systems; the function included Ohm's law for fluids, the law of conservation of mass and descriptions of a few specialized physiological processes; the system was designed to analyze physiological behavior, identify the effects of abnormalities, suggest appropriate therapies, and predict results of therapy. In the complicated field of molecular biology, Koton developed a model-based approach to solve a greater variety of problems and more difficult problems than was possible using traditional expert systems [Koton 85]. Coulson describes use of linked AI natural resource and resource management models [Coulson 87]. There has been interest in facilitating knowledge acquisition, such as described in [Weiss 78]. Finally, the methodology described in this paper has been applied in diverse application areas including scheduling, capacity analysis, planning, design and diagnosis. Each of these motivations is an attempt to relax restrictions of classical expert systems and to create methodologies for building knowledge systems which are more powerful and flexible.

Analysis of structure and function has inspired a substantial theoretical literature on reasoning. For example, Kuipers discusses qualitative simulation of behavior which can be represented as differential equations and continuously differentiable functions [Kuipers 86], and deKleer's work in assumption-based truth maintenance systems (ATMS) was inspired by efforts to develop techniques which will be useful in analyzing behavior and diagnosing faults in complex devices by analyzing structure and function [deKleer 86]. This paper presents an engineering approach to building knowledge systems which suggests that analysis of structure and function is a methodology which can be followed effectively in creating applications. The methodology exploits the strengths and extends the engineering notion of modeling and expert systems, and there are significant potential benefits to using this methodology. The reasoning techniques of qualitative analysis and the ATMS can be used effectively with this methodology for building knowledge systems using model-based reasoning, and for some kinds of problems they are helpful or crucial. The methodology recommends *what* to represent and manipulate -- structure and function -- and exploits whatever representational and reasoning technique seems to be most appropriate for the particular application.

All of these systems exploit descriptions of structure and function and knowledge of how to analyze it. Thus, the situations or configurations possible within a domain are implicit, while the structure and function of the domain are explicit. Thus, they share domain descriptions and reasoning processes which allow them to analyze different situations. In contrast, compiled heuristic knowledge attempts to describe all possible situations explicitly and to classify individual situations as one of the explicitly identified situations. In such expert systems, the domain structure and function are implicit in the explicitly described situations. Some authors have characterized the knowledge of the structure and function of a domain as "deep" knowledge, to contrast it with the empirical associations which are characterized as "shallow" knowledge.

Model-based reasoning systems all share an explicit structural and functional model of a domain. Reasoning methodologies all work with respect to an explicit model of the parts of a modeled system and connections among those parts. Thus, the reasoning is separated from domain descriptions of circuits, factories, or systems. The model-based reasoning systems have more or less knowledge of the principles which govern function in the domain. This knowledge of behavioral principles is most useful when represented explicitly using some language which is natural for the domain. Finally, depending upon the completeness of the knowledge of principles, the model-based reasoning systems may be built using relatively small or large amounts of the heuristic knowledge which is the hallmark of classical expert systems. In general, research projects attempting to push model-based reasoning as far as possible have avoided use of heuristics, and systems which have a more engineering-orientation have exploited heuristics when they seemed useful. Thus, the model-based approach is characterized by use of a domain model which explicitly represents structure and function of the modeled system separately from control of the reasoning process, but the approach allows a range of kinds of knowledge of behavior varying from principles to heuristics.

Most applications have multiple users, such as developers, collaborating experts, executives, operators, trainers and trainees. Applications built using model-based reasoning and interface methodology can support these various users consistently, so that the presentation of model structure and results of analyses can be presented consistently in different ways at differing levels of detail. Similarly, the use of shared structural and behavioral models facilitates viewing problems from different perspectives, such as control flow, information flow and material flow, each presented at various levels of detail.

Use of natural graphical metaphors to explain models contributes significantly to transparency of the model and of the model-based reasoning. The most useful graphical representations use natural graphical metaphors of a domain, such as circuit diagrams and bar charts. The graphical representation helps users to understand the fidelity of the model because they can compare models with their personal understanding of modeled systems. Knowledge contained in a model can be modified relatively easily because it is represented explicitly and is accessible through an interactive model editor [Nardi 86]. Model editors can also be used to support input and output of data, both by supporting simple table entry associated with individual components of the model and by allowing structure modification such as with editors which allow connecting and disconnecting model components graphically. As knowledge of modeled systems change, models need to be made more complex. Model-based reasoning facilitates managing that complexity because knowledge in a model is explicit and public and is thus accessible to many users. In addition, because it is represented explicitly, it tends to be relatively visible to both developers and users, and because it is built on public knowledge, both developers and users can suggest appropriate changes.

Symbolic models and model-based reasoning and interfaces provide new methodologies for knowledge engineering. Building models is a directed activity: developers must seek to identify those aspects of the structure and function of the system which are useful for analyzing particular sets of problems. The fundamental knowledge to be encoded is the public knowledge of users and designers of the modeled systems; specialized heuristic knowledge can be used as it is found to be necessary or convenient.

7. Conclusions

There are significant opportunities for advancing the state of the art in developing model-based reasoning systems. The cost to develop these systems can be imposing: in many cases, there is no formal description of the components of a process and the way that it operates. Such descriptions are passed informally to new employees and learned, but those descriptions often tend to be informal rather than formal, and thus large amounts of careful and thoughtful analysis is sometimes needed to formalize a domain and to critique the formalization.

We find that it is usually relatively straightforward to describe the structure of a domain. Experts are facile at identifying conceptual and concrete objects such as parts, machines, measurable parameters and operational states. The representational formalism we use most frequently for representing structure, namely frames, seems to work effectively. Important research issues include ways to automate representation of structure and representation of different perspectives on a system in coherent ways, such as representing the structural, electrical and kinematic properties of a motor.

Specification of the function of conceptual and particular objects of a domain is much more difficult, however, than specification of domain structure. For example, in a factory application, it might be necessary to describe how are (and should) parts be routed; and how are (and should) parts be classified as acceptable or defective. This kind of functional description can be difficult to specify, and the description can be complicated once specified. In addition to the cognitive and organizational complexity, the representational formalisms which are available for describing function, rules and methods, require relatively more skill and tenacity to use effectively than frames and graphics. Important research and development issues include improved representation for knowledge of function, and creation of generic libraries which can be customized and extended.

Testing is, in our judgment, the most fundamental issue concerning development of model-based systems. Is a model valid, and how can the developer even ask the question of whether the model is valid? Testing is a fundamental issue in all complex computing systems. The difficulty and importance of this issue is exacerbated in model-based systems because of the complexity of the models which can be built. Is a model accurate enough for its intended purpose. If a change is made, are the model and its analysis still accurate? Empirical testing is the only methodology we now have for validating model-based systems. It is necessary to create test cases which describe both the inputs to a model-based analysis and the expected results. Then the model can be analyzed to determine whether the actual and the expected results are close enough. Formal program verification techniques do not yet seem applicable for systems of the complexity of typical model-based applications. Major research and development issues concerning testing include the methodology for testing, design of the procedures which support creation and analysis of test cases and comparison of expected with actual results, and value attribution.

Acknowledgment: Greg Clemenson, Fred Cummins, Allen Cypher, Theresa Farrah, Nick Lance, Ray Levitt, Jane Malin, Ed Payne and large numbers of anonymous people initially conducted numerous model-building and interface experiments and later graciously provided important critiques of many of the ideas discussed in this paper.

References

[Barrie 84] Barrie, D.S., Paulson, B.C.
Professional Construction Management.
McGraw-Hill, New York, 1984.
Second Edition.

[Buchanan 84] Buchanan, B.G., and Shortliffe, E.H. (editors).
Rule-based Expert Systems.
Addison Wesley, 1984.

[Coulson 87] Coulson, R.N., Folse, L.J., Loh, D.K.
Artificial Intelligence and Natural Resource Management.
Science 237:262-267, 17 July 1987.

[Davis 84] Davis, R.
Diagnostic Reasoning Based on Structure and Behavior.
Artificial Intelligence 24:347-410, 1984.

[deKleer 84] de Kleer, J.
Choices Without Backtracking.
In *Proceedings of the National Conference on Artificial Intelligence*, pages 79-85. 1984.

[deKleer 86] deKleer, J.
Problem Solving with the ATMS.
Artificial Intelligence 28(1), 1986.

[Duda 83] Duda, R.O., Shortliffe, E.H.
Expert Systems Research.
Science 220:261-268, 1983.

[Eddy 82] Eddy, E.M., Clanton, C.H.
The Art of Diagnosis.
New England Journal of Medicine 306:1263-1268, 1982.

[Fegley 84] Fegley, K.A.
Modeling and Simulation -- an Engineering Outlook.
In *Modeling and Analysis in Biomedicine.* World Scientific, 1984.

[Feigenbaum 77] Feigenbaum, E.A.
The Art of Artificial Intelligence: Themes and case studies of knowledge engineering.
In *Proceedings of the International Joint Conference on Artifical Intelligence, 1977*, pages 1014-1029. 1977.

[Genesereth 84] Genesereth, M.R.
The Use of Design Descriptions in Automated Diagnosis.
Artificial Intelligence 24:411-436, 1984.

[Gido 86] Gido, J.
Project Management Software Directory.
Industrial Press, Inc., New York, NY, 1986.

[Hayes-Roth 83] Hayes-Roth, F., Waterman, D.A., Lenat, D.B. (editors).
Building Expert Systems.
Addison-Wesley, Reading MA, 1983.

[Hutchins 85] Hutchins, E. L., Hollan J. D., and Norman, D. A.
Direct Manipulation Interfaces.
Technical Report 8503, Institute for Cognitive Science, University of California, San Diego, May, 1985.

[Koton 85] Koton, P.A.
Empirical and Model-Based Reasoning in Expert Systems.
In *Proceedings of the International Joint Conference on Artifical Intelligence, 1985*, pages 297-299. 1985.

[Kuipers 86] Kuipers, B.
Qualitative Simulation.
Artificial Intelligence 29:289-338, 1986.

[Kunz 83] Kunz, J.C.
Analysis of Physiological Behavior Using a Causal Model Based on First Principles.
In *Proceedings of the National Conference on Artifical Intelligence, 1983*, pages 225-228. 1983.

[Kunz 84] Kunz, J.C., Kehler, T.P., Williams, M.D.
Applications Development Using a Hybrid AI Development System.
AI Magazine :41-54, Fall 1984.

[Kunz 88] Kunz, J.C.
Model Based Reasoning in CIM.
In Michael Oliff (editor), *Intelligent Manufacturing: Expert Systems and the Leading Edge in Production Planning and Control.* Addison Wesley, 1988.

[Levitt 85] Levitt, R.E., Kunz, J.C.
Using Knowledge of Construction and Project Management for Automated Schedule Updating.
Project Management Journal :57-81, December, 1985.

[Malin 85] Malin, J.T., Lance, N.
An Expert System for Fault Management and Automatic Shutdown Avoidance in a Regenerative Life Support System.
In *ISA Proceedings, 1985.* 1985.
ISA 1985 - paper #85-0333.

[Malin 87] Malin, J.T., Lance, N.
Processes in Construction of Failure Management Expert Systems from Device Design Information.
IEEE Transactions on Systems, Man and Cybernetics , November, 1987.

[Nardi 86] Nardi, B.A., Simons, R.K.
Model-Based Reasoning and AI Problem Solving.
In *Tools for Knowledge Based Systems.* 1986.
Sponsored by AAAI, OLAIR and DARPA, October 6-8, Columbus Ohio.

[Stelzner 88] Stelzner, M., Michael D. Williams.
The Evolution of Interface Requirements for Expert Systems.
In (editor), *Expert Systems: The User Interface.* Ablex Publishing Corporation, 1988.

[Weiss 78] Weiss, S.M., Kulikowski, C.A., Amarel, S., Safir, A.
A model-based method for computer-aided medical decision making.
Artificial Intelligence 11:145-172, 1978.

Topics in Expert System Design
G. Guida and C. Tasso (Editors)

AN INTEGRATED APPROACH TO THE CONSTRUCTION OF KNOWLEDGE-BASED SYSTEMS: EXPERIENCE WITH ADVISE AND RELATED PROGRAMS

Arthur B. BASKIN (°) **and Ryszard S. MICHALSKI** (°°)

Department of Computer Science (°)
University of Illinois
Urbana, IL, USA

Department of Computer Science (°°)
George Mason University
Fairfax, VA, USA

1. INTRODUCTION

Over the last few years, knowledge-based systems have clearly demonstrated the potential for substantial impact in a number of diverse areas. The successful construction of such knowledge-based systems has required that it be possible to encode sufficient domain expertise within a machine manipulable form to support intelligent problem solving behavior. A number of different approaches have been taken to the problems of knowledge acquisition, knowledge representation, uncertainty propagation and problem solving methodology. Choosing an architecture for a particular

---

The research program outlined in this paper has been supported by a number of sources. The primary support has come from the Office of Naval Research, N00014-92-K-0186, with additional support from DARPA, N00014-85-K-0878 and N00014-87-K-0874, and the Alcatel European Support Center's Artificial Intelligence Group, 85-ESC-5004.

expert system application requires not only domain knowledge but, also, the ability to match aspects of the problem domain with the characteristics of different competing paradigms for knowledge-based systems [1].

In proposing an integrated approach to the construction of knowledge-based systems, this paper presents the generalization of experience gained by designing and implementing the ADVISE system at the University of Illinois [2]. By integrating different, apparently competing, knowledge-based system techniques together with powerful machine learning techniques for knowledge acquisition and refinement, knowledge-based systems of a qualitatively different character can be constructed.

The emphasis in the ADVISE effort has been to develop a unified approach to the construction of knowledge-based systems incorporating multiple control schemes, multiple knowledge representations, different uncertainty propagation schemes, and extensive learning capabilities. The integrated approach described here goes beyond the degree of integration which was achieved with the actual implementation of ADVISE but is, none the less, grounded in the practical experience gained with that system.

The next section discusses two of the major design issues which influenced the original ADVISE effort and the current integrated approach as well. The discussion of an integrated approach to knowledge representation is followed by a discussion of the variety of machine learning tools and problem solving methods which can be brought to bear on knowledge organized in the form of networks, rules, and relational tables of data. The paper concludes with a description of an integrated language for knowledge-based systems called $KBVL_2$.

2. MATCHING THE PROBLEM TO THE SOLUTION

The advent of an increasing number of expert system shells for computers ranging from a personal computer to large main frames has produced an interesting phenomenon. In most cases, users of expert system shells are people with a solution in search of a suitable problem. That is, the knowledge representation and problem solving capabilities of the system are predefined by the choice of shell, and in that situation, the knowledge engineer is searching for a problem suited to the solution technique already chosen.

The knowledge structuring and manipulation operations supported by a given expert system shell limit or foster the description of domain knowledge for inclusion in the knowledge base as they clash or conform to the natural expression of the domain knowledge. For instance, when large numbers of facts and simple relationships between them characterize the domain, then posting and retrieving simple assertions on a blackboard can be quite natural. In other situations where the domain knowledge is best expressed as a non-deterministic exploration of a group of possibilities at each step in the solution, the concept of exploring *multiple worlds* can be much more concise. Finally, when causal or associational reasoning chains are known, then standard production rule systems are most natural.

Frequently, the enforced regimen of constructing a knowledge base is, itself, a contribution to the domain being studied. When the representation for the knowledge is ***cognitively close*** to the way that domain knowledge is already expressed and manipulated, then the construction of the knowledge base is simple, the validation of correctness is more likely, and the knowledge base can be used by itself as a ***distillation*** of knowledge in the domain. It is important to note that there is no such thing as a single ***best*** knowledge representation or problem solving paradigm. The different approaches have evolved as part of experience with different classes of problems and reflect a response to the requirements of different domains.

Matching solution technique to problem is made more complex by the cost and complexity of building the knowledge bases in complex domains. Once domain experts and knowledge engineers have been trained on a particular system, they are not generally able to use another system with differing primitives for knowledge structuring. It is as though each separate system is a different foreign language and retraining on radically different (and therefore potentially more suitable) approaches is simply not feasible. This problem is especially important because, in many cases, knowledge acquisition and refinement are the limiting factors in the construction of knowledge-based systems.

3. LIMITATIONS OF CURRENT EXPERT SYSTEMS

At present, the technology of expert systems is undergoing very rapid growth and is being applied to a wide spectrum of practical problems. Although the application of existing expert system techniques to practical problems can now produce useful expert systems, the current techniques have different limited areas of applicability and do not work together well.

Current expert systems suffer from a number of limitations that restrict their usefulness. They typically employ only one form of knowledge representation, have no learning capabilities, use only one type of inference procedure, employ only a single control strategy, and often do not deal with data or situations that are time-dependent [3] [4, 5]. Many of the techniques explored in today's expert system shells have been extensively studied and have known areas of applicability as well as known deficiencies. For a discussion of specific problems or limitations with individual techniques consult [1].

Limiting an expert system to both a single knowledge representation and a single control scheme is a common way to simplify the construction of the expert system. Unfortunately, different problem domains and even different aspects of a single domain may not be well suited to the same knowledge representation or the same problem solving control scheme. Limitations in an expert system technique which do not correspond to requirements of a particular domain do not hinder the operation of the system, but subproblems with different requirements will frequently not fit a single paradigm.

Single paradigm approaches impose their particular assumptions about the nature of the data, the knowledge representation, and the problem solving in the given domain. Assumptions about the nature of the data commonly made include assumptions about:

- distribution of training examples in the space of possible situations
- conditional dependence/independence of individual findings
- time dependence/independence of data
- ambiguity, reproducibility, completeness, and redundancy of data
- ability to influence data collection
- level of specificity, timeliness, and reliability of the data
- data and situations do not change during the consultation.

Complex domains which are uniformly structured according to one version of all of the assumptions listed above are quite rare. All too often, portions of the problem solving process or areas of the domain will require conflicting assumptions.

Current expert system shells make a number of assumptions about the nature of the knowledge to represent and the best approach to that representation. In some cases, blackboards form ideal models for communication between cooperating problem solving processes but do not form good representations for intermediate decision making. Some domains are data driven and easily organized for constraint propagation or spreading activation; other domains may contain procedural knowledge which is properly represented by rules, while still others are underconstrained and benefit from a hypothesize and test approach.

Domains which are highly goal directed or diagnostic in nature are well suited to backward chaining while domains such as mechanical component design are much less well structured and require some construction of the goal itself. Explicit representation for some control information is also a requirement not always met by current techniques. Quite often in industrial design applications (such as switching system configuration), a domain expert will know not only detailed information about the design process, but also general approaches and precedence relations defined over data collection, problem decomposition, and candidate solutions to try before conducting a search. This strategic information needs to be separated from the more tactical information normally incorporated in non-deterministically scheduled rulebases so as not to loose the strategic information in a sea of tactical rules for intermediate decision making.

Knowledge acquisition is perhaps the most important part of the construction of any intelligent system. The rate at which domain knowledge can be captured is directly limited by the suitability of the knowledge representation primitives to the domain and to the level of detail at which the domain knowledge is specified. Generally, high level non-deterministic descriptions of the desired problem solving process are the most concise to acquire. Knowledge acquisition that depends on ***learning by instruction*** has been a major factor in the development of expert systems to date. Such an approach can be extremely limiting when general heuristics are not known or domain expert time is at a premium. Machine learning techniques can be used to reduce the dependence on pre-digestion of the problem solving process by domain experts and to refine knowledge bases regardless of their source.

4. INTEGRATED APPROACH TO KNOWLEDGE-BASED SYSTEMS

The expert system shells currently in the marketplace are predominantly built upon the expert systems research of the middle to late 1970s. More recent attempts to build ***knowledge-based systems*** reflect the need for even more knowledge intensive paradigms for constructing intelligent computational models of real world expertise. Thus, while current knowledge-based system research is grounded in earlier work in expert systems, it should not be considered as merely an extension of the that earlier work.

There have been a number of efforts to develop special purpose knowledge representations and/or problem solving strategies for knowledge-based systems. Rather than attempt to develop another radically different approach, the ADVISE effort centered around using a variety of existing techniques within a single knowledge-based system paradigm. Thus, the knowledge representation and problem solving strategies could be selected from among the range supported by the system.

Most knowledge-based systems emphasize the deductive application of the knowledge base to a presenting problem in order to produce a result. Our efforts to develop an integrated approach are different in that they have emphasized the incorporation of machine learning techniques to build and modify the knowledge base.

Figure 1 shows the three knowledge representation techniques supported in our unified approach and the inference operations defined over them. The arrows represent inferential transformations which operate on one representation and produce another. Thus, the traditional expert system operation is depicted as a deductive application arrow from the rulebase to a particular database element (a database tuple consisting of the presenting data and the deductively produced result). Similarly, the arc from data to rules represents the learning from examples arc and depicts the inductive generalization of rules from examples of the decision. The remainder of this paper consists of more detailed presentation of information about each component of the integrated approach to knowledge-based systems portrayed in Figure 1.

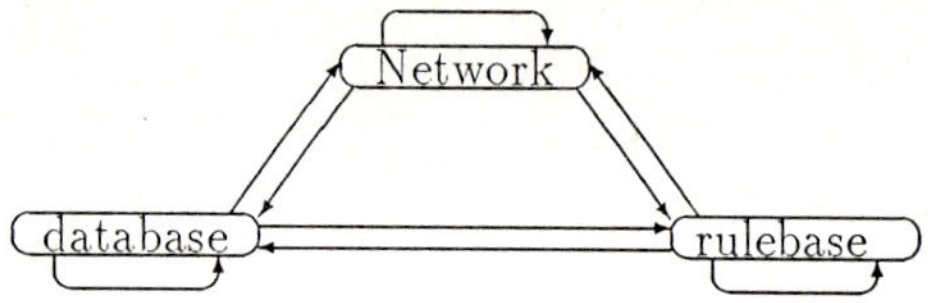

FIGURE 1
Knowledge representation alternatives and transformation operations linking them.

Each arc in Figure 1 corresponds to a transformation operation which takes in one form of knowledge from the knowledge base and produces a potentially different knowledge representation. Some of the transformations shown in Figure 1 correspond to inductive learning operations and some correspond to deductive application of the knowledge base for problem solving. A few arcs such as the one from database to database can be both inductive learning and deductive problem solving. The meaning of the various arcs is briefly outlined in the remainder of this section and described in greater detail in sections 6 and 7 below.

4.1. Learning Transformation Operations

Figure 2 shows the subset of the transformation arcs from Figure 1 which represent learning components of the integrated approach. Each of these arcs corresponds to inductive learning operators which operate on a portion of the knowledge base to inductively derive revised or additional knowledge base contents. The learning transformation operations are:

database ⟶ database — used to reduce database complexity by selecting most representative data examples (called events) and/or by eliminating unnecessary attributes from further consideration;

network ⟶ network — used to reason by analogy and produce a revised or extended network structure from an existing network structure;

rulebase ⟶ rulebase — used to derive improved or extended rules from inefficient or overly restrictive rules;

database ⟶ network — used to organize data elements together into groups (conceptual clusters) and to derive hierarchies of such groups;

rulebase ⟶ network — used to organize the rules together into groups and to derive hierarchies of such groups;

database ⟶ rulebase — used to derive rules which summarize the decision behavior implicit in a set of examples taken from the database.

Among the learning transformation operations shown in Figure 2, the learning of rules from examples has received the most attention and is the most developed.

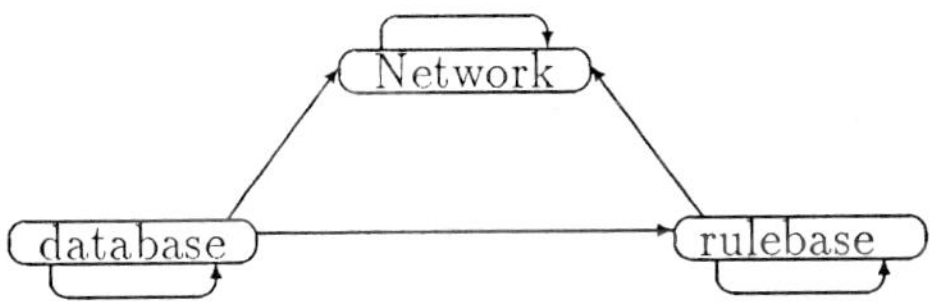

FIGURE 2
Transformation operations which involve learning.

4.2. Problem Solving Transformation Operations

Figure 3 shows the subset of the transformation arcs from Figure 1 which represents the use of portions of the knowledge base for problem solving. Each of these transformations corresponds to one or more (usually deductive) operators which applies the general knowledge in the knowledge base to a specific situation. The problem solving transformations are:

database ⟶ **database** — direct retrieval of a solution from the fact base;

network ⟶ **network** — plausible reasoning and/or reasoning by analogy to determine network relationships which hold for the present problem;

rulebase ⟶ **rulebase** — rule-based reasoning about the control over which rules to use and in which order to pursue them;

network ⟶ **rulebase** — network-based reasoning about the control over which rules to use and in which order to pursue them;

rulebase ⟶ **database** — the application of the rulebase to the situation at hand to define solution (and, thus, an event in the database).

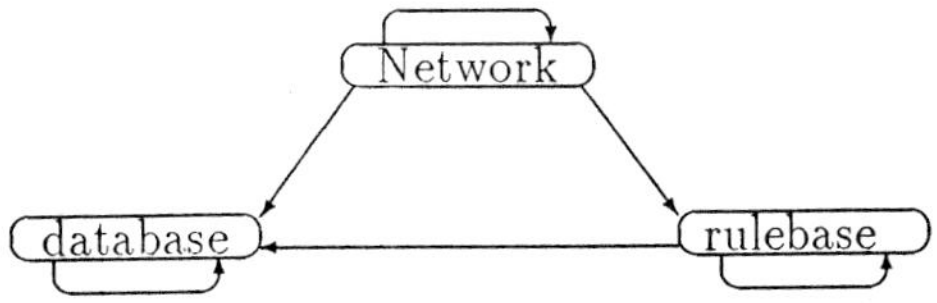

FIGURE 3
Transformation operations for problem solving.

Before discussing the transformation operations shown in the figures above in greater detail, additional information about the various knowledge representations must be presented.

5. MULTIPLE KNOWLEDGE REPRESENTATIONS

In our integrated approach to knowledge representation, we identified three different knowledge representation techniques, each well suited to a different role:

- networks of objects
- relational database of facts
- and a rulebase for more procedural information.

A unified underlying access protocol is used to support these conceptually different forms of knowledge. The knowledge base is structured into segments for ease of management and efficiency of some inference operations. A segment is merely a subset of the knowledge base and can either contain only information of one type or can span all three types of representation. Finally, a segment can itself contain segments to as many levels as needed.

The network of objects is used to contain strategic information about the domain and is used for planning during problem solving. The relational database stores facts or assertions about the problem at hand and facts about the domain or about specific decisions (usually examples supplied by a human expert). Finally, the rulebase is used to store detailed procedural information about the domain and the solution to problems.

5.1. Networks of Objects

The network component of the knowledge base consists of network links between objects used to capture general domain knowledge about interrelationships among various conceptual units. For example, it can include hierarchies of attributes from the application domain indicating the level of generality of such attributes (a ***generalization tree***), a representation of the structure of the rulebase, and precedence relations defined over queries to the user. Links between nodes in the network represent ***static*** relationships between concepts. The network organization is a form of the ***Logic Net*** formalism described in [6].

Each conceptual unit in the knowledge base behaves like an object in an object oriented programming environment. Thus, each object can have attached attributes and procedures. The networks of objects are used to capture not only the traditional object oriented inheritance hierarchies but also knowledge engineer designed relationships between concepts.

In combination with the notion of knowledge base segments, which can themselves be conceptual objects, the networks of objects portion of the knowledge base provides a powerful structuring mechanism. Rules can be gathered together into segments and structured as networks; individual findings can be associated together in a network with inference defined over the links, and structure within the range of values of a variable or among a group of variables can be captured as a generalization tree.

Although the original ADVISE system, on which this integrated approach is based, only supported construction of static network structures, the generalization to dynamic structures is quite desirable. The concept of ***worlds*** common to a number of expert system shells amounts to the dynamic management of subsets of facts in the knowledge base. In a similar manner, the dynamic management of segments containing rules is a way to provide for adjustment of the knowledge base to changing situations or a predictable temporal evolution.

5.1.1. Instance Variables

A knowledge engineer uses predefined objects and knowledge engineer defined objects in describing a domain knowledge to the system. The instance variables of an object behave like the slots in a frame and the instance variable inheritance is similar to slot inheritance in a frame hierarchy. When defining an object, the knowledge engineer can start with the predefined ***object*** which contains nothing and buid an object entirely to suite the situation at hand, or the knowledge engineer can build upon the predefined object classes.

An instance variable of an object may be a full object itself or simply a value. A simple value behaves like an object with a single instance variable called ***value***. Predefined object classes for variables used in logic rules such as ***integer, real***, and ***string*** have instance variables used to contain: a prompt string, a default value, whether or not the variable is askable, the range of values the variable is allowed, and the units with which the variable is measured. These properties may be modified or extended by changing the object oriented ***core*** of the system.

5.1.2. Methods

Unlike most object oriented systems where the methods on objects are specified in some programming language, the methods on objects are here defined using the same rule format used to define the segments of rules in the rulebase. The methods are deterministically scheduled rules which are investigated in the order in which they occur in the method. These logic rules may modify instance variables and they may also modify knowledge engineer defined variables which are also used by the rules in the rulebase segments.

A number of predefined methods exist for uncertainty management, rule scheduling in the rule segments, data collection, and presentation of results. These methods may be modified or extended by defining new methods. In general, the predefined methods provide higher performance than the knowledge engineer defined methods because they can be *pre-compiled* into the system rather than being interpretively executed.

5.1.3. Using Networks of Objects

The simplest network of objects used in the system is the inheritance hierarchy for the classes of objects defined within the system. This hierarchy provides for default structure of objects, default methods, and default values for individual instance variables. In addition to the predefined inheritance hierarchy, the knowledge engineer can define additional networks for use in the problem solving process. For instance, a goal tree can be defined to capture a static problem decomposition and a method can be defined to traverse the tree in a case specific order. A knowledge engineer can also define a specificity hierarchy of attributes where such a structure exists for the domain or can be derived using the learning techniques discussed in the next section. Separate specificity hierarchies can be used for attributes themselves and for structure within the range of values of an attribute.

Network-based problem solving can take the form of *spreading activation* where changes in values or certainties are propagated along network links. Methods attached to network segments control this form of problem solving in a similar way to the rule scheduling methods attached to rulebase segments. In general, the network portion of the knowledge base is best suited to describing general properties or organizational principles of the domain and not detailed problem solving. The network structures can provide partial orderings of goals to pursue and/or data to solicit.

5.2. Rule base

The rulebase is the most commonly used knowledge structuring for knowledge-based systems. It is best suited to capturing tactical information. Individual rules or groups of rules can be used to answer specific questions or differentiate among a small number of alternatives.

5.2.1. Generalized Decision Rules

The rule format supported by the ADVISE system is based on the GVL rule syntax developed by Michalski [7]. As with most decision rules, the rules are divided into condition/action pairs. The condition can be a disjunction of multiple conjunctions of constraints on attribute values. The action portion of a rule contains one or more assignments of values to attributes. The rulebase consists of rules of the following basic form:

$$\text{CTX: CONDITION} \Rightarrow \text{CONCLUSION} : \alpha, \beta$$

where:

CTX is an experssion describing the context within which the rule is applicable;

CONDITION is a formal expression (in VL_2 [8]) which involves elementary conditional statements (called *selectors*), linked by various logic operators (including quantifiers);

CONCLUSION defines the decision or action which is executed when the CONDITION is satisfied by a given situation;

α is the strength of the evidence which supports the CONCLUSION when the CONDITION is completely satisfied ($0 \leq \alpha \leq 1$) and

β is the strength of the evidence which supports the CONDITION when the CONCLUSION is completely satisfied ($0 \leq \beta \leq 1$).

The rule above is read: In the context CTX, CONDITION implies CONCLUSION with forward strength "α" and backward strength "β". Specifically, the rule states that: if the context and the left hand side (LHS) of the decision assignment operator ($\Rightarrow$) are satisfied, then the right hand side (RHS) is asserted with a degree of confidence α, and if the context and the RHS are both satisfied, then the LHS is asserted with a degree of confidence β. The decision assignment operator is equivalent to logical implication when $\alpha = 1$ and $\beta = 0$, and is equivalent to logical equivalence when $\alpha = 1$ and $\beta = 1$. Thus, by providing both "α" and "β" for each rule, it is possible to use rules in both forward and backward directions.

5.2.2. Application of Reversible Rules to Design Problems

Reversible logic rules pose some problems in that they necessarily support the same logical operations on both sides of the decision assignment operator. When nested disjunctive operations are supported in both the CONDITION and the CONCLUSION some form of *world* management is required. Despite these difficulties, reversible rules support a very important class of problems as can be illustrated briefly here.

Particularly in mechanical design, there are deep models and mathematical simulation programs which can predict an outcome from specified design parameters. For instance, the stress or wear on a given metal can be predicted from a simulation of the known behavior of the metal in a given environment. Such outcome knowledge can be captured in a knowledge-based system as, for instance, production rules which specify α to a great degree of precision. Unfortunately, design problems rarely present in this form. All too often, the design problem takes the form of a desired outcome (say lack of metal fatigue) and the problem is to find the design parameters which lead to that conclusion. Once those parameters have been found, they can be *validated* with the *forward* logic.

The reversible rules described above directly address the design problem. In particular, the rules are initially constructed from the deep knowledge to run in the *forward* direction. Later the β values are added and the rules are actually used in the *reverse* direction to solve a design problem. Once a candidate solution has been obtained, it can be evaluated by using the same rules in the *forward* direction. It should be noted that not all rules are reversible (as signified by either $\alpha = 0$ or $\beta = 0$) and that the definitions of *forward* and *backward*, while they must be used consistently for a given domain, are arbitrary.

5.2.3. Options for Uncertainty Management

The term *strength of evidence* used above was intentionally vague. In much the same way that the original ADVISE system sought to solve the problem of choosing the correct knowledge representation by supporting multiple representations which could be chosen based on the problem, it also supported multiple mechanisms for uncertainty propagation. Thus, both the CONDITION and CONCLUSION portions of rules allowed several different strategies to be used to propagate uncertainty. Each attribute (similar to an assertion in a blackboard system) to which a value can be assigned can also be assigned a strength of evidence supporting that value. In the case that there are multiple values possible, each may have its own strength of supporting evidence. The strengths of evidence are all assumed to increase with increasing evidence and decrease with decreasing evidence; only the Bayesian control scheme uses a strict probabilistic interpretation of strengths of evidence. By choosing among the predefined methods for combining strengths of evidence (or writing new methods), the knowledge engineer can utilize a range of uncertainty managements including probabilistic, MYCIN-like certainty factors, and normalized/unnormalized fuzzy logics.

Each constraint on an attribute within a rule (called a selector) can be parameterized with an α-weight and a β-weight analogous to the α and β of an entire rule. The weights indicate the importance of the attributes to the truth or falsity respectively of the term in which they occur. The weighted strength of evidence of each constraint may be linearly combined with the weighted certainty of other selectors to form a linear module. Individual selectors or linear modules may be *anded* or *ored* together in any combination to form the strength of evidence of the condition.

The combining of the strengths of evidence for a variable with the weight on the selector and the subsequent folding together of the weighted strengths of other selectors can be done using any of several different uncertainty propagation schemes. The conjunction of strengths of evidence may consist of maximum, average, probabilistic sum or Bayesian updating of strengths. Similarly, disjunction may be minimum or average. The uncertainty propagation scheme may be changed for every rule within the knowledge base, but usually all rules within a single knowledge base segment will use the same uncertainty propagation scheme.

In general, the difficulty with utilizing different uncertainty propagation mechanisms within a single system lies in combining strengths of evidence arising from different sources and calculated using different assumptions. Unfortunately, there is no simple solution to this problem. The problem can be mitigated by using homogeneous propagation mechanisms within a knowledge base segment and, thus, minimizing the exchange of strengths arising from different assumptions. For instance, a knowledge base segment might be used to derive a rank ordered list of candidate hypotheses for investigation by another segment which utilizes the partial ordering and not the actual strengths of evidence. In such a case, there is no need for the uncertainty management to be the same in the two segments.

5.3. Relational Database of Facts

The relational database contains relational tables which represent any factual information, e.g., examples of experts' past decisions. Also, the operation of the deductive inference component of the system essentially produces additional examples which can be stored in the relational tables — these are results of the operation of the machine-based expert. A modified relational algebra has been developed using constructs from Variable-valued Logic in order to integrate database operations concisely into the knowledge base formalism.

The relational database serves as the starting point for all inductive learning from examples. In many ways, the relational database of facts forms the bridge between the inductive learning process and the largely deductive problem solving process. Logic-based relational operations can be performed interactively by a knowledge engineer to control knowledge acquisition and refinement programs, or these same operations can be controlled from within logic rules during problem solving.

5.3.1. Table Creation

Relational tables can be constructed as part of batch loading of a knowledge base, operation of rules during problem solving, and interactive knowledge acquisition from a human expert. In any case, the table must be named and the attributes (columns) of the table must be defined. In addition, *key* attributes may be specified along with whether or not the table is normalized. The key attributes may be used to select rows from the table and to sort entries. A normalized table requires that all rows (corresponding to events or examples) must have unique values for the keys for that row. An unnormalized table by have duplicate values for the key fields in two or more rows.

The predefined object class, *table*, can be used to define a new table. Either a new class of table can be defined by adding properties to the system *table* or an instance of the predefined table can be created. For example, the table for holding information on blood tests might contain information about the specimens and laboratory result such as:

labvals : table (spec#, MCV : integer; Hgb : real; RBC_morph: string) key = spec#

where the spec# is the specimen number used to retrieve the results for the test and the additional attributes represent the mean corpuscular volume, hemoglobin, and red cell morphology respectively.

The ***table, integer, real, and string*** objects used in the table declarations above are not just simple data types. They are predefined object class definitions which the knowledge engineer can modify or extend. For instance, each has default methods for soliciting values from the user and a default prompt string to be used when requesting a value. The ***key*** instance variable is an instance variable of the object ***table*** which is used to contain the set of attribute names which are keys for the table. It is initialized to contain one attribute in the example above.

5.3.2. Operations on Tables

The system table object comes with a number of default methods which operate on the tables and behave as simple operators. These operators include the following editing operations: **add** — appends a new row onto a table, **change** — modifies selected rows in a table, **delete** — removes the selected rows from a table, and the following relational data operations:

union — the union of two relational tables is a table containing all of the rows (without duplication) from the two input tables. The input tables for union, intersection and difference must have ***identical attribute lists.***

intersect — the intersection of two tables is a table containing only the rows common to the two tables.

difference — the difference of two tables is a table made up of the rows of the first table which are not also rows of the second table.

product — the Cartesian product of two tables is a table made up of the concatenation of each row from the first table with all of the rows of the second table.

select — a selection from one input table is a table formed from the input table by applying a logical constraint rule to each row in the input table. Only rows which meet the logical constraint are included in the output table.

project — the projection of a table is a table containing only the indicated columns (with duplicate rows removed).

join — the join of two or more tables is a table containing a row for each row containing identical values for the shared attributes among the tables. The resultant row is formed by concatenating the input rows and using only one copy of the shared attributes. When the input tables share no attributes, then the result is the same as for the Cartesian product of the input tables.

The operations listed above can be used to manipulate tables of data either for problem solving or for submission to various learning operations which use tables. In either case, the operations can be incorporated into the rulebase or used interactively by the content expert in building or refining the knowledge base.

6. Learning Capabilities

Inferential learning techniques (largely inductive) can be used for knowledge acquisition and refinement. The inclusion of machine-based inference as a part of the knowledge acquisition process is intended to reduce the burden on human experts who would otherwise have to directly encode the contents of the knowledge base. By defining inference procedures over each component of the knowledge base, the system no longer relies on the human expert to organize and present a complete, concise, and error free knowledge base. In much the same way that the relational table operators have been incorporated into the rule formalism as operators which can operate directly on the knowledge base, the learning operators can be interactively invoked or invoked from within rules during problem solving.

Recent progress in the area of machine learning [9] opens a number of possibilities for improving knowledge acquisition methods for knowledge-based systems. Various experiments have demonstrated that it is possible to learn the decision rules from examples of experts' decisions, and that these rules perform as well, and sometimes even better than rules obtained by encoding the experts' rules e.g., [10].

Important progress has been made recently in studying other machine learning strategies, such as learning by analogy [11, 12, 13] and learning from observation and discovery [14, 15]. These findings indicate possibilities for developing new techniques for knowledge acquisition for knowledge based systems using learning techniques.

The discussion of learning capabilities for integrated knowledge-based system building below is organized according to the transformations from Figure 2. Additional details about each category of transformation are provided below. In principal, there is no limit to the number and variety of inferential operators that might be included in this integrated approach. The discussion below has been limited to a meaningful length by only including those inferential operations which we have explicitly explored rather than all possibilities.

6.1. From Data to Rules – Learning from Examples

Inductive derivation of rules from expert supplied sets of examples is one of the most classic applications of machine learning to knowledge acquisition as demonstrated by such programs as AQVAL [16], INDUCE [17], and ID3 [18]. Such programs are usually used to ***differentiate*** among outcomes and produce rules which summarize tables of examples of the desired decision. In our work, we have investigated rule inference in three different areas: attribute-based decision rules – differentiate, structural descriptions – structure, temporal process prediction – predict. Each of these efforts has lead to an operator in the integrated approach.

6.1.1. Differentiate

We have explored the differentiate operation using the programs GEM, and AQ11 [19]. The GEM program takes in two or more relational tables each containing a set of examples of a decision class and produces as output a set of consistent and optimized decision rules expressed as statements in the ***attribute calculus*** known as VL_1 (Variable-valued Logic system 1) [16]. The output of the induction process is a collection of decision rules which can be stored in the knowledge base. The GEM operator can be used to interactively generate optimized decision rules when only examples of the decisions are well known. It has been used to generate soybean diagnosis rules from examples. In that situation, the generated rules outperformed the rules which were hand-crafted from expert knowledge [20]. The AQ11 and AQ15 programs take a number of event classes and attempt to find the conceptually simplest rules that will determine the class of each event. These programs use the same basic ***Aq*** algorithm which is used in GEM but support a more extended knowledge representation than that supported by GEM.

6.1.2. Structure

The program INDUCE/3 is able to learn structural descriptions of classes of objects from examples. It can solve learning problems similar to those solved by GEM, but unlike GEM, it processes structured examples described in an extended predicate calculus (system VL_2). The program incorporates an inference mechanism of ***constructive induction*** for applying background knowledge rules to examples to produce new descriptors. The INDUCE program can be used to generate decision rules when examples of the decisions are available and the examples have internal structure.

6.1.3. Predict

The SPARC family of programs generate rules describing processes which evolve over time (temporal process prediction). Examples of temporal processes can be represented in a conceptual network, or in ***Annotated Predicate Calculus***. In previous research [21], the program was used to play the card game Eleusis in which the goal is to discover a card sequence prediction rule to direct the play of the cards. The program has recently been extended to solve a more general problem of process prediction.

6.2. From Data to Data – Event and Attribute Selection

Transformations of tables of data elements into other tables of data elements are common operations during knowledge acquisition and refinement. The relational table operations such as project, join, and select can be used to build new tables from existing tables. Also, a table can be extended or modified to reflect new information. In addition to these interactive operations, there are two inductive operations we have investigated: attribute (variable) selection – VARSEL, event (example) selection – ESEL. If the table of examples is organized with the attributes across the top as column headers and the examples themselves as rows, then these operations correspond to selecting a subset of the columns or rows for further use. Selecting a subset of the available examples can be particularly important for time saving with computationally intensive learning algorithms.

6.2.1. Attribute Selection

The VARSEL operation invokes the program called PROMISE [22] which selects the most ***promising*** attributes for differentiating between classes of events. Its output is therefore intended for use with the Differentiate operation described above.

The VARSEL operation takes two or more relational tables each containing examples of a particular class and selects a projection of the tables which consists of relevant selected variables. A variable is relevant if its values contribute significantly to differentiating the examples in one class from those in another class. The output consists of tables containing the same examples as the input, but with columns of values for only the relevant attributes. The VARSEL operator is used to reduce the complexity of example sets in the relational database by removing attributes which are irrelevant.

6.2.2. Event Selection

The ESEL operation invokes the program ESEL/2 [23], a program that takes a large number of examples and selects a small subset of examples that is most representative of the larger group. The smaller sample will require less computation when used as input to other inductive operators. Large numbers of examples (more than 200) can require substantial processing time when used as input to other inference operators.

The ESEL operator takes one or more relational tables containing examples and selects a subset of examples which are most representative of the set. Several different selection algorithms are available, based on conceptual measures similar to the conceptual cohesiveness measure used by the CLUSTER operator (described below). The ESEL operator is used to scale down large example sets while trying to retain the embedded knowledge.

6.3. From Rules to Rules – Incremental Rule Refinement

In our experiments, we have not developed separate tools devoted to incremental rule refinement, but we have used other existing tools to meet this need. We have identified two different cases for rule refinement: Refinement based on experience – Refine, Refinement from consistency checking – Consistency. Each of these cases involves taking in a segment of rules and producing a revised segment of rules that are more consistent or more general.

6.3.1. Refine

When additional examples are provided or the results of problem solving are critiqued, errors in the problem solving behavior of the system can be detected. Ignoring for the moment the substantial problem of blame assignment, rules in the knowledge base can be modified with special exception clauses which specifically exclude the known counter examples from the more general terms in the rules. This form of knowledge base update can be performed by storing a table of exceptions to check first or by modifying individual rules.

As rules accumulate exception clauses, they become cumbersome to manipulate and are less likely to fully represent the structure of the original problem. Either the original training set of examples can be modified to include the new examples for an entirely new inductive learning process, or the rules can be incrementally modified. Incremental modification of rules preserves as much of the previous solution as possible while improving the performance, understandability, and predictive value of the refined rules. (The INDUCE operation provides limited support for this function.)

6.3.2. Consistency

A knowledge base can be refined by analyzing it for consistency and completeness [24]. A segment of rules can be inspected for its coverage of the full range of input values (completeness) or for the uniqueness of its reported result for any given input pattern (consistency). When inconsistencies or omissions are detected, additional rules can be generated to force the supplied rule segment to be either complete or consistent. Usually, such rules will need to be inspected by an expert with domain knowledge to evaluate the suitability of including the inductively derived rules into the knowledge base.

The consistency and completeness operations are combined in a single program which is invoked by the consistency operator [24]. This operator takes a rule segment and returns a (potentially) modified rule segment where rules have been modified or added to make the knowledge base more complete or consistent. The rulebase is made complete by simply constructing a rule (or rules) which explicitly enumerate the incompleteness by explicitly assigning the decision variable(s) to undefined. Rules are added or modified to produce a consistent rulebase by eliminating competing rule chains that produce conflicting results.

6.4. From Rules to Networks – Completeness

The completeness operator described above is also capable of detecting structure within a rulebase. The operator groups rules together into functional groups which share access to common variables and participate in common rule chains. The result is similar to that produced by Jacob and Froscher [26] but is based upon the intermediate results of the consistency analysis. The grouping of the rules is structured as segments defined within the original segment and these segments are organized in a tree structure using the network of object primitives.

6.5. From Data to Networks – Conceptual Clustering

The purpose of the *cluster* operation is to divide a collection of objects into smaller groups of similar objects based upon some criterion or measure of similarity. Clustering is the process of developing a taxonomy or classification scheme for the objects of a study. The program invoked by the *cluster* command is called *CLSUTER/paf* [25]. Unlike most numerical taxonomic techniques, this program uses a *concept-based* method of clustering that produces descriptions of the clusters (categories) that it derives. It also permits the user to specify the criteria which are to be used to evaluate clusters.

The *cluster* operation takes one relational table containing examples and automatically builds classifications of the examples. A classification is a hierarchy of conjunctive concepts expressed in the *attribute calculus* of VL_1. A more powerful extension of the operator invokes the CLUSTER/S program which accepts a collection of structured objects and automatically builds classifications composed of conjunctive statments in the extended predicate calculus (VL_2). The CLUSTER operator is used to organize and give conceptual structure to a collection of examples. This can improve ease and speed of access to the data, the efficiency of subsequent inferential operations, and can reveal to the domain expert underlying patterns.

6.6. From Networks to Networks

In the work on ADVISE, we have not explored machine learning as applied to refining network structures from networks. Michalski and Collins, however, have explored the use of transformation operators which operate to produce a form of plausible reasoning [27]. The application of the theory of plausible reasoning they have outlined can produce organizations of new material based on reasoning over existing knowledge. Thus, a specificity hierarchy can serve to guide the construction of a similar hierarchy using transformation operators such as generalization, specialization, similarity and dissimilarity as applied to both attributes and their values.

7. Problem Solving Using Multiple Representations

The reason for supporting an integrated approach to problem solving over multiple knowledge representations is to allow the selection of the knowledge representation which most suits the problem domain. By choosing the knowledge representation and associated problem solving technique most natural for a problem or subproblem, the knowledge engineer can minimize the distance between the way that information about the problem is presented in the outside world and recorded in the knowledge base.

This section explores the problem solving transformations shown in Figure 2. In most cases, we have explored these problem solving strategies as separate components of the ADVISE system. A brief outline of problem solving over each knowledge representation is presented in the subsections which follow. Additional information about some of the problem solving methods is presented in the example applications in the next section.

7.1. From Data to Data – Deductive and Inductive Retrieval

Deductive retrieval represents the simplest and most straight forward method for conducting problem solving (unfortunately it is seldom sufficient). The relational commands supported over the knowledge base provide for simple deductive retrieval of examples. When an example in the knowledge base (such as the exceptions discussed under learning from rules to rules) is directly retrieved based on a match between the presenting information and the present case, the stored decision can be used. Although direct retrieval is not a good general purpose way to implement a machine-based problem solver, it can be used to encode exceptional, prototypical, and exemplary cases for use in problem solving, generalization, and explanation.

The deductive retrieval process can be implemented as part of the problem solving process, e.g. a preamble to more traditional machine-based reasoning techniques or as an end in itself. If deductive retrieval is included, then it is quite natural to provide for relaxed criteria matching on the retrieval and, thus, support inductive retrieval. In the case of inductive retrieval, other than a perfect match between the presenting data and the retrieved data can be used to generate a decision. The amount of the generalization allowed in the inductive retrieval can be controlled and used to decide whether additional methods should be used to verify a given result. When the results of the inductive retrieval are themselves stored back in the knowledge base, then a form of incremental learning results.

7.2. From Rules to Data – Deductive Rule Application

Deductive rule application is the most common form of problem solving for expert systems. In our experiments with ADVISE, we have investigated the use of multiple control schemes for scheduling rules and multiple mechanisms for propagating uncertainty. Reinke [28] empirically investigated the role of uncertainty propagation mechanisms within the ADVISE approach and constructed tools for executing ADVISE rules in batch mode for analysis.

The notion of a rulegroup in the ADVISE system has been generalized to a knowledge base segment in this integrated approach. A rule group forms a unit of uniform scheduling and uncertainty propagation scheme and usually corresponds to a subproblem in a task decomposition. Support for multiple schemes for conducting deductive inference over the rules allows the problem solving to be tailored to the problem domain.

7.3. From Rules to Rules – Rule-based Scheduling

Reasoning from rules to rules is equivalent to reasoning about the control of rule exploration using rules. In our integrated approach, we have used the concept of a rulegroup (here generalized to a knowledge base segment) as a rulebase structuring element. An entire rule segment appears like an encapsulated logic operation which has a similar external structure to that of a rule. Thus, an entire rule segment can be invoked in a rule of another segment much like a function call. The acquisition of the value of the function is scheduled in the same way that scalar attribute collection is scheduled (e.g. based on cost, frequency, strength of implication, etc.).

In its most basic form, an invocation of a rule segment from within a rule segment looks like a single rule which summarizes the behavior of the the invoked rule segment. This use of rule segments and their encapsulation can provide a simplification of knowledge base management similar to that afforded traditional programs by equivalent software engineering techniques [26].

7.4. From Networks to Data – Network Problem Solving

Although experiments with purely network-based problem solving were conducted with the BABY system (described below), true network-based problem solving was never incorporated into the ADVISE system. Systems such as AL/X and PROSPECTOR in addition to numerous efforts involving spreading activation indicate that such techniques should be part of the integrated approach.

When reasoning from networks to data, the problem solving strategy consists of a traversal of the network in order to evaluate the possible conclusions in light of the prevailing evidence. The acquisition of evidence can be controlled by the topology of the network linkages and sequential Bayesian updating of probabilities or analogous operations on certainty factors of various kinds can support reasoning over uncertain evidence.

7.5. From Networks to Rules – Network-based Scheduling

Reasoning from networks to rules is similar to reasoning from rules to rules in that it amounts to a form of rule scheduling. This option for rule scheduling was used extensively in the BABY system described in the next section to support an evolution of the reasoning process.

Spreading activation or sequential Bayesian traversal of the network can be used to evaluate what amount to preconditions on the invocation of rule segments or individual rules. In either case, rule sequencing information has been included in the network. This approach is particularly well suited to situations where data arrives naturally in the course of operation of the system and does not need to be solicited. Temporal progressions or developing situations can be described by the network and appropriate rules to react to the evolving situation can be activated by the the individual nodes in the network.

7.6. From Networks to Networks – Plausible Reasoning

Reasoning from networks to networks amounts to reasoning from known structure of the problem domain (or the problem at hand) to a new structure of the problem at hand in light of available evidence. Such reasoning can take at least two forms: reasoning by analogy and responding to changing situations. These two distinct problem solving activities can share a common knowledge representation and many of the operations over that representation. Reasoning by analogy as a part of plausible reasoning was discussed in the section on inference of networks from networks above and is more fully discussed in [27].

When reasoning from networks to networks is used to respond to changing situations, network descriptions of the structure of the various possible situations must be constructed. These descriptions serve to guide the instantiation of sub-networks which provide detailed descriptions of the evolving situations.

8. Experiments Using the Integrated Approach

The range of applicability of many of the ideas presented in this integrated approach can be seen from three example knowledge-based systems which were developed in the ADVISE approach and an application of the ESSAI system (which incorporates many ideas from the integrated approach). The system which was most fully developed was the PLANT/ds which serves as a consultant for soybean disease diagnosis. The PLANT/cd system predicts the cutworm damage to corn and the BABY system was developed as a consultant for the neo-natal intensive care unit. The ESSAI system, derived from the original ADVISE system, was applied to the problem of configuring a System 12 switching system. Each of these systems made use of different knowledge structuring primitives and different problem solving strategies.

8.1. PLANT/ds

The PLANT/ds system uses data about the condition of plants in a soybean field to predict which of the 19 most common disease(s) may be present [29]. The questions the system asks are organized in a collection of forms which allow many related questions to be answered at one time. The selection of the forms to present to the user is determined by evaluating the *utility* of all of the variables for which a value is not known. The form containing the more useful variable is then presented to the user and the form is filled out. The evaluation of the utility measure for the next variable to select uses all of the data volunteered on the previous forms in evaluating variables and rules.

The PLANT/ds control scheme has been used with expert derived rules and rules derived from machine induction. A version of PLANT was developed that used both expert and machine rules to arrive at a diagnosis. In addition, the utility measure control scheme was also used in a project to develop a turf management expert system using expert rules.

8.2. PLANT/cd

The PLANT/cd expert system uses data about insects and corn plants to predict the damage to corn due to cutworms [30]. The control scheme for PLANT/cd is a traditional backward chaining theorem proving model. Rules, and, finally variables are selected for evaluation based on the potential strength of implication of the rules. The PLANT/cd system is disjunctive because of its use of an external climatologic database and a deep model of insect growth. These two sources of information external to the expert system itself were consulted in much the same way that the human user was asked a question. Because of the nature of backward chaining, questions were asked serially and there was limited ability for the user to volunteer data.

8.3. BABY

The BABY system is a consultant that is intended to monitor on-line data, laboratory data, and clinical data in a neo-natal intensive care unit [31]. (The system used transaction files to simulate direct connection to a premature infant.) Data is supplied to BABY as it is generated and the majority of the data input into the system comes automatically. Clinical findings which a doctor might specify are requested by the system when they would be important for a diagnosis. Unlike the other systems, BABY must contend with data that arrives at different time intervals and with differing levels of detail and reliability.

BABY uses input data that changes in time as normal (or abnormal) bodily functions proceed in the infant. In addition, the situations (the patterns of normal and abnormal physiology) change with the age of the infant. Because BABY is intended to operate over long periods of time with little operator intervention, it handles data and situations that change in time.

The control scheme for BABY is a hybrid of a forward chaining and a network-based partial sequential Bayesian updating of certainty factors. Rules are used to recognize patterns in the data and a causal network is used to identify physiologic states that should cause medical intervention or further investigation. Changes in certainty that result from evaluation of rules are propagated through the network using a modified sequential Bayesian updating of the odds for each node in the network.

As part of the management of time, each certainty factor associated with a variable is *aged* if the value is not supplied again. The aging factor used is tailored to the normal rate of change of each variable. The changing situations are managed using context arcs in the Bayesian network. The context arcs control the portions of the graph that are instantiated at any given time. The instantiation (or deinstantiation) of portions of the network also control the rules that are evaluated. Thus, it becomes possible for the system to properly recognize that patterns of findings that would signal alarm for a full term infant are *normal* for premature infants. Similarly, in the presence of known problems, expected patterns of abnormality are not pointed out, but those that should not be expected under the circumstances are.

8.4. ESSAI

The ESSAI system, incorporating many of the ADVISE ideas, was developed by the Tools and Technology Group of the telecommunications company, Alcatel, at their base in Paris, France. It was applied to the customer application engineering (CAE) process whereby the exchange requirements of a telephone administration are translated into detailed design and layout specifications needed for the exchange installation. The CAE process is naturally subdivided into 20 major functional units — each of which can be associated with a knowledge base segment. The equipment placement portion of the CAE process is concerned with determining a valid placement within a building for the various items of equipment that constitute a System 12 telephone exchange. This equipment includes the telephonic equipment such as the suites into which are placed the racks, power supplies, and the main distribution frame containing peripheral equipment. The placement process involves knowledge of physical constraints affecting equipment position and access as well as knowledge of exchange design rules affecting power supplies and cabling requirements.

The object oriented nature of the system has proven particularly effective in supporting end user interaction. Here, the major challenge was to enable the end user to prepare a representation of the building plan using a high resolution graphics workstation. The building plan supplies the physical space dimensions of each of the rooms in the building and shows the psoition of physical obstacles, such as pillars, doors, and location of windows; the plan may also indicate customer preferences for positioning equipment, access points, and a specification of more detailed aspects of the switching room. The layout produced by the expert system is stored in a tabular database to enable extensions or modifications to the plan by the customer, and the layout can be printed on a plotter to produce a scale drawing of the floor plan.

The experience with ESSAI has shown the value of an integrated paradigm which combines features of rule-based systems with those of object oriented programming. This combination enables a high degree of control and configurability without losing the advantages of declarative representations and non-deterministic problem solving.

9. Design of a Language for Integrated Knowledge-based Systems

The integrated approach described here is of little value unless all of its components can be unified in a single knowledge-based system. At first glance, it is not apparent that the diverse operations and representations described in the integrated approach can coexist within a single formalism. The Knowledge Base Variable-valued Logic system 2 ($KBVL_2$) has been developed to provide a unifying syntax and semantics for expressing operations and knowledge within the integrated approach. This section discusses a few major design constraints on $KBVL_2$ and illustrates major components of the language with simple examples.

9.1. Requirements for $KBVL_2$ Design

The $KBVL_2$ language is intended to support the three representations which are part of the integrated approach, the inductive learning operations defined over them, and the problem solving operations defined over them. This formalism is intended to integrate the various operations and knowledge base representations as much as possible rather than simply merge otherwise separate systems for rules, networks, and data. The $KBVL_2$ formalism is intended to support batch operation in which a knowledge base can be described and tested [28] as well as interactively constructed and refined [32, 24]. Finally, all knowledge structuring primitives as well as inferential operators must be available to operations coded in the knowledge base language itself.

The last constraint on the design of $KBVL_2$ is implicit within the entire integrated approach. In many knowledge-based system environments, the logic of the control of the problem solving is implicit within the design of the system itself and is not subject to change by the knowledge base builder. Because of limitations in the knowledge representation and because of this implicit definition of the control information, considerable portions of sophisticated exert systems for real world problems must be encoded directly in a procedural language of some form rather than be captured in the knowledge base itself. This problem arises when the implicit procedural control of problem solving does not match the explicitly required problem solving behavior of a portion of the solution to a complex problem.

The theme of explicitly encoding problem solving control information within the knowledge base runs through the integrated approach (see reasoning from networks to networks, networks to rules, and rules to rules above). The $KBVL_2$ formalism is intended to directly address the need to provide for explicit declaration of the sort of problem solving control information which is traditionally implicit within a particular expert system shell. Thus, the knowledge base builder can construct a knowledge-based system where strategic knowledge about how to go about the problem solving process can be integrated within the knowledge base formalism along with the traditional tactical information about the problem at hand.

9.2. Knowledge Base Objects

In KBVL$_2$, each atomic entity and all of the composite enties are viewed as objects. That is, they can have instance variables and methods attached. Instance variables themselves may be objects and methods are rules which are executed when the method is invoked. A few objects such as integer, real, string, and a generic object with no properties are predefined in the system. Additional objects for manging networks, rules, and a relational database are described below.

In KBVL$_2$ there is a distinction between class definitions and instances as found in most object oriented systems. A class definition and instance definition are represented as:

```
< new_class_name >=< existing_class_name > with < object options >
< new_class_name > : < existing_class_name > with <object options>
```

respectively where the *with <object options>* is optional and defines additional instance variables and methods if required for the new object. Thus, to define a class of integer valued laboratory tests which can be performed on one of two different instruments with a cost per test which is dependent on the instrument used, one would write:

```
two_instruments=integer with
   {instrument:nominal(instrument1,instrument2);
    cost_instrument1 : real; cost_instrument2 : real;
    price : method {[instrument = instrument1] ⇒ [price = cost_instrument1];
                    [instrument = instrument2] ⇒ [price = cost_instrument2]; } }
```

where the method called *price* calculates the price of the test by sequentially scheduling the rules in the body of the method for evaluation and potential execution. The class called *two_instrument_test* is formed from the builtin class *integer* by adding the indicated instance variables and methods. In order to define two instances of the new class and initialize their costs, one would write:

```
test1:two_instrument_test with cost_instrument1 = 2.34, cost_instrument2 = 3.45;
test2:two_instrument_test with cost_instrument1 = 3.31, cost_instrument2 = 2.05;
```

where the two instances differ from each other only in their initial values for their costs based on each instrument. Using these structuring primitives, a knowledge engineer can construct concept descriptions which are natural to the domain and tailor them to individual problems by changing initial values, adding instance variables, or adding methods.

9.3. Structuring the Knowledge Base – Segments

A large knowledge base can quickly become unmanageable if representations for knowledge base structuring are not used. In $KBVL_2$, knowledge base segments are defined and used to delineate portions of the knowledge base which behave as structural units. (The method definition in the previous subsection is an example of a knowledge base segment nested within the definition of a knowledge base ***object***. In keeping with the three forms of knowledge representation, there are three predefined knowledge base segments which can be instantiated by a knowledge base builder.

The class and instance definitions shown above cannot stand alone; they must be included in a knowledge base segment. The class definition would most naturally be included in a network segment of class definitions linked by the ***subclass*** and ***superclass*** relations. The individual laboratory tests would be included in a table of other attributes and both might be included together in a knowledge base ***segment*** called ***test_kb***:

```
test_kb : {class : network (subclass, superclass) {
          two_instrument_test = integer with
          {instrument : nominal (instrument1, instrument2);
          cost_instrument1 : real; cost_instrument2 : real;
          price:method {[instrument = instrument1] ⇒ [price = cost_instrument1];
          [instrument = instrument2] ⇒ [price = cost_instrument2]; }
          }}
          attribute : table(name : string, value : object) {
          test1:two_instrument_test with cost_instrument1 = 2.34,
                                         cost_instrument2 = 3.45;
          test2:two_instrument_test with cost_instrument1 = 3.31,
                                         cost_instrument2 = 2.05;
          }}
```

Multiple knowledge base segments can be constructed for subproblems and each can use concept descriptions from global segments as well as individualized knowledge representations and problem solving techniques.

The example above shows a knowledge base segment containing different kinds of knowledge. A rule segment could be added which produces interpretive reports for the two laboratory tests and the segment would form a solution to the subproblem of generating reports. Segments can be used to define structure within the knowledge base or to portray its organization. For instance, given a class definition for a blackboard as a table with ***post***, ***remove***, and ***search*** methods operating on blackboard entries, a structured blackboard can be constructed by creating a network of sub-blackboards. The decomposition of the blackboard can parallel decompositions within the rulebase or can simply reflect structure within the solution to the problem and not the manner of problem solving.

9.4. A More Complete Example – The Monkey and the Banana

The $KBVL_2$ language can be illustrated with a simple example of a knowledge base for solving a problem. The problem and solution shown in this section have been constructed to present a range of features of $KBVL_2$ and not with the intent of presenting an ***optimal*** solution.

The monkey and banana problem has been used frequently to illustrate machine-based problem solving systems. The $KBVL_2$ language is well suited to describing both the problem and its solution. The problem to be solved is that of instructing a monkey alone in a room with several objects of furniture and a bunch of bananas suspended from the ceiling. The monkey's goal is to assemble the furniture into a pile so that the bananas can be reached by climbing on the furniture. The instructions can be presented as a sequence of commands to move about within the room, carry objects, pile objects, climb on, and grasp objects. The $KBVL_2$ object classes and objects which can be used to define the monkey and banana problem arc (omitting the optional ***object with*** from the declarations):

location = {zpos : integer; xypos: {xpos,ypos:integer}}
movable_object = {height:integer;
    identity : nominal(table, stool, box, banana);
    xyzpos:location;}
room : {objects : set of movable_object;
    banana : location with identity : nominal(banana); }
monkey : movable_object with {grip : movable_object;}

where the operations grasp, climb_on, moveto, and release are also defined as truth-valued functions that return true if their indicated function was accomplished by the monkey. The situation can be defined by initializing the instance variables for each movable_object in the room and placing them in the set of objects associated with the room. The goal of the monkey can be stated as an attempt to make the logical condition [***identity of grip of monkey*** = ***banana***] be true. The named rules which define the possible actions of the monkey are:

GRASP :For_all obj in objects of room [grip of monkey = empty]
    and [location of monkey = location of obj]
    ⇒ [grip(obj)] ⟶ [grip of monkey = obj]

MOVE :For_all obj in objects of room [xypos of obj ≠ xypos of monkey]
    ⇒ [moveto(xypos of obj)]⟶ [xypos of monkey = xypos of obj]

CLIMB :For_all obj in objects of room [location of obj = location of monkey]
$\Rightarrow$ [climb_on(obj)] $\longrightarrow$ [zpos of monkey = zpos of monkey + height of obj]

RELEASE : [grip of monkey $\neq$ empty] $\Rightarrow$ [release] $\longrightarrow$ [grip of monkey = empty]

where the implication arrows on the right hand side of the rules describe the side effects of the instructions to the monkey. (The syntax of the quantification has been altered slightly for the purposes of readability in this example.) The rules above constitute both a statement of the degrees of freedom of the monkey and the solution to the problem. Taken together with the logical statement of the goal, the rules non-deterministically define a solution to the problem at hand. Unfortunately, neither a forward nor a backward chaining search will produce a solution to this problem with a short search.

While the rules above accurately portray the solution to the problem, they do not lend themselves to its rapid solution. The performance of the rules can be substantially improved by incorporating information about the goal directly into them. In the event that the rules of behavior are modified to include information pertinent to the monkey's search for the banana, the rules become less useful for other purposes. Indeed, it is just such a mixing of tactical and strategic information that the integrated approach is intended to avoid.

Information about good strategies to employ can be readily incorporated into a network structure which can direct the search. For instance, the concept of ***carry*** can be represented as ***release*** $\rightarrow$ ***move_to*** $\rightarrow$ ***grasp*** $\rightarrow$ ***move_to***. Similarly, the concept of ***pile*** can be constructed as a loop involving ***carry*** $\rightarrow$ ***climb*** $\rightarrow$ ***release***. Finally, the overall strategy can be specified as ***pile*** followed by grasping the banana.

Separating the strategic information from the rules about the world of monkies and bananas allows the strategic information to be treated as only one of many possible annotations on the group of rules. Different annotations can be added and kept distinct from each other as well as distinct from the rules themselves.

A data table (not shown in the example above) can be used to accumulate a trace of the actual commands issued to the moneky. In the event that a correct solution which can be correctly executed is derived, then the table will contain a trace of the monkey's steps in obtaining the banana. In any case, the tabular trace, or tables of such tables, can be used to inductively derive the sort of strategic information discussed above.

10. Bringing It All Together – QUIN

The original research on the ADVISE system which emphasized the use of multiple knowledge representations, multiple control and uncertainty propagation schemes, together with a major learning component has been generalized to form the integrated approach to knowledge-based systems presented here. The integrated approach emphasizes the construction of knowledge bases using the best problem solving and representational tools at hand rather than using a single prescribed representation and problem solving scheme. The approach emphasizes the integration of machine learning tools directly within the knowledge base language and within an interactive user interface for knowledge acquisition and refinement.

The $KBVL_2$ language was developed as part of this integrated approach and provides for description of libraries of knowledge base segments which can be integrated into a single knowledge-based system or used as building blocks for defining a family of knowledge-based systems. The $KBVL_2$ language directly supports the definition of problem solving control information separated from tactical decision rules. This separation together with the rich combination of network, rule and database structuring primitives for knowledge representation provides a more widely useful knowledge-based system tool than would otherwise be possible.

The QUery and INference system, QUIN, provides interactive access to the knowledge represented in a $KBVL_2$ knowledge base. QUIN is primarily a marriage between relational database and inductive learning technologies [33]. Its purpose is the management of large amounts of data for input to and output from the inductive transformation operators shown in Figure 1. The system provides rudimentary access to problem solving using the knowledge base for deductive and inductive retrieval as well as learning.

QUIN may be used for the management and analysis of data as well as to browse through a knowledge base. Management here refers to the creation, retrieval, and modification of the data, while analysis refers to activities that attempt to discover more about 1) interrelationships within the data and 2) phenomena that produce those interrelationships. Although the QUIN interface was originally developed to operate only on tables of relational data, some editing and display operations on networks and rules have been added in this integrated approach.

The operations in QUIN provide access to the inductive inference, analysis, and problem solving transformations shown in Figure 1. In general, each operation requires an options object in addition to the table(s) of input data on which to operate. Output from the inferential process in the form of tables, networks or rules can be inspected by the user and introduced into a new segment or stored over the information in the segment from which it came. (Details about each operation can be found in sections 6 and 7 above.)

The induction operations within QUIN interact to form a set of utilities that can be used in sequence or in cycles. The databases used to test and experiment with these learning algorithms are more easily handled with database management techniques that store, modify, and restructure data for eventual input to the inference programs. The cycle of knowledge refinement by iteration of the mechanized inference with a human critic produces better results than either alone.

The integrated approach to the construction of knowledge-based systems discussed in this paper brings together interactive application of machine learning techniques, variations in knowledge representation, problem solving strategy, and uncertainty management in a single paradigm. The integrated approach, while not fully realized in any existing system, has been substantially incorporated in experimental meta-expert system tools and has demonstrated its potential for qualitative improvement in knowledge-based system technology.

REFERENCES

[1] Klein, P.J. and Dolins, S. B., *Choosing Architectures For Expert Systems*, CCSC Technical Report # 85-01-001, Texas Instruments Incorporated, Dallas, TX, 1985.

[2] Michalski, R.S., Baskin, A.B., Uhrik, C. and Channic, T., *The ADVISE.1 Meta-Expert System: The General Design and a Technical Description*, UIUCDCS-F-87-962, Department of Computer Science, University of Illinois, Urbana Illinois (DCSUI), 1987.

[3] Davis, R. and King, J., *An Overview of Production Systems*, in: Elcock and Michie (eds.), Machine Intelligence, 1976.

[4] Buchanan, B.G. and Duda, R.O., *Principles of Rule-base Expert Systems*, Advances in Computers, **22**, Academic Press, 1983.

[5] Drazovich, R.J., McCune, B.P., and Buchanan, B.G. *Characteristics of hypothesis formation systems*, Technical Report, Advanced Information and Decision Systems, Mountain View, Ca, Project Number 3003, May 27, 1981.

[6] Baskin, A.B., *LOGIC NETS: Variable-valued Logic plus Semantic Networks*, Policy Analysis and Information Systems, No. **3**, 1980.

[7] Michalski, R.S., *Pattern Recognition as Rule-Guided Inductive Inference*, IEEE Transactions on Pattern Analysis and Machine Intelligence, Vol. PAMI-2, No. **4**, 1980.

[8] Michalski, R.S., *Pattern Recognition as Knowledge-Guided Computer Induction*, Report No. 927, DCSUI, 1978.

[9] Michalski, R.S., Carbonell, J.G., and Mitchell, T., (eds.), *Machine Learning, An Artificial Intelligence Approach, Vol II.*, Morgan Kaufman Publishers, Inc., Los Altos, CA, 1986.

[10] Michalski, R.S., Mozetic, I., Hong, J., and Lavrac, N., *The AQ15 Inductive Learning System: An Overview and Experiments*, UIUCDCS-R-86-1260, ISG 86-20, DCSUI, 1986.

[11] Winston, P.H., Binford, T.O., Katz, B. and Lowry, M., *Learning Physical Descriptions from Functional Definitions, Examples and Precedents*, in: Proceedings of AAAI-83, Washington, D.C., 1983.

[12] Carbonell, J.G., *Derivational Analogy in Problem Solving and Knowledge Acquisition*, in: Proceedings of the International Machine Learning Workshop, University of Illinois Allerton House, Urbana, Illinois, 1983.

[13] Burstein, M.H., *Concept Formation by Incremental Analogical Reasoning and Debugging*, in: Proceedings of the International Machine Learning Workshop, University of Illinois Allerton House, Urbana, Illinois, 1983.

[14] Lenat, D.B., *Case Study 2: The Eurisko Program; Heuristics Used to Develop New Heuristics*, in: MACHINE LEARNING: An Artificial Intelligence Approach, R.S. Michalski, J. Carbonell, and T. Mitchell (eds.) TIOGA Publishing Co., Palo Alto, CA, 1983.

[15] Stepp, R.E. and Michalski, R.S., *Conceptual Clustering: Inventing Goal-Oriented Classifications of Structured Objects*, in: Machine Learning: An Artificial Intelligence Approach, Volume II, Morgan Kaufman Publishers, Inc., Los Altos, CA, 1986.

[16] Michalski, R.S., *AQVAL/1 - Computer Implementation of a Variable-valued Logic System* VL_1, in: Proceedings of the First International Joint Conference on Pattern Recognition, Washington, DC, 1973.

[17] Larson, J., *INDUCE-1: An Interactive Inductive Inference Program in* VL_{21} *Logic System*, Report No. UIUCDCS-R-77-876, DCSUI, 1977.

[18] Quinlan, J.R. *Discovering Rules from Large Collections of Examples: A Case Study*, in: Expert Systems in the Micro-Electronic Age, Michie, D. (ed.), Edinburgh University Press, Edinburgh, 1979.

[19] Michalski, R.S. and Larson, J.B., *Selection of Most Representative Training Examples and Incremental Generation of* VL_1 *Hypothesis: The Underlying Methodology and the Descriptions of Programs ESEL and AQ11*, Report No. 877, DCSUI, 1978.

[20] Michalski, R.S. and Chilausky, R.L., *Knowledge Acquisition by Encoding Expert Rules versus Computer Induction From Examples: A case study involving soybean pathology*, International Journal for Man-Machine Studies, No. 12, 1980.

[21] Dieterich, T., and Michalski, R.S., *Discovering Patterns in Sequences of Events*, Artificial Intelligence Journal, Vol**25**, No.2, 1985.

[22] Baim, P.W., *Automated Acquisition of Decision Rules: The Problem of Attribute Construction and Selection*, Masters Thesis, DCSUI, 1984.

[23] Cramm, S., *ESEL/2: A Program for Selecting the Most Relevant Training Events for Inductive Learning*, ISG 83-1, UIUCDCS-F-83-901, DCSUI 1983.

[24] Riedesel, J.D., ***Consistency and Completeness: An Exercise in Knowledge Base Validation***, Masters Thesis, DCSUI, 1988.

[25] Michalski, R.S., ***Knowledge Acquisition Through Conceptual Clustering: A Theoretical Framework and an Algorithm for Partitioning Data into Conjunctive Concepts***, International Journal of Policy Analysis and Information Systems, Vol. **4**, No. 3, 1980.

[26] Jacob, R.J.K., and Froscher, J.N., ***Developing a Software Engineering Methodology for Knowledge-Based Systems***, Technical Report NRL REport 90919, Naval Research Laboratory, 1986.

[27] Collins, A. and Michalski, R.S., ***THE LOGIC OF PLAUSIBLE REASONING: A Preliminary Report***, Report No. UIUCDCS-F-85-951, DCSUI, 1986.

[28] Reinke, R.E., ***Knowledge Acquisition and Refinement Tools for the ADVISE Meta-Expert System***, Masters Thesis, DCSUI, 1984.

[29] Michalski, R.S., et. al., ***PLANT/ds: An Expert System for the Diagnosis of Soybean Diseases***, European Conference on Artificial Intelligence, 1982.

[30] Boulanger, A.B., ***The Expert System PLANT/cd: A Case Study in Applying the General Purpose Inference System ADVISE to Predicting Black Cutworm Damage in Corn***, Masters Thesis, DCSUI, 1983.

[31] Rodewald, L.E., ***BABY: An Expert System for Patient Monitoring in a Newborn Intensive Care Unit***, Masters Thesis, DCSUI, 1984.

[32] Spackman, K.A., ***QUIN: Integration of Inferential Operators within a Relational Database***, ISG 83-13, UIUCDCS-R-83-917, DCSUI, 1983.

[33] Michalski, R.S., Baskin, A.B., and Spackman, K.A., ***A Logic-based Approach to Conceptual Database Analysis***, in: Proceedings of Sixth Annual Symposium on Computer Applications in Medical Care, Washington, D.C., 1982.

Topics in Expert System Design
G. Guida and C. Tasso (Editors)

KNOWLEDGE BASE DESIGN AND CONSTRUCTION: FROM PROTOTYPING TO REFINEMENT

Casimir A. KULIKOWSKI

Department of Computer Science
Rutgers University
New Brunswick, NJ, USA

1. Introduction

As the second generation of expert systems moves towards maturity, the problems of knowledge acquisition and knowledge base construction still present many open methodological questions. From a practical point of view, these processes have been well systematized for expert systems that fall within a clearly defined problem solving paradigm. Many diagnostic, action selection and advice-giving consultation problems can be treated as classification problems [1], and most succesful expert systems fall into this category. There are, however, a few notable exceptions which do not fit the classification paradigm, like the DNA experiment planning system MOLGEN [2], and the computer configuration system R1[3].

Explicit methodologies for knowledge base construction were first outlined in a systematic way at the workshop on expert systems held in

words, it is the careful distinction of different *types of facts, and types of heuristics, used selectively in a particular context* of the problem solving that makes it possible to distinguish expert-level from apprentice-level and general problem solving. For example, in medical diagnosis there are specific distinctions in the confidence attached to the inferences made from symptoms elicited from the patient, the signs observed by the physician, and the test results obtained from more "objective" measurements. Another characteristic of expertise is that much of it has been *compiled* in special forms for efficient use in different contexts - reasoning from first principles is a strategy of last resort for the expert in the midst of the complex and possibly threatening situations where his skills are required. Thus, there are certain compiled "review of (medical) systems" questions always asked by an experienced practitioner so as not to miss any unexpected problems not obviously related to the chief complaint of a patient.

The control strategies used in rule-based systems can be distinguished according to whether they are automatic, allow interactive user control, or are of a mixed initiative type. In any practical expert system that needs human intervention from time to time, the latter is the most advisable. When in automatic mode, reasoning has been traditionally designed to be either *data-driven(or event-driven)*, responding to the results of observed events or data as they are acquired, or *goal-driven*, following a top-down view of rational problem solving as pre-planned by the human expert. In some of the early work on rule based systems, particularly MYCIN [13], this latter mode was emphasized almost exclusively. In contrast, traditional pattern recognition methods were completely data-driven, and our own CASNET [14] system was predominantly responsive to whatever new patterns of observations were presented to the system. It is now recognized that realistic problem solving involves a mixed strategy of goal-driven and event-driven reasoning, depending on the stage and context of problem solving.

The other important components of an expert rule-based system are the knowledge acquisition and explanation subsystems. In addition, a general interface facility is needed to connect the inference engine to the user and other systems from which it might acquire data (such as sensors, instruments, etc), or to which it might pass results (other expert systems or instruments being directly controlled by the expert system. The overall 'generic' architecture of such a system is illustrated in Figure 1.

4. Selected Examples of Rule-based Expert Systems

Before abstracting general principles about the process of knowledge base design and construction, it may be helpful to consider several systems that have been of practical use, so that they can be used subsequently as examples in the more general discussion. The first two were initiated and developed by our expert systems research group at

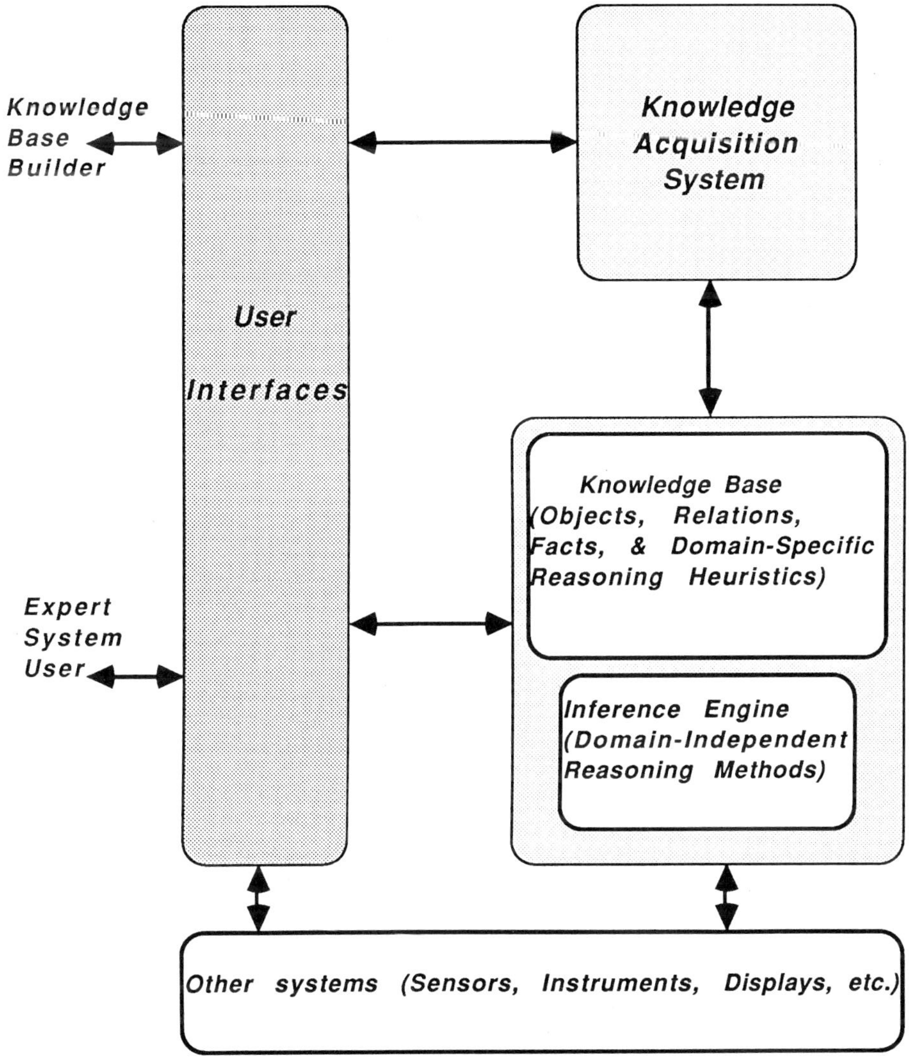

Figure 1: Architecture of a Generic Expert System

Rutgers in collaboration with researchers in industry, so I can share some of the insights that went into their design and construction. The first is the SPE/EXPERT system for serum protein electrophoresis interpretation, which was the first expert system on a chip, integrated into an instrument, and widely disseminated on a commercial basis [8, 15]. The second is the ELAS system for controling the use of an oil-well log interpretation software package. This served as the basis for a significant software redesign by a major oil company: Amoco [6,16]. The third system is R1/XCON [3, 17] a system developed by Digital in collaboration with John McDermott's group at Carnegie-Mellon University. This has become the major "success story" among industrial applications due to Digital's long-term commitment, and the productivity improvements that the system has yielded [18]. The final system considered is ONCOCIN, developed at Stanford [19], which represents a major effort in custom-crafting an expert system to an application with most careful attention paid to the human interfaces and the role of the system within an existing, complex medical work environment.

In what follows I will review these systems, contrasting their problem solving goals, and knowledge-level descriptions, as well as their implementation differences, and the implications for knowledge base construction.

4.1 SPE/EXPERT - A Small Rule-based Signal Interpretation System

The serum protein fractions obtained from scanning an electrophoresis pattern by a densitometer constitutes the most frequently used clinical laboratory test for distinguishing acute from mild and chronic infections. Because of this important screening function and because only the five protein fractions (an example waveform is shown in Figure 2) plus the patient's age are important in determining how to proceeed with subsequent laboratory testing, our collaborator Dr. Robert Galen, suggested that it would make a good example of a small rule-based system which might have commercial application. This was in 1979, when, despite six years of work on knowledge-based systems, none had progressed beyond the prototype stage.

Our own experience with CASNET and that of the other AIM (A.I. in Medicine) groups suggested that the limiting factor was less a matter of knowledge base size as of function. That is, would an expert system find a natural and indispensable niche within an existing health care system? At the 1977 AIM Workshop held at Rutgers, Dr. Raj Reddy from CMU suggested that packaging a knowledge-based system within an instrument might represent just such an opportunity . In the serum protein application we felt that we had found just the right example of such a system. In addition, we had just developed the EXPERT shell for representing rule-based reasoning [20], and wanted a new but circumscribed application that would test its capabilities (it had already succeeded in re-representing the glaucoma knowledge from CASNET, and the thyroid knowledge base which I had previously used in

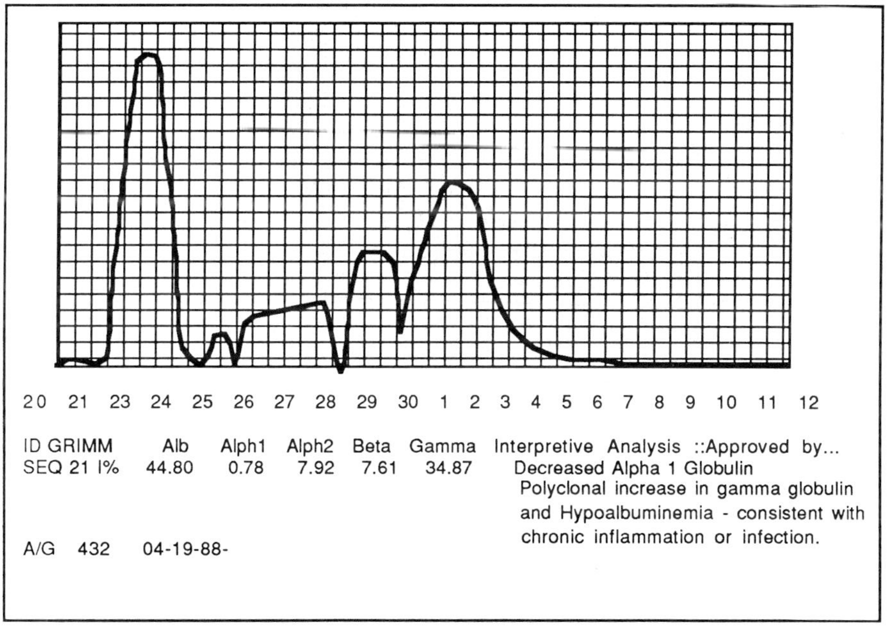

Figure 2: Example of Data Input & Interpretive Output of the SPE/EXPERT System

statistical and pattern recognition systems for consultation [21]).

The first step was to develop a prototype knowledge base, for which Dr. Galen served as the expert. He provided Sholom Weiss and me with the information needed to expand a first simple model of 10 end-points (advice-giving conclusions about the probable status of the patient and the need for further testing) into one that had 25 conclusions and 50 inference rules. After satisfying ourselves that the prototype (written in the EXPERT rule-based formalism), worked correctly on several dozen classical cases, we demonstrated it to the president of Helena Laboratories of Beaumont, Texas, who was the manufacturer of the most widely used scanning densitomenter - the Cliniscan (TM). He was sufficiently impressed with the prototype that he agreed to include the interpretive model in his Cliniscan if the knowledge base could be expanded and tested to cover all necessary patterns of findings and conclusions that could be reached using the instrument's results. As a consequence, Dr. Galen was able to enlist the help of Dr. Ritzman, an emminent specialist who had written the major textbook on the interpretation of serum protein tests, and together they produced a sufficiently large set of solved cases for building and testing a realistic knowledge base.

After working for only six months, Dr. Weiss and I were able to structure the intermediate hypotheses in such a way that only 82 well chosen rules were needed to cover the approximately 100 or so significant patterns of findings that the experts had identified to reach 38 conclusions. A key confirmation of what we had already experienced in some of the earlier medical domains was that only some of the tests needed to be stratified by age (or gender), and that the choice of summarizing intermediate hypotheses was critical in reducing the conceptual complexity and size of the rule set. We were dealing here with a simple classification problem for which all the reasoning could be carried out in a data-driven fashion. In building the knowledge base, we identified three different types of rules: those that established constraints among the data items themselves, those that encoded the patterns of inference of intermediate hypotheses and final conclusions from data patterns (data abstraction process), and those which led to final conclusions from patterns of intermediate hypotheses (classification step).

Figure 3 illustrates the structure of the rule base in a schematic fashion, together with an example of one of the data abstraction rules. Note the mix of direct data interpretation with a pre-abstracted hypothesis (elevated Gamma fraction, the interpretation of which is dependent on age) in the antecedent component of the rule. The definition of such intermediate hypotheses is a useful technique for simplifying rule base construction.

An important technical decision made in conjunction with Helena Labs was that of not including a more sophisticated pattern recognition module within the system. We had originaly proposed to handle unusual patterns of the serum protein waveform by extracting some statisticaly discriminating features, and automatically using them in the reasoning.

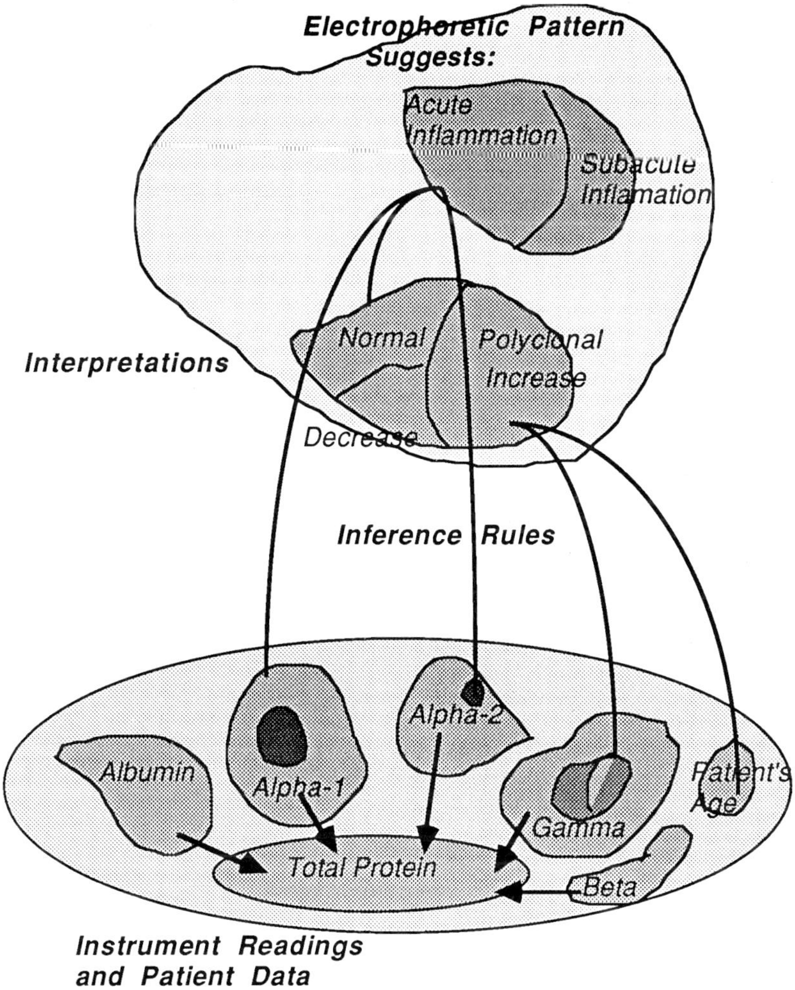

If: The Alpha 1 fraction is greater than 1.3 and the alpha 2 fraction is greater than 2.0, and the Gamma fraction is elevated,
Then: The electrophoretic pattern suggests subacute inflammation

Figure 3: Schematic Rule Base of SPE/EXPERT with typical rule

It was the judgment of our clinical advisors and of the company that such a system would be less likely to be accepted than one where the pathologist selected the unusual pattern manually, and told the system whether it was present or not. This decision further reduced the complexity of the system, and probably helped in its ultimate acceptance.

The development of the second SPE prototype showed us the advantages of rapid prototyping that could be obtained with a rule based representation like EXPERT. It also led us to consider moving to the next, technology-transfer phase, by developing an automatic translation system from the EXPERT model to the microprocessor logic. This was carried out by Sholom Weiss, who was able to restrict the class of EXPERT rules used by the SPE model to three levels of uncertainty, thereby reducing the complexity of the logic, and making it possible to automatically compile the EXPERT rule set into an algorithmic form (in the BASIC language). He then developed a second translator to take the resulting decision algorithm and produce the assembly language code needed for programming the Motorola 6809 processor within the Cliniscan. This double translation process enabled us to produce an instrument-based system ready for field testing in approximately one year from the time the first knowldge base was attempted. The EXPERT model on the DEC2060 at Rutgers allowed us to rapidy experiment with changes in logic suggested by the clinical experts, while the automatic translation permitted quick production of a new compiled model for the microprocessor. The final knowledge base was tested against 256 cases provided by Dr. Ritzman, and worked correctly on all. Our approach represented a dramatic increase in productivity over previous efforts to directly encode the decision logic on a microprocessor, and helped Helena produce the first example of an interpretive instrument system, which continues to be cited as one of the few examples of expert systems widely and commercially disseminated beyond its laboratory of origin [22]. As of 1986, the Cliniscan with the interpretive capabilities is reported to be in use at over 400 hospitals world-wide.

4.2. ELAS (Expert Log Analysis System) - A Medium Size Rule-Based System for On-Line Software Control

Shortly after we had our first sucess with the SPE/EXPERT prototype, we decided that it was time to tackle a more ambitious project, particularly one in which the rule base methodology might need extending or varying. In discussions with the Amoco Production Company Laboratories management at Tulsa, Oklahoma, we found that they had developed a sophisticated programming package, called INLAN [23], for analyzing oil well logs. These logs are the electric, magnetic, sonic, and nuclear signals characterizing the rock formations through which an oil well is drilled. Amoco management also felt that it might be useful to supplement the statistical and graphical analysis methods by an expert system component in order to make these techniques more widely and easily available to their analysts. Besides this goal of disseminating expertise, they wanted to formalize the experience of their best experts in using computer-based analysis systems, including their heuristics for applying different methods in different geological environments, and drilling contexts. Since expert log analysts are widely sought after and in short supply in the oil industry, and often move from company to company, there is a clear advantage in capturing this expertise in a knowledge base.

Weiss and I started by using the EXPERT formalism for encoding well-log interpretation patterns, thus capturing the most salient features that were described to us by the expert analyst, Jay Patchett. However, it soon became clear that to use INLAN and other analysis programs, the expert would also have to provide us with the heuristics of subproblem decomposition, which he had developed in choosing the parts of the computer-based analysis that had to be performed at every stage of the analysis. Then we found that since there were so many different types of signals providing often redundant and sometimes discrepant information about the same oil-well, consistency analysis rules grew into a whole new component of the model.

At this point we were joined by Chidanand Apte, who was carrying out doctoral research in our group. He became the "knowledge engineer" for this problem, and spent many weeks at Tulsa and months at Rutgers developing the needed rule base. After about a year, he had produced a prototype that integrated many of the analysis and display subprograms from INLAN, and communicated with an EXPERT model under the control of specialized code (Figure 4). The system allowed the user to carry out a well-log analysis session, and only be interrupted by advice if he made an incorrect assumption in the choice of method or parameters. It also provided for summarizing interpretations at key stages of a session. We called the system ELAS, and first presented it at the National AI Conference in Pittsburgh in 1982 [6]. Apte subsequently generalized the representational framework for encoding knowledge for this kind of expert system, by creating a frame-based scheme for separating out each of the major methods used in analyzing the oil well-log data. He was able to describe the problem solving of an expert at the *knowledge level* in the form of a cyclic flow-graph relating key states of reasoning. Associated with each of these states was a method and a set of rules encoding how it could be applied and updated. The final interpretation would be obtained when all significant inconsistencies were taken care of, and when the system provided a consistent interpretation of the data and the problem solving flow employed by the user of the software package. In the process of restructuring and generalizing ELAS's knowledge base, Apte had to compile many of the INLAN macros into context-specific sequences of steps used by the domain expert for particular types of oil-well interpretation problems. The context depended on the site of the oil-well, the associated lithology, and the conditions under which the data was obtained (i.e. known or assumed noise from wash-outs in drilling, distortion of signal characteristics due to the type of rock-formation, etc.). To make the state of problem solving obvious to the user at a glance, a spread-sheet format was adopted to summarize the critical parameters of the logs for each of the regions suspected of bearing hydrocarbons (oil and gas). This was quite an innovative step at

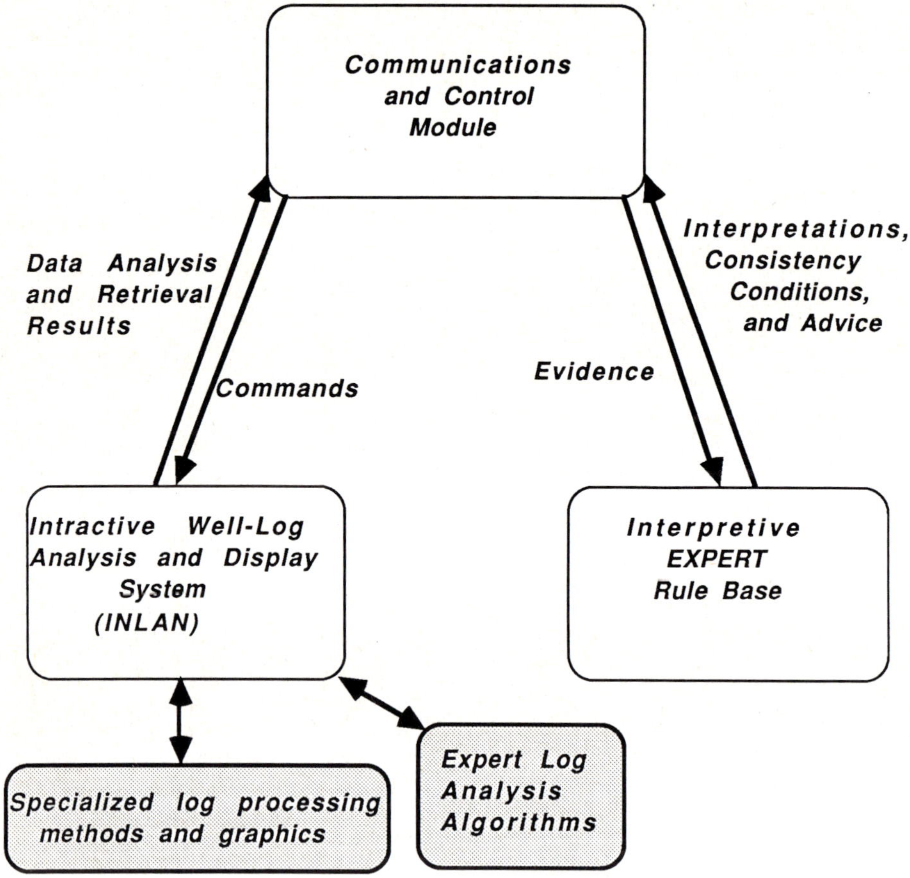

Figure 4 : Overview of the ELAS System

the time, since Visicalc had just introduced the concept. Figure 5 shows an example of such a spread sheet.

In terms of problem solving methods, ELAS combines a first stage of data-abstraction followed by classification in terms of interpretive consistency conditions, and the propagation of these to conclusions about the state of the user's problem solving. These are monitored together with the state of the "background" interpretation provided by the system, and when sufficiently complete results about the presence or absence of hydrocarbons are obtained, a final conclusion is produced for each foot of depth of the well. These results are then integrated over defined zones of interest, and the overall estimate of oil and gas within the zone obtained. There are, in effect, two models: one of the well-log interpretation status, and the other of the user's problem solving status.

As part of his doctoral dissertation, Apte also developed a generalized knowledge-acquisition scheme for helping structure the information about methods through standardized input forms, which represented in a frame the title, assumptions, input-output, controlling, interpretive, consistency, and reporting requirements associated with one of the expert methods of log analysis [24].

To summarize, it took 2 years to produce the first robust prototype of ELAS, and about 4 years to complete the first field-testing of the system. This resulted in a new representation of knowledge for expert systems that control software which can be organized into its domain-specific methods of analysis. As result, a modified frame-based shell was built, enabling graphical entry of knowledge in the frame format, and interfacing with other programs. For Amoco, the system highlighted changes needed in their well-log data base, which was modified accordingly. The expert system was made available on a test basis in two of their geological regions, but the downswing in oil prices in the mid-80s delayed further active development.

4.3. R1/XCON - A Large-Scale Rule Based System for Configuring Computer Systems

The R1/XCON system is probably the best known expert system after MYCIN. It showed that the OPS rule-based language [25] could be used to build a large scale rule base with specialized reasoning facilities taking advantage of the basic recognize-act rule evaluation cyle of OPS. The application differed somewhat from the previous type of consultative system, since it was aimed at producing a configuration layout for a VAX system specified by the customer. XCON was expected to evaluate the ordered parts for consistency, suggest additions and deletions, and produce a layout diagram. After many years of evolutionary development, estimated to have taken 50 man-years of effort [26], the system was able to handle incrementally most of the changes required as new generations of VAXes were added. For efficiency, the OPS version was re-implemented in BLISS, and was recently reported to contain over 3,500 rules.

HIGHLAND PARK WELL NO.77			
SURFACE TEMP	55.	TEMP. GRADIENT	0.017
RMF	2.000	RMFT	60.
RM	2.000	RMT	60.
		BITSIZE	8.50

ZONE	1	2	3	4	5
BACKGROUND					
TOP	1040.	1925.	2574.	3520.	4132.
BOTTOM	1280.	2467.	3347.	4010.	4628.
LITHOLOGY	CLEAN SAND	CLEAN SAND	CLEAN SAND	CLEAN SAND	CLEAN SAND
FLUIDS	GAS WATER	GAS WATER	GAS WATER	GAS WATER	GAS WATER
DISCRIMINATORS					
BAD HOLE					
MAX. POROSITY	45.	45.	45.	45.	45.
LITHOLOGIC					
SP GREATER THAN	-9.	-4.	-9.		-12.
GR GREATER THAN		& 45.			
POROSITY					
METHOD/INTERPRET.	HOUSTON	DP	VALESKE	NP-DP XPLT	DP
RHOG		VARIABLE	VARIABLE		2.75
RHOF		1.0	1.0		1.0
RHOGAS			0.25		
ZONE			0.29		
RW INITIAL					
RW QUALITY	UNKNOWN	UNKNOWN	UNKNOWN	FAIR	UNKNOWN
RWT	100.	100.	100.	100.	100.
RWUSED	5.000		1.8134	0.1415	0.3100
RW METHOD	1/SW HSTGM	INITIAL	1/SW HSTGM	PICKETT	INITIAL
SW EQUATION	ARCHIE'S	ARCHIE'S	ARCHIE'S	ARCHIE'S	ARCHIE'S
N INITIAL	2.0	2.0	2.0	2.0	2.0
M	1.60	1.40	1.35	1.40	1.75

Figure 5: Master Panel of ELAS
(Spread-Sheet Summary of Problem Solving Status)

From a problem solving perspective, XCON carries out a rule-based constraint satisfaction process, checking whether the specified order conforms to an acceptable type of order. This could be viewed as a diagnostic classification subtask, with the excess and missing components being the "faults" of the requested system, and the resulting suggestions for deletions and additions being the remedial or "therapeutic" actions. Producing an acceptable layout is a somewhat different task. While it does involve some classification in terms of what represents acceptable or even optimal layouts, the process of putting together the layout chart involves a synthetic and constructive element of reasoning which goes beyond the determination of layout pattern.

The current version of XCON is reported to automatically configure about 97% of the VAX orders processed by Digital, and has increased the productivity of its technical editors considerably. An additional advantage cited is that the system produces a more consistent style of configuration than do human editors.

4.4. ONCOCIN - Rule-based Treatment Planning

Integrating an expert system into the routine provision of health care is not easy, and an alternative to the instrument-based approach we took with SPE/EXPERT has been taken by Shortliffe and his group at Stanford's SUMEX-AIM Resource. The goal was to encode the protocols for cancer treatment and produce a system for reviewing administered medications, checking for consistency with the protocol and suggesting improvements. In order to make the system fit "seamlessly" into the existing clinical environment, data entry reproduced on the screen the the same paper forms' that were being filled out by the physicians in following their patients progress. These consisted of spread-sheets that summarized patient status and treatment, and graphics displays to indicate the sites of tumors and their changes over time. The system applied a MYCIN-like rule base to suggest a treatment plan integrated uniformly with the prior data on the patient [27]. From a problem solving perspective ONCOCIN carries out a lot of consistency checking of proposed treatment steps against those allowed in the plan protocol. It does some classification of expected outcomes, and matching against possible alternatives from the protocol.

The system has now been installed on the wards of the Stanford Medical Center, and is used routinely. It took 4 to 5 years of development beyond the initial prototype to obtain a high level of performance, and combine the system with optimized advice on the treatment planning tasks. Several graphical summarization and knowledge acquisition techniques have been made available so that the ONCOCIN knowledge base can be updated through a system called OPAL [28], while experiments in planning alternative therapies are carried out with the ONYX system [29].

5. Knowledge Acquisition and the Construction of Rule-based Systems

From the very beginning of work with knowledge-based systems, it was recognized that extracting the knowledge from an expert was difficult and usually produced the greatest delays in building a knowledge base. The TEIRESIAS system [30] developed as early as 1975 by Davis, tried to make it easier to test and modify the MYCIN knowledge base through the use of meta-heuristics that suggested changes in a rule or group of rules whenever the system performed poorly on a case.

As the first generation of knowledge based systems was developed, knowledge acquistion became known as the major bottleneck in the construction process. Many expert systems shells were built with a panoply of knowledge acquisition tools, including the use of induction modules in order to overcome this bottleneck [31]. It was soon found out that capturing static pieces of knowledge (including the apparently dynamic problem solving heuristics) did not present a problem in any of the representational frameworks - whether rule-based, frame-based, logic-based or otherwise. The difficulty always lay in capturing how the knowledge was used in complex problem solving situations - where the context was not well defined, and where the invocation and articulation of rules, or frames was not easily or uniquely specified by the human expert. These real dynamics of problem solving still present an obstacle to knowledge-base construction today, particularly for medium-to-large size systems where there are a wide variety of reasoning modalities employed, and where knowledge is at times redundant, incomplete, and uncertain.

However, for small-to-medium size systems with relatively simple representational structures (like rule bases), and simple knowledge level descriptions (data abstraction, classification and plan selection), the well-established techniques of knowledge base construction will enable the builder to overcome the knowledge acquisition bottleneck. In what follows we trace the various steps by which a knowledge base is designed and constructed, concentrating on the factors that makes the process as easy and repeatable as possible. At the conclusion of this paper I concentrate on issues of testing and validation of rule-based systems for which our own empirical learning approach embodied in the SEEK family of systems have proven to be most valuable.

6. Phases of Knowledge Base Design and Construction

As discussed at the beginning of the present paper, the major stages of knowledge base design and construction include: problem identification, conceptualization, formalization, implementation, and testing. These can be further elaborated by recognizing that formalization may result in several different options in terms of possible choices of knowledge representation, thereby constituting a distinctive step that has to be completed before a specific implementation is embarked upon. Likewise, the testing step combines the substeps of a first, in-house critique and evaluation under friendly circumstances, followed by knowledge base refinement, and possibly reformulation (if the original representation is found to be inadequate), after which full scale field testing is reasonable. Further refinements and even reformulations of the knowledge base may follow these, as hard reality and unsympathetic judges decide whether the system lives up to its expectations. Each of these steps will now be considered in greater detail, together with its expected outcomes. The entire process is illustrated in Figure 6.

6.1. Problem Identification Phase

Whether a problem qualifies for solution by expert systems techniques depends on many factors, not least of which are those having to do with what is expected from an automated or semi-automated expert system. Is it supposed to replace an existing human specialist under present circumstances of operation? Is it meant to augment and help an existing expert by automating some of his routine duties? Is it designed to apply an expert's knowledge in situations which he cannot currently reach? The goal for a proposed expert system may be well defined, or it may only be incompletely and uncertainly defined, and it may be defined differently by the different people who identified the opportunity for using expert system methodologies.

The participants in the identification stage usually come from one or more of the following groups:

. management, at several possible levels,

. domain experts, or the technical staff currently carrying out the specialized problem solving,

. knowledge engineers, or the technical staff in computer science, mathematics or engineering disciplines who currently help the domain experts in formalizing and automating their methods,

. knowledge brokers, who are usually middle management personnel, possibly having been themselves domain experts at an earlier stage of their career, and who now see the opportunities of improving the productivity of the domain specialists or introducing new, automated techniques.

Depending on who initiates an expert systems project it will have different chances of success, but regardless of this, it is the combination of enthusiasm by sufficiently highly placed management that will ensure rapid funding of the project. The enthusiastic

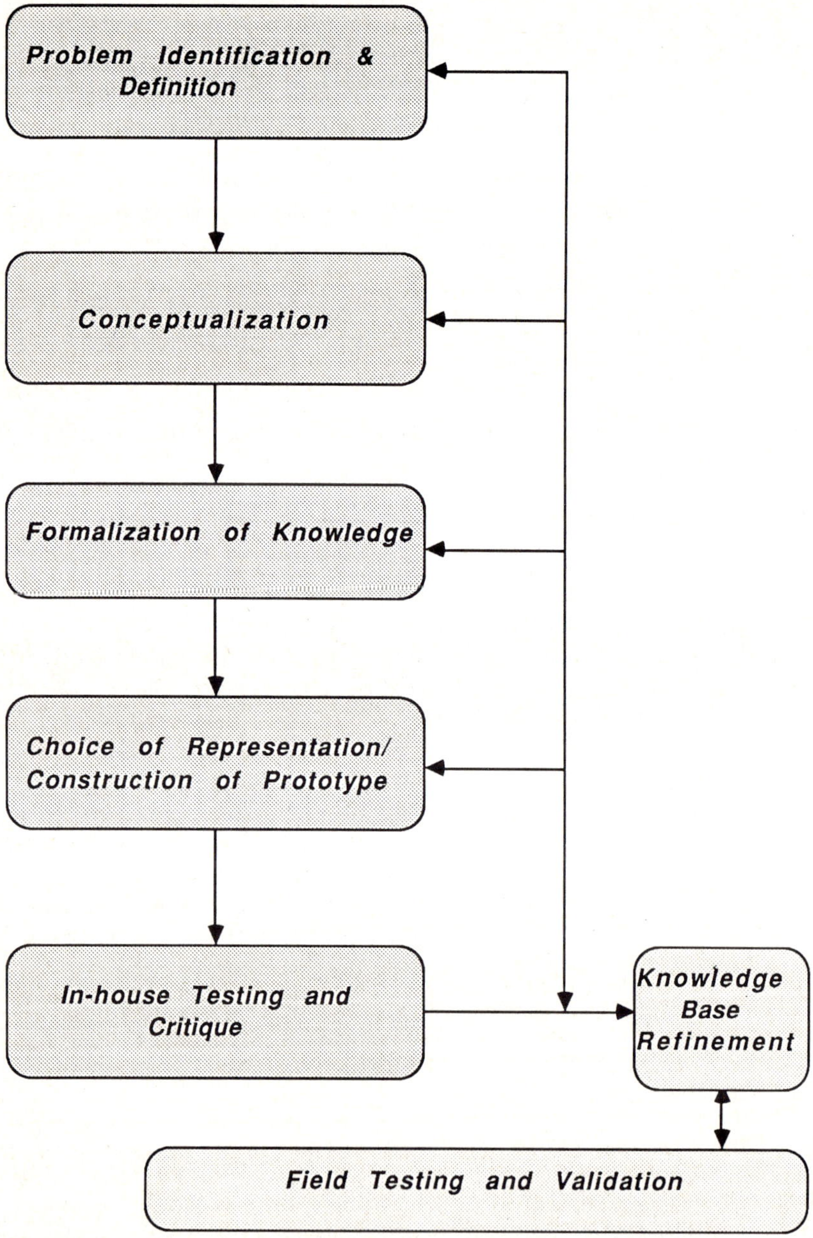

Figure 6: Phases of Knowledge Base Construction

involvement of at least one (and preferably more) domain experts is important if the first prototype is to be successful. Likewise, the services of a good knowledge engineer (assuming he is distinct from the domain expert) is also needed. Finally, if the project is to be sheperded through the hurdles of in-house and field tests, a knowledge broker in a middle management position who is sympathetic to the project will help enormously.

The *knowledge sources* that are typically available for building an expert knowledge base are:

. human expertise, for which the existence and availability of a recognized and respected expert is indispensable,

. textbooks or manuals of operation detailing any problem solving knowledge that has been already formalized,

. examples of solved problem cases, preferably already encoded and stored in a data base on a computer.

While much attention has been given to the first two sources, little is usually said about the third, which is critical if the expert system is to be validated, tested, and its knowledge base refined in a systematic fashion. Most institutions cannot boast of a history of methodical record keeping on the details of problem solving, so it is highly unlikely that the hoped for data base will actually exist. Even in situations like medical diagnosis, where patient records are routinely kept, the chances of them being computerized, and containing accurate and uniformly gathered data are very small. Thus, it is often the task of the knowledge engineer and domain expert to develop a data base system and gather cases of solved problems as they are constructing the knowledge base. This has the advantage of making it possible to adapt the recorded description of the problem to the needs of the explicitly documented problem solving, but it has the disadvantage that considerable extra effort is involved. The best approach is then to commission the gathering of solved cases to an "auxiliary expert", preferably someone who is enthusiastic about standarization of observations, and is likely to produce a good, independent set of cases on which to test the system.

Having identified the nature of the problem and the sources of knowledge, the expert and knowledge engineer must work together to produce a first informal problem description. This should consist of specifications of the goals, motives, and rationales of the problem solving; how the anticipated formalization and automation of reasoning will affect current human-mediated systems, together with a listing of all relevant knowledge sources and the identification of those component reasoning tasks which are essential and those which are not essential for the succesful completion of the problem. These can be considered as the minimum requirements for any knowledge base to be built, and serve as input to the next step of conceptualizing the problem solving process used by the domain experts. It is certainly a good idea to have them reviewed and accepted by upper management before proceeding with much work at the next stage.

6.2. Problem Conceptualization Phase

Even after the problem's main characteristics have been identified, more detail is needed, in terms of how the expert actually solves typical examples and abstracts from them the general rules that he claims to be applicable in different contexts.

The first and most important outcome of this phase is to obtain a decomposition of the overall problem into subproblems. These in turn should be likewise succesively decomposed, until the knowledge engineer has produced a top-down hierarchical view of the problem solving process, down to its most basic or primitive reasoning and operational parts. A different, but related job is to obtain from the expert an outline of the information flow used in solving the problem. In other words, the expert must be able to specify when and how each knowledge source is being used to solve the problem.

With the problem hierarchically decomposed, and the elements in the information flow identified, the knowledge engineer can then proceed to characterize each major reasoning task, together with the main concepts by which it is defined. Distinctions between evidence, hypotheses, and actions to be taken at each step must be carefully specified. Finally it is desirable at this step to assess the expected difficulty of problem solving for the major subproblem components, and to produce a cost/benefit analysis of alternative ways in which an automated system could help assist or replace the human expert. All the above still represent an informal, though detailed conceptual map of what the expert system is expected to do. It is essential if the next step of formalization is to proceed smoothly.

6.3. Knowledge Formalization Phase

At this point the knowledge engineer is ready to consider alternative formal reasoning schemes that can be used to model the individual problem solving components identified and conceptualized at the earlier stages.

Various prototypical problem solving processes have been identified, such as classification, data abstraction, temporal aggregation, and causal attribution. While there is no uniform agreement on the "generic" nature of these, it is worthwhile to match the expert's problem solving steps against them, so as to obtain a better idea of the complexity of the overall problem solving process, and a partial specification of what the first working prototype is supposed to do. It is also at this stage that the knowledge engineer should insist that the expert produce a few good solved examples for testing the prototype.

6.4. Knowledge Representation Phase

Once the formalization phase has yielded the knowledge level description of the problem solving process, the builder of a knowledge basc has to choose a representation that will lead to the first implementation prototype of the system.

The questions that immediately arise are the folowing:

. *Do the types of problem solving involved make one particular representation a natural choice over all others?* For instance, if we are dealing with a signal interpretation problem where data has to be monitored and interpreted continuously so that there is no delay in the detection and identification of a hazardous signal, it is natural that the knowledge base be designed with an event-driven recognizer, which can be easily implemented with a rule base using a forward chaining strategy.

. *Is the expressive power of the chosen representation a more important consideration than simplicity in knowledge acquisition?* In the example given above, if signal detection and recognition is to be carried out as by a stand-alone system, and human operators are to take whatever subsequent action is deemed necessary, a simple rule-based system may be a quite adequate representational framework to handle the straightforward classification problem involved. Knowledge acquisition for such a representation could take advantage of the rule refinement methods discussed later in this paper quite simply and effectively. On the other hand, if the signal recognition is but the first stage of a complex automatic system or subsequent reaction to and control of the hazardous state (as in a large industrial power plant, a medical intensive care unit, etc.), then it will probably be necessary to consider more complex representations, like a blackboard system, to control the problem solving and reasoning with different sources of knowledge.

. *Is the problem size and efficiency of processing a major concern?* Here again, much depends on whether the problem can be broken down so that subproblems can be handled efficiently, often with a compiled submodel of reasoning, or whether complex interactions have to be anticipated, and the entire "state-of-the-world" (of problem solving) has to be always recomputed after each reasoning step (or major cycle of steps).

. *Is a good development environment essential to hire or retain the knowledge engineers or experts working on the system?* This may sound like a strange question, but as long as both experts and knowledge engineers are in short supply and strong demand, companies are likely to find that they will move to greener pastures unless they are provided with the best state-of-the-art in programming environments, workstations, or other technological tools that they need (or feel they need) to be competitive. As some types of expert system building becomes more routine (for classification problems, for instance), this situation is likely to change, but on the frontiers of real expert system design, the problem is likely to remain with us for the forseeable future.

. *Are resources available to build a new system in-house, or is the purchase of a commercially available shell desirable?* As prices of expert system shells come down, and their availability on PCs increases, it becomes easier for companies to buy (after often first testing on a trial basis) many alternative representational frameworks and products. However, it may often turn out, that after experimenting with several of them, a specific project will be best implemented in-house with a specialized representation that involves a selection of the components that are most appropriate to the knowledge level description of the problem being handled.

6.4.1. Selection of Implementation Tools

There are many different factors that affect the choice of a particular implementation tool. These involve primarily the issues of knowledge level description of the problem to be solved, as described above, but also independent questions about the hardware on which the expert system must run, the possible cost/benefits of various hardware and software combinations, and the availability of personnel to develop and run the prospective system. Major issues that seem to arise repeatedly are:

. *Should the choice of representational framework be dictated by the need for a flexible development environment, or an efficient final system?* Clearly the answer depends in part on what business the developers are in. If they are going to be routinely developing expert systems, it will be wise to consider development flexibility, cost, and effectiveness as paramount, but if it is a one-time, or occasional enterprise, then clearly final system considerations will be as important or or even more important than the development issues.

. *Importance of knowledge acquisition facilities and user interfaces* - the first is most directly of concern to a group that expects to build many expert systems, the second to anyone who expects to turn out a workable, easy to use, and understandable system.

. *Long term maintenance and support factors.* This is again crucial if a final product is to be delivered. Users of shells will be concerned with the reliability and long term support of their software environments - which in today's rapidly changing market can be rarely assured. In-house developers need to get management's support for enough personnel to maintain and update the system. This can represent an investment ranging from one or two specialists, to a whole new group in the company! As usual, success breeds success, and often a company will be willing to invest in a large enterprise with high visibility (like in the R1/XCON case).

6.5. Prototype Implementation Phase

After the tool has been selected, it is important to begin building a prototype. The groundwork has already been laid during the previous phases of problem identification, conceptualization, and formalization, which should have produced quite a few pages worth of material on the expert reasoning needed to solve the problem. However, when faced with actually building a system that must work, the designer needs to establish his own approach to the construction of the prototype:

.First, he must choose the scope of subproblems to be covered by the prototype: Are they to be typical, extreme, or marginal problems, or a sampling from all of these types? How are they to be selected - by difficult, by rarity of occurence, or in some kind of representative manner? Are cases of solved problems for testing already available, and if not is it feasible to obtain them quickly? The best practical advice is that a prototype is just that - it should concentrate on one or two exemplary subproblems, and not try to cover so many as to be a full-fledged system. The choice of prototype subproblems is important: they must be representative, but also sufficiently intricate that the results of prototype testing will not be dismissed as an exercise in trivia.

. Once the subproblems have been formalized and represented within the chosen framework, changes in the formalization will innevitably appear. Experts will typically produce a first set of rules that is overgeneral, and need to be specialized. In some cases they may require some specific procedural attachments, and the original formalization may no longer be quite as applicable as it first seemed.

. The actual domain knowledge provided by the expert in the first conceptualization and formalization phases will almost invariably be incomplete, and often surprisingly incorrect - after all, it is only a first try. Considerable depth of detail is typically needed beyond what the expert originally provided to build a working prototype.

. The acid test comes when the prototype is tested with the first solved test cases - now the initial reasoning will have to be modified and any domain knowledge or even general inference heuristics modified to get the system to work. Really serious questions about the adequacy of the chosen representation typically show up at this stage. However, the knowledge engineer must be on the alert for red herrings produced by the experts or their associates. These are often test cases that appear to fit the subproblems modeled, but are in fact representative of some other special kind of problem, often an interaction with some particularly difficult and almost completely unrelated subproblem that could trick all but the very advanced expert, but is not at all representative of what the prototype was designed to capture. Since initial prototypes should shy away from all but the most indispensable interactions among subsystems, such a case, while representing an important landmark for future development of the knowledge base, should be set aside in the early stages. The determination of what is an important and what an "accidental" system interaction can, however, be quite subtle, and it is easy f or the novice knowledge engineer to be misdirected, paticularly by a pet case of a very persuasive expert. This same advice applies even more strongly to the expert himself: beware of personal experiences that won't have wider appeal. Choosing test cases so that they will help prove the worth of the prototype to others is the key consideration - "selling" the prototype to the expert should not be a primary consideration by this stage, unless they have opposed the system all along.

6.6. In-House Critique Phase

The first efforts at evaluation should always be carried out within a friendly and supportive environment, which should, nevertheless, be critical enough to identify and help correct flaws in the system in a constructive manner. The scope of the prototype and the adequacy of the test samples should be reviewed by an independent expert, and expanded or changed as needed. The logical and expressive adequacy of input and output should be reviewed by some representative future users of the system, or people that can simulate their expectations and behavior (this latter alternative is, of course, not without dangers). The adequacy of the explanatory facilities and the justification of the reasoning should be assessed. While much work should not be devoted to the explanation component at this time, any warning signs of future limitations should be noted. If prototype interfaces are poor and are likely to result in disappointing performance when the system is presented to management or others who will decide on the future of the project, it is usually advisable to put some effort into interface design at this stage. However, the temptation to cover up inadequacies of the prototype's reasoning with excessive "bells and whistles" should be resisted, lest managers get the wrong impression about what constitutes substance, and what is surface polish.

This phase is particularly critical in determining whether the original goals of the project are likely to be met. In expert systems design it is not infrequent to change the objectives of the project as the reality of what can really be built versus what people vaguely imagined could be built sinks in. Experts and knowledge engineers who may see that original expectations were excessive or misdirected (possibly expecting too much from a fully automated system, where a judicious blend of human interaction with partially automated reasoning might be more effective and much more productive) should not hesitate to tell their superiors about the feedback from the prototype construction. Just demonstrating what was originally proposed, and failing to make clear its broader implications on the choice of problem and solution methods would be a great disservice. However, when the prototype does indeed vindicate the original problem identification and formulation, the prototype will serve as the first stage in the design and construction of the larger system. This leads to the next step of expanded prototype development and knowledge base refinement.

6.7. Knowledge Base Refinement and Prototype Expansion Phase

Deciding how to expand, test, and refine the original prototype often requires a different frame of mind and organizational set-up. In most cases it is no longer feasible to rely strictly on a single expert to cover a truly representative and broad scope of problems. This involves a difficult job - having to select a group of experts who will work well together and with the knowledge engineer(s). While they may differ on the knowledge base details for specific subdomains, they must agree to work together towards a consensus in constructing the entire system. This is most important if the ultimate system is to work, since having many pieces that do not interact because the experts fail to agree on how they should reason together will lead quite predictably to a poor outcome, regardless of how sucessful the prototype was.

In any case, it is also a good idea to introduce the mechanism of external, independent reviewers, who will be brought in after the first comprehensive prototype is completed. This should make the contributing experts aware that, not only must they display their "virtuoso" best in building their individual subcomponents of the knowledge base, but must also address issues of overlap and interaction with the other experts' subcomponents. Since evaluation with test cases will continue at this stage it is also important to secure a commitment from each expert to supply these, or to have some associate do it for them. If this is not done from the beginning, there is a high probability that testing will be done in a patchwork manner, leading to a system that is well tested in some subareas, and barely at all in others. When the independent reviewers carry out their evaluation, the results will be predictably uneven, and the system may fail to pass to the next stage.

The potential for speeding up the process of knowledge base construction by *automatic refinement* becomes a reality as soon as enough representative test cases have been gathered and captured in a data base. Unfortunately, most expert knowledge base frameworks do not lend themselves easily to large scale automated refinement because of the complexity and flexibility of the structures they allow. This flexibility makes it possible to mix many different types of problems at the knowledge level, with a resulting nonhomogeneity that blocks the application of consistent and powerful knowledge refinement heuristics. However, in those cases where a more uniform representation is used, and where the problem types are restricted, to classification problems it is indeed possible to combine heuristic and statistical methods to automatically refine and improve the performance of the prototype. Our group at Rutgers has pioneered the empirical approach to knowledge base refinement, starting with the SEEK system [9], and progressing through a number of more structured and general schemes for refinement, like SEEK-2 [10].

6.7.1. Automatic Empirical Refinement, and the SEEK Family of Systems

In the late 1970s, after we had completed the CASNET prototype and produced the EXPERT shell, we saw that it was necessary to develop a methodology to systematically validate, evaluate and refine a knowledge base. At first we produced a number of ancilliary testing and evaluation modules which were attached to EXPERT, and tried them out with early versions of the AI/Rheum [5] knowledge base. It soon became clear that a more comprehensive knowledge acquisition and testing scheme would be desirable. Peter Politakis was the knowledge engineer on the rheumatology project in collaboration with the University of Missouri, and he expanded the original modules to take advantage of the kind of decision structure that was used by the specialists on this project. A breakthrough came when he recognized that the distinction between major and minor criteria within diagnostic classification tables (developed by the American Rheumatological Association, and elaborated in greater detail by the Missouri research team of Dr. Gordon Sharp and his associates for the connective tissue diseases), could serve to rank rule modification experiments. Whereas before it was difficult to see how machine learning methods could be applied to the very noisy medical data, it now seemed that at least some heuristics could be developed to generalize and specialize rules to correct for their mistakes over a data base of solved cases. This led to the main idea behind the SEEK (System for the Empirical Experimentation with expert Knowledge) system [9], in which Politakis and Weiss proposed to analyze the performance of rules and sets of related rules on a statistical basis, rather than carrying out the single-case analysis that had been characteristic of refinement in TEIRESIAS [30] and other systems until then.

The major assumption in SEEK is that a knowledge base provided by the expert should be considered as a first approximation, which is a candidate for successive refinement as it is progressively challenged with more and more independently obtained test cases. Weiss and Politakis developed the first set of heuristics based on the classification criteria of AI/RHEUM, and produced an interactive system that proposed a variety of *knowledge base modification experiments* to the designer. These were ranked according to expected improvement yield over the data base of test cases, and the expert could then decide between experiments that promised to yield excellent results but might be construed to be of a "curve fitting" variety, versus those which might not give quite as good results for the existing cases but were more attuned to the underlying semantics of the domain knowledge. Thus, SEEK served as a system for evaluating performance and intelligently suggesting refinements of the knowledge base. It was most successful in helping build and refine the AI/RHEUM knowledge base, and also served an independent research group at the University of Missouri in building a dermatology knowledge base [32]. For its innovative contributions SEEK was awarded a prize at the first International AI in Medicine Workshop at Pavia in 1985 [33].

After completing the work with AI/Rheum it was natural to try to find out whether the ideas of combining performance-based heuristics with knowledge base refinement could be generalized to a broader class of rule-based systems, like the classification models in EXPERT. Another possibility was to automate the choice of experiments so as to make best use of the computer in searching over the large space of possible rule modifications and select the best automatically.

This work was carried out by Ginsburg and Weiss, and resulted in the SEEK-2 system, which successfully replicated the interactive SEEK results but also produced a number of additional and alternative rules which got better performance out of the original rheumatology cases [34].

While the system does take quite a long time in searching the space of possible rule modifications, using some generalized pruning heuristics, this is quite reasonable given the accelerating trend of substantial annual increases in computer memory size and speed. The heuristics chosen by Ginsburg were initially a generalization of the ones in SEEK. While these gave good results, it soon became clear that performance measures might be specified in different ways by different users, and that domain knowledge might also provide additional useful constraints on modifications of the rule base because of underlying causal, hierarchical, or temporal relations. For these reasons our group has taken the approach of designing metalanguage facilities to represent such constraints. Ginsburg produced a prototype for expressing the SEEK-2 heuristics [10].

Research is currently proceeding on a very important related issue: how to get the most out of a finite data base of test cases. The statistical approach to this problem involves resampling methods such as jacknifing and bootstrapping [35]. In rule-bases, however, we are dealing with highly modular knowledge bases, where it is difficult to predict rule interactions, and as result the decision model is considerably more complex than anything attempted statistically. Nevertheless, it is possible to apply heuristic methods that rely on resampling techniques to get more reliable estimates of performance than those that might be obtained with the usual methods of dividing a sample into design and testing subsamples. It is this approach that our group at Rutgers has taken in trying to produce realistic methods for evaluating expert system performance [36].

7. Expert System Evaluation and Knowledge Base Validation

While the first and most necessary component of an expert system evaluation must be a measure of the system's performance, this represents only a small part of the overall evaluation. The degree to which the system has fulfilled the goals and objectives set for it in terms of practical application, integration within (or replacement of) existing systems, and its economic, social, and individual payoffs (and trade-offs) will constitute the general parameters of an evaluation. Because the future of the system will often depend on the outcome of the evaluation, it is important to not only carefully define *what* is being evaluated, but also *by whom*, and *when* [37].

Expert systems are different from most other types of systems in that they are based primarily on human reasoning, for which there are few, if any well-agreed upon standards of definition, measurement, or comparison. It is common to compare the system's conclusions with those reached by human experts who are presented with comparable data. This is a reasonable approach as long as some care is taken in selecting the experts, and measuring their degree of agreement on the conclusions. Only in this way will it be possible to tell whether their degree of agreement with the expert system's conclusions is reasonable or not. To be confident in the representativeness and impartiality of the results it is best to include experts from outside the laboratory that produced the system that is being tested. In addition, it is always best to design a blind test of the system where the assessors will be unable to outwardly distiguish between the computer and human generated conclusions, and therefore avoid any bias due to this distinction.

A major problem in designing an evaluation arises when it is found that the experts differ on their standards for *validation* of the knowledge base. That is, they may start out by superficially appearing to agree on the definition of decision outcomes, criteria of evidence, and even methods of analysis, but, when confronted with the system's performance on specific cases, discover that they actually differ in subtle (and sometimes unsubtle) ways on definitions, criteria, and the relative importance and context of application of analytical methods. When experts come from different schools of thought or training backgrounds, it is particularly important to separate out the parts of the knowledge base that constitute shared factual knowledge, and those that involve the experiential and judgmental components of reasoning, which are bound to show greater inter-expert variability.

Validating expert knowledge is particularly difficult for problems involving decision making under high risk circumstances and with large degrees of uncertainty in the data. Although decision analytical methods can be applied to small subproblems with well-defined statistics, there is an increasing awareness of the subjective nature of decision costs or utilities [38], and of the frequent deviation of individual human behavior from the traditional assumptions of rational, risk-averting behavior that underlies the formal expected utility models [39]. This raises important issues for validating decision rules in knowledge bases, since ultimately someone has to take responsibility for any prescriptive advice given by the expert system. The ethical dimension of expert systems applications has barely begun to be discussed except in the most general of terms.

In deciding on how to validate the knowledge base it is essential to decide on the role of test cases and how they are to be selected. While they must they come from different, independent sources to assure a representative sampling of all expected problem types, they must neverthless have had their data gathered and recorded according to a common protocol, so as to ensure comparability of results. The consistency and criteria of verifiability for underlying models that use causal, hierarchical, or mathematical relations presents interesting open research problems related to ongoing A.I. research in qualitative reasoning and simulation [40,41]. Unlike case data, a relation or submodel is a synthetic construct which must be supported scientifically by experimental results and a coherent fit within existing theory. Research in theory formation is still in its infancy, despite considerable progress in retrospective analysis of reasoning for major scientific discoveries [42]. The next step, of validating how experts apply theoretical knowledge in practical problem solving instances in a prescriptive manner is also a completely open research problem.

Because expert systems are typically experimental (no previous comparable mode of automation is likely to have been tried), it is important to determine the phase of development during which the system is to be evaluated. Most reported evaluations of expert systems have been at the end of the prototype phase, or after several cycles of prototyping [43,44,45,46]. This means that the most useful outcome is a set of recommendations on improvements of the knowledge base, or on how the system's goals might be modified to ensure greater acceptance or more realistic outcomes [47].

8. Conclusions

In this paper I have tried to provide a mixture of information about "established practices" in knowledge base design and construction, while also pointing to open areas of research, particularly related to expert system evaluation and knowledge base validation. Insofar as the ultimate success of an expert system depends on acceptable proof that it is helping solve a problem more efficiently and effectively than available, though possibly non-expert human counterparts, simple measurement of economic gain may suffice to demonstrate the advantages of the technological solution. However, because of the social repercussions of automation, and the ethical concerns about the correct application of codified human judgments, it is essential that the technical advances of the present generation of expert systems not obscure the great need for new insights into knowledge representation, reasoning, and the underlying semantics of knowledge bases.

It is particularly important that a more systematic understanding of problem solving tasks be developed in relation to both surface models of compiled expertise and underlying models of scientific reasoning. Only in this way will new, knowledge-based paradigms for reasoning under risk and uncertainty be developed. While the availability of new technology in the form of parallel and distributed systems with powerful graphics interfaces promises to open the horizons for practical expert systems even further, the basic issues of formalizing experiential knowledge, and applying it prescriptively in the correct context requires a combination of pattern recognition and knowledge-based approaches which will keep researchers busy for many years to come.

References

[1] Weiss, S.M. and Kulikowski, C.A., *A Practical Guide to Designing Expert Systems*, Rowman & Allanheld, Totowa, NJ, 1984.

[2] Stefik, M. An Examination of a frame-structured representation system, *Proc 6th Int Joint Conf on Artif Intell*, pp.923-925, 1979.

[3] McDermott, J., R1: A rule-based configurer of computer systems, *Artif Intell Journal*, v. 19, pp. 39-88, 1982.

[4] Buchanan, B.G., Barstow, D., Bechtal, R., Bennet, J., Clancey, W., Kulikowski, C., Mitchell, T., and Waterman, D.A., Constructing an expert system, in *Building Expert Systems* (Hayes-Roth, F., Waterman, D.A., and Lenat, D.B., eds.), pp. 127-167, Addison-Wesley, Reading, MA, 1983.

[5] Lindberg, D.A.B., Sharp, G.C., Kay, D.R., et al. The expert consultant as teacher, *Moebius*, v. 3, pp. 30-36, 1983.

[6] Weiss, S.M.,Kulikowski, C.A., Apte, C., Uschold, M., Patchett, J., Brigham, R., and Spitzer, B., Building expert systems for controlling complex programs, *Proc AAAI-82*, pp. 322-326, 1982.

[7] Kastner, J.K., Dawson, C.R., Weiss, S.M., Kern, K.B., and Kulikowski, C.A., An expert consultation system for frontline health workers in primary care, *Journal of Medical Systems*, v. 8, pp. 389-397, 1984.

[8] Weiss, S.M., Kulikowski, C.A., and Galen, R.S., Developing a microprocessor based expert model for instrument interpretation, *Proc 7th Int Joint Conf on Artif Intell*, pp. 853-855, 1981.

[9] Politakis, P., and Weiss, S.M., Using empirical analysis to refine expert system knowledge bases, *Artif Intell Journal*, v. 22, pp. 23-48, 1984.

[10] Ginsberg, A., A metalinguistic approach to the construction of knowledge based refinement systems, *Proc AAAI-86*, pp. 436-441, 1986.

[11] Feigenbaum, E.A., The art of artificial intelligence: Themes and case studies of knowledge engineering, in *Proc Nat Computer Conf*, New York, AFIPS, 1978, pp. 221-230.

[12] Chandrasekaran, B., Generic tasks in knowledge-based reasoning: High-level building blocks for expert system design, *IEEE Expert*, pp.23-30, Fall 1986.

[13] Shortliffe, E.H., *Computer-based consultations:MYCIN*, Elsevier,New York,NY, 1976.

[14] Weiss, S.M., Kulikowski, C.A., and Safir, A., Glaucoma consultation

by computer, *Computers in Biology and Medicine*, v.8, pp. 1-25, 1978.
[15] Weiss, S.M., Kulikowski, C.A., and Galen, R.G., Representing expertise in a computer program: The serum protein diagnostic program, *Journal of Clinical Laboratory Automation*, v.3, pp. 383-387, 1983.
[16] Apte, C., and Weiss, S.M., A framework for expert control of interactive software systems, Report CBM-TR-144, Laboratory for Computer Science Research, Rutgers University, New Brunswick, N, October, 1984.
[17] McDermott, J., Building expert systems, in *Artificial Intelligence Applications for Business* (W. Reitman, ed.), Ablex, Norwood, NJ, 1984.
[18] van de Brug, A., Bachant, J., and McDermott, J., The taming of R1, *IEEE Expert*, pp. 33-39, Fall 1986.
[19] Shortliffe, E.H., Medical expert systems: Knowledge tools for the physician, *Western Journal of Medicine*, v.145, pp. 830-839, 1986.
[20] Weiss, S.M., and Kulikowski, C.A., EXPERT:A system for developing consultation models, *Proc 6th Int Joint Conf on Artif Intell.*, pp. 942-950, 1979.
[21] Kulikowski, C.A., and Ostroff, J., Constructing an expert knowledge base for thyroid consultation using generalized A.I. techniques, *Proc 4th SCAMC*, pp. 175-180, 1980.
[22] Waterman, D., *A Guide to Expert Systems*, Addison Wesley, Reading, MA, 1986, p. 216.
[23] Martner, S., and Brigham, R., An interactive computer system for well log analysis, *Proc SPWLA 16th Annual Logging Symposium*, pp. 1-14, 1975.
[24] Apte, C. , *A Framework for Expert Control of Interactive Software Systems*, doctoral dissertation, Rutgers University, 1984.
[25] Forgy, C.L., OPS5 user's manual, Report CMU-CS-81-135, Computer Science Department, Carnegie-Mellon University, Pittsburgh, PA, July 1981.
[26] Bachant, J., and McDermott, J., R1 Revisited: Four Years in the Trenches, *AI Magazine*, v. 5, 1984.
[27] Shortliffe, E.H., Computer programs to support clinical decision making, *JAMA*, v. 258, pp. 61-66, 1987.
[28] Mussen, M.A., Fagan, L.M., Combs, D.M., and Shortliffe, E.H., Facilitating knowledge entry for an oncology therapy advisor using a model of the application area, *Proc MEDINFO-86*, pp. 794-798, 1986.
[29] Langlotz, C.P., Fagan,L.M., Tu, S.W., Sikic, B.I., and Shortliffe, E.H., Combining artificial intelligence and decision analysis for automated therapy planning assistance, *Proc MEDINFO-86*, pp. 794-798, 1986.
[30] Davis, R., Interactive transfer of expertise: Acquisition of new inference rules, *Artif Intell Journal*, v. 12, pp. 121-158, 1979.
[31] Michalski, R.S., and Baskin, A.B., Integrating multiple knowledge representations and learning capabilities in an expert system: the ADVISE system, *Proc Int Joint Conf Artif Intell*, pp. 256-258, 1983.
[32] Vanker, A., and Van Stoeker, W., An expert diagnostic program for dermatology, *Computers and Biomedical Research*, v. 17, pp. 241-247, 1984.
[33] DeLotto, I. and Stefanelli, M., *Artificial Intelligence in Medicine*, North Holland, Amsterdam, 1985.
[34] Ginsberg, A., Weiss, S.M., and Politakis, P., SEEK-2: A generalized approach to automatic knowledge base refinement, *Proc 9th Int Joint*

Conf on Artif Intell, pp. 367-374, 1985.
[35] Efron, B., *The Jacknife, the Bootstrap, and Other Resampling Plans*, SIAM, Philadelphia, 1982.
[36] Weiss, S.M., Minimizing error rates for induced production rules, *Unpublished*, 1988.
[37] Buchanan, B.G., and Shortliffe, E.H., The Problem of Evaluation, Chapter 30 in *Rule Based Expert Systems: The MYCIN Experiments of the Stanford Heuristic Programming Project*, Addison-Wesley, Reading, MA, 1984.
[38] Pauker, S.G., The acquisition and use of patient attitudes in clinical decision-making, *Proc. 4th Illinois Conf. Med. Info. Systems*, 1978, pp. 130-145.
[39] Machina, M.J., Decision-making in the presence of risk, *Science*, v.236, pp. 537- 543, 1987.
[40] Bobrow, D.G., *Qualitative Reasoning about Physical Systems*, MIT Press, Cambridge, MA, 1985.
[41] Kuipers, B., Qualitative Simulation, *Artif. Intell. Journal*, v.28, pp. 289-338, 1986.
[42] Langley, P., Simon, H.A., and Bradshaw, G.L., Rediscovering Chemistry with the BACON system, in *Machine Learning, An Artificial Intelligence Approach* (Michalski, R.S., Carbonell, J.G., and Mitchell, T.M.,eds.), Tioga, Palo Alto, CA, pp. 307-330, 1983.
[43] Yu, V.L., Fagan, L.M., Wraith, S.M., Clancey, W.J., et al., Antimicrobial selection by computer: A blinded evaluation by infectious disease experts, *J. Amer. Med. Assoc.*, v. 242, pp. 1279-1282, 1979.
[44] Miller, R.A., Pople, H.E., and Myers, J.D., INTERNIST-I, An experimental computer-based diagnostic consultant for general internal medicine, *N. Engl. J. Med.*, v. 307, pp. 468-472, 1982.
[45] Weiss, S.M., Kulikowski, C.A., and Galen, R.S., Developing microprocessor-based expert models for instrument interpretation, *Proc. 7th Int Joint Conf on Artif Intell*, pp. 853-855, 1981.
[46] Kingsland, L., Sharp, G., Capps, R., et al., Testing a criteria-based consultant system in rheumatology, in *Proc MEDINFO-83*, pp. 514-517, 1983.
[47] Miller, P.L., The evaluation of artificial intelligence systems in medicine, *Computer Methods and Programs in Biomedicine*, v. 22, pp. 5-11, 1986.

PART 4

Development tools

Topics in Expert System Design
G. Guida and C. Tasso (Editors)

EXPERT SYSTEM BUILDING TOOLS

James L. ALTY

The Turing Institute
Glasgow, United Kingdom

1. INTRODUCTION

As with any other building process the construction of an expert system can be made considerably easier and more cost-effective through the use of tools. Tools can assist in many different areas such as knowledge acquisition, system construction, validation and testing. This paper concentrates upon tools which assist in the actual system construction process rather than in knowledge acquisition or validation though some tools can of course be useful in more than one area (for example a shell can provide a useful environment for knowledge acquisition). A large number of tools already exist either in research laboratories or as commercial systems. Waterman[1], for example, lists about a hundred tools which he divides into System Building Aids (24), Frame Based Languages (16), Logic Based Languages (9), Object Orientated Languages (6), Procedural Languages (9) and Rule Based Languages (32). About a quarter of these are available commercially.

A tool is only useful if it can be applied across a number of domain areas. In the early days of Artificial Intelligence a great deal of effort was expended in the search for general purpose problem solvers (for example GPS, Newell and Simon [2]). However it was rapidly realised that human beings commonly utilise a knowledge-based approach rather than a general purpose approach to problem solving. A small amount of high level knowledge about a particular domain can make problem solving highly efficient and rapidly convergent. For example, a human being crossing a busy road could, by using Newton's laws of motion, work out a safe way to reach the other side. The approach would involve a large set of complex calculations which would be continually repeated as the situation changed. However the use of some high level knowledge about how cars normally move together with a set of reasonable expectations makes the problem solving process almost effortless.

A knowledge based approach is therefore very economical but it has a drawback. What works for one situation is often not relevant to another. Problem solving becomes domain dependent and in the extreme case this would mean that every expert system solution would probably be unique. Fortunately, many domains exhibit similar problem solving characteristics - for example, diagnosing a fault in one domain may use a similar underlying representation to that of determining a fault in another apparently dissimilar domain. Thus whilst it is not possible to construct a general purpose tool, a range of tools can be provided which can be used in a wide variety of domains so that as with any other building process part of the secret of success is using the correct tool in the right situation.

There is one common thread which runs through the design of all Artificial Intelligence tools - one of programming under uncertainty or "programming when you don't know what you are doing" (Shiel [50]). Because of the complexity of the domain all development is exploratory, thus the designer must be able to change his or her mind easily. Gone is the traditional design-specify-code process. The key is a deferred commitment approach, that is final committment to code is delayed as long as possible. This results in the absence of "typing" and a lack of distinction between program and data.

One of the earliest tools used in expert system building was LISP. LISP is a versatile language and can support a rich variety of representational structures and most of the early expert systems such as MYCIN, PROSPECTOR etc. were built using some dialect of LISP. From a computer science point of view LISP is a high level language, but in Artificial Intelligence it is regarded as being more like an Assembler. With LISP the designer has total freedom of control over building decisions and the types of representational structures required. However an intimate knowledge of LISP is necessary and the expert system must effectively be built from scratch. This is thus a fairly expensive option so that these days LISP on its own is not extensively used for expert system building but is often used as part of a larger tool set such as KEE (Knowledge Engineering Environment). In this paper we shall follow the history of tool development in the Expert Systems area which led to the initial development of a number of spin-off tools, and later to languages, toolkits, shells and special purpose toolkits.

Building an expert system involves the correct choice of a knowledge representation strategy and an inferencing process. Early on in the development of expert systems it was realised that a clean separation of these two aspects was important - "keep the knowledge base separate from the inference engine" (Davis [3]). The developers of MYCIN (Shortliffe et al [4]) realised that with such a reasonably clean separation the same representation formalism and inference engine could be used in a number of apparently different domains. This resulted in the development of one of the first expert system building tools EMYCIN (i.e. Empty MYCIN, Van Melle et al [5]). This might be said to be the start of the "spin-off" era of expert system tool development. Tools were normally developed from an existing specific expert system development

2. SPIN-OFF TOOLS

EMYCIN is essentially the MYCIN system with all the domain dependent knowledge removed. What remains is an empty representational shell or set of knowledge templates into which different domain knowledge can be inserted. The system can be used in other problem domains provided that the representational formalism is suitable and the inference mechanism is appropriate. The representational scheme employed in EMYCIN embraces production rules, knowledge triples, a context tree to guide the consultation and an uncertainty handling mechanism based upon measurements of belief. The inference mechanism used a fairly exhaustive depth-first backward chaining strategy and provides extensive explanation facilities. There is no conflict resolution. A comprehensive set of system support facilities are provided such as user interface options, knowledge-based rule editors and debugging aids. A varied set of domains were exploited using EMYCIN, including CLOT (Bennet and Goldman [6] for blood disorders), PUFF (Aikens et al [7] pulmonary malfunction) and SACOM (Bennet and Engelmore [8] Structural Engineering Calculations). Certainly the use of EMYCIN considerably speeded up the process of expert system construction in these domains and some of the basic mechanisms of EMYCIN have been adopted in a number of more recent shells (e.g. Personal Consultant and LEONARDO). The EMYCIN approach is only suitable for problems of a classification nature. It is not well suited to problems involving planning, synthesis, design, constraint satisfaction, multiple goals or model based reasoning.

Shortly after the MYCIN team had announced their first results work began on the PROSPECTOR expert system, to aid geological prospecting, (Duda et al, [9]). Because of the nature of the domain a different representational scheme was adopted - a set of production rules in the form of an inference net. Overlaid on this net was a semantic network connecting different objects in the domain in a geologically meaningful way. The inference engine was again mainly backward chained and a different uncertainty mechanism based on Bayes Rule was adopted. The developers again created a shell out of this work called K.A.S. (Reboh [10]). The HYDRO system (Gaschnig et al [11]) which assists a geologist in using a watershed simulation program was developed using K.A.S and a number of more recent shells have also adopted the formalism (for example SAVOIR [12]).

The CASNET expert system which exploited causal mechanisms was developed for treating Glaucoma (Kulikowski and Weiss [13]), and out of this the EXPERT shell was developed. The rules in EXPERT are written in a high level language which is compiled into FORTRAN for reasons of portability and efficiency. EXPERT divides its data memory into "findings" and "hypotheses". The former are measurements or observations and the latter are inferences made by the system. Like EMYCIN there is a mechanism for handling uncertainty (confidence values). The rules in the system are divided into three basic types - those which deduce findings from findings (called FF rules), those for deducing hypotheses from findings (HF rules) and those which deduce hypotheses from hypotheses (HH rules). FF rules basically control questioning by relating findings already known to others not yet known. The FH and HH rules are rather similar in nature and generate new hypotheses with varying levels of confidence. Rules can be grouped by context. The inference mechanism cycles and a cycle commences with information gathering. During a cycle the HH rules are evaluated once in the order specified by the programmer so that in contrast to some other tools the rule order is very important. New findings trigger FF rules which then cause the cycle to be repeated. The control strategy is therefore basically data-driven. For a more detailed explanation of the handling of confidence factors see Weiss and Kulikowski [14]. EXPERT has been quite widely used and applications include Well Log Analysis (ELAS, Apte and Weiss [15]), Rheumatology (AI/RHEUM, Lindberg et al [16]) and in Serum Protein Diagnosis (Weiss et al [17]).

Whilst the rule-based approach has proved to be relatively successful in diagnostic situations it does have a number of limitations. A number of other new representational formalisms have therefore been explored together with alternative control mechanisms. For example, the development of the INTERNIST expert system (Miller et al [18]) was based on the frame-based abduction mechanism. In this approach the domain knowledge is represented in descriptive frames of information and the inference mechanism uses hypothesis-and-test cycles. From an initial set of observations a set of potential hypotheses is generated. These are then checked to see if they account for all observed features and new questions are generated in order to narrow down the set of possible hypotheses. A very readable account of a modification of this approach - the set covering model - is given in Reggia et al [19]. It is said that frames are natural and easy to write and their content can often be taken directly from paper or textbooks. Furthermore such systems can cope with multiple causes and diseases. Other systems which have used the approach include PIP (Pauker et al [20]) and IDT (Shubin and Ulrich [21]). Out of this approach more general tools have been developed. One such system is KMS which provides frame-based abduction alongside the rule based approach (Reggia and Perricone [22]). One system built using

KMS was System D - a large expert system for diagnosing patients with dizziness (Reggia et al [19]).

Even though there has been a great deal of work carried out using the above differing representation and control schemes, little has been reported about the relative advantages or disadvantages of the different approaches. Ramsey et al [23] have made a comparative evaluation of three building approaches - Bayesian Classification, Rule Based Deduction and Frame-Based Abduction. Eighteen systems were studied including six rule based, two statistical, five frame based and five mixed approaches. They found that all methods could be adapted to any problem involving the selection of a set of different alternatives and they all showed reasonable performance in a wide range of application domains. Each had a strong theoretical foundation and all could support answer justification. They pointed out however that all three are limited in their ability to support spatial and temporal information and that the mappings between problem features and solutions are "shallow" in nature.

In particular the statistical methods suffer from a lack of available probabilities and some of the assumptions of the Bayesian approach (for example mutually exclusive outcomes) are unrealistic. The rule based approach does not represent descriptive knowledge satisfactorily. Another problem with rules is that all the required contexts for their application must be included in the IF part and some features are very context dependent. Ramsey et al identified the experimental nature of Frame-Based Abduction as an important disadvantage of the method. It has not yet been studied in sufficient depth in real world situations for an objective assessment to be made. Furthermore they raised questions about the reasoning mechanism itself. A pure frame based abduction approach might follow a line of reasoning and determine a solution which accounts for all the observations but it might never ask about some unrelated symptom which actually exists. Ramsey reported on two prototype expert systems developed to aid software engineering management, one rule based and the other frame based. The two systems were deliberately built to be as consistent with each other as possible. It was found that the rule based system performed rather better than the frame based one and provided more interpretations. They concluded that in an area as ill-defined as software engineering a rule based approach was more applicable.

There is one other well documented comparison of the usefulness of some early expert system building tools - the environmental crisis management handling problem at Oak Ridge National Laboratory (Waterman and Hayes-Roth [24]). This Laboratory complex occupies 200 square miles of space involving over 200 buildings many of them storing oils and chemicals. The whole site is drained by a tree-like drainage system which eventually empties into White Oak Creek. Any discharge detected at the Creek causes an emergency program to be initiated to determine the location of the spill. The designers of the eight successful expert system tools were invited to Oak Ridge to spend no more than three days interacting with the experts in hazardous chemical spills. No team knew the nature of the problem before arrival. Although the imposition of a short time scale was rather artificial it was expected that the test would show the relative strengths and weaknesses of the tools. Five of the eight teams produced executable models within the three day timescale.

The problem has certain features which might favour one tool over another. In particular the problem was expected to pose particular problems for diagnostic tools. Another feature of the problem was multiple parallel and assynchronous goals. EMYCIN had great difficulty in implementing a drainage basin search mechanism. This was because of the heavy emphasis on backward chaining and a lack of iterative facilities in the language. It also had difficulty in processing multiple goals such as simultaneously locating the spill and identifying its nature. KAS likewise did not address the drainage basin search problem and even the comparatively simple problem of retrieving a list of buildings and filtering it by identity and volume of polutant was beyond KAS. This was done by writing LISP functions. However a simple model was built which exhibited plausible behaviour. EXPERT used forward chaining but solved the problem of drainage basin search with a FORTRAN routine. Although the multiple goal problem was not addressed a working model was produced which allowed the user to interrupt and either volunteer data or change previous answers. This test illustrates the importance of matching a tool's capabilities to the characteristics of the problem and of having access to external language facilities.

3. KNOWLEDGE ENGINEERING LANGUAGES

At the end of the 1970's the second phase began - that of developing special purpose languages without reference to some pioneering system. LISP, for example, can be used to create an intermediate environment between the basic LISP language and the expert system shell. One example of this is the programming language called OPS4 (later OPS5, Forgy [25]) which is an implementation language for a Production System. The developers of R1 (or XCON, McDermott [26]) chose OPS5 as a development medium. The system, written in LISP, is forward chained with a simple representation scheme. However it has powerful matching facilities and a set of useful system construction aids. It is not a true expert system shell but rather an implementation of the production system approach with a choice of two conflict resolution strategies called LEX and MEA. The OPS family of languages provide a powerful environment for implementing an efficient system and the conflict resolution strategy can be used to support meta-rules. However there are no uncertainty handling facilities and no in-built explanation facility. The developers of OPS5 later produced OPS83 (Forgy [27]). This is a rather different approach to OPS5 and employs procedural language constructs.

Another early general purpose knowledge engineering language built in LISP was ROSIE - "Rule Oriented System for Implementing Expertise" (Fain et al [28]). This combined a rule-based approach with a procedural language. It supports both standard programming constructs and pattern matching techniques. Facts and Relationships are described in a limited English language syntax involving class membership, predication, verbs, complements and phrases. This makes the underlying knowledge in the system more readable and understandable. Similar techniques have been used in many later shells. An important feature of ROSIE is the capability of dividing rules into rulesets. Three types of ruleset are supported - procedure, generator and predicate - and these act on imperative verbs, nouns and comparative verbs. A special program called a monitor is associated with each ruleset and this specifies the order in which the rules will be executed (sequential, cyclic or random). ROSIE has been used in a number of applications including legal decision making (Waterman and Peterson [29]), Tactical Air Target Recommender (Callero et al [30]), and a system to assist combat operations decision makers (Beebe et al [31]).

At about this time a new general purpose expert system building language PROLOG, became more generally available. PROLOG was developed mainly in Europe and has been steadily gaining in popularity ever since. Its widespread adoption has been hampered by the lack of good development environments (in contrast with LISP which exists in a number of excellent environments) but the situation is now rapidly improving with implementations such as Quintus PROLOG. PROLOG offers a somewhat higher level language approach than LISP. It provides a backward chained production system environment in which rules, facts and relationships can be naturally expressed. However, as with LISP considerable expertise is needed and most of the required facilities have to be programmed in. It is therefore again an expensive option. It is often provided as part of a more comprehensive toolkit, for example in the POPLOG environment (Hardy [32]).

POPLOG is a multi-language development environment which supports PROLOG, Common LISP and POP-11. All three languages are integrated within a virtual machine and are implemented as incremental compilers. A facility is also provided for interfacing to other conventional languages. The whole toolset is packaged into a WIMP (Windows, Icons, Mouse and Pointers) interface and runs on conventional reasonably low cost hardware. POPLOG is available on a number of systems including VAX, APOLLO, Hewlett-Packard and SUNs. A window manager provides a set of primitives for building sophisticated Interfaces but the support is at a fairly low level so a complicated visual interface will require a lot of hard work. However there are plans to provide better window facilities based upon "X" windows.

PROLOG (like LISP) can be used to provide higher level environments, indeed it is an ideal language for implementing a meta-language approach. Additional predicates can be added to provide user-querying facilities, explanation facilities, uncertainty handling and other system debugging facilities. Examples of such systems include APES (Hammond and Sergot [33]) and YAPES (Niblett [34]). This type of tool appeals to the knowledge engineer who wishes to have a combination of some higher level facilities combined with access to the primitives built in to the tool that they use. Prolog has the advantage that the specification is the implementation so specifications can be run almost immediately. However there is often a trade-off between efficiency and legibility. The separation of control and logic allows refinements to be made which considerably improve efficiency. The resulting programs are however often less intelligible.

In APES standard PROLOG is extended by the addition of over sixty modules to provide the following facilities:

> the controlled handling of undefined relationships which could be satisfied by querying the user. Normal PROLOG would simply fail so without this facility a designer would have to use direct calls to PROLOG input/output primitives from within rules
>
> primitives for handling HOW and WHY explanations
>
> interface design primitives providing default forms which ease interface design.

The designers of APES emphasise its roots in Logic Programming and stress its declarative reading. However they admit that it is very easy for designers versed in conventional program control to succumb to the high level features and develop programs which are correct but inefficient.

YAPES, developed at the Turing Institute, is a similar approach. It provides additional primitives for handling user queries such as HOW (how did you reach this conclusion ?), WHY (why are you asking this question ?)and WHY NOT (why did this goal fail ?). It also supports an extended version of Horn Clause logic which use a plausible reasoning scheme. Another advantage of the extended PROLOG approach stems from the use of a uniform representational language. In YAPES, for example, the shell is written in the same language as the representation language interpreted by the shell. This means that the designer can alter the meta logical control language used by the interpreter (in YAPES this contains only 8 clauses). The designers claim that such changes do not affect the explanation capabilities or the plausible reasoning facilities of the shell. Howcver alterations to the basic interpreter require the designer to be fully competent in PROLOG, thus PROLOG extensions such as APES and YAPES assume that a heavy investment in PROLOG has already been made. For those not versed in PROLOG this approach can be an expensive one.

LISP was the original language of AI but PROLOG has begun to challenge it in a number of areas. In a sense they are not strictly comparable since PROLOG provides facilities at a higher level. PROLOG has its origins in Europe and it is still more extensively used there. Recently however the Japanese endorsement of PROLOG in the "Fifth Generation Project", has increased interest. One of the primary reasons for this preference by the Japanese was the inherent ability of PROLOG to operate in a parallel environment. True Logic Programming exhibits both "AND" and "OR" parallelism and although this is not so easy to achieve in PROLOG, versions have been developed which can offer some parallelism (e.g. PARLOG). PROLOG does offer a more natural style for representing structures and rules but often implementation details blur the situation. LISP however is still the most popular language and one of its advantages is the rich set of environments in which it is available. Arguments between LISP and PROLOG are probably sterile. It is likely that each will be found suitable for specific applications.

A third interesting area in language environment developments has been the emergence of Object Orientated Programming languages. The original work was carried out at the Xerox Palo Alto Laboratories and resulted in the environment Smalltalk (Goldberg and Robson [35]) but the approach has been adopted in a number of LISP based systems such as LOOPS (Stefik et al [36]) and FLAVORS though these systems incorporate other paradigms as well. In the Object-Orientated world objects contain their own procedures and data and communicate via messages. A second key concept is that of inheritance which is a major part of the Frame-based representation approach which will be discussed shortly. Object Orientated languages have also contributed significantly to the expert system tool set by providing greatly enhanced user interfaces. Interface design is now accepted as a key development area since it is generally agreed that poor interface design has held back expert system exploitation.

Both ROSIE and OPS5 were subjected to the Oak Ridge National Laboratory Spill problem mentioned earlier, but a team of LISP programmers was unable to attend at the last moment. This was unfortunate since it would have given an interesting comparison between the tools and the basic language approach. With hindsight it might also have been interesting to have teams of FORTRAN or C programmers present on the test as well. One of the strengths of ROSIE was its English-like syntax. This speeded program development and very readable rules. ROSIE was also able to perform the drainage basin search. It also simulated assynchronous processing of multiple goals. Later the model was redesigned without time constraints and this solution is often quoted. It is a nice solution but took much longer than three days(Fain [28]). OPS5 was able to carry out the drainage basin search effectively and processed multiple goals. However it could not process new data on arrival (no interupt facility). Also the interface was rather weak and it could not explain it's reasoning. The languages therefore did rather better on the spill problem than the more specialised tools such as EMYCIN.

4. TOOLKITS

It is normally desirable to have additional structure in the knowledge base particularly if it is large. Frames provide a convenient way of doing this. The term was first introduced by Minsky [37]. A frame gathers together both declarative and procedural knowledge about an "object" of interest. Thus as well as containing normal data values it may also have within it rules and procedures. The attributes (or slots) can also have default values and slots can point to other frames. Thus the knowledge base normally contains a set of frames in some form of hierarchy. This corresponds to the real life situation where knowledge is never in isolation but is always connected with other knowledge. Frames may also inherit properties from other frames so that specific objects can inherit characteristics from other more generalised objects. The scheme provides an economical way of representing knowledge. Frames are used in the object orientated paradigm where objects communicate via messages. The early Frame-based tools such as KRL (Bobrow and Winograd [38]) and FRL (Roberts and Goldstein [39]) focussed on structural descriptions. However the development of CENTAUR (Aikins [40]) led to the integration of frames and rules to provide both structural descriptions and the control of reasoning. Another development at this time was SRL+ (Fox [41]). The armoury of the knowledge engineer therefore now consists of rules, rulesets, demons, contexts, semantic nets, frames, inheritance, active values and a variety of control mechanisms. This variety has led to the development of Artificial Intelligence Toolkits - collections of the various paradigms which can be used when and where required. Because of the complexity of this knowledge representation process such tools have normally been provided in highly visual environments using high quality bit-mapped screens. Examples of such tools include LOOPS, KEE (Fikes and Kehler [42]) , ART and Knowledgecraft. Such "toolkits" provide a rich environment for expert system development but are normally provided on special purpose hardware.

Because the toolkit approach is quite general it lacks a focus, so the knowledge engineer using such a system has to decide which paradigm (or combination of paradigms) to use in his or her application. This implies a much greater knowledge of the knowledge engineering process than with, say, shells. Such toolkits, however, are excellent for prototyping new systems and it not unknown for an expert system to first be developed on an A.I. workstation and then re-coded into PASCAL or C for implementation. Such an approach gives the productivity and flexibility of the toolkit with the efficiency and portability of conventional languages. This portability issue is an important one. If the expert system is to run in many locations the target system would not normally be an expensive A.I. workstation.

The three main toolkits in the marketplace are KEE (Knowledge Engineering Environment), ART (Automated Reasoning Tool), and Knowledge Craft. KEE was the first in the field and is therefore the most used of the three. All three are based on LISP so the designer is free at any time to program in LISP. It also means that to use these packages one needs to be an expert LISP programmer.

ART is a conceptual successor to OPS5. It provides a rule-based perspective based upon a blackboard architecture. Declarative knowledge is stored in schemata or contexts and relationships between schemata are defined. Hierarchies are created via rules. ART provides a Truth Maintenance facility which allows non-monotonic reasoning to be used. A record is kept of the inferencing chains, so if a fact becomes invalid any consequent facts or clauses can be retracted. Another nice facility in ART is "alternative" worlds. The system can simultaneously consider a number of viewpoints and reason about them providing temporal and hypothetical context representation and reasoning. The viewpoints approach provides a natural mechanism for representing real-world temporal problems. It has therefore been used in Critical Path Resource Allocation (Jackson and Maletz [43]). ART is probably the fastest of the three tools.

Knowledge Craft was developed at Carnegie-Mellon out of the SRL language. It allows the creation of multiple hypotheses. It has a full implementation of CRL-PROLOG which combines the deductive power of PROLOG with the representational power of Object Orientated Programming. It has an excellent schema representational language which allows complex inheritance paths to be defined through user-defined relations and grammars of inheritance paths. It supports Access-orientated programming via demons. Reasoning is provided through CRL-OPS rules which bring the reasoning power of OPS5 to the system, but the pattern matching capability has been considerably improved over OPS5. Knowledge Craft has a good user interface with graphical schema editors and two debugging workbenches, one for PROLOG and one for OPS5.

KEE, being the best established, and oldest, of the three probably has the best knowledge designer interface. It is based on UNITS which provides frame based representational formalism and it has an excellent graphics interface. Reasoning is based upon rules which are represented as KEE objects. The reasoning direction can be both forward and backward. The underlying object oriented paradigm provides powerful access orientated programming approach. This provides such facilities as active values (or demons) and Active images which allow graphics images to be attached to units slots. The user interface is very friendly. There is a graphics Units editor, a graphical backward chaining explanation facility and plenty of window information explaining what the system is doing.

Because of the different facilities offered by these tools and the variable match between these and user requirements, it is not really meaningful to state which is the best tool. An interesting review of the three tools can be found in Laurent et al [44]. They conclude that "KEE is a nice tool to use, especially because of its user interface, but the user is quickly limited by the weakness of KEE's inferential features and by its slowness...It seems difficult to develop professional and large applications with the software..". However since this paper was written Key Worlds has become available and some speeding up of the systems has been achieved. As far as ART was concerned they felt that "..ART seems to be the most suitable tool for complex applications, and especially for real time applications. ...ART combines the power of Knowledge Craft with the clean integration of KEE". They concluded that "Knowledge Craft has various interesting features which make it significant for people looking for the maximum at the best price". They include a readable tabular comparison of the three tools. Although two years have now passed this still makes interesting reading

5. PURPOSE BUILT SHELLS

The original shells were developed as spin-off products from existing systems. More recently however shells have been purpose-built. They vary from small scale shells running on personal computers and costing a few hundred pounds to sophisticated shells running on mainframes and costing many thousands of pounds. Some require no programming expertise at all whilst others, to be used effectively, need familiarity with LISP or PROLOG. The early shells had very limited interfacing facilities and had virtually no connection with the outside world. More recently these factors have become important and many shells have been upgraded to enable the designer to have more flexibility with the interface design and to give him or her access to external data files and even programming languages. The representational schemes offered vary from rules to frames to a mixture of both. Both forward and backward control strategies are available but not always in the same system. Uncertainty handling is provided at a number of levels or not at all.

The variety offered by the market in 1988 can be seen in Table 1. This table contains some of the more popular or interesting shells with some limited information about their representation and control strategy. The market is very volatile and the nature of the table changes rapidly. The table is therefore only intended to illustrate the scope and the variety of offerings. Anyone interested in finding out more about any package can find the contact address in any of the recent survey papers (e.g. Hewett and Sasson [45]).

SHELL	MANUFACTURER	REPRESENTATION	CONTROL
Advisor II	Expert Systems International	Rules	Back Chain
EXSYS	Exsys Inc.	Rules	Back Chain
Super Expert	Intelligent Terminals Ltd.	Induction	
GURU	Micro Data Base Systems Inc.	Rules	Back Chain Limited For'd Chain
KES II	Software A&E	Rules, Classes	Back Chain Limited For'd Chain
LEONARDO	Creative Intelligence	Rules, Frames Procedures	Back and Forward Chain
Xi Plus	Expertech	Rules Induction	Control over direction
Goldworks	Goldhill Inc.	Rules, Frames Objects, Inheritance	Control over direction
Nexpert	Neuron Data Inc.	Rules	Forward Backward Chain
ESE	IBM	Rules	Back Chain

Table 1 - Some Expert System Shells

The shells can be divided into small PC based shells, large PC based shells and mainframe shells. The facilities offered vary markedly and the price ranges from a few hundred pounds to over ten thousand pounds. Mainframe or VAX shells cost a lot more than the PC shells but, of course, they can be run on many distributed terminals. When judging whether a shell is or is not suitable for an application a number of factors have to be taken into account.

5.1 Handling of Uncertainty

Some shells offer no facilities (e.g. Xi Plus, Nexpert) others a very limited (and perhaps inadequate) form (e.g. Exsys) some offer a Baysian approach (e.g. Savoir), others offer a MYCIN certainty factor approach (e.g. Personal Consultant Plus) and some offer both a MYCIN certainty factor approach and a Baysian approach (e.g. LEONARDO and KES2).

5.2 Reasoning Control

Shells also vary in the type of reasoning control offered. Some offer straightforward backward chaining (e.g. Exsys, although a limited form of forward chaining can be done indirectly) , Others offer backward chaining with a limited form of forward chaining (e.g. Insight2). Some shell offer a fair amount of control over the reasoning direction (e.g. Xi Plus) and others allow the designer to control the reasoning direction explicitly (e.g. KES, Savoir). A common form of designer control is achieved through the use of demons (WHEN... THEN...). Finally Nexpert offers a very flexible forward and backward chaining mechanism.

5.3 Inductive Reasoning

Inductive shells use the concept of Machine Induction to assist in the knowledge acquisition process. The domain expert decides upon a set of possible results, a set of relevant attributes , and then gives a set of examples within these attributes each giving a particular result class. The inductive system then induces a rule (Michie D [46]) and this rule can then be used in the expert system under construction. Induced rules tend to be much more complex than the rules extracted from experts and it is important that the rules are still regarded as meaningful by the expert giving the examples. Some inductive shells are relatively simple. SuperExpert, for example allows a rule to be induced and offers some simple structuring facilities with which to connect this induced rules to other rules giving rule chains. However the representational facilities in the shell are very limited. Other inductive shells are more complex. EXTRAN for example will induce rules from examples and these can be combined with rules extracted from the expert by more conventional techniques. A sophisticated set of structuring facilities is provided and there are extensive links to other languages and sensors. The benefits of inductive shells have been reported in a number of places [47]. Recently the conventional shell manufacturers have been augmenting their shells with inductive add-ons. One example of this is Expertech who have recently added Xi-Rule onto Xi-Plus.

5.4 Representational Power

Shells vary widely in their representation facilities. Some of the smaller ones offer only attribute-value pairs, simple sets and rules to process them. More sophisticated shells allow variables in rules (for example Xi Plus or APES), and simple hierarchical structures such as is-a or simple frames (LEONARDO). At a higher level again a full frame system may be implemented with truth maintenance facilities (e.g. GOLDWORKS). In most shells considerable efforts have been made to keep the representation English-like. In some cases spaces are allowed in both identifiers and values, and operators can be redefined to make the reading easier (e.g. Xi Plus).

5.5 External Connections

Connecting to external data bases or language facilities has become increasingly important. On the one hand it is difficult to solve problems in isolation from conventional data and on the other hand access to a language can often make up for deficiencies in the shell. Integration can be achieved in three ways - by invisibly embedding the expert system within a conventional language, by constructing an integrated environment between the expert systems development tool and other systems such as dBase III or Lotus, and thirdly as a separate system which can access external files and programming languages. Most systems now offer this last alternative and many offer access to Lotus and/or dBase III (Insight2, PC easy, VP expert, 1st Class etc..). KES and M.1. can be used in the manner of the first approach.

5.6 Knowledge Engineering Interface

Most shells offer a specialised Knowledge Engineering Interface. In some it is offered directly in the package (e.g Xi Plus, APES) in others the designer uses an off-line editor or Word Processing package (e.g. Savoir, VP Expert, KES, M.1.). Some shells offer both (GURU). Direct interfaces usually give on-line syntax checking and some of the off-line approaches have knowledge checkers (for example SAVOIR's probability checker).

5.7 User Interface Facilities

The early shells offered rudimentary facilities for communicating with the user. In some cases this was little more than scrolled question - answer output. Recently this matter has received attention from most tool manufacturers. It is now quite common to be able to design screens often within the constructs of the system. Some systems now allow access to graphics routines to provide reasonable quality picture output. Window interfaces are now quite common. For example a pop-up window will be used to show an explanation. One has to remember however that the majority of shells are targetted at solving advisory and diagnostic problems which fit neatly into a sequential dialogue.

5.8 Explanation Facilities

The quality of Explanation Facilities varies widely. If the rule formalism allows variables it is extremely useful to have the current instantiation of the variables in the explanation. Some systems offer this (e.g. APES) but others (e.g. Xi Plus) do not. Some systems offer only a form of canned text. In systems using probabilities it is important to have traces of the progress of the probability calculations. This is not only useful for debugging but is also of considerable assistance to the expert when developing an understanding of probabilities and their manipulation. A "What If" facility is also extremely helpful both during debugging and normal operation.

5.9 Hybrid Tools

Some tools are now being developed which are mid-way between the full toolkit approach and the shell approach. One good example is the system GOLDWORKS. This system offers many of the facilities of the large toolkits at a fraction of the price (£5000). It runs on the PC/AT but it helps to have as fast a machine as possible (e.g. the COMPAQ 386). GOLDWORKS offers frames, rules and contexts within a LISP environment. In theory the designer need not know LISP and interacts through a menu interface, however for serious system building a knowledge of LISP is probably essential. Another nice feature of GOLDWORKS which may become more common is the end-user interface. A screen is regarded as a frame. This mean that the I/O interface can be reasoned about in the same way as other facts and relationships in GOLDWORKS and this could enable some very sophisticated interfacing to be done. Nexpert Object is another hybrid tool.

6. SPECIAL PURPOSE TOOLKITS

Once the general toolkits became available it was inevitable that special purpose tools would be offered on top of them. This is a rather new area of development but it is expected to grow in importance. One well-known example is PICON (Knickerbocker et al [48]) whose area of interest is continuous real time control. The application area covers network management, space station control and the process industries. PICON attempts to provide on-line control and advice (most expert systems to date in this area have been exclusively off-line). The requirements which PICON is expected to meet include :

high-speed context sensitive rule activation
maintenance of sensor histories
remembering what matters and forgetting what does not matter
communication between multiple expert systems

High speed rule activation is achieved through a hierarchical rule organisation which provides a means for managing the many subsets of rules typical of a complex real time operation. The reasoning power of an LMI system is used to focus in on the appropriate rule set. The system is written in LISP. One problem with real time expert systems is that the data coming from sensors can be of varying quality. PICON therefore provides facilities for checking sensor input over time and for comparing measured and derived values.

The design of PICON assumes upto 20,000 measuring points and alarms. However information is passed to the expert system when requested rather than on a fixed scan basis. The system supports both forward and backward chaining. There is an element of parallelism in the system. A 68010 processor evaluates the first level of reasoning and higher level reasoning is carried out in the LISP machine.

PICON has been used in a number of applications. One of these is alarm management at a coal fired power station (Taunton, [51]) and another, the control of a satellite electrical power system (Leinweber and Gidwani [52]).

Other tools of this nature either available or planned include:

Pilotex - for real time control of process which change over time
ISS Three - computer capacity management for large IBM systems
Trillium - A prototyping environment for Interface design

There is no doubt that this area of tool development will be an interesting one to watch and it is expected to grow.

7. LANGUAGE, SHELL OR TOOLKIT ?

The shells provide the upper level of a stratum of tools, the lower level being the basic languages and the middle level comprising the toolkits. Figure 1 attempts to draw out some of the differing properties of the language, toolkit and shell approaches. Languages are applicable quite generally. Virtually any type of expert system can be produced. Shells on the other hand tend to be rather specific in applicability. Indeed one of the main ingredients for success in using a shell is a good match between its facilities and the problem to be addressed. A sophisticated toolkit like KEE or ART has the generality of the language approach but also contains specific representations and control strategies. The degree of abstraction is, as expected low in the language approach and medium in the shell approach (often fairly simple rules and/or frames). Toolkit once again provide a rich set of abstractions. Facilities are also most rich in the toolkit, medium in the shells and limited in the language approach, but of course any facility missing in a language can be provided by programming.

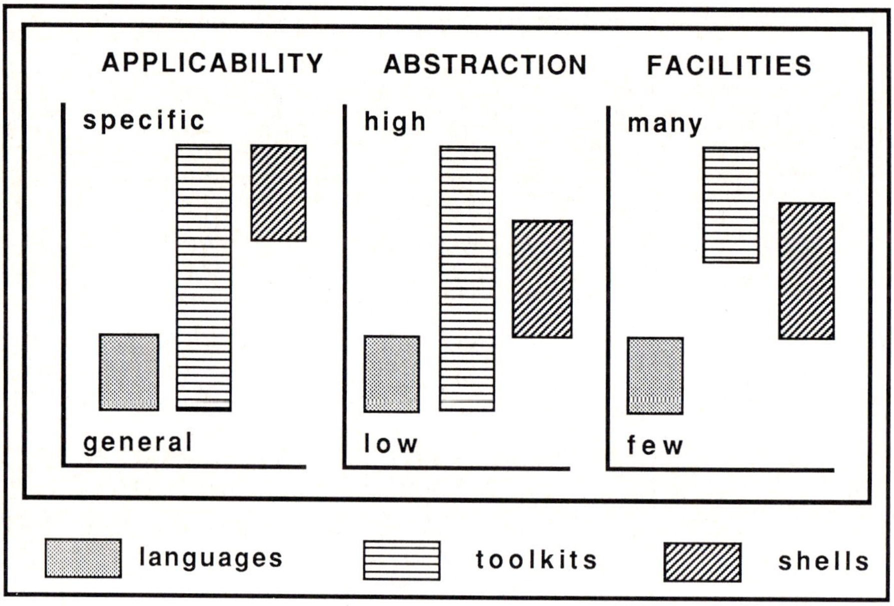

Figure 1 Properties of the Tool Stratum

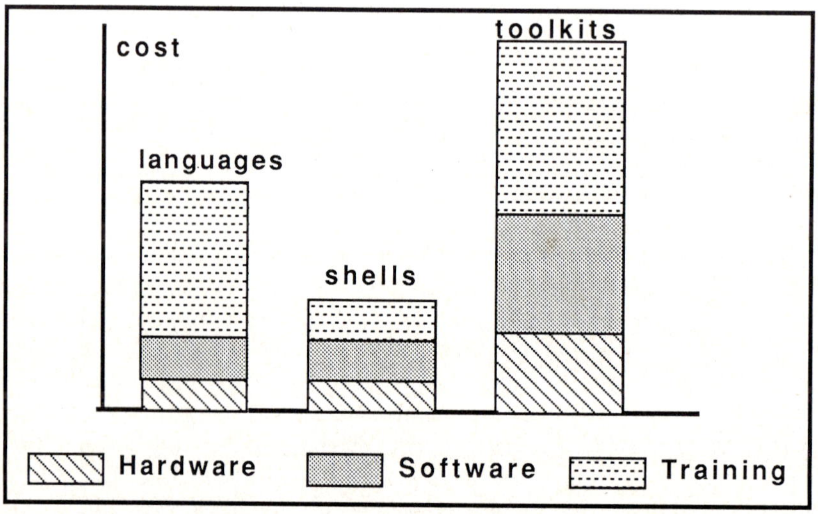

Figure 2 Costs of Hardware,Software and Training

From Figure 1 the toolkit approach appears to win handsomely over the other two, however other factors have to be taken into account. Important factors include cost of hardware, cost of software and cost of training. These are illustrated in Figure 2.

The hardware costs for the language and shell approaches is normally quite low. Most language implementations and shells will operate on Personal Computers or workstations like the SUN. On the other hand the toolkits often require specialised hardware such as the SYMBOLICS, Xerox 1186 or the Texas Instrument's Explorer. Even when they do run on more conventional systems like the SUN they require large amounts of main store and backing store. In contrast to both languages and shells the software is also very expensive. The shells usually require a fairly short training period (obviously this does depend on the shell) but the required investment in training someone in PROLOG or LISP is much greater. The toolkits, being very sophisticated collections of software require a long and intensive training period. Another problem with toolkits is the target machine. Although some suppliers (e.g. KEE) have announced run-time only versions of the software these still are expensive and require fairly large systems to support them. KEE have announced that their system will be available on the PC but this must presumably mean a more limited functionality.

The relative ease with which shells can be used makes them ideal for "playing" with early ideas about expert systems. In a relatively short time a shell can give someone not familiar with A.I. a useful overview of the technique (and its problems). For reasonably small, well-defined problems a shell can work well. In the Turing Institute, a Mechanical Engineering Ph.D. student with no previous knowledge of Artificial Intelligence was able to construct a 1200 rule system using Xi Plus. The rules were extracted from the planners and the system had external connection to the Computer-Aided-Design database as well as the scheduling data base. Interestingly, the main help sought from Institute staff was not in Artificial Intelligence but in machine connection. The system has achieved a 30% saving in a planning process on the factory floor. For larger problems where a successful prototype is needed the Toolkit approach is excellent. Toolkits certainly reduce the prototyping time and greatly assist the designer in controlling the complexity of the system. Finally the language approach is often best when a real system of considerable complexity has to be implemented from the prototype and a portable version is required.

8. THE FUTURE

Spang Robinson [49] report that the number of installed toolkits at the end of 1987 was KEE (1743), ART (700), and Knowledge Craft (400) bringing in revenue in excess of £23 million. However there were signs that sales of large toolkits were slowing down partly because of aggressive marketing and improved facilities being offered by smaller shells. For example the shells VP-Expert , Personal Consultant and GURU had sales of 15,000, 10,000 and 5,000 systems respectively and revenues were $15 million, $4.5 million and $12 million respectively.

The tool situation has certainly not stabilised. In the future there will be a move to more sophisticated shells with a wide range of facilities at reasonably affordable prices. There will then have to be changes at the toolkit end of the market possibly with cut down versions of the tools becoming more readily available on general purpose machines. Finally, it is likely that special purpose tools like PICON will become more commonplace. These will be tools customised by domain specialists and knowledge engineers for fairly specific knowledge domains. They will have a high performance and their interfaces will be highly targetted at the specific domain and will thus be easier to use. Tools will have to move nearer to the users if we are to sustain exploitation of expert system techniques.

REFERENCES

[1] Waterman D.A., "A Guide to Expert Systems", (Addison Wesley, Reading, Mass. 1986)

[2] Newell A., and Simon H., "Human Problem Solving", (Englewood Cliffs, NJ., Prentice Hall 1972).

[3] Davis R., "Expert Systems: Where are We ? and Where do We Go from Here ?, AI Memo No. 665, MIT AI Laboratory ,1982.

[4] Shortliffe E.H., Axline S.G., Buchanan B.G., Merrigan T.C., and Cohen S.N., "An Artificial Intelligence Program to Advise Physicians Regarding Antimicrobial Therapy", Computers and Biomedical Research, Vol 6 (1973), pp 544 - 560 .

[5] Van Melle W., Shortliffe E.H., and Buchanan B.G., " EMYCIN: a Domain Independent System that Aids in Constructing Knowledge Based Consultation Programs", Machine Intelligence, Infotech State-of-the-Art Report 9, No. 3 (1981), pp 249 - 263.

[6] Bennet J.S., and Goldman D., "CLOT: a Knowledge based Consultant for Diagnosis of Bleeding Disorders", Report HPP-80-7, Computer Science Dept., Stanford Univ., Stanford, Calif, (1980).

[7] Aikens J.S., Kunz J.C., and Shortliffe E.H., "PUFF: an Expert System for Interpretation of Pulmonary Function Data", Computers and Biomedical Research Vol 16 (1983), pp 199 - 208.

[8] Bennet J.S., and Engelmorc R.S., "Experience using EMYCIN", in Buchanan B.G., and Shortliffe E.H., (eds.), Rule Based Expert Systems,Addison-Wesley,Reading, Mass. (1984), pp 314 - 328.

[9] Duda R., Hart P.E., Nilsson N.J., Barrett P., Gaschnig J, Konolige K., Reboh R., and Slocum J., "Development of thc PROSPECTOR Consultation System for Mineral Exploration" SRI Report, Stanford Research Institute, 333 Ravenswood Ave., Menlo Park, Calif. (1978).

[10] Reboh R., "Knowledge Engineering Techniques and Tools in the PROSPECTOR Environment", SRI Tech. Note 243, Stanford Research Institute, 333 Ravenswood Ave., Menlo Park Calif ,(1981).

[11] Gaschnig J., Reboh R. and Reiter J., "Development of a Knowledge Based Expert System for Water Resource Problems", SRI Report 1619, AI Center, SRI international, Menlo Park, Calif, (1981).

[12] Savoir "SAVOIR: expert systems meet the video mass market", Expert Systems, Vol 1, No. 2, (1984), pp 105 - 106.

[13] Kulikowski C.A., and Weiss S., "Representation of Expert Knowledge for Consultation: the CASNET and EXPERT projects", in Szolovitz P. (ed.), Artificial Intelligence in Medicine, Boulder, Colorado, (Westview Press, 1982), pp 21 - 55.

[14] Weiss,S.M. and Kulikowski, C.A., "A Practical Guide to Designing Expert Systems", (London: Chapman and Hall, 1983).

[15] Apte C.V., and Weiss S., "A Knowledge Representation Framework for Expert Control of Interactive Software Systems", Report CBM-TR-144, Lab. for Computer Science Research, Rutgers Univ. New Brunswick, NJ.,(1984).

[16] Lindberg D., Sharp G., Kingsland L., Weiss S., Hayes S., Ueno H. and Hazelwood S., "Computer based Rheumatology Consultant" in Proc. 3rd World Conf. on Medical Informatics, (North Holland 1980), pp 1311 - 1315

[17] Weiss S., Kulikowski C., and Gallen R., "Developing Microprocessor based Expert Models for Instrument Interpretation", in Proc. 7th Int. Joint Conf. on A.I., Vancouver, Canada (1981), pp 853 - 855.

[18] Miller R.A., Pople Jr., H.E., and Myers, J.D., "INTERNIST-1, an Experimental Computer Based Diagnostic Consultant for General Internal Medicine", New England Journal of Medicine, Vol 307, No 8 (1982), pp 468 - 476, .

[19] Reggia, J.A., Nau D.S., and Wang P.Y., "Diagnostic Expert Systems Based on a Set Covering Model", Int. J. Man-Mach. Studies, Vol 19, (1984), pp 437 - 460.

[20] Pauker S., Gorry G., Kassirer J., and Schwartz W., "Towards the Simulation of Clinical Cognition", American J. of Medicine,, Vol 60 (1976), pp 981 - 986.

[21] Shubin H., and Ulrich J., "IDT: an Intelligent Diagnostic Tool", Proc. Nat. Conf. on AI, (1982), pp 290-295.

[22] Reggia J.A., and Perricone B., "KMS Reference Manual", Technical Report TR-1136, Computer Science Department, University of Maryland (1982),.

[23] Ramsey C.L., Reggia J.A., Nau D.S., and Ferrentino A., "A Comparative Analysis of Methods for Expert Systems", Int. J. of Man Mach. Studies, Vol 24, (1986), pp 475 - 499.

[24] Waterman D.A.,and Haycs-Roth F., "An Investigation of Tools for Building Expert Systems", inHayes-Roth F., Waterman D.A., and Lenat D.B.,(eds.) Building Expert Systems, (Addison Wesley, Reading, Mass., 1983), pp 169 - 215.

[25] Forgy C.L., "OPS5 User Manual. Report CMU-CS-81-135, Computer Science Dept, Carnegie-Mellon Univ, Pittsburgh, PA (1981).

[26] McDermott J., "R1: an Expert in the Computer Systems Domain", Proc. AAAI-80, (1981).

[27] Forgy C.L., "Overview of OPS83", Computer Science Dept. Report, Carnegie-Mellon Univ., Pittsburgh, PA., (1983).

[28] Fain J., Hayes-Roth F., Sowizral H., and Waterman D.A., "Programming in ROSIE: An introduction by means of examples", Tech Report N-1646-ARPA (Rand Corp. Santa Monica, Calif ., 1982).

[29] Waterman D.A., and Peterson M.A., "Models of Legal Decision Making", The Rand Corporation, R-2717-ICJ, (1981).

[30] Callero M., Waterman D.A., and Kipps J.R., "TATR: A Prototype Expert System for Tactical Air Targeting", The Rand Corporation, R-3096-ARPA, (1984).

[31] Beebe H.M., Goodman H.S., Henry G.L., and Snell D., "The Adept Workstation - a Knowledge based System for Combat Intelligence Analysis", in Proc. 7th MIT /ONR workshop on C3 Systems, MIT. Cambridge, Mass, (1984).

[32] Hardy S., "A New Software Environment for List-Processing and Logic", in O'Shea T.,and Eisenstadt M., (eds.), "Tools, Techniques and Applications", (Harper and Row ,1984).

[33] Hammond P., and Sergot M, "The Apes User Manual", Logic Based Systems Ltd., Richmond, Surrey, UK. (1985).

[34] Niblett T, "YAPES: Yet Another Prolog Expert System Shell", Machine Intelligence News, No. 7, (Turing Institute, Glasgow, 1984), pp 24 - 50.

[35] Goldberg A and Robson D., "Smalltalk80: The Language and its Implementation", (Addison-Wesley, Reading. Mass, 1986).

[36] Stefik M., Bobrow D.G., Mittal S., and Conway L, "Knowledge programming in LOOPS: Report on an experimental course", Artif. Intel. Vol 4., No 3, (1983), pp 3 - 14.

[37] Minsky M., "A framework for representing knowledge", in. Winston P., (ed.), "The Psychology of Computer Vision", (McGraw Hill, New York 1975).

[38] Bobrow D.G., and Winograd T., "An overview of KRL, a knowledge representation language", Cognitive Science, Vol 1, (1977) , pp 3 - 46.

[39] Roberts R.B., and Goldstein I.P., "The FRL Primer: Memo No 408, A.I. Laboratory, MIT, Cambridge, Mass. 1977.

[40] Aikens J., "A Representational Scheme Using both Frames and Rules", in Buchanan B.G., and Shortliffe E.H., (eds.), Rule Based Expert Systems, (Addison Wesley, Reading., Mass., 1984), pp 424 - 452.

[41] Fox, M., On Inheritance in Knowledge Representation", IJCAI, (1979), pp 282 - 284.

[42] Fikes R., and Kehler T., "The Role of Frame Based Representation in Reasoning", Comms ACM, Vol 28, No 9, (1985).

[43] Jackson P.C., and Maletz M.C., "Critical Path Resource Allocation using ART Viewpoints", 6th Int. Workshop on Expert Systems and their Applic., AVIGNON 86 , (1986), Agence de L'Informatique, Paris, France.

[44] Laurent J., Ayel J., Thome F., and Ziebelin D., "Comparison evaluation of three expert system development tools: KEE, Knowledge Craft and ART", The Knowledge Engineering Review, Vol 1, No 4, (1986), pp 18 - 29.

[45] Hewett J., and Sasson R., "Expert Systems 1986: USA and Canada", (Ovum Ltd, London, England, 1986).

[46] Michie D., "The state of the Art in Machine Learning", in Michie D., (ed.),Introductory readings in Expert Systems, (Gordon and Breach, New York 1982),.

[47] Razzak M., Michie D., and Ahmad A., "Case Studies of Building Expert Systems using EXTRAN", Proc. Conf. AI and Advanced Computer Applications, Wiesbaden, (TCM Expositions, Liphook, 1986), pp 12

[48] Knickerbocker C.G., Moore R.L., Hawkinson L.B., and Levin M.E., "PICON Expert System for Process Control", in Expert Systems and their Applications, Avignon , (Agence de l'Informatique, Paris, France, 1985) , pp 59 - 65.

[49] Spang Robinson , "The Spang Robinson Report on Artificial Intelligence, Vol 3, No 14, December 1987

[50] Sheil B., "The Artificial Intelligence Tool Box", in Reitman W., (ed.), Artificial Intelligence Application for Business, (Ablex , Norwood, New Jersey, USA, 1984), pp 287 - 295.

[51] Taunton J.C., "Real Time Process Management", in KBS 87, (Online Publications, London, 1987), pp 223 - 231.

[52] Leinweber D.L., and Gidwani K., "Real Time Expert System Development. Techniques and Applications", Robinson G.S., and Cook M.S., (eds.), Proc WESTEX-86, Anaheim, Calif., (IEEE Computer Society, Los Angeles, 1986), pp 69 - 77.

Topics in Expert System Design
G. Guida and C. Tasso (Editors)

EXPERT SYSTEM TOOL EVALUATION

Jeff ROTHENBERG

The RAND Corporation
Santa Monica, CA, USA

1. Introduction

The expert system paradigm has spawned a host of new "expert system tools" (or "shells") for building expert systems. The proliferation of these tools can be very confusing to a system developer or project manager who must decide which (if any) tool to use for building a new expert system. The tools are typically large, complex systems themselves, requiring major investments of time, money and effort to acquire, learn and use. Even developers with considerable experience in building traditional systems may feel understandably lost when confronted with this new paradigm. It is therefore important to develop guidelines for evaluating and choosing expert system tools. Evaluation requires discovering which tool characteristics are best suited to accomplishing a given task.

This paper presents a framework of evaluation criteria and a methodology for selecting an expert system tool, given a task. This summarizes the results of a study reported in Rothenberg, et al. [1]. The framework is adaptable to fit virtually any domain, problem and set of available tools, but it is only a starting point: it must evolve as the field and the tools mature. The methodology applies this framework to select the most appropriate tool (or tools) for a given task; it is intended to be general enough to apply to any problem and any potential set of tools for the foreseeable future (recognizing that this is rarely very long in computer science).

In addition, the framework reveals the strengths and weaknesses of individual tools and of the current generation of available tools in general. It therefore serves as an indicator of the maturity of the field and as a guide for designing improved tools and for choosing promising areas for research.

Evaluation can never be entirely mechanical. The skills and knowledge of the expert system developer will have a significant effect on the outcome; but the framework and methodology presented here should provide a point of departure.

The next section provides background for the framework and methodology presented in Sections 3 and 4. Section 5 presents conclusions.

2. Background

This section defines some terminology, discusses recent surveys of expert system tools, and provides motivation for the evaluation framework presented in the next section.

The term **expert system** is used here to mean any system built with a knowledge-based approach, i.e., utilizing expert knowledge applied to difficult, real world problems. The term **expert system tool** (or simply **tool**) is used to mean any software intended to help design, build, field (i.e., deliver to the end-users' environment) or maintain an expert system. This is taken to comprise not only the software environment but more generally all aspects of the software entity and its use, including training, documentation, ease of use, vendor support, cost, etc. This broad viewpoint is necessary to evaluate tools in a meaningful way; for example, the viability of the company supporting a tool may be just as important as the concrete functionality of the tool.

The terms **tool developer** and **expert system developer** are used to distinguish the builders of a tool from its users. The term **user** is used to mean the user of a tool, while the term **end-user** is used to mean the user of the target expert system produced with a tool. The term **development environment** is used to mean the environment in which a tool is used to design and implement an expert system. The expert system developed with a tool and delivered to its end-users is referred to as the **target (expert) system**, and the environment in which it runs is referred to as the **target** or **delivery environment**.

Many recent studies have addressed the evaluation of expert system tools and technology. They fall into four broad categories, as follows.

Catalogs of tools. Bundy [2] provides a catalog of over 250 software products and AI techniques. Waterman [3] gives short descriptions of over

95 tools and offers insight into the understanding and selection of tools. Walker and Miller's book [4] provides short descriptions of more than 70 tools and is updated yearly.

Feature comparisons across large numbers of tools. Gevarter [5] identifies the features of tools that are important for solving certain types of problems and compares 20 tools with respect to features and problem types. Gilmore and Howard [6] identify important criteria for the selection of both large and small-scale tools. Harmon and King [7] organize tools into classes, evaluate 17 tools with respect to knowledge representation and inference and control strategies, and identify the best tools for particular problem types.

Detailed comparisons of tools that fall into the same class. The monthly newsletter "Expert Systems Strategies" edited by Harmon [8] reviews expert systems by categories. The volume addressing PC tools evaluates 8 tools across a number of characteristics and presents a technique for deriving the value of small tools for practical business applications on the IBM-PC™. Beach [9] compares KEE™, ART™, S.1™, and KnowledgeCraft™ by implementing the same prototype problem with each tool. Richer [10] also compares these four tools and develops five criteria for evaluating tools: basic features, development environment, functionality, support, and cost.

Comparisons of tools with respect to an application area. Culbert [11] determines the tool features most critical to NASA expert system development projects and evaluates 16 tools with respect to those features. Mayer et al. [12] define expert system tool capabilities required by the specific needs of manufacturing applications and identify shortcomings of existing tools in order to direct research toward developing new tools. They also discuss the issues to be considered in deciding to acquire an expert system tool and in selecting the proper tool. Wall et al. [13] compare KEE, ART, and KnowledgeCraft with respect to those tool characteristics most critical to a Navy command and control system, by implementing a prototype problem.

Some of these studies (Beach, Gilmore, Harmon, Harmon and King, Richer, Ruby) evaluate tools in the abstract. This is not well suited to choosing a tool for a particular application, since it does not focus on the aspects of the tool and its environment that are relevant to a specific application. This type of evaluation also quickly becomes outdated; tool developers can release new versions of tools faster than new studies can be performed and published. Many studies (Beach, Culbert, Gevarter, Mayer, Wall) develop lists of tool features or capabilities that are relevant to a particular application or class of applications and then rate how well each tool supports each needed feature or capability. The value of such studies depends on the extent to which they focus on capabilities of tools rather than features, as discussed below.

Expert system tools include very high level programming languages called **knowledge engineering languages** and an assortment of support facilities such as debugging aids, explanation facilities, run-time data acquisition facilities, and knowledge base editors. They provide convenient ways to represent and organize complex, high-level concepts from the domain. Barr and Feigenbaum [14] summarize the standard set of knowledge representation techniques. The representations most widely used in current expert system tools are **rules** and **frames**.

Although general definitions of these techniques are widely accepted, there are many shades of meaning and variations in their specific application and interpretation. For example, in KEE, frames are called **units**, properties of units are called **slots**, and properties of slots are called **facets**. In S.1 on the other hand, frames are called **classes**, properties of classes are called **attributes**, and properties of attributes are called **slots**. Similarly, a **rule** in ROSIE™ is not the same as a **rule** in ART, and both of these are different from a **rule** in RuleMaster™. The presence of a given feature name in a tool's documentation is not sufficient to conclude that the tool supports the representational paradigm normally denoted by that name.

The value of feature comparison for expert system tools is therefore limited by the lack of meaning behind these feature names and the tendency to focus on superficial aspects that miss the essential issues. Furthermore, enumerations of current features (e.g., "backward chaining") are of short-lived value and may not apply to future tools. It is important to focus on the capabilities these features provide (e.g., "goal-directed reasoning") instead of the features *per se*. These capabilities are themselves an evolving set, but they are at a higher semantic level than features and should follow a slower obsolescence curve.

The framework presented below shares many elements with the studies cited above, but it adds three additional dimensions: metrics, assessment techniques, and contexts. Rather than comparing features of tools in the abstract, it recommends using specific assessment techniques to evaluate specific metrics of the capabilities of various tools in a particular context, given the relevant characteristics of the application. Though the additional dimensions make evaluation more complex, they also make it more meaningful and therefore more useful.

3. The Tool Evaluation Framework

Evaluating and choosing a tool involves more than "matching a tool to a problem", as is often suggested. It must include all aspects of the problem domain, the problem itself, and the anticipated project, i.e., "matching a tool to *its intended use*". This section presents a framework for performing expert system tool evaluation. Section 4 presents a methodology for using this framework.

The framework and methodology are intended to apply both to existing tools and to new tools as they appear; for example, they allow for tool capabilities that are not present in any current tools. Similarly, they are intended to apply to a number of tasks including: evaluating and selecting tools, comparing tools, designing tool enhancements, suggesting future generation tools, and focusing research in expert system technology.

Although the framework includes a large number of criteria, these can be pruned by identifying items of particular significance to a project. Furthermore, most of the dimensions can be prioritized. Pruning and prioritizing should make evaluation manageable. This is discussed further in Section 4.

3.1. Framework Overview

Tool evaluation involves five distinct dimensions:

Application Characteristics
Tool Capabilities
Metrics
Assessment Techniques
Contexts

Application Characteristics represent the problem, its domain, and the project; Tool Capabilities represent the functionality of the tools being considered; Metrics represent measures for evaluating the capabilities of tools; Assessment Techniques represent ways of applying metrics; Contexts represent the different requirements for using a tool in different phases of expert system development.

These dimensions are used in the following way to evaluate a tool for building a given application:

> *Given the relevant* ***application characteristics****, apply* ***metrics*** *by means of* ***assessment techniques*** *to evaluate particular* ***capabilities*** *of a tool in particular* ***contexts****.*

A concrete example of evaluating a single aspect of a single tool might be:

> *A two person-year project is proposed to develop an expert system to locate spills in a chemical plant. Application characteristics include the size and experience of the development team, their computing environment and funding level, the expected end-users and delivery environment, and all relevant problem and problem domain constraints. Evaluate the flexibility of tool X's knowledge acquisition capabilities in the development context, by analyzing case studies.*

The schema shown in Figure 1 summarizes the above. It is to be read as a sentence.

Use an **assessment technique**
to evaluate a **metric**
of a tool's **capability**
in a **context**
given the **application characteristics**.

Figure 1: Evaluation Schema

The following discusses these dimensions in detail, presenting a rationale for those criteria to be considered. These criteria represent only a starting point; they must be pruned and extended as appropriate for a given evaluation.

One particularly crucial concept, namely *integration*, straddles the framework. It can be viewed as an application characteristic (e.g., requiring integration of a tool into the development environment, or of the target expert system into the delivery environment), a tool capability (e.g., supporting the integration of expert systems into existing environments), or a metric to be applied to other tool capabilities (e.g., measuring how well a tool's representational paradigms are integrated). Integration is a multi-faceted concern that pervades tool evaluation.

3.2. Application Characteristics

This dimension represents the impact of the application on tool evaluation. Though the problem domain and problem may be ill-defined, it is crucial to determine as many of the following characteristics as possible to derive appropriate requirements and constraints.

This dimension overlaps traditional requirements analysis; the following focuses on those aspects that are unique or crucial to expert system development.

- Application Characteristics
  - Problem Characteristics
    - Problem Domain
      - Kinds of knowledge
      - Constraints
    - Problem to be solved within the domain
      - Special processing/knowledge/representation
      - Problem type
      - Other problem attributes
    - Knowledge Acquisition/Expertise
      - Characteristics and constraints
    - Target Environment
      - Constraints
      - End-users
  - Project Characteristics
    - Scope
      - Goals and budget
    - Development Environment
      - Constraints
    - Development Team
      - Characteristics

3.2.1. Problem Characteristics

Developing an expert system involves many tasks beyond analyzing the problem and solving it. These include identifying experts and other sources of expertise in the domain, acquiring and validating the required knowledge, identifying and understanding end-users and their environment, and organizing and managing the development effort. As a concrete example,

Figure 2 shows some problem characteristics of the NEOMYCIN system (Clancey [15]; Hasling, Clancey, and Rennels [16]).

Problem Domain
  Infectious Blood Diseases.
  Medical knowledge: relating infecting organisms with patient history, symptoms, and laboratory test results; drug treatment procedures; diagnostic problem-solving methods.
Problem to be solved within the domain
  Diagnosis of and therapy recommendation for hospital patients with bacteremia, meningitis, and cystitis infections. Also intended to use knowledge-base for teaching medical students.
Knowledge Sources
  Existing MYCIN knowledge base; medical practitioners/diagnosticians; medical textbooks.
Target Environment
  End-Users: Physicians; Medical students.

Figure 2: Problem Characteristics of the NEOMYCIN System

Many of the requirements for a target expert system imply requirements for the tool used in building it. For example, the ability to implement a given end-user interface for the target system may be sharply constrained by the tool used. Similarly, issues such as portability of the target system or its ability to integrate with existing databases, software, or hardware may derive requirements for the tool. Though many of the issues discussed here should be obvious to anyone with extensive design experience, they are included for completeness and as an aid for those who may not have such experience.

Few expert system development efforts are well formulated in advance. Expert system technology comes into its own in situations where the problem domain is complex, domain knowledge and expertise are ambiguous, and the problem itself can only be understood after considerable exploration and experimentation, possibly involving several iterations of prototyping and design.

This produces a chicken-and-egg problem: choosing an appropriate tool can only be done after understanding the requirements imposed by the problem, but this may only be possible after experimenting and building a prototype expert system, which requires choosing a tool. In some cases it may be necessary to choose an initial tool for experimental purposes and then choose a (possibly different) tool based on what is learned from prototyping. Choosing different tools for prototyping and development (for example) might also result from different requirements for these phases of a project, rather than from a change of direction produced by the refinement of requirements during the prototype phase. This is discussed further under Project Characteristics. Similarly, it is possible that no single tool will handle all aspects of a problem, requiring multiple tools to be used and interfaced. However, the investment required to use multiple tools makes it impractical in many cases.

Expert system tools may also be evaluated without a specific problem—or even a specific domain—in mind. Many organizations are exploring the technology simply to understand it and to see whether it is applicable to any relevant problems. In these cases, the domain and problem characteristics may be indirectly determined by the selection of a particular tool.

Problem Domain. The kinds of knowledge and processing that characterize a domain may provide useful criteria for choosing among tools. For example, applications in earth science or military simulation may require spatial reasoning; financial or legal applications may require strict accountability; and process control, nuclear power or space systems may have real-time and critical reliability requirements.

In some cases a tool may incorporate specific mechanisms and knowledge oriented toward a particular domain. For example, a tool for building financial expert systems might incorporate concepts and computational techniques such as tax tables or amortization algorithms. Similarly, some existing tools are tailored toward process control and real-time data acquisition, whereas some provide automated rule induction for domains where expertise consists of examples rather than explicit rules. New tools may emerge with utility packages or knowledge bases tailored to specific domains. Pre-packaged domain knowledge of this kind may become an important consideration in choosing a tool, just as the availability of subroutine libraries for statistics, graphics, or database access is a consideration in choosing a programming language.

Problem to be solved within the domain. The problem to be solved may involve special kinds of knowledge, processing or representational requirements that may lead to special requirements for a tool. The problem also establishes requirements and constraints for the capacity, performance and delivered cost of the target system, as well as for its availability, reliability, robustness, and maintainability.

Many problems require that a target expert system communicate and integrate with special databases, software, and hardware (e.g., sensors or effectors) in the target environment. This can be crucial due to the difficulty of building such interfaces.

It is tempting to try to characterize a problem according to its "type" (e.g., diagnosis, classification, planning, etc.), but most problems consist of combinations of such types. For example, since many expert system tools evolved from early research in medical diagnosis, there has been a tendency to think of diagnosis as a coherent problem type, spanning many domains. Whether this is more than superficially true is questionable. Nevertheless, an appropriate taxonomy of primitive types might prove useful in selecting tools. An attempt to define such a taxonomy is currently underway in the research community (see, for example, Chandrasekaran [17]), but results so far are inconclusive.

Additional problem attributes that should be considered include: expected complexity and storage requirements; operational constraints such as execution speed, real-time requirements, compatibility requirements, physical environment, hardware portability requirements, or the need for formal verification or proof of correctness; and formal properties such as decomposability, the degree to which the problem lends itself to algorithmic vs. heuristic solution, and symbolic or numeric requirements.

User-machine interaction is also important both in terms of the required tool interface for the expert system developer and the required tool support for building the end-user interface for the target expert system. The degree of autonomy of the target system (i.e., whether it is to be used as a decision aid or as an autonomous controller) also affects its end-user interface requirements.

Knowledge Acquisition/Expertise. It is important to identify any special characteristics or constraints that may apply to knowledge acquisition or the sources of expertise in the application domain, including the need for multiple knowledge sources or coordination of multiple knowledge bases.

Target Environment. The target environment for an expert system determines its delivery hardware and its need to integrate with existing hardware, software, databases and networks. It also establishes requirements and constraints for the capacity, performance and delivered cost of the target system, as well as its availability, reliability, robustness and maintainability. Similarly, the characteristics of the expected end-users of the target system (their level of experience with computers, domain expertise, educational background, etc.) determine user interface and explanation requirements for the target system and therefore for the tool.

3.2.2. Project Characteristics

These include characteristics of the expert system project, its development environment and its development team.

Scope. The scope, goals and budget of an expert system effort are the most important factors in determining what kind of system will be built, and therefore what kind of tool is required. In particular, the scope of a project will determine which phases are targeted (e.g., prototyping, development, etc.), as represented by the context dimension discussed later in this section.

Most expert system tools provide support for the entire process of building and delivering expert systems, but a given project may focus on certain phases of the process. For example, if a project is concerned with prototyping a system, or showing the feasibility of a solution to a problem, or exploring representations without producing a running system, then a tool might be chosen for maximum representational flexibility and ease of building prototypes, with no emphasis on large-scale development support or delivery to end-user environments.

On the other hand, if a project has already defined its problem and already has a representation or even a knowledge base, then a tool might be chosen to launch a development and delivery effort, without concern for knowledge acquisition or prototyping. The phase or phases targeted may also interact with problem characteristics as well as project characteristics. For example, the prototyping phase focuses on sources of expertise and problem formulation, whereas the fielding phase is concerned with robustness, integration, performance and end-user interfaces.

Closely tied to scope is the question of budget. Ideally, more powerful tools allow a given expenditure of effort and money to produce more results, but the tools themselves cost money and time to learn and use effectively. Especially for the first project using a given tool, the cost of climbing this learning curve limits the scope that can be undertaken within a given budget. Cost is often an overriding (or at least vetoing) factor in choosing a tool. Well-funded projects tend to consider only high-end tools, under the assumption that these will deliver the greatest power. Low-budget efforts tend to consider only low-end tools, either because they are the only ones affordable, or under the assumption that the greater power of a more expensive tool will not be worth its greater cost.

Development Environment. The development environment delimits the hardware and software on which a tool must run as well as the network and database interfaces it must provide during development. These factors may be given, or a project may have some control over them (i.e., be free to choose hardware based on the preferred tools).

Development Team. The composition of the development team must also be taken into account. If the team is large, the cost of bringing all the developers up the learning curve for a tool may be prohibitive. Similarly, the size of the team may generate requirements for a tool to support cooperative development, configuration management, shared databases, etc.

The background, preferences and previous experience of the team is also important, and will become increasingly so as tools begin to accrue significant user communities. Though not always homogeneous across the team, this "mindset" is often a determining factor in the choice of a tool in cases where an existing team has strong preferences. Similarly, characteristics of the knowledge engineering team (such as their computer sophistication) will affect the kinds of tool support required for knowledge acquisition.

3.3. Tool Capabilities

The tools currently on the market provide many features supporting a wide range of capabilities. In addition, there are a number of other desirable capabilities, some of which are provided to a certain extent by some existing tools while others are merely wishful thinking.

It is important to focus on the capabilities of a tool, rather than the specific features the tool provides for achieving (or "supporting") those capabilities. (For example, a tool may support the capability of representing object type hierarchies by means of different features, such as frames or rules.) Focusing on capabilities emphasizes the functionality of a tool rather than the specific implementation of that functionality. Users generally require a particular capability without caring which features are used to provide it.

As expert system technology and its tools evolve, the list of relevant capabilities will evolve and expand with it. This is therefore a very dynamic dimension. The following is a list of examples of capabilities and representative features that support them. This list is far from exhaustive, and the examples of supporting features are merely illustrative; many additional features supporting these capabilities can be found in current tools.

Capability	Examples of Supporting Features
Arithmetic processing	*arithmetic operators, extended floating point*
Certainty handling	*certainty factors, fuzzy logic*
Concurrency	*distributed processing, parallel processing*
Consistency checking	*knowledge base syntax checking*
Documenting development	*assumption/rationale history, code/data annotation*
Explanation	*execution trace, knowledge base browsing*
Inference & control	*iteration, forward/backward chaining, inheritance*
Integration	*calling other languages, interprocess calls*
Internal access	*tool parameter setting functions, source code*
Knowledge acquisition	*rule induction, model building aids*
Knowledge-base editing	*structure editors, graphic rule lattice*
Life Cycle	*tool support for target system life cycle support*
Meta-knowledge	*rules controlling inference, self-organizing data*
Optimization	*intelligent look-ahead, caching, rule compilation*
Presentation (I/O)	*text, graphics, windows, forms, mouse*
Representation	*rules, frames, procedures, objects, simulation*

The set of capabilities relevant to a given evaluation must be identified on the basis of the given application characteristics. This dimension will therefore normally be filled in only after analyzing the application characteristics of the task at hand.

3.4. Metrics

Metrics are applied to particular capabilities of a tool using the assessment techniques described later in this section. The aggregated metrics shown here capture most of the relevant qualities of a tool in a relatively small number of measures. Explicit metrics allow analyzing tools in depth by looking at different facets (such as the flexibility, efficiency, or ease of use) of their capabilities, rather than evaluating them according to a single measure.

The aggregate metrics are:

Cost
Flexibility
Extensibility
Clarity
Efficiency
Vendor Support

The "Relative Importance of Metrics across Development Phases" shown in Figure 3 suggests the qualitative relationships of importance for five of these six metrics (excluding cost, which behaves rather differently). The graph shows typical relationships among these metrics, though these relationships may vary for different projects. The following paragraphs discuss these metrics and their relative importance.

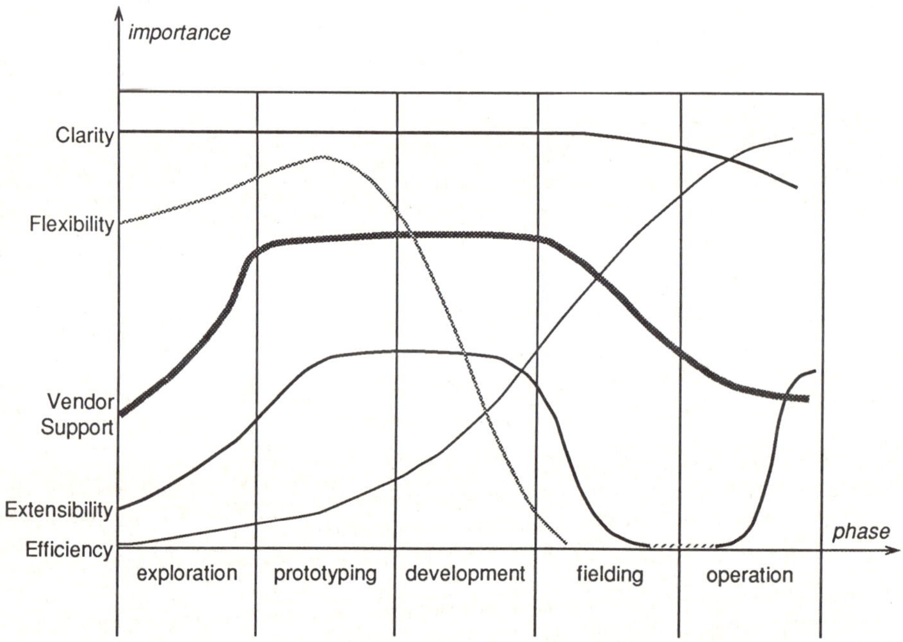

Figure 3: Relative Importance of Metrics across Development Phases

Cost includes hidden expenses such as costs of training and integration, as well as the purchase price and support costs of a tool. Cost may be in terms of money, person-power, machinery, supplies, computation used, elapsed time, etc. The importance of cost is felt throughout the life cycle, but for evaluation purposes its relevance peaks at the transitions between phases, where a project either commits to switching tools or stays with what it has. For this reason it has been omitted from Figure 3.

Flexibility includes representational power (data structures and reasoning mechanisms), adequacy to the given task or tasks, breadth of applicability, and sophistication. Note that flexibility may be antithetical to clarity (e.g., maintainability). Flexibility is most important in the initial stages of tool use, peaking during the prototyping phase. As implementation decisions get locked in, flexibility decreases in importance and may actually become a negative factor in later phases as the need for maintainability leads to the requirement that the system be stable.

Extensibility includes breadth of applicability, access to system parameters, defeatability (i.e., the ease with which system parameters or functions can be overridden), ease of integration, portability, scalability, and subsetability. Extensibility peaks during design and implementation, and decreases in importance during fielding, by which time the system should be fairly stable. Its importance may rise again later if maintenance requires new extensions or reintegration.

Clarity includes the ease of understanding and using a tool, cognitive efficiency (i.e., how many concepts must be kept in mind to use the tool), maintainability, modularity, learnability, coherence of the tool's features, and how appropriately the tool responds. Clarity is important in all phases, and its sacrifice can only be justified once the system is operational, if the need for performance (efficiency) becomes dominant.

Efficiency includes speed of response and utilization of computational and memory resources. During development, the efficiency of a tool manifests itself in terms of compilation speed, response time and knowledge base memory requirements, all of which impact the development process. However, the ability of a tool to produce an efficient target system tends to overshadow the efficiency of the tool itself. The importance of efficiency therefore tends to remain low until the target system is operational, though there are cases in which it may be crucial from the start of a project (i.e., for efficient development).

Vendor Support includes vendor philosophy, system availability, reliability, portability, and robustness. The importance of vendor support rises as users begin to learn a tool, and stays high until the target system has been delivered, at which point the burden of support shifts to the target system developer who must generally support the delivered system for its end-users.

3.5. Assessment Techniques

For some metrics, assessment techniques seem obvious and straightforward. Evaluating the initial cost of a tool, for example, is simply a matter of asking for its price; however, even in this highly quantitative realm, evaluating learning cost, long-term cost or cost-effectiveness is often far from trivial. Similarly, feature comparison is often performed by simply asking whether a tool has a given feature. Vendor sales departments encourage this technique by publishing checklists of features for their products. However, as pointed out above, this kind of comparison can be quite misleading.

There is a great deal of suspicion about any measurement technique that claims to be objective, especially if it is also quantitative. For example, performance benchmarks tend to be resisted by tool developers and users alike as being too easily "faked" or distorted by implementing special shortcuts or "comparing apples and oranges that are both named tangerines" (e.g., showing relative speeds for processing "rules", where the granularity and power of a rule may vary widely among tools).

The assessment techniques suggested here do not attempt to produce quantitative measures, but instead produce textual results. When a metric is applied using one of these techniques, the result will require intelligent interpretation. This is an advantage, rather than a disadvantage, since it gives the decision maker valuable information.

The assessment techniques that seem the most promising are:

Direct comparisons
Benchmarks
Interviews, questionnaires and personal advice
Library of case studies and development efforts
Knowledge-based system for tool evaluation

3.5.1. Direct comparisons

Direct comparisons among tools can be valuable, provided that they focus on corresponding capabilities of tools and that they make explicit the ways in which these capabilities are different or incomparable. Comparison with an abstract standard or with "conventional" AI approaches (e.g., using LISP or Prolog) may also be useful.

3.5.2. Benchmarks

In the expert system context, this should *not* mean a quantitative performance measure such as how fast a tool can run the Sieve of Eratosthenes, or a feature-based comparison such as how many rules a tool can process per second. Instead, a benchmark should be a well-formulated statement of a more or less fragmentary problem. Ideally, for each tool under consideration, the solution of the benchmark (or the impossibility thereof) should be published along with any relevant performance data or development statistics.

Benchmarks can be small or large. Small benchmarks need not have much data associated with them: the style of the published solution constitutes the result. Larger benchmarks can include performance data or statistics, such as the time required to implement a solution using a given tool, but the emphasis should still be on the content and style of the published solution: the evaluator should always be responsible for interpreting any numeric data in terms of the quality of the solution.

Small benchmark problems can be used to compare specific capabilities of tools (for example, testing how well a tool can represent a class hierarchy), provided they are interpreted on the basis of the style of their solutions rather than their performance. Implementing larger benchmarks using a number of different tools may be warranted prior to a major tool commitment. The key to the success of benchmarks is to formulate problems that are specific but do not require a particular implementation.

3.5.3. Additional techniques

Interviews, questionnaires and personal advice from other developers, tool users and colleagues can provide useful information which is often more credible than the results of formal evaluation studies. A library of case studies and expert system development efforts can be a valuable source of evaluation data, if it can be (a) large enough to be representative, (b) kept up to date as tools evolve and experiences change, and (c) accessible by a wide range of potential tool users and indexed according to application characteristics.

A knowledge-based system for tool evaluation could be used to recommend relevant criteria or to help synthesize a decision based on the results of evaluating various tools according to various criteria. Though a general purpose system of this kind is unlikely to be feasible for some time, an organization engaged in choosing tools on a recurring basis in a relatively constrained domain may be able to formalize some of its evaluation expertise in an expert system of this kind.

3.6. Contexts

This dimension represents the contexts in which a tool can be used. Each context is named for the development phase in which it is dominant, but a given context may apply across several development stages: for example, tool requirements for "fielding" may be felt early in the conceptual design stage of a project. Representing these contexts as a separate dimension emphasizes this independence and allows applying the concerns of each context (and the resulting tool evaluation criteria) to all stages of development. Delimiting contexts as a fixed set of points must not obscure the transitions between development phases, which can be just as important as the phases themselves.

The evaluation contexts that are relevant to a given development effort are derived from the project scope and the problem to be solved. The potential contexts (and development phases) are:

Conceptualization
Prototyping
Development
Fielding
Operation/Maintenance

Conceptualization emphasizes a tool's support for conceptualizing, formalizing and decomposing a problem, and for identifying and organizing key concepts and defining the problem's scope. This may involve exploration of feasible approaches and representations as well as conceptual design.

Prototyping emphasizes a tool's facilities for guiding rapid development, eliciting different approaches and representations, and quickly trying alternative implementations.

Development considers a tool as it is used to develop an expert system. The tool's support for software development (including debugging facilities, configuration management, etc.) are emphasized here.

Fielding emphasizes a tool's facilities for porting from the development environment to the delivery environment and for integration and end-user interface support.

Operation/Maintenance emphasizes a tool's support for the performance, maintainability and supportability of target expert systems in their delivery environments.

4. Methodology

The framework presented in Section 3 can be applied to a particular evaluation task by means of the steps shown in Figure 4. Though many tool evaluation studies use an implicit methodology (such as "rate the tools with respect to these criteria, weight the criteria, and use this to choose a tool"), the explicit and objective methodology presented here avoids prejudice and browbeating. The steps of this methodology are examined in detail, following some caveats.

1. Determine application characteristics.
2. Identify relevant contexts.
3. Derive relevant tool capabilities.
4. Identify discriminating metrics & assessment techniques.
5. Identify available tools.
6. Filter available tools to identify candidate tools.
7. Prune & prioritize each framework dimension.
8. Apply the framework schema to evaluate & select tools.

Figure 4: Evaluation Methodology

4.1. Evaluation Caveats

There are several questions that should be asked prior to performing an evaluation. If satisfactory answers cannot be found, the validity of the evaluation process may be impugned.

(1) Does the evaluation have an identified **consumer**?

Evaluations for use by managers, technical staff or end-users will each have different requirements. The eventual consumer of the evaluation should be identified at an early stage to avoid producing superfluous or misleading results.

(2) Will the evaluation be impartial and objective?

Though impartiality may be relative to the needs of the consumer, it is nevertheless important to ask whether those performing the evaluation can be expected to be impartial. Intentional biases should be made explicit to avoid an evaluation's being used by unwitting consumers.

For all but the most informal purposes, evaluation must be objective if it is to have any credibility. This requires that priorities, importance weights and evaluation algorithms be established in advance, if at all possible, by domain experts or other disinterested parties who are not prejudiced as to the outcome of the selection process. Once weights and algorithms have been chosen, they should be considered inviolable unless they are found to be untenable, in which case they should be formally redefined or relaxed. An evaluation in which such initial decisions are never made or are relaxed whenever they become inconvenient or are subjected to pressure is a meaningless exercise.

(3) How will the evaluation be monitored for accuracy or bias?

In other words, who evaluates the evaluator? If no such monitoring is to be performed, the consumer should be made aware of the possibility of errors and biases.

(4) Will the evaluation be timely?

The evaluation process must be designed to deliver its results in time to be of use. Since tools evolve rapidly, the results of an evaluation may quickly become obsolete unless precautions are taken to update them. It is important to make explicit mention of versions and release dates of the tools evaluated, to give consumers of the evaluation an explicit basis for judging its timeliness.

4.2. The Eightfold Path to Evaluation

In this section, we examine the eight steps listed in Figure 4 for performing tool evaluation and selection.

Step 1: Determine application characteristics

Even though the application domain and problem may be ill-defined, it is necessary to determine the application characteristics as far as possible, since the required tool capabilities are largely derived from these characteristics. It is equally important to determine project characteristics at this point, defining the goals, scope and budget of the development effort, and characterizing the development team and development environment. The scope of the project determines the contexts to be targeted, whereas the development team and environment supply additional constraints for tool selection.

Application characteristics should be weighted as to certitude and importance. The scope and goals of a project will determine which characteristics of the problem and domain represent obligatory requirements and which ones are negotiable.

Step 2: Identify relevant contexts

The contexts targeted for a project supply the other major factor for determining required tool capabilities. It is particularly important here to be realistic about which phases of development are to be undertaken. Targeting only the initial exploratory or prototyping phases may lead to choosing a tool that encounters a dead end if the development process is extended into later phases. On the other hand, targeting all phases when only some of them are likely to be undertaken will overconstrain the selection process.

Step 3: Derive relevant tool capabilities

The tool capabilities are derived from the application characteristics and the relevant contexts. It is important to weight these capabilities along a scale from *required* to *desired*, for use in filtering the available tools in Step 6. These weights are derived from the application characteristic weights determined in Step 1.

Step 4: Identify discriminating metrics & assessment techniques

It will often be the case that certain metrics, such as cost, may have high discriminating (or vetoing) power in choosing a tool. If there are any such metrics for a project, they should be identified here, along with the best available assessment techniques for applying them in this early stage of the evaluation (there may be better assessment techniques that are not available at this stage due to the cost or time required to apply them). If no such discriminating metrics are appropriate for a project, this step has no effect.

Step 5: Identify available tools

This step may necessarily involve some implicit filtering, since it is difficult to find all available tools, but it is desirable to make this survey as complete as possible, filtering explicitly in Step 6 instead.

Step 6: Filter available tools to identify candidate tools

Using the *required* capabilities derived in Step 3 and the discriminating metrics (if any) identified in Step 4, the available tools are filtered to produce a set of candidate tools to be evaluated in further detail.

Step 7: Prune & prioritize each framework dimension

Each dimension of the framework should be pruned to eliminate irrelevant or inapplicable criteria, and the remaining items should be prioritized or weighted. Attempting this prioritization earlier in the process would be difficult due to lack of focus. At this point enough should be known about the application characteristics, contexts, capabilities and available tools to prioritize each framework dimension separately. For example, if cost filtering has already resulted in a set of candidate tools whose costs are very similar, then using cost as a high-priority metric at this stage would be ineffectual.

In most cases, strict prioritization will be inappropriate. For example, cost might be a more important metric than efficiency, but a *very* efficient tool might be worth *some* extra cost. Therefore "prioritization" is intended in a general sense here, meaning that weights are assigned to the items in a dimension to reflect their relative importance within that dimension.

With one exception, each dimension should be prioritized in terms of the expected importance and relevance of each item in that dimension. The "Assessment Techniques" dimension is somewhat different: these techniques must also be prioritized in terms of their availability, applicability, timeliness, cost, and believability by the intended consumers of the evaluation.

Step 8: Apply the framework schema to evaluate & select tools

Finally, the prioritized dimensions are applied to the candidate tools using the schema shown in Figure 1. That is, the appropriate assessment techniques are used to evaluate the relevant metrics applied to each capability of a particular tool in each context, given the relevant application characteristics. Since the dimensions have already been pruned prior to this step, the cross-product of evaluations to be performed here will be minimal (i.e., as small as possible, though not necessarily small). There may still be a large number of individual evaluations required, but this is unavoidable.

The thoroughness and formality with which these evaluations are made (and with which their weighted results are combined and compared in order to select a tool or tools) is left to the discretion of the evaluators and the consumers of the evaluation. In some cases it may be preferable to display multi-dimensional heterogeneous results like these by means of a graphic presentation mechanism such as the Colored Scorecard Technique described in Goeller, et al. [18] and Miser and Quade [19].

As noted previously, the credibility of an evaluation depends on how formally and objectively it is done. This methodology is not intended to tell developers how to interpret the results of their evaluations, but simply to produce useful data for their decisions.

5. Conclusions

The multitude of tools supporting the new expert system paradigm makes it important to develop guidelines for evaluating these tools and choosing among them. Evaluating and choosing a tool requires "matching a tool to *its intended use*", including all aspects of the problem domain, the problem itself, and the anticipated project.

Due to the evolving and inconsistent terminology in this new field, comparing features of different tools is of limited utility (and limited longevity). Instead, the capabilities provided by these features must be analyzed, evaluated, and compared. The framework presented above shows how to use specific assessment techniques to apply specific metrics to specific capabilities of a tool for a specific application in a specific context. The associated methodology shows how to perform this evaluation in an objective way.

Expert system development is first and foremost *software engineering*. This is reflected in the importance of such issues as integration, database access, portability, fielding, maintainability, robustness, reliability, concurrent access, performance, user interface, debugging support and documentation. The relationship between expert system development and software engineering is symbiotic. The new paradigm has already made at least two significant contributions to the traditional software engineering discipline. First, it has shown how to encode knowledge explicitly and declaratively rather than implicitly and procedurally, thereby making programs more understandable and maintainable. Second, it has pioneered the new software development strategy of prototyping and refinement, as opposed to the traditional cycle of specification, design and implementation.

Though the difficulty of comparing and selecting tools may be daunting to a developer faced with a decision, this difficulty is largely a result of the richness of the field and the bewildering pace at which new ideas are being incorporated into tools. The evaluation approach presented here is offered, not as a final answer to a fixed problem, but as a strategy for dealing with a dynamic problem whose complexity reflects the health of a research area whose impact on software engineering is only beginning to be felt.

REFERENCES

[1] Rothenberg, J.G., J. Paul, I. Kameny, J.R. Kipps, M. Swenson, *Evaluating Expert System Tools: A Framework and Methodology*, The RAND Corporation, R-3542-DARPA, 1987.

[2] Bundy, A. (ed.), *Catalogue of Artificial Intelligence Tools*, Second Revised Edition, Springer-Verlag, New York, 1986.

[3] Waterman, D. A., *A Guide to Expert Systems*, The Teknowledge Series in Knowledge Engineering, Addison-Wesley, Reading, Massachusetts, 1986.

[4] Walker, T. C., and R. K. Miller, "Tools for Building Expert Systems", Chapter 3 in *Expert Systems 1986*, SEAI Technical Publications, Madison, Georgia, 1986.

[5] Gevarter, W. B., *The Nature and Evaluation of Commercial Expert System Building Tools*, NASA, Ames Research Center, NASA Technical Memorandum 88331, June 1986.

[6] Gilmore, J. F., and C. Howard, "Expert System Tools for Practitioners", presented at the First Australian Artificial Intelligence Conference, Melbourne, Australia, November 1986.

[7] Harmon, P., and D. King, "Commercial Tools", Chapter 8 in *Expert Systems*, John Wiley and Sons, Inc., New York, 1985, pp. 92-133.

[8] Harmon, P. (ed.), *Expert Systems Strategies*, Arlington, MA, September 1985 through present time.

[9] Beach, S. S., "Evaluating Expert System Tools", *The Spang Robinson Report*, Volume 2, Number 10, October 1986, pp. 1-8.

[10] Richer, M. H., "An Evaluation of Expert System Development Tools", *Expert Systems*, Volume 3, Number 3, July 1986, p. 166-183.

[11] Culbert, C. J., *Expert System Building Tools*, NASA, Lyndon B. Johnson Space Center, FM7(86-19), February 11, 1986.

[12] Mayer, R. J., et al., *A Characterization of Expert System Development Tools for Manufacturing Applications*, Knowledge Based Systems Laboratory, Department of Industrial Engineering, Texas A&M University, June 10, 1986.

[13] Wall, R. S., et al., *An Evaluation of Commercial Expert System Building Tools*, Texas Instruments Inc., Computer Science Laboratory Technical Report 85-30, November 9, 1985.

[14] Barr, A., and E. A. Feigenbaum (eds.), *The Handbook of Artificial Intelligence*, Volume I, William Kaufmann, Inc., Los Altos, California, 1981.

[15] Clancey, W. J., *Methodology for Building an Intelligent Tutoring System*, Department of Computer Science, Stanford University, STAN-CS-81-894, October 1981.

[16] Hasling, D. W., W. J. Clancey, and G. Rennels, *Strategic Explanations for a Diagnostic Consultation System*, Department of Computer Science, Stanford University, STAN-CS-83-996, November 1983.

[17] Chandrasekaran, B., "Generic Tasks in Knowledge-Based Reasoning: High-Level Building Blocks for Expert System Design", *IEEE Expert*, Volume 1, Number 3, Fall 1986, pp. 23-30.

[18] Goeller, B. F., et al., *Protecting an Estuary from Floods—A Policy Analysis of the Oosterschede: Volume I, Summary Report*, The RAND Corporation, R-2121/1, December 1977, pp. 8-13 and 126-129.

[19] Miser, H. J., and E. S. Quade (eds.), *Handbook of Systems Analysis*, North-Holland, New York, 1985, pp. 89-109, 230-233.

PART 5

Knowledge acquisition and modeling

Topics in Expert System Design
G. Guida and C. Tasso (Editors)

COGNITIVE TASK ANALYSIS: AN APPROACH TO KNOWLEDGE ACQUISITION FOR INTELLIGENT SYSTEM DESIGN

Emilie M. ROTH (°) **and David D. WOODS** (°°)

Department of Engineering and Public Policy (°)
Carnegie-Mellon University
Pittsburgh, PA, USA

Department of Industrial and Systems Engineering (°°)
The Ohio State University
Columbus, OH, USA

1. INTRODUCTION

Advances in computational technology are making it possible to build intelligent machines that can apply rich knowledge and reasoning power to the solution of problems. While these tools create new opportunities for decision aiding, they create new challenges as well. Artificial Intelligence (AI) technology provides flexible mechanisms for knowledge representation and powerful problem-solving heuristics but is mute with respect to how these machine problem-solving capabilities should be deployed.

Questions such as what constitutes effective use of machine power (e.g., should the intelligent machine attempt to solve the problem for the user, or should it serve in a support staff role, compiling and synthesizing information for the human domain practitioner), and what knowledge is relevant to expert performance and advice, fall outside the purview of AI technology. There is a need to develop paradigms for effective intelligent decision support and methodologies for building these systems. These constitute important challenges for the field of *cognitive engineering*, which draws on knowledge and techniques of cognitive psychology and related disciplines to provide the basis for principle-driven design of person-machine systems (Norman, 1981; Woods & Roth, 1988a).

This paper examines issues in the design of intelligent systems from a cognitive engineering perspective. A primary underlying premise is that in real applications intelligent problem-solving systems almost always function as advisory or decision support systems that depend on substantial interaction with (and/or supervisory overview by) a human practitioner for effective performance. Few intelligent systems in actual operation function as true autonomous problem-solvers (e.g., autonomous vehicles that navigate without any human input or intervention). Most intelligent systems derive solutions through extensive interaction with a human practitioner (e.g., question/answer dialogue). Even in the case of systems that do not require extensive interaction with a person to generate outputs, such as R1 that configures VAX computers (Bachant & McDermott, 1984) and PDS that diagnoses turbine generators based on analysis of sensor data (Osborne, 1986), the intelligent machine outputs are treated as "recommendations" that need to be reviewed and approved by a human practitioner before being acted upon. These systems are properly viewed as a subset of advisory and decision support systems, and should be analyzed, built and evaluated from that perspective.

In this paper we discuss some of the common pitfalls that arise in building intelligent support systems and describe a pragmatic knowledge acquisition approach for defining and building effective intelligent support systems. An implicit assumption often made in building intelligent systems is that intelligent support is synonymous with outputting an "answer" -- that is solving the problem *for* the user. The primary design focus is on developing a stand-alone machine expert that can generate problem solutions. The guiding model is a human expert solving a problem in isolation. In this view the objective of knowledge acquisition is to collect and encode "nuggets" of knowledge elicited from the human expert with the ultimate goal of developing a system that can mimic how the human expert goes about solving the problem. We have seen many intelligent systems built using this approach in industry. While the system designers often succeeded in building small prototypes that could solve a narrow range of problems, in almost all cases the systems failed to handle a sufficiently broad range of problems to have practical impact, and the projects were ultimately abandoned. One of the main reasons the systems failed is that the designers took too narrow a view of the knowledge acquisition task. They focused on mimicking how experts solved specific problems rather than attempting to develop a formal specification of the range of problems that arise in the domain and the factors that contribute to problem difficulty.

In this paper we argue that knowledge acquisition for intelligent system development needs to be defined more broadly. From a cognitive engineering perspective, knowledge acquisition is first about understanding the factors that make problem-solving in the domain hard (for any agent -- human or machine) and how machine intelligence could be used to support task performance. Only after the problem space has been mapped out, do questions about what specific domain knowledge needs to be encoded in the machine expert and how that knowledge can most efficiently be obtained become relevant.

First, we describe some of the major shortcomings of systems that can occur when the designer focuses too narrowly on extracting specific bits of knowledge from domain experts. Second, we present an approach to knowledge acquisition based on a cognitive task analysis of the domain that we have developed and successfully applied in building intelligent support systems (e.g., Woods & Hollnagel, 1987; Roth & Woods, 1988; Woods & Roth, 1988b).

2. PITFALLS IN BUILDING INTELLIGENT SYSTEMS

We have had the opportunity to participate in and/or observe the development of several intelligent systems for industrial application. In some cases we participated in the design and building of the systems (e.g., Roth, Elias, Mauldin & Ramage, 1985; Roth & Woods, 1988; Woods & Roth, 1988b), in others we participated in evaluation of the systems (e.g., Roth, Bennett & Woods, 1987). Some of the projects succeeded and the systems are being commercialized, but in more cases the systems failed, in the sense that work never went beyond a demonstration system. This provided us with a unique opportunity to observe where and how things can go wrong in building intelligent systems for an actual application. This section reviews some of the major pitfalls.

2.1. Failing to Appreciate the Demands of the Task

One of the most common ways intelligent systems fail is that they are unable to solve a sufficiently large proportion of the hard problems that arise in the domain to have a practical impact. The weakness in performance is often due to an overreliance on an iterative refinement approach to developing the intelligent system knowledge base. Iterative refinement is one of the standard recommendations for how to build intelligent systems (Hayes-Roth, Waterman & Lenat, 1983). The strategy is to begin with a small set of example cases, discuss the cases with a human domain expert, and encode the rules the expert used to solve those cases in the AI system. The resulting knowledge base is then tested on a new set of cases. If problems in performance on the new test cases are found, the knowledge base is modified to resolve them, and the process then is repeated. The philosophy is that over time, as more cases are observed and the system is modified to handle them, the knowledge base will evolve to deal with all the major cases. While in principle, given enough time and cases, the iterative refinement technique could work, in practice it merely encourages a piecemeal approach to knowledge acquisition and is a major contributor to brittle machine problem-solvers. There are two main reasons for this. First, the amount of time and resources typically available for system development in industry does not allow for the long term evolution of systems entailed by the iterative refinement approach. There is pressure to put systems in the field early. Second, as experience with building intelligent systems has increased, there has been a growing realization that knowledge base architectures that are built based on consideration of a core set of examples will often not have the necessary structural hooks and processing mechanisms to deal with new cases that have complex aspects that had not been represented in the original set (Bachant & McDermott, 1984). As a result, correctly handling these new cases will often require major restructuring of the knowledge base rather than minor tuning. The pragmatics of corporate system development projects frequently does not allow for large scale redesign in midstream.

Iterative refinement is not only an inefficient approach to knowledge base development, it encourages a piecemeal approach to knowledge acquisition with several negative consequences. First, there is a tendency to develop systems that can handle the straightforward cases (since they are typically the ones included in the core development set), but fail to handle the complex cases (e.g., ignore multiple faults, intermittent faults, miscalibrated sensors, situations where test equipment is malfunctioning or unavailable) that are characteristic of the kinds of real problems confronted in the field. A case in point was an expert system for troubleshooting that we had an opportunity to test in the field (Roth, Bennett and Woods, 1987). In spite of the fact that the system developers thought the AI system was sufficiently mature to go into the field following several iterative refinement cycles, the system, unaided by the technician, was only able to handle a small portion (less than a fourth) of the problems that arose in the field. The problem was that the system developers were too focused on developing the knowledge base to handle specific cases and never developed a formal description of the space of problems that could arise in the domain and that an effective system would need to handle.

A second symptom of the same problem is that system designers who use an iterative design approach are often unable to clearly delineate the range of problems that the system can handle and the classes of problems that fall outside the system's boundaries. It is not uncommon for system designers, when asked what classes of problems their system can currently handle, to respond with an enumeration of the specific cases encoded in the knowledge base. The reason this is a serious problem is that the system designer is then unable to give potential system users any guidance as to the conditions under which it will be profitable for them to access the system, and when not. This problem arose in the case of the troubleshooting AI system investigated in Roth et al. (1987). The system was placed in the field and technicians were directed to use it, but they were given no clues as to which of classes of malfunctions the system would be useful for. The result was that they tried the system on all problems, observed a low success rate, and quickly lost confidence in the value of the system. If the designers of the AI system had had a clearer definition of the total space of malfunctions that the system would eventually need to deal with and focused on exhaustively handling a clearly bounded subset of difficult problems as a first phase, the resulting system could have had a better chance of succeeding.

Another danger of piecemeal knowledge acquisition is that it can lead to an oversimplified representation of the total set of goals and constraints that the target user is attempting to meet. This has the consequence of producing AI systems that optimize on one dimension of the user's problem, by ignoring (and therefore in some cases sacrificing) the other performance goals that the user is attempting to satisfy. A case in point was an AI system we worked on that was designed to support operators in a process control task (i.e., maintaining level in a boiler during a plant startup). Because poor performance on this task had severe economic consequences (i.e., when level exceeded limit values the plant shut down), it was assumed by those who commissioned the AI system that it should be built exclusively from the perspective of optimizing performance on this one goal. However, by performing an upfront analysis of the goals and constraints of the larger task the operators confronted (i.e., starting up the plant and preventing plant shutdown from multiple sources of which boiler level was only one), it was found that under some circumstances it was appropriate for operators to accept non-optimal performance on the boiler level goal (i.e., take actions that brought them closer to the shut down set points) in order to meet a more pressing goal (i.e., preventing the plant from an automatic shut down on some other criterion). The system we ultimately built accommodated such goal tradeoffs (Woods & Roth, 1988b). We might have failed to appreciate these goal interactions had we not begun with an upfront analysis of the demands of the complete task.

2.2. Failing to Support the Human Problem-Solver

Effective intelligent systems must be able to deal with the actual range of problems that arise in real world applications, and cognitive task analysis can increase the range of situations within a system's performance boundary. However, for both practical and theoretical reasons, situations unanticipated by the original system designers will inevitably arise (cf., Roth et al., 1987; Woods & Roth, 1988a) -- for example, the inherent variability present in real world situations such as normal variation in physical devices, multiple interacting faults or processes, test equipment faulty or unavailable, people misunderstanding or misexecuting instructions. This means that another critical element for effective intelligent systems is that they provide some mechanisms to facilitate the detection and resolution of cases that fall outside their bounds.

One of the major failure modes that we have observed in AI systems is to not provide support for the human problem-solver to handle cases where the AI system is beyond its bounds. This point was made salient in the case reported by Roth et al. (1987). The study examined actual technicians attempting to troubleshoot broken electro-mechanical devices with the aid of an expert system designed to lead them through the diagnostic process. Deviation from the solution path anticipated by the designers of the machine expert turned out to be the norm (80% of the cases) rather than the exception. This provided the opportunity to observe human-machine interaction when novel situations arise (problems outside the machine's competence), when adaptation to special conditions is required, in the face of underspecified instructions, and when recovery from human or machine errors is demanded. The study revealed the brittle performance that can result when systems do not support the human in adapting problem-solving to different sources of unanticipated variability.

The AI system used the conventional expert system question and answer style of interaction. The technician was asked to choose from a list of symptoms the one that best describes the trouble with the device (the machine uses the answer to this type of request to narrow its search to certain kinds of disturbances or to certain areas of the device). The machine then directed the user to make observations about the device's behavior and to take measurements from internal test points. When sufficient evidence accumulated, the expert system drew a conclusion as to the possible malfunction and reported it together with a confidence value computed for that hypothesis. The technician had the option of either accepting the hypothesis as the solution and terminating the session, or rejecting the hypothesis (in which case the machine continued its search for another candidate solution). This process continued until either the correct solution was reached or the machine's search paths were exhausted.

The expert system design assigned the human a passive role of following instructions. When (as in the majority of cases) situations deviated from the expected path, it took substantial participation by the technician to detect that the system was off track and redirect it in a productive path. The more the human functioned as a passive data gatherer for the machine, the more performance was degraded. Those who passively followed the directives of the machine expert dwelled on unproductive paths and reached dead-ends more often than participants who took a more active role.

Active human participation in the problem-solving process led to more successful and rapid solutions. The active technicians attempted to cope with unexpected conditions, to monitor machine behavior, to recognize unproductive directions, and to redirect the machine to more productive paths (within the limited means available) based on activities and judgments formed *outside* of the machine's direction. However, the design of the expert system not only failed to support an active human role, it actually retarded technicians from carrying out an active role. The machine expert provided few cues as to its intentions in pursuing a line of diagnosis and few possibilities for redirecting its resources. Furthermore, the machine expert did not provide even the most basic user support functions such as an external memory on the results of the diagnostic tests performed up to that point.

When the technician reached a point where the line of questioning seemed to be focused in an unproductive direction or the system generated a hypothesis that was suspect, the technician had to decide whether the machine expert was still on track or not. The technician did not have access to the machine's perceptions of current world state or to its troubleshooting strategy. Consequently, he had no way of knowing whether the system was systematically working through hypotheses and would eventually reach the correct one, whether the machine expert misperceived the state of the device (possibly because of an input error on the technicians part), or whether the system was beyond its boundary of competence. Failing to find an input error, the only basis for evaluating whether the system was on track was to judge the plausibility of the line of reasoning based on his own perceptions of device state and his assessment of plausible lines for diagnosis and tenable hypotheses under those conditions. Thus, he was forced to work through the diagnosis process independently and in parallel rather than build on top of the information processing work carried out by the machine.

There are several simple steps that can be taken to increase the ability of the joint person-machine system to adapt to unanticipated situations. First, it is important to ensure that the person will have sufficient information about the machine's situation assessment and intentions to detect cases where the machine is off track and situations beyond the machine's competence. One way to accomplish this is to make the machine's knowledge about the state of the device, viable hypotheses, and diagnostic directions available to the human (Fitter & Sime, 1980, Roth, Butterworth, & Loftus, 1985; Woods & Roth, 1988b). By having access to the same information as the machine expert, the user is in a better position to evaluate the soundness of the situation assessment that served as input to the machine expert's decisions. This, combined with explicit statement by the machine expert of the intended objectives of recommended responses (e.g., the information objective behind a particular diagnostic test), improves the human's ability to follow the line of reasoning and evaluate the quality of the advice. This *common frame of reference* concept for explaining the behavior of intelligent machines was employed in building an intelligent advisory system for a process control task (Woods & Roth, 1988b).

Another step in improving the capability of the person-machine system to adapt in the face of unexpected variability, is to provide more capabilities for human control of the machine's reasoning. This includes mechanisms for the human problem-solver to add to or change the information or knowledge that the machine is using about the state of the device and regions where the fault may lie (Roth, Elias, Mauldin & Ramage, 1985; Rasmussen, 1986). More ambitious use of machine power can provide the human with facilities to explicitly manipulate the attention of the machine expert (e.g., to redirect the diagnostic path) in much the same manner as two people would interact in the course of handling a difficult problem (Gadd & Pople, 1987).

2.3. Assigning the Person Responsibility But Not Control

Another problem, related to the lack of ability to monitor and control intelligent system performance, is that users often have ultimate responsibility for system performance without being given sufficient resources to accurately gauge system performance and take effective control (Woods, 1986). It is common to assert that the AI system merely provides "recommendations" that can be over-ridden. However, in many cases the authority is illusory, and the person is placed in a double-bind situation because he or she is not provided with effective mechanisms to oversee system performance. We had an opportunity to witness the responsibility/authority conflict this can produce in an actual case -- the introduction of the expert troubleshooting aid (described above) in the field. The expert system was designed to troubleshoot a device which, when broken, carried significant consequences for the customer and therefore required immediate repair. The intention was that the expert system would perform the troubleshooting for the technician, and a management decision was made to minimize training on the device being serviced. As described earlier, the expert system provided virtually no information about its diagnostic strategy and basis for its conclusion; consequently when the system failed to correctly diagnose the malfunctioning device, the technician had no information to guide him in understanding why the expert system failed. Furthermore, since he had limited training on how the device functioned, he was not in a position to fix the device himself. Technicians immediately recognized the double-bind they would be placed in -- they would be accountable to the customer for failures to repair the malfunctioning device in a timely fashion without having any control over the troubleshooting and repair process.

2.4. Mimicking Suboptimal Coping Strategies

Another common error in building intelligent systems is to assume a priori that the way to achieve optimal performance is to mimic slavishly how the people who are best at the task go about doing it. The problem here is that often times the strategies displayed by even the best practitioners can be convoluted, suboptimal, or developed in response to an impoverished task and support environment.

A case in point was an intelligent advisor which we were asked to build to support boiler level control during plant start up. The problem formulation for the project was to elicit from experts how they controlled boiler level and encode those rules in an expert system. However, when we performed the cognitive task analysis (cf., Roth & Woods, 1988), including the dynamics of boiler level behavior and the data available for assessing the state of the different variables that contribute to boiler level behavior, it became clear that there was not sufficient state information available for any agent, person or machine, to perform the boiler level control task well. The best operators were better at interpreting indirect measures of process behavior, and therefore could control boiler level somewhat better than other operators, but they were all operating under a severe handicap.

While we could have built an AI system that modeled faithfully the microstrategies used by the best operators to extract process state information from indirect measures, we chose a different strategy. First, we developed new more accurate sources of state information. Second, this information was used to build a better situation assessment for the human (via new displays) and for an AI machine advisor which recognizes the current factors driving level behavior, recognizes the degree of exposure to automatic shutdown, and generates response strategies for avoiding or negotiating high exposure regions (Woods & Roth, 1988b). The underlying computational mechanisms in no sense replicated the surface strategies that the expert operators were forced to employ to extract process state information from the existing impoverished system representation. Also, the response strategies that the human experts employed given the impoverished representation were no longer relevant given the new representation. The results of preliminary testing showed that the new joint cognitive system design improved the performance of less skilled operators and increased the range of situations that could be handled, even by the expert operators.

3. WHAT MAKES FOR GOOD ADVICE? LESSONS FROM HUMAN-HUMAN ADVISORY ENCOUNTERS

The multiple cooperative agents metaphor is often invoked in considering the interaction between intelligent machines and their users. Typically, the metaphor is to a human expert providing advice to someone with less experience in the task at hand. There have been a number of studies that examine human-human relationships in multi-person problem-solving or advisory situations and then to transpose the results to human-intelligent machine interaction (e.g., Coombs and Alty, 1984). This strategy has produced significant insight into the high degree of interaction involved in effective advisory encounters, and the factors that influence whether advice is meaningfully integrated and applied.

Human-human advisory encounters have been examined in a number of different contexts including face-to-face advice on using a local computer system (Alty & Coombs, 1980; Coombs & Alty, 1980; McKendree & Carroll, 1986; Aaronson & Carroll, 1987) and radio talk show "call in" advice on finance management (Pollack et al., 1982) as well as other domains (Belkin, Brooks and Daniels, 1987; Isaacs & Clark, 1987; Hill & Miller, 1988). The results uniformly indicate that good advice is more than recommending a solution. Good advisory interactions involve cooperative problem-solving. The advisor does not merely respond to the immediate request of the user, rather he/she aids the user in problem formulation and plan generation (especially with regard to obstacles, side effects, interactions and tradeoffs). The advisory encounter aids the user to determine the right questions to ask; how to look for or evaluate possible answers; and how to develop or debug a plan of action to achieve his goals. This is in marked contrast to the machine directed problem-solving observed in the case of the troubleshooting expert aid studied by Roth et al. and described above.

Alty and Coombs (1980; Coombs & Alty, 1980), who examined consulting interactions on the use of a computer system, found that in more successful advisory interactions, two partial experts (experienced computer user with a domain task to be accomplished and a specialist in the local computer system) cooperated in the problem-solving process. Control of the interaction was shared in the process of identifying the important facts and using them to better define the problem. In this process each participant stepped outside of his own domain to help develop a better understanding of the problem and, as a consequence, appropriate solution methods. Interestingly, the advisor does not need to generate a complete solution to a problem in order to provide effective advice. For example, Perkins & Martin (1986) found that one third of the errors made by student programmers were corrected with general hints that did not require knowledge of correct solution or the specific error.

In contrast, Alty and Coombs found that unsatisfactory human-human advisory encounters were strongly controlled by the advisor. The advisor asked the user to supply some specific information, mulled over the situation, and offered a solution with little feedback about how the problem was solved. While a problem was usually solved, it was often some proximal form of the user's real problem (i.e., the advisor was guilty of a form of solving the wrong problem: solving a proximal case of the user's fundamental problem). The advisor provided little help in problem definition.

Analyses of human-human advisory interactions like the studies described above clearly reveal the elements of good advice and point to the features required for effective joint cognitive systems. Machine decision support must be more than a solution plus justification. It must be structured around the problem-solving process and involve close cooperation with the human practitioner in formulating the problem and in identifying and evaluating solution paths. The function of an "advisor" (man or machine) is to broaden the user's horizons, to raise and help answer questions like: What would happen if? Are there side effects to this response? What are the pre-conditions (requirements) and post-conditions for a particular response (given the responses, what consequences must be handled)? Are there other possibilities which should be considered (hypothesis generation)? At the same time an important function of the user is to monitor, probe, and contribute information to the advisor to ensure that the advisor's recommendations are based on an accurate representation of the problem situation that the user is facing and the full set of constraints that a viable solution must meet (McKendree & Carroll, 1986).

This analysis of good and poor advisory encounters emphasizes that effective advice is not simply a matter of solving the problem for the practitioner. This does not mean that advisory systems should never provide directive advice or lead the problem-solving activity. Decisions with respect to how the person and intelligent machine should interact should be guided by the goal of maximizing the ability of the total person-machine system to respond to the breadth of problems and changing circumstances that inevitably arise.

The main insight to be gleaned from the studies of person-person and person-machine interactions is that the user of an intelligent advisory system has a substantial role to play in the problem-solving process and attempts to eliminate the human from the problem-solving process will inevitably lead to inefficient and brittle problem-solving systems. As the "person-on-the-scene", the human practitioner is best equipped to recognize aspects of a situation or the constraints on a problem solution that deviate from the assumptions and expectations of the machine expert. His ability to recognize faulty assumptions on the part of the machine and take constructive action to correct machine misconceptions will depend on the facilities available for viewing (or probing) the machine's perception of the problem state and redirecting machine problem-solving.

3.1. Challenges in Formulating Advice

The analysis of good and poor advisory models provided above emphasizes that there are many useful functions an advisor can serve that do not entail autonomous problem solutions. In fact, advisors rarely are in possession of sufficient information about the problem to solve it for the client. Providing insights and suggestions that broaden the set of options and/or constraints considered by the client in drawing his own conclusion is often more effective than attempting to dictate a complete solution. Our experience in designing machine advisors has led us to the same conclusion. It is often more effective to design advisory systems that contribute partial results toward a solution than to attempt to generate complete solutions under all conditions.

There are several challenges in characterizing effective advice for a particular application. (1) What is the appropriate level of context-sensitivity and specificity to aim for in generating advice: should the system generate highly specific micro-responses or should it generate more global information leaving the practitioner degrees of freedom in deciding how to instantiate the advice? (2) When should the machine advisor interject advice: should the system attempt to generate advice under all conditions or only for those situations where the person is clearly unable to cope and the appropriateness of the advice can be assured? (3) Should the system provide an explanation for the advice it presents, and if so what are the elements of a good explanation (Berry and Broadbent, 1987)? Developing coherent strategies to cope with these challenges should also be a part of the knowledge acquisition process because the answers can have large impacts on the processing mechanisms, knowledge representation and interface features of the AI based advisor.

One challenge for building advisory systems is specifying the appropriate *unit* or *grain* of advice. Highly specific advice is likely to be most effective (i.e., ensuring an optimal response) provided the recommended action is correct; However, generating accurate micro-advice can be very difficult because the most appropriate specific response often depends on extensive context-specific information, some or most of which may be beyond the bounds of the machine expert (e.g., historical data, sounds associated with malfunctioning equipment). If all of the contextual factors are not taken into account, highly specific advice is more likely to be in error. In contrast to micro-advice, global advice is likely to be more robust, in the sense that the advice will be correct at some level, but it risks the danger of being vague or stating the obvious. The problem is how to define a level of advice that is specific enough to be useful without being over-specific and risking the danger of brittleness -- incorrect advice due to a failure to consider all the relevant contextual variables.

A prime example of the risks of overly-specified advice is the case where the practitioner's role demands parallel processing of multiple factors or goals, and the machine expert focuses on only one of these in generating advice. A preferable strategy is to generate more global advice that alerts the practitioner to constraints and defines objectives, but leaves the practitioner degrees of freedom in responding to the situation. A specific example arose in the case of an advisory system we developed for a process control task (Woods & Roth , 1988b). The main focus of the advisor was to provide guidance in the control of level in a boiler. While the machine advisor could have been made to generate highly specific advice designed to optimize on that goal (i.e., maintain boiler level within tight bounds around the target), the operators' behavior was often guided by other goals that were beyond the capabilities of the system to detect (e.g., a need to control a second process affected by boiler level). Consequently, the machine advisor generated a broad target band rather than an "optimal" target value as its recommendation. The operator then had the flexibility to select a specific target within that band that satisfied his multiple goals.

A related issue is determining *when* the machine expert should intervene. If the machine expert attempts to generate advice under all conditions, it will be prone to two major pitfalls: stating the obvious under the routine conditions, and generating erroneous advice in particularly difficult cases that fall beyond its bounds.

There are several strategies that can be adopted to make the machine expert more selective in the nature and timing of its advice. For example, in dynamic worlds one can take advantage of the fact that as the situation worsens the degree of potential ambiguity about what are appropriate responses decreases. Thus, the machine advisor can be quiescent when the situation is relatively stable or normal and gradually output stronger and more specific response advice as the situation worsens. This is the concept of ***severity dependent variations in the grain and timing of advice.*** It balances several constraints on what is good advice: deliver advice in those situations where one can generate clearly appropriate information, but interject advice only when it is needed (which implies an understanding of the state and likely future course of the problem-solving process and which tends to be an inverse function of how easy it is to generate relevant advice), and preserve the practitioner's initiative and flexibility in responding to situations beyond the capacity of the advisor (Woods & Roth, 1988b).

A more ambitious, though related strategy for governing when to intervene, relies on user intent modeling. In this approach the person is given the primary responsibility for all decisions as long as his or her behavior meets a reasonableness criterion. The machine expert tracks the person's behavior and attempts to construct a model of the person that identifies goals and strategies based on the decisions the person makes (as reflected in his actions). As long as the human appears to be handling the situation in a reasonable manner (i.e., the machine is able to construct a rational explanation for the behavior), the machine expert remains in the background. If the machine recognizes the user's intentions and identifies more effective means for carrying them out, it interjects with a suggestion. In this approach, as long as the machine expert can construct a model of the user's behavior that is coherent and rationale (the "reasonableness" criterion) the machine expert does not impose its recommendations, with the assumption that the practitioner's behavior may be governed by contextual factors beyond the bounds of what the machine is able to consider. However, interjections are more directive, if the person's behavior fails to meet the reasonableness criterion. The intent modeling approach is similar to "critiquing" systems that take the form of a machine agent who comments on the human's problem-solving process (e.g., Coombs & Alty, 1984; Langlotz & Shortliffe, 1983; Miller, 1983)

Another issue in building advisory systems is the problem of explanation -- how to communicate to the user why the system has determined that the recommended action is needed and how the action it suggests will achieve the desired outcome. While the importance of explanation is generally recognized, advisory systems often fall short in this respect. Typically, explanation consists of a justification of the machine's decision in the form of a trace of the detailed process by which the machine generated the advice. Furthermore, the human-in-the-loop must decide, based on his own assessment of the world and without any support, when to question the machine's advice and to call for an explanation. The problems with this approach have been detailed elsewhere (e.g., Woods, 1986; Roth et al., 1987).

An alternative approach to explanation is to present advice in the context of the assessment of current (and future) state of the world in order to create a *shared frame of reference for the person and machine.* Having access to the same information as the machine expert, allows the practitioner to evaluate the soundness of the machine's state assessment. This, coupled with explicit statement of intended objectives of recommended responses, enables the practitioner to evaluate the quality of the advice (cf., Woods & Roth, 1988a; 1988b).

4. COGNITIVE TASK ANALYSIS

The potential pitfalls in building intelligent systems and the elements of effective advice make clear the importance of understanding what makes a domain task hard and what are the sources of good and poor human performance as a prerequisite for determining how machine intelligence should be deployed. What knowledge acquisition techniques are available for mapping the domain demands and for understanding the basis of human skill and error at the task?

It is widely acknowledged that building intelligent systems involves an intensive knowledge acquisition effort (e.g., Barr and Feigenbaum, 1982; Hayes-Roth, Waterman & Lenat, 1983; Prerau, 1987). There has been a great deal of interest in developing tools and techniques to increase the efficiency of the knowledge acquisition process (e.g., Boose & Gaines, 1987). Efforts have gone in two directions. One approach has been to look to behavioral science research for insight into how human experts represent and utilize domain knowledge and the techniques available for eliciting this knowledge and organization from experts (e.g., Ericsson & Simon, 1984; Gammack and Young, 1985; Hart, 1986; Hawkins, 1983; Hoffman, 1987). A second approach has been to develop computational tools (e.g., editors; graphic displays of the knowledge encoded computationally; mechanisms to detect and flag inconsistencies in the knowledge encoded) to facilitate the encoding of knowledge into a particular computational formalism (e.g., Boose, 1984; Boose & Bradshaw, 1987; Eshelman, Ehret, McDermott & Tan, 1987; Kahn, Breaux, DeKlerk & Joseph, 1987).

In general, these approaches to the knowledge acquisition problem have focused primarily on the issue of how to extract the particular knowledge and strategies of a domain expert so that they may be encoded in the intelligent machine. While this is a legitimate element of the knowledge acquisition problem, it is only one aspect of the problem.

The real design goal in the development of an intelligent system is to improve the performance of the joint person-machine system (Woods, 1986). This means that knowledge acquisition must be more than acquiring the knowledge fuel for a particular computational engine. Thus, from a cognitive engineering point of view, there are two distinct stages of knowledge acquisition. The first is a *problem formulation or cognitive task analysis* stage. During this stage the cognitive engineer is attempting to define what makes the domain problem hard, what errors domain practitioners typically make and how an intelligent machine can be used to reduce or mitigate those errors or performance bottlenecks. In this stage domain experts are not the sole subject of focus. Understanding the knowledge and strategies currently employed by average and low skill practitioners is equally important. Understanding the limitations of the knowledge (e.g., incomplete or inaccurate mental models of the domain) and strategies (e.g., failures to consider multiple interacting goals in plan formulation) across the range of domain practitioners for whom the intelligent advisor is intended is a prerequisite for defining how machine intelligence can be deployed to enhance their performance.

One of the important outcomes of the problem formulation stage is an accurate assessment of the dimensions of task complexity and the cognitive demands imposed by the world that any intelligent agent will have to deal with. The same factors that make the task hard for people usually will make it a challenging task for a machine problem-solver as well (e.g., the possibility of multiple interacting failures). Appreciating the range of complexity that the person-machine system will confront is necessary to identify what computational mechanisms are necessary for this application and to specify the range of cases that the system will be able to handle.

The product of the problem formulation stage is a description of the cognitive demands imposed by the domain, the knowledge and problem-solving strategies required to meet those demands, and the reasons for poor performance (e.g., limitations in knowledge, ineffective strategies) observed in the current environment. This enables an informed decision about what kind of support system needs to be built, what the range and boundaries of problems that the system will need to be able to handle, what computational tools to adopt (i.e., knowledge representation techniques, inference strategies), and what specific knowledge needs to be collected and encoded in the intelligent machine.

Too often the problem formulation stage is completely bypassed. The problem of knowledge acquisition is viewed as a problem of gathering and translating specific domain knowledge into the syntax of a particular computational formalism (e.g., production system rules). This view is reinforced by the computational tools made available to system developers. Typically, expert system development software include tools to facilitate encoding and manipulating specific bits of information (e.g., graphic representations of the knowledge base; editors; consistency checks), but no conceptualization aids are provided to help the system developer define and bound the design problem. The danger is that it encourages piece-meal development without explicit analysis of the requirements for machine competence or the existing boundaries of competence.

Detailed knowledge acquisition can only meaningfully take place once a cognitive mapping of the problem-space and an explicit definition and bounding of the scope of machine competence has been completed. This provides an umbrella structure of domain semantics that organizes and makes explicit what particular pieces of knowledge mean about problem-solving in the domain (Woods, 1988). At this point a second, *knowledge encoding* stage is entered. It is during this stage that issues of how to efficiently elicit specific information from domain experts and encode it in a specific computational formalism becomes relevant.

There are a number of available reviews of tools and techniques that support the second stage of detailed, computationally-driven knowledge acquisition (cf., Boose, 1984; Boose & Gaines, 1987; Eshelman, Ehret, McDermott & Tan, 1987). Below we focus on knowledge acquisition strategies to support the cognitive task analysis carried out during the problem formulation stage.

Cognitive task analysis is used to derive a description of the cognitive demands imposed by a task and the sources of good and poor task performance (Woods & Hollnagel, 1987). The method relies on two mutually reinforcing analyses. One analysis focuses on building a description of the cognitive demands imposed by the world that any intelligent agent would have to deal with. It involves a formal analysis of the kinds of problems that can arise, independent of the methods by which they are solved. The output provides a model of the requirements for competent performance in the domain, i.e., *a competence model.* This provides a framework to guide the second analysis: an empirical investigation of how practitioners, both experts and less skilled individuals, respond to the task demands. The output of the second analysis is a *performance* model that describes the knowledge and strategies that characterize good and poor performance in the domain. For a specific example of the application of this methodology to the development of an intelligent decision support system see Roth & Woods (1988) and Woods & Roth (1988b).

To build a cognitive description of a complex world the first hurdle is to escape from the language of the application and to characterize the kinds of cognitive demands that arise in the course of performing domain tasks (Clancey, 1985; Gruber & Cohen, 1986; Newell, 1982; Woods & Hollnagel, 1987). One approach is to start from the constraints imposed by the design and proper function of the system in question via a kind of goal directed analysis (e.g., Rasmussen, 1986; Woods & Hollnagel, 1987). A goal-directed representation is constructed by structuring domain tasks in terms of the goals to be accomplished, the relationships between goals (e.g., causal relations, constraints) and the means to achieve goals (how a process functions, alternative means, pre-conditions, post-conditions). Included in the goal-directed representation is a description of the information either actually (given a particular man-machine interface) or potentially (given a proposed man-machine interface) available to the agent for assessing current world state, detecting and resolving goal competition, and determining courses of action.

The goal-directed representation serves as a framework or problem space that is used to describe the kinds of cognitive situations that arise in the course of carrying out domain tasks (Mitchell & Miller, 1986 and Moray, 1987 describe related techniques for cognitive task analysis of worlds made up of many, highly interactive parts) and the quality of information available to the agent to support his decision making tasks. The goal-directed representation aids in the identification of complex situations that will be difficult for any agent, human or machine to handle. Cases include situations with multiple constraints where a course of action should simultaneously satisfy all of the constraints, and cases where the available evidence is too weak or uncertain for any agent to make a definitive situation assessment.

The results of the goal-directed analysis define the requirements for *competent performance* or a *model of the problem-solving environment*: what kinds of problem-solving situations can arise in this world? what must people know and how they must use that knowledge to solve these problems (what are the difficult cognitive demands)? what information must be obtained (or derived) for monitoring and situation assessment? what knowledge must be accessed and utilized to select goals, to form intentions to act, to monitor and adapt plans (Woods, Roth & Pople, 1987)?

In addition to understanding the cognitive demands imposed by the task, it is important to identify what practitioners do, both successfully and erroneously, in response to these demands in the *current* problem-solving environment. This requires a second level of analysis focused on developing *performance* models. Performance modeling examines the cognitive resources that practitioners bring to the task, including the task relevant knowledge they possess and the processing strategies they have evolved. This analysis describes ineffective strategies that lead to poor performance (i.e., a model of error) as well as the adaptive strategies that have been developed by skilled or "expert" practitioners to cope with task demands, given the current world representation (i.e., a model of skill). The former results localize which aspects of the task are the largest contributors to poor performance -- and thus where performance aiding efforts should be concentrated. The latter results define candidate strategies for expert performance that may be useful to transfer to less experienced practitioners, for example, through on-line advice.

Data collection techniques for performance modeling can vary from informal interviews, retrospective analyses of actual incidents (Flanagan, 1954; Klein, in press), observation of practitioners as they attempt to perform domain task (e.g., Bainbridge, 1979; Hawkins, 1983; Gadd & Pople, 1987), to formal behavioral studies that attempt to uncover the problem-solving strategies underlying task performance under highly controlled conditions (e.g., Belkin, Brooks, and Daniels, 1987; Kuipers & Kassirer, 1983; Larkin, McDermott & Simon, 1980; Lesgold, Rubinson, Feltovich, Glaser, Klopfer & Wang, 1986). The choice and combination of methods employed depend on the depth of modeling required and the resources available.

The distinction made here between models of competence and models of performance is analogous to the distinction between competence and performance originally made by Chomsky (1968) with respect to human language understanding capabilities. A linguistic competence model provides a description of the system of rules that relate sound to meaning in a particular language (i.e., the grammar of that language). It provides a structural analysis of the grammatical distinctions and regularities of the language that fluent speakers must be able to handle in order to understand and generate utterances in that language (i.e., the demands imposed by the language). Speakers of the language may not necessarily be able to articulate these rules of grammar, but their linguistic performance demonstrates an "implicit" knowledge (i.e., they are behaving "as if" they knew the rules). While competence models describe requirements for effective performance (i.e., what speakers must be able to do), they do not account for the process by which speakers generate and understand utterances in actual situations (i.e., how they do it). The actual cognitive processing strategies by which fluent speakers achieve these competencies (or in many cases fall short, resulting in ungrammatical utterances) are described by performance models.

One critical role that competence models perform is to guide and provide discipline to the development of *performance models* -- models of how domain practitioners actually perform the task -- by providing a formal specification of the set of competencies that need to be accounted for. Competence models also enable discrimination between aspects of task performance that result from "surface" characteristics of the current work environment (e.g., an impoverished representation) and fundamental task demands. When a new support system is introduced it often changes the representation of the world (though not the underlying problem-solving demands). Advice generated strictly from observation of task performance in the original task environment may not apply or may be incomplete after the work environment is changed by new support systems (cf., Woods & Roth, 1988b for examples). A second danger of over-reliance on analysis of performance in the existing environment, is that aids will be devised to enhance the ability to carry out strategies that merely cope with the "surface" demands created by the impoverished representation of the current work environment instead of helping practitioners directly meet the underlying task demands.

Taken in combination the analyses reveal the sources of task difficulty and enable identification of options to produce a better match between the cognitive demands of the task and the available resources. They serve to discriminate between difficulties that derive from the inherent structure of the domain (e.g., the fact that there are multiple competing goals that must be balanced) from those that arise because of characteristics of the current environment (e.g., the quality of information currently available). They provide the basis for specifying what new information, representations, and advice should be provided.

5. TACTICS FOR KNOWLEDGE ACQUISITION

The fundamental difficulty in knowledge acquisition is the bootstrapping problem -- knowing what question to ask domain experts (or what situations to observe their behavior in or how to analyze their behavior) can depend on considerable domain knowledge. Furthermore, there is the problem of how to interpret the answers given (or the behaviors observed) -- are they only descriptions of particular cases ("war stories") or are they instances of more general kinds of categories of situations that can arise in the world in question.

This section describes some of the pragmatic issues in gathering domain knowledge and outlines an approach for mapping the cognitive demands imposed by the world and developing performance models. The approach consists of a multi-phase progression from initial informal interview techniques to derive a preliminary mapping of the semantics of the domain, to more structured knowledge elicitation techniques to refine the initial semantic structure, to controlled experiments designed to reveal the knowledge and processing strategies utilized by domain practitioners. The methodology is designed to reveal the cognitive demands imposed by the task, the kinds of errors that less skilled practitioners are subject to, and the factors that contribute to those errors, and the knowledge and skills required for expert performance.

The first phase is exploratory and is intended to provide a preliminary cognitive description of the task to guide further analysis. The objective is to learn enough about the task itself to be able to ask the right questions about how people do the task (and how to understand the answers given). A preliminary mapping of the semantics of the domain is built from interviews with different people having different perspectives of the basic task and from existing documentation on the task. The objective here is to get a broad overview of the basic concepts, procedures, range of problems and sources of complexity involved in performing the task. A real danger in this early phase is that discussions between the cognitive engineer and the domain expert focus prematurely on eliciting detailed information (e.g., specific rules) that either forms no coherent picture (e.g., a set of arbitrary rules with no cohesion), or worse, produce a distorted picture of the true bounds of the task, "missing the forest for the trees" (Berry and Broadbent, 1986). One stra to avoid this problem suggested by Gammack and Young (1985) is to h the domain expert prepare and give an overview presentation. This is likely to be a more effective approach to gain broad perspective of the demands of the domain than the approach typically recommended of having the expert select and discuss a small set of examples (Hayes-Roth, Waterman & Lenat, 1983). Focusing prematurely on a small set of example problems selected before the cognitive engineer has a broad overview of the range of problem cases that can arise in the domain, risks the danger of a biased, atypical, or overly bounded sample that provides a distorted picture of the true range of complexity inherent in the domain. An important part of the initial phase is to use the knowledge gained to begin to build the competence model of the domain. This helps to avoid "missing the forest" by forcing one to think of specific cases as general instances of more general categories of situations (Woods & Hollnagel, 1987; Woods, 1988).

Once the cognitive engineer has developed an overview of the semantics, major players, methods, and demands of the domain, a second more structured phase of knowledge acquisition can begin. While the first phase is primarily focused on understanding the domain itself, the second phase begins the process of understanding how domain practitioners actually perform the tasks. Structured knowledge elicitation techniques are employed to build an initial model of what makes the task hard (or when is it hard), how experienced practitioners avoid, cope, or surmount the task difficulties, and how less experienced practitioners fail in the face of these difficulties. At this stage, one begins to acquire the specific knowledge used by practitioners to perform the task effectively.

In this second phase there is a greater reliance on observation and analysis of actual task performance. The cognitive engineer is now in a position to select (or construct) challenging problem-solving situations and analyze how domain practitioners deal with them. Analysis may take the form of review of critical incidents for which data on actual practitioner performance is available. It may involve discussions with practitioners of past challenging cases they confronted and how they dealt (or failed to deal) with them (i.e., retrospective analyses of actual cases). Or it may involve selecting or constructing test cases and observing domain practitioners as they try to solve them.

One method that has proved highly effective and highly efficient is to convene an "expert panel" session that brings together several domain practitioners identified as experts by their peers for focused group discussion and controlled observation (cf., Roth & Woods, 1988 for a detailed discussion of this technique). Note that one typical practical hint for knowledge acquisition has been to recommend starting with only one domain expert. The motivation for this "maxim" is that it makes the knowledge encoding stage easier (for example, it can reduce difficulties in knowledge base integrity and avoids the need to integrate different problem-solving strategies). In contrast, we have found that bringing multiple experts together in the appropriate format is a highly effective technique for the purposes of cognitive task analysis. Expert panel sessions are an extremely efficient way to obtain a corpus of challenging cases that have arisen in the field and to identify the critical elements that contribute to problem difficulty and the strategies for adequately handling those cases.

In the expert panel technique, the preliminary cognitive description of domain demands is used to provide a conceptual framework for focusing panel discussion on a common functional plane rather than on superficial characteristics that may vary across the experiences of the experts and blur fundamental commonalities. It also provides an essential framework for interpreting and integrating the information provided by the experts.

The results of structured interviews and observations of task performance provides a sufficient level of understanding to design more formal observations to examine, under more controlled conditions, the knowledge and problem-solving strategies utilized by experts. Various methods from cognitive psychology then can be used to isolate the role of different types of knowledge in different problem situations. The model of difficulties and corresponding strategies derived from these studies can point to the kinds of knowledge and decision aids which should improve performance.

Below we discuss a sampling of performance-based techniques that can be used to understand the knowledge and strategies that underlie practitioner performance.

5.1. Protocol Analysis

Cognitive Science research on the nature of expertise (e.g., Chi, Glaser & Farr, 1986) and the structure and representation of semantic memory (e.g., Smith & Medin, 1981) offer a number of effective paradigms for extracting the conceptual structure of experts' domain knowledge and the cognitive processes that underlie expert performance. Knowledge acquisition techniques from this tradition can be used to derive an accurate model of the structure of the knowledge representation of experts and their processing strategies. These techniques have been successfully employed to develop models of expert performance in a variety of domains. (Roth, et al., 1987; Woods, Roth & Pople, 1987; Lesgold, Rubinson, Feltovich, Glaser, Klopfer & Wang, 1986; Clancey, 1986). These techniques reveal external cues and internal *conceptual structures* used by domain practitioners to characterize the problem and guide problem solution.

One of the basic paradigms is *protocol analysis.* The domain practitioner is presented with a task to perform, and a careful record is taken of all the operations he performs and verbal statements he makes during the task. These are then analyzed using a variety of techniques (e.g., Ericsson & Simon, 1984) to develop a formal, often computer-executable model of knowledge and processes involved in performing the task.

The power of the methodology for revealing the knowledge and strategies that underlie task performance comes from (1) manipulations in the nature of the task, (2) what process measures are collected during task performance, and (3) observation of performance of individuals at multiple levels of expertise.

One of the most critical elements is the selection of cases to be presented. Presenting ambiguous situations, that can be interpreted in multiple ways, provides the opportunity to observe which interpretations come to mind most readily, the extent to which the domain practitioners entertain multiple interpretations simultaneously, and the practitioner's ability to *revise* his interpretation as new information comes in that either supports or is inconsistent with his current interpretation. In most actual applications, there already exists a large amount of pre-planned material (doctrine, procedures, standard operating practices) on how to recognize a situation and how to respond to it, if it is identified. This pre-planned guidance can serve as a resource in selecting cases. One heuristic is to select cases that go beyond or challenge the pre-planned material for that domain. Examples of such complicating factors are underspecified instructions, human execution errors, bugs in the plan, impasses (where the plan's assumptions about the state of the world or the context are violated), secondary failures, multiple major failures, and novel events for which no pre-planned material exists.

A second major task manipulation is whether the practitioner is allowed to control information gathering himself during problem-solving or whether the content and timing of information presentation is controlled by the cognitive engineer. Both techniques are valuable and provide complementary insights. The advantage of the first method is that the expert generates the list of relevant information under cued retrieval conditions and provides data on his diagnostic search process (Bruner, Goodnow & Austin, 1956; Brooke & Duncan, 1981). The second method allows more control over the content and timing of information acquisition. This enables observation and analysis of the effect of particular kinds of information in guiding the interpretation process. By controlling the order information is provided, it is possible to examine how the availability of a given piece of information biases the interpretations called to mind. By withholding critical information until after preliminary hypotheses have been formed, it is possible to examine the ability of domain practitioners to re-evaluate and revise their interpretation as new evidence comes to light. One of the signature characteristics that distinguishes experts from less experienced practitioners is their *flexibility* in revising an interpretation as the evidence requires it (Woods & Roth, 1988a; Lesgold et al., 1986).

A third powerful manipulation in protocol analysis techniques, is to compare the performance of individuals at different levels of expertise. The contrast in strategies employed, contextual evidence requested and utilized, kinds of interpretations entertained, and ability to revise interpretation in light of conflicting evidence displayed by individuals at different levels of expertise, provide strong cues for isolating what aspect of expert knowledge and processing characteristics account for their superior performance (Chi et al., 1986). As an additional advantage, analyzing the performance of less experienced domain practitioners enable isolation of the factors that contribute to weak performance and provide insight into how intelligent aids can be utilized to enhance performance.

The success of the protocol methodology depends critically on the ability to track the cognitive processes of the domain practitioner as he or she performs the task. Several techniques can be used to externalize processing activities. These include: encouraging the experts to "think-aloud" as they perform the task, using eye-movement equipment to track the pattern in which the practitioner searches for data and thus infer focus of attention at each stage in the problem-solving process (e.g., Lesgold et al., 1986) and forcing the practitioner to explicitly ask for each piece of information.

5.2. Techniques for Eliciting Domain Concepts and Organization

The protocol methodology outlined above provides information about how domain practitioners access and utilize knowledge during problem-solving. There are other techniques derived from semantic memory research paradigms that can be used to reveal how experts structure their knowledge of the domain (i.e., the domain concepts they possess, and how they are organized). Techniques for deriving the taxonomic structure of memory include: the repertory grid technique (Kelly, 1955; Boose, 1984) that is used to elicit the set of concepts or classes into which the domain expert breaks up the world and the dimensions that he/she utilize in drawing similarities and distinctions among the concepts; classification sorts (e.g., group pictures or problem descriptions into meaningful classes and subclasses); "call to mind" studies where the expert is requested to list subordinate and superordinate categories; and typicality ratings, where the expert is asked to judge how "typical" a particular case (e.g., a configuration of symptoms) is of a concept or class (Smith & Medin, 1981; Roth & Shoben, 1983).

Another useful technique for externalizing the conceptual structures domain practitioners employ is *reconstruction.* In the reconstruction technique, pictures depicting domain situations, or situation descriptions are presented for a fixed (usually brief) period and the practitioner is asked to reconstruct (i.e., draw or otherwise describe) the information presented. Memory distortions (omissions; insertions) reveal the conceptual framework (i.e., schemata) that the practitioner was employing in interpreting the information displayed (Bartlett, 1932). The reconstruction techniques can be generalized to other tasks than recall of the material presented in the study phase. Generalized reconstruction techniques include using discrimination, problem-solving and extrapolation tasks during the test phase.

These techniques all serve to reveal what concepts practitioners use to think about the domain (i.e., how they parse the world) and how they organize their knowledge of the domain. This can be useful in guiding the design of the knowledge base of intelligent systems (i.e., what concepts to include and how to organize them). For effective communication it is important that the machine expert and the people who interact with it share a common conceptual framework.

5.3. Factors Facilitating Knowledge Elicitation

In determining how to obtain knowledge from domain practitioners it is important to understand what information a person can easily access and verbalize about his or her own knowledge and thought processes and what are the circumstances that most facilitate the knowledge elicitation process. This section provides a brief overview of some of the dimensions of the knowledge elicitation task that affect the accuracy and completeness of the information obtained. Other reviews of the issues involved and the empirical data that speak to these issues can be found in Ericsson & Simon (1984) and Leplat (1986; this volume).

Three important dimensions that affect the accuracy of the knowledge elicited are: (1) the specificity of the information being elicited, (2) how closely the conditions under which the information being requested resembles the "usual conditions" under which the expert accesses or uses that knowledge (i.e., the fidelity or realism of the retrieval context), (3) the length of time between when the information was attended to by the expert and the time he is asked to report it.

Specificity of Information Being Requested.
In attempting to elicit information from experts, the more specific the information request, the more accurate the results will be. For example, experts will be more likely to describe their reasoning and problem-solving strategies in the context of a specific example than in response to being asked a general question such as "How do you generally approach a problem?" or "How do you go about diagnosing a malfunction?"

The reason is that problem-solving strategies are not likely to be represented explicitly in memory. When the expert is asked to exercise his reasoning on specific problems, the processes are reactivated and the cognitive engineer is then in a position to observe and analyze them in order to abstract out general principles and strategies. Asking general questions puts the burden of analysis on the expert himself. A large body of data suggest that when people are asked to theorize about their own cognitive processes, the results are likely to be inaccurate (Nisbett & Wilson, 1977; Ericsson and Simon, 1984).

An expert is also more likely to recall accurately characteristics of specific cases or problems he has encountered, than generalizations about the characteristics of classes of problems. This is particularly true if the generalization the expert is asked for is not something that he has thought about before and can directly remember. If the expert has to produce the generalization on the spot, by trying to recall specific instances, and generalizing based on them, the result is likely to be biased (Ericsson & Simon, 1984). For example, there is likely to be an *availability bias* (Tversky and Kahneman, 1982). When trying to recall specific instances, "typical" cases that arise frequently, are likely to come to mind. Therefore the generalization will tend to hold for the "typical" or "canonical" case, but not the less frequently occurring exceptions. A case in point is when people are asked to give definitions of concrete nouns such as "fruit" or "chair". Their definitions tend to hold only for the more typical examples of the category (e.g., a chair is something you sit on that has four legs and a back) but not for atypical examples (e.g., a bean-bag chair) (Rosch & Mervis, 1975). It is therefore preferable to ask the expert to recall specific "typical" and "atypical" cases that he has encountered. The knowledge engineer can then abstract out the the generalities, commonalties, and provisos that may apply through more explicit analysis.

Fidelity of Retrieval Context.

A second important factor influencing ease of knowledge transfer, is how similar the knowledge elicitation context is to the actual "field" context in which the expert normally functions. The higher the fidelity of the context, the more successful the knowledge acquisition will be.

The more the acquisition context allows the expert to reproduce his behavior, rather than speculate on what it would be, the more valid the results will be. However, the knowledge acquisition situation need not be high fidelity in all respects. A mixed fidelity, or part-task situation, can also be effective, provided it successfully recreates those aspects of the actual performance context that are relevant to the decision processes being examined. For example, successful knowledge acquisition has been obtained by presenting experts with detailed scenario descriptions of problems requiring diagnosis. The tasks are structured in such a way that the expert is presented with only the information that he decides is relevant and requests (e.g., history, test results). This ensures that the expert *exercises* his information gathering and problem-solving skills. This technique has been successful employed in the development of medical expert systems where detailed case histories of actual patients are available (Clancey, 1984; Kuipers and Kassirer, 1983; Kuipers, Moskowitz, & Kassirer, 1988; Johnson, Moen & Thompson, in press).

In attempting to establish the problem-solving skills employed by an expert, it is important to ensure that the task presented taps the problem-solving skills he normally employs. For example, if the question of interest is how the expert goes about diagnosing a specific disease or malfunction "X", it is inappropriate to ask the expert that question directly (i.e., "suppose a person came in with disease "X", how would you diagnose it?") because in a normal diagnostic situation the expert would not know at the start what the actual problem was. Knowing the outcome of the diagnosis at the start distorts the diagnostic process (Fischhoff, 1982). It would be preferable instead to present the expert a case to solve where the symptoms given are the ones typically associated with the disease or malfunction of interest, and to observe what information the expert asks for, and what hypotheses he considers, in the process of isolating the malfunction.

A high fidelity retrieval context is also important in attempting to access knowledge that is explicitly stored in long term memory, such as specific cases encountered, and experience-based generalizations or "rules of thumb". Retrieving information from long term memory is an active process that depends on having (or generating) good retrieval cues that trigger recall or the *activation* of knowledge. Retrieval is most facilitated when the recall context matches closely the context in which the information was originally acquired, or is normally used (e.g., Bransford, Sherwood, Vye & Rieser, 1986)

Time Interval Between Event and Verbal Report.

The third important variable that affects the completeness and accuracy of knowledge elicitation is the time interval between when the particular event or piece of information being described is experienced or attended to by the expert and when he is asked to report it. *Retrospective* reports are descriptions of tasks or events that are provided after-the-fact. *Concurrent* reports are verbal descriptions that are provided *at the time* the task is being performed. Concurrent verbalizations are more reliable than retrospective reports since memory retrieval is not involved. The person is reporting information that he is currently attending to and thinking about. Retrospective reports are subject to memory failures and biases (Hoc & Leplat, 1983; Ericsson & Simon, 1984).

Memory for past events is reconstructive in nature (Bartlett, 1932). People use inferences based on related information acquired either before or after the event to fill in memory gaps. These inference processes are generally "unconscious" so that the individual is unable to distinguish retrieved from inferred information (Spiro, 1977). That verbal reports provided after-the-fact can be notoriously poor are attested to by numerous studies of eyewitness testimony (Loftus, 1979). One case in point (Loftus & Palmer, 1974) is a study where people were shown a film of an auto accident. After the film some were asked to estimate the speed of the cars when they "collided", others were asked for the speed when they "smashed". One week later, all participants were asked whether they had seen broken glass (the film had not shown any broken glass). The people in the "smashed" condition were more likely to claim they saw glass than the other group. Thus, information provided after-the-fact distorted memory of the event.

Retrospective reports can be improved by providing effective retrieval cues. Hoc and Leplat (1983) had people describe how they went about solving a problem while they watched a videotape of themselves during the problem-solving task. They found that this *cued retrospective* report methodology produces precise and accurate descriptions. Presenting videotapes of the actual problem-solving task serves to re-introduce the contextual cues of the original situation, thus enhancing recall.

Techniques that can be used to obtain knowledge from experts range from holding informal interviews and discussions with the expert, to more formal performance-based techniques where the expert is asked to solve a problem or perform a task. We have described just a sample of these. Larger scope reviews can be found in (Hart, 1986; Hoffman, 1987; Leplat, 1986; this volume; Kidd and Welbank, 1984). A cognitive engineer responsible for obtaining information from an expert should be prepared to use a mix of techniques. Knowledge elicitation is difficult for the expert. The more retrieval cues that are provided to activate relevant memories, the more complete and accurate the knowledge obtained will be.

The dimensions discussed above should be kept in mind in selecting a mix of knowledge elicitation techniques to employ. For example, informal interview techniques, which tend to be weak on all three dimensions, need to be complemented by performance-based techniques.

6. CONCLUSIONS

While AI tools increase the potential power of decision aiding systems, the fundamental challenges facing designers of support systems remain the same: defining the cognitive demands that make the problem situation challenging; understanding what knowledge and problem-solving strategies allow human experts to perform well; understanding what kinds of errors of performance occur and the basis for those errors; and specifying what information or advice would reduce those errors and make for effective decision support.

Because AI systems can encode expert human problem-solving heuristics, there is a temptation to assume that they have a special status and that upfront analysis of the problem domain can be bypassed. This belief is based on an implicit assumption that meaningful advice will be generated automatically by an autonomous machine problem-solver that faithfully mimics how a human expert performs the task. In this paper we have tried to show the inadequacy of this assumption, and the corresponding need to broaden the view of what is effective advice and to broaden the scope of knowledge acquisition in the development process via the cognitive task analysis process. Also, we have tried to show how cognitive task analysis can be carried out practically.

The cognitive task analysis provides an umbrella structure of domain semantics that organizes and makes explicit what particular pieces of knowledge mean about problem-solving in the domain (e.g., Clancey, 1985; Woods & Hollnagel, 1987; Gruber & Cohen, 1987; Woods, 1988). Acquiring and using such a domain semantics is essential (1) to specify what kinds of cognitive support functions are needed, (2) to specify what kinds of computational mechanisms are capable of providing such functions, (3) to clearly delineate machine performance boundaries, and (4) to build less brittle machine problem-solvers, for example, through features that enable the human problem-solver to extend and adapt the capability of the system to handle unanticipated situations. This is in contrast to technology-driven approaches where knowledge acquisition focuses on describing domain knowledge in terms of the syntax of particular computational mechanisms; in other words, the language of implementation is used as a substitute for a cognitive language of description (Newell, 1982). As a result, semantic questions are displaced either to whomever selects the particular computational mechanisms or to the domain expert who enters knowledge.

The cognitive task analysis approach redefines the knowledge acquisition problem: knowledge acquisition, first, is about deciding what kinds of intelligent systems would make a difference and, second, about what domain specific knowledge is needed to fuel those systems.

ACKNOWLEDGEMENTS

This paper was partially written while the authors were at the Westinghouse Research and Development Center. Many of the ideas for what constitutes effective decision aids and the cognitive task analysis approach to knowledge acquisition were originated in the context of developing AI based decision support systems at Westinghouse. We gratefully acknowledge our colleagues who collaborated on the design of these systems, especially William Elm, James Easter, Craig Watson, and John Gallagher Jr., of Westinghouse Nuclear Technology Systems Division, and Kevin Bennett formerly of the Westinghouse Research and Development Center.

REFERENCES

Aaronson, A. & Carroll, J. M. The answer is in the question: A protocol study of intelligent help. *Behaviour & Information Technology*, 1987, *6*, 393-402.

Alty, J. L. & Coombs, M. J. Face-to-face guidance of university computer users--I: A study of advisory services. *International Journal of Man-Machine Studies*, 1980, *12*, 390-406.

Bachant, J. & McDermott, J. R1 Revisited: Four years in the trenches. *The AI Magazine*, Fall 1984, *4*, 21-32.

Bainbridge, L. Verbal reports as evidence of the process operator's knowledge. *International J. of Man-Machine Studies*, 1979, *11*(4), 411-436.

Barr, A. & Feigenbaum, E. A. *Handbook of Artificial Intelligence.* Los Altos, CA: William Kaufmann, 1982.

Bartlett, F. J. *Remembering: A Study in Experimental and Social Psychology.* London: Cambridge University Press, 1932.

Belkin, N. J., Brooks, H. M., and Daniels, P. J. Knowledge elicitation using discourse analysis. *International Journal of Man-Machine Studies*, 1987, *27*(2), 127-144.

Berry, D. C. & Broadbent, D. E. Expert systems and the man-machine interface: 1. Knowledge acquisition. *Expert Systems*, 1986, *3*, 228-231.

Berry, D. C. & Broadbent, D. E. Explanation and verbalization in a computer-assisted search task. *The Quarterly Journal of Experimental Psychology*, 1987, *39A*, 585-609.

Boose, J. H. Personal construct theory and the transfer of human expertise. In AAAI (Ed.), *Proceedings of the Fourth National Conference on Artificial Intelligence.* American Association for Artificial Intelligence, 1984.

Boose, J. H. & Bradshaw, J. M. Expertise Transfer and Complex Problems: Using AQUINAS as a knowledge-acquisiton workbench for knowledge-based systems. *International Journal of Man-Machine Studies*, 1987, *26*(1), 3-28.

Boose, J. H. & Gaines, B. R. (Eds.). *Knowledge Acquistion for Knowledge-Based Systems.* Academic Press, in press. Also published as 5 special issues of the journal *International Journal of Man-Machine Studies*, 1987.

Bransford, J., Sherwood, R., Vye, N. & Rieser, J. Teaching and problem solving: Research foundations. *American Psychologist*, 1986, *41*, 1078-1089.

Brooke, J. B. & Duncan, K. D. Effects of system display format on performance in a fault location task. *Ergonomics*, 1981, *24*, 175-189.

Bruner, J. S., Goodnow, J. J. and Austin, G. A. *A Study of Thinking.* New York: Wiley, 1956.

Carroll, J. M. & McKendree, J. Interface design issues for advice-giving expert systems. *Communications of the ACM*, 1987, *30*, 14-31.

Chi, M., Glaser, R., & Farr. *The Nature of Expertise.* Hillsdale, NJ: Erlbaum, 1986.

Chomsky, N. *Language and mind.* New York: Harcourt Brace Jovanovich, 1968.

Clancey, W. J. Methodology for Building an Intelligent Tutoring System. In W. Kintch, J. R. Miller, and P. G. Polson (Ed.), *Method and Tactics in Cognitive Science.* Hillsdale, New Jersey: Lawrence Erlbaum Assoc., 1984.

Clancey, W. J. Heuristic Classification. *Artificial Intelligence*, 1985, *27*, 289-350.

Clancey, W. J. Acquiring, representing, and evaluating a competence model of diagnostic strategy. In M. Chi, R. Glaser & Farr (Ed.), *The Nature of Expertise.* Hillsdale, NJ: Erlbaum, 1986.

Coombs, M. J. & Alty, J. L. Face-to-face guidance of university computer users--II: Characterising advisory interactions. *International Journal of Man-Machine Studies*, 1980, *12*, 407-429.

Coombs, M. J. & Alty, J. L. Expert systems: An alternative paradigm. *International Journal of Man-Machine Studies*, 1984, *20*, 21-43.

Ericsson, K. A. & Simon, H. A. *Protocol Analysis: Verbal Reports as Data..* Cambridge, Mass.: MIT Press, 1984.

Eshelman, L., Ehret, D., McDermott, J. & Tan, M. MOLE: a tenacious knowledge acquisition tool. *International Journal of Man-Machine Studies*, 1987, *26*(1), 41 54.

Fischhoff, B. For those condemned to study the past: Heuristics and biases in hindsight. In Kahneman, D., Slovic, P., & Tversky, A. (Ed.), *Judgment Under Uncertainty: Heuristics and Biases.* New York: Cambridge University Press, 1982.

Fitter, M. J. & Sime, M. E. Responsibility and shared decision making. In H. T. Smith & T. R. G. Green (Eds.), *Human Interaction with Computers.* London: Academic Press, 1980.

Flanagan, J. C. The critical incident technique. *Psychological Bulletin*, 1954, *51*, 327-358.

Gadd, C. S. & Pople, H. E. An interpretation synthesis model of medical teaching rounds discourse: Implications for expert system interaction. *International Journal of Educational Research*, 1987, Vol. *1*.

Gammack, J. G., & Young, R. M. Psychological Techniques for Eliciting Expert Knowledge. In M. A. Bramer (Ed.), *Research and Development in Expert Systems.* Cambridge, England: Cambridge University Press, 1985.

Gruber, T. & Cohen, P. Design for Acquisition: Principles of knowledge system design to facilitate knowledge acquisition. *International Journal of Man-Machine Studies*, 1987, *26*, 143-159.

Hart, A. *Knowledge Acquisition for Expert Systems.* New York: McGraw-Hill Book Company, 1986.

Hawkins, D. An analysis of expert thinking. *International Journal of Man-Machine Studies*, 1983, *18*, 1-47.

Hayes-Roth, F., Waterman, D. A. and Lenat, D. B. *Technowledge Series in Knowledge Engineering.* Vol. 1: *Building Expert Systems.* Reading, Massachusetts: Addison-Wesley Publishing, 1983.

Hill, W. C. & Miller, J. R. Justified advice: A semi-naturalistic study of advisory strategies. In E. Soloway, D. Frye & S. Sheppard (Ed.), *CHI'88: Conference on Human Factors in Computing Systems.* Washington, D.C.: ACM/SIGCHI, 1988.

Hoc, J. M., and Leplat, J. Evaluation of different modalities of verbalization in a sorting task. *International Journal of Man-Machine Studies*, 1983, *18*, 283-306.

Hoffman, R. The problem of extracting the knowledge of experts. *AI Magazine*, Summer 1987, *8*(2), 53-68.

Isaacs, E. & Clark, H. H. References in conversation between experts and novices. *Journal of Experimental Psychology: General*, 1987, *116*, 26-37.

Johnson, P. E., Moen, J. B. & Thompson, W. B. Garden path errors in diagnostic reasoning. In M. J. Coombs & L. Bolec (Ed.), *Expert Systems.* New York: Springer-Verlag, in press.

Kahn, G. S., Breaux, E. H., De Klerk, P. & Joseph, R. L. A mixed-initiative workbench for knowledge acquisition. *International Journal of Man-Machine Studies*, 1987, *27*(2), 167-180.

Kelly, G. A. *The Psychology of Personal Constructs.* New York: Norton, 1955.

Kidd, A. & Welbank, M. Knowledge Acquisition. In J. Fox (Ed.), *Infotech State of the Art Report on Expert Systems.* Infotech. Pergamon, 1984.

Klein, G. A. Recognition-primed decisions. In W. B. Rouse (Ed.), *Advances in Man-Machine Research, Volume 5.* Greenwich, CT: JAI Press, in press.

Kuipers, B. and Kassirer, J. P. How to discover a knowledge representation for causal reasoning by studying an expert physician. In IJCAI (Ed.), *International Joint Conference on Artificial Intelligence-83.* International Joint Conferences on Artificial Intelligence, Inc., 1983.

Kuipers, B. Moskowitz, A. J., & Kassirer, J. P. Critical decisions under uncertainty: Representation and structure. *Cognitive Science*, 1988, *12*, 177-210.

Langlotz, C. P. & Shortliffe, E. H. Adapting a consultation system to critique user plans. *International Journal of Man-Machine Studies*, 1983, *19*, 479-496.

Larkin, J., McDermott, D. P., & Simon, H. A. Expert and novice performance in solving physics problems. *Science*, 1980, *208*, 1335-1342.

Leplat, J. The Elicitation of Expert Knowledge. In Hollnagel, E., Mancini, G. & Woods, D. D. (Eds.), *Intelligent Decision Support.* New York: Springer-Verlag, 1986.

Lesgold, A. M., Rubinson, H., Feltovich, P., Glaser, R., Klopfer, D., & Wang, Y. Expertise in a complex skill: Diagnosing X-ray pictures. In Chi, M. T. H., Glaser, R., & Farr, M. (Ed.), *The Nature of Expertise.* Hillsdale, NJ: Erlbaum, 1986.

Loftus, E. F., & Palmer, J. C. Reconstruction of automobile destruction: An example of the interaction between language and memory. *Journal of Verbal Learning and Verbal Behavior*, 1974, *13*, 585-589.

Loftus, E. F. *Eyewitness Testimony.* Cambridge, MA: Harvard Univ. Press, 1979.

McKendree, J. & Carroll, J. M. Advising roles of a computer consultant. In Mantei, M. & Oberton, P. (Ed.), *Human Factors in Computing Systems: Chi'86 Conference Proceedings.* ACM/SIGCHI, 1986.

Miller, P. L. ATTENDING: Critiquing a physician's management plan. *IEEE Transactions on Pattern Analysis and Machine Intelligence*, 1983, *PAMI-5*, 449-461.

Mitchell, C. & Miller, R. A. A discrete control model of operator function: A methodology for information display design. *IEEE Systems, Man, and Cybernetics*, 1986, *SMC-16*, 343-357.

Moray, N. Intelligent Aids, Mental Models and the Theory of Machines. *International Journal of Man-Machine Studies*, 1987, *27*, 619-629.

Newell, A. The knowledge level. *Artificial Intelligence*, 1982, *18*, 87-127.

Nisbett, R. E. & Wilson, T. D. Telling more than we can know: Verbal reports on mental processes. *Psychological Review*, 1977, *84*, 231-259.

Norman, D. A. *Steps towards a cognitive engineering* (Tech. Rep.). University of California at San Diego, Program in Cognitive Science, 1981.

Osborne, R. L. Online, artificial intelligence-based turbine generator diagnostics. *The AI Magazine*, Fall 1986, *6*, 97-103.

Perkins, D. & Martin, F. Fragile Knowledge and Neglected Strategies in Novice Programmers. In E. Soloway & S. Iyengar (Eds.), *Empirical Studies of Programmers.* Norwood, NJ: Ablex, 1986.

Pollack, M. E., Hirschberg, J. & Webber, B. User participation in the reasoning processes of expert systems. In *Proceedings of the National Conference on Artificial Intelligence.* Pittsburgh, PA: American Association of Artificial Intelligence, 1982.

Prerau, D. S. Knowledge acquistion in expert system development. *AI Magazine*, Summer 1987, *8*(2), 43-52.

Quinn, L. & Russell, D. M. Intelligent interfaces: user models and planners. In Mantei, M. & Oberton, P. (Ed.), *Human Factors in Computing Systems: Chi'86 Conference Proceedings.* ACM/SIGCHI, 1986.

Rasmussen, J. *Information Processing and Human-Machine Interaction: An Approach to Cognitive Engineering.* New York: North-Holland, 1986.

Rosch, E. & Mervis, C. B. Family resemblances: studies in the internal structure of categories. *Cognitive Psychology*, 1975, *7*, 573-605.

Roth, E. M, & Shoben, E. The Effect of Context on the Structure of Categories. *Cognitive Psychology*, 1983, *15*, 346-378.

Roth, E. M., Butterworth, G. & Loftus, M. J. The Problem of Explanation: Placing Computer Generated Answers in Context. In *Proceedings of the Human Factors Society.* 29th Annual Meeting, 1985. Vol. II.

Roth, E. M., Elias, G. S., Mauldin, M. L., & Ramage, W. W. Toward Joint Person-Machine Cognitive Systems: A Prototype Expert System for Electronics Troubleshooting. In *Proceedings of the Human Factors*

Society. 29th Annual Meeting, 1985. Vol. I.

Roth, E. & Woods, D. D. Aiding human performance: I. Cognitive analysis. *Le Travail Humain*, 1988, *51*(1), 39-64.

Roth, E., Bennett, K. & Woods D. D. Human Interaction with an 'Intelligent' Machine. *International Journal of Man-Machine Studies*, 1987, *27*, 479-525.

Smith, E. E. & Medin, D. L. *Categories and Concepts*. Cambridge, Massachusetts: Harvard University Press, 1981.

Spiro, R. J. Remembering information from text: The state of schema approach. In R. C. Anderson, R. J. Spiro, and W. E. Montague (Ed.), *Schooling and the Acquisition of Knowledge..* Hillsdale, N.J.: Lawrence Erlbaum Assoc., 1977.

Tversky, A., & Kahneman, D. Availability: A heuristic for judging frequency and probability. In Kahneman, D., Slovic, P. & Tversky, A. (Ed.), *Judgment Under Uncertainty: Heuristics and Biases*. Cambridge, Mass.: Cambridge University Press, 1982.

Woods, D. D. Paradigms for Intelligent Decision Support. In Hollnagel, E., Mancini, G. & Woods, D. D. (Eds.), *Intelligent Decision Support in Process Environments*. New York: Springer-Verlag, 1986.

Woods, D. D. Coping with Complexity: The Psychology of Human Behavior in Complex Systems. In L. P. Goodstein, H. B. Andersen & S. E. Olsen (Eds.), *Mental Models, Tasks and Errors*. London: Taylor & Francis, 1988.

Woods, D. D. & Hollnagel, E. Mapping Cognitive Demands in Complex Problem Solving Worlds. *International Journal of Man-Machine Studies*, 1987, *26*, 257-275.

Woods, D. D. & Roth, E. M. Cognitive Systems Engineering. In M. Helander (Ed.), *Handbook of Human-Computer Interaction*. New York: North-Holland, 1988. (a).

Woods, D. D. & Roth, E. Aiding human performance: II. From cognitive analysis to support systems. *Le Travail Humain*, 1988, *51*(2), 139-171. (b).

Woods, D. D., Roth, E. & Pople, H. *Cognitive Environment Simulation: An Artificial Intelligence System for Human Performance Assessment*. Washington D. C.: U. S. Nuclear Regulatory Commission, 1987. (NUREG-CR-4862).

Topics in Expert System Design
G. Guida and C. Tasso (Editors)

MODELS OF EXPERTISE IN KNOWLEDGE ACQUISITION

Joost BREUKER and Bob WIELINGA

Department of Social Science Informatics
University of Amsterdam
Amsterdam, The Netherlands

1. The Knowledge Acquisition Problem

Although the last decade has seen a rapid growth of capabilities in building knowledge based systems, knowledge acquisition still constitutes a major factor that impedes a well controlled knowledge based systems (KBS) life cycle. We define knowledge acquisition as the elicitation and analysis of data on expertise with the aim of building a knowledge based system. In order to understand the problems in knowledge acquisition we will discuss elicitation and analysis activities in more detail. Our main conclusions will be the following. First, problems in eliciting knowledge do not constitute the true bottleneck, for the simple reason that we would not know how to represent the implicit, detailed knowledge of a human expert. The way expert systems reason rather simulates an articulate novice who is extremely well informed, than an expert who relies on detailed experiences. Therefore, limits on how deep we can probe into the knowledge of an expert can be considered as a limit to construct a system given our current know-how, rather than as a bottleneck. Second, the data obtained are in general extensive, qualitative and not systematically ordered, so that major problems of interpretation arise. Therefore, the problems appear to be due to lack of adequate methods, tools and conceptions for analysing these data. In this section we will also review several approaches to support the analysis of data on expertise, including the KADS methodology.

1.1. Knowledge acquisition as mining

Accounts by experts of how they solve problems and what knowledge they use seem very unsystematic and incomplete. The mental eye has no direct access to all the details of the problem solving processes, or it may be difficult to report what is going on. Elicitation techniques differ in effectiveness (Burton et al, 1987). This is due to at least

The research reported here is partially funded by the ESPRIT Program of the European Community under contract P1098. Partners in this project are: University of Amsterdam, SCICON, STC, Cap Sogeti Innovation, KBSC and SCS (since 1988: NTE).

two factors: accessibility and reportability. In an interview, where the expert is asked to tell how he solves a problem, the accessibility may be very low, because there are no active problem solving processes available for inspection: these have to be obtained from selections in long term memory (cf Nisbett & Wilson, 1977 vs. Ericsson & Simon, 1979). On the other hand, thinking aloud techniques facilitate accessibility, because the problem solving trace is fresh, but reportability may suffer because presenting an on line report is easily limited by central processing capacities.

Some other elicitation techniques are aimed at the uncovering of apparently inaccessible or "implicit" knowledge by inducing structures from regularities in behaviour: in particular by using rating or sorting tasks (Gammack, 1987; Neale, 1987). The repertory grid method (Kelly, 1955) is one of the most popular ones, as for instance used in knowledge acquisition systems like ETS/AQUINAS (Boose, 1986), or PLANET (Shaw & Gaines, 1986).

Attributing the knowledge acquisition bottleneck to problems of elicitation represents a *mining* view (Kidd, 1987; Hayward, 1987). This view has two variants: an optimistic and a pessimistic one. The first assumes that by deeper digging not only more, but also new, and probably essential elements may be discovered which form the key to what the domain expertise is really about. Extensive elicitation and observation may provide these keys and is exemplified in "deep immersion" practices, where "jewels of knowledge" are uncovered (Feigenbaum & McCorduck, 1983). The more pessimistic version of the mining view says that the tools and techniques for elicitation will not allow for deeper digging: the essence of expertise remains implicit. With growing expertise the knowledge becomes automised and compiled out, and is no longer directly accessible for inspection. Minsky (1985) presents an illuminating, and somewhat more pessimistic account of our reflexive competences. Inaccessibility of compiled out knowledge is also a popular theme among critics of the AI enterprise in general (Dreyfus & Dreyfus, 1986; Winograd & Flores, 1986).

Let us assume that this pessimistic view is true. What consequences does this have for knowledge engineering? Before discussing this question, we should be careful not to make a carricature of this view. It does not state that all knowledge is inaccessible. Otherwise, we would not be able to answer an endless variety of factual questions, ranging from telling one's name, to describing recent events, or the use of formulas in solving physics problems. Moreover, it will probably also maintain that we are able to give a very detailed account of *reasoning* processes. For instance, in solving seriation problems (e.g. A > B; B < C; D > C; A ? D) a thinking aloud protocol reveals almost all of the successive steps. This is classical problem solving behaviour which is characterised by successive, and explicit reasoning steps. It requires effort and concentration, and proceeds relatively slowly. However, that is not what many people, and in particular the 'pessimists' consider to be expertise. A novice may slowly obtain a solution by reasoning, but an expert does so by understanding the problem and 'seeing' or refining the solution. The process of understanding, seeing, etc. is so immediate that it appears to be inaccessible. In that respect, expertise resembles common sense reasoning as in understanding mundane stories. In understanding, inferences are made almost automatically and very fast. They are far more rich than those produced by reasoning steps.

Understanding and reasoning are both involved in problem solving in 'semantically rich' domains. Reasoning may control understanding, and understanding provides most of the facts on which reasoning is based (Breuker, 1981). The relative contribution of understanding to reasoning to problem solving varies with the type of domain, and in particular with the degree of expertise. With growing experience successive steps are compiled out, as for instance modelled in current theories on explanation based learning (e.g. Mitchel et al., 1986: see also v.d. Velde, 1988). At the same time, a large knowledge base of cases is created, by which the problem solving process may be replaced by memory look up, pattern recognition and constrained analogical reasoning. For instance, expertise in chess is highly dependent on the recognition of similarities and differences between the current position and those in known matches (De Groot, 1966). The master chess player has access to thousands of previous cases to constrain plausible alternatives for reasoning, while novices can only rely on some general strategic principles in order to constrain the time consuming calculations of consequences of potential moves.

Looking at the current formalisms for representing knowledge and reasoning in KBS, it is obvious that these are more suited to perform reasoning operations than to enable understanding processes. In fact, we can only speculate about the nature of these understanding processes, which seem to require other, probably analogical instead of symbolic representations and distributed processing (for some precise hypotheses: see Steels, 1988). Therefore, we may safely say that an expert system reasons, rather than understands. A KBS seems to solve problems in the way a very well informed and systematic novice would do. rather than mimicing a real expert. Note that this does not imply that a KBS will yield less valid results because it uses other methods than real life experts do. In some respects the explicit model of expertise that is implemented in a KBS may lead to formally better controlled inferences than human expertise.

The validity of the outcomes of a KBS may be equal to or better than that of a human expert, but the performance is not as flexible. Reasoning when based upon analogies, local dynamics and a large variety of available cases is far more flexible than when explicit domain theories and global processes are used. Flexibility affects the range of problems in a domain that the system can adequately cope with and in this respect KBS are noteworthy brittle (Hayes-Roth et al., 1983). However, flexibility may not only be created at lower levels by the use of large and finely tuned memories, but may also come from reflexive exploitation of domain 'principles' (Maes & Nardi, 1988) as applied in second generation expert systems (Steels, 1987). Problem solving that is based on reasoning rather than compiled out skills may also support a secondary, but important function of KBS: the knowledge that is used is often also suited to provide justification of solutions (cf. XPLAIN, Swartout, 1983; van der Velde, 1986; NEOMYCIN, Clancey & Letsinger, 1981). It also leads to well structured and maintainable knowledge bases. Therefore, these second generation KBS which use metaknowledge and have different types of knowledge can provide the required flexibility (Wielinga & Breuker, 1986).

The point of this is that while we are capable of building well performing, and even flexible KBS, these systems are not based upon *all* the types of knowledge that a human expert uses. Our thesis is that there is a strong correlation between the accessibility of human expertise and the feasibility for designing a KBS for a particular domain. Elicitation is not a bottleneck, but a very practical limiting factor in building expert systems. If we were able to obtain the detailed data of the knowledge that drives human expert behaviour, we would not know how to handle it. This correlation may not be accidental at all. Implementability in the machine and accessibility in the mind may be two sides of the same coin. Many AI techniques have been developed by reflection, induction, and in particular construction. Although AI, and knowledge engineering, are not concerned with psychological plausibility the criterion for the validity of an inference is whether 'reasonable' people will assert it to be the case, (or whether a robot performs the intended action in the physical world). Evidence for this thesis is also the fact that in the practice of building KBS those domains are selected for which there exists explicit and abstract knowledge, e.g. for those domains for which we have formal education, etc. For instance, it appears that it is more feasible to construct a system which plans advanced biochemical experiments (Stefik, 1981), than a system that plans the preparation of a meal consisting of various dishes (De Greef et al., 1988b).

If the knowledge acquisition bottleneck is not to be located in the elicitation of data, then the analysis of these data seems the potential source of problems. De Kleer (1985; review of Hayes-Roth et al., 1983) rejects the mining view for the following reason:

"Expert systems are not applicable for every task. Only a limited number of techniques are available and these only work on limited classes of problems. The major task for an expert systems project is not "extracting knowledge" but problem selection: identifying that valuable task for which applicable techniques exist" (p 106).

This shifts the attention to the artefact -the KBS- rather than the data. The elements from which this artefact is constructed are the (AI) techniques. However, as we shall see in the next sections, the relationship between tasks and AI techniques is not a simple one.

1.2. Modelling: the abstraction and transformation of data

An alternative view on developing an expert system, or knowledge based system (KBS), is that it is essentially a modelling activity. In the modelling view, a KBS is not some container filled with extracted knowledge, but a model that behaves in a specific way analogous to a system in the real world (Clancey, 1985). The building of a KBS is a mapping from an understanding of behaviour in the real world to a description in the form of an artifact: an engineering construct. In this view, the bottleneck consists of the fact that the mapping between the (verbal) data on expertise and the implementation formalisms is not a simple, one to one correspondence. Even if one can identify simple, individual rules, facts, problem solving states, etc., the context of use, and the interdependencies are in general not explicit. In other words: besides the fact that the data have to be *transformed* into implementation elements, the assessment of their relevance and the identification of structures has to be obtained by *abstraction*. Analysis of data on expertise consists of performing these two functions.

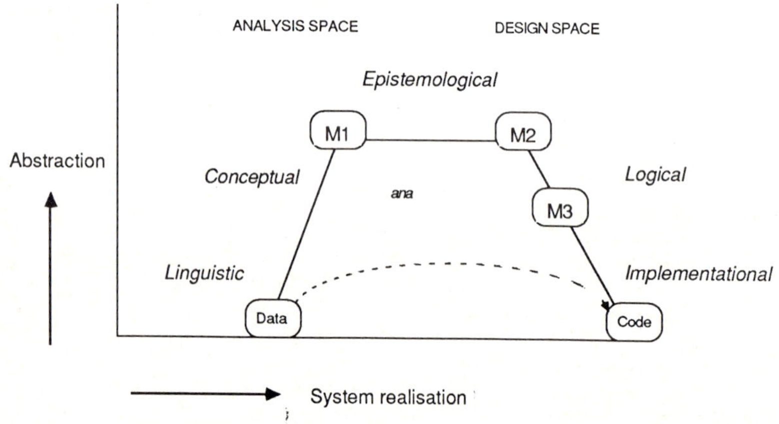

Figure 1: Models and the development space of expert systems

The straight lines mark the KADS trajectory: from DATA, passing through M1 (conceptual model) via M2 (design model) and M3 (detailed design) to the artefact (CODE). The italic labels are Brachman's (1979) levels of analysis. The dotted line symbolises prototyping. (see text for explanation)

In figure 1. abstraction and transformation are represented as two dimensions of this mapping or modelling space. The higher we get in this space, the more we abstract from individual data or elements and the more the structure becomes explicit. In this space one can represent the 5 levels Brachman (1979) has distinguished in describing what various semantic network formalisms (languages) try to capture. The highest level of abstraction in this figure is marked: epistemological.

> "The epistemological level of semantic network permits the formal definition of knowledge-*structuring* primitives, rather than particular knowledge primitives.." (Brachman, 1979, p206).

At this level one attains a degree of abstraction at which we are only concerned with types of structures. The lower levels are either closer to a conceptual interpretation of data (conceptual, linguistic), or to constructs that are machine interpretable (logical, implementation). These levels can also be used to describe levels or stages in the development of a KBS (Wielinga & Breuker, 1984; 1986). The KADS trajectory passing through the M1, M2 and M3 points in Figure 1 will be described in more detail in the next sections.

1.2.1. Bottom-up approaches

By abstracting from the detailed data, the structures which constitute the expertise in a domain can be laid bare. Of course, there is not one, 'natural' structure in data. The structures that are revealed are to a large extent dependent on what we consider relevant and less relevant attributes. Abstraction succeeds when these distinctions can be made in a systematic way. In abstracting we preserve only relevant attributes of elements. What is relevant is dependent on our aims or view. Three major types of tools or techniques have been developed to support bottom-up KBS construction.

Prototyping
In developing a KBS in a purely bottom up way this view is both dependent on the available implementation elements ('solutions') and what the data constrain as possible interpretations of expert problem solving in a domain. It is clear that such a double sighted view is far too complex to handle in obtaining a coherent and efficient mapping. In a purely bottom up practice, e.g. in AI research, the way out is eclectic and experimental: by *prototyping*. In knowledge engineering this (rapid) prototyping practice has been adopted too (cf Bratko and Kahn et al., this volume). Rapid prototyping means that as soon as the KE has understood how some of the data can be structured, solutions are applied and a system is constructed (see the dotted line in Figure 1). Because the implementation formalisms do not reach beyond the "logical" level, the required abstraction is relatively low. In domains of a reasonable complexity this is insufficient to acquire a coherent view on the structure of the expertise. In rapid prototyping in KBS development the structures are chains of reasoning which are instances, rather than generic descriptions of the problem solving process. *) As a consequence, rapid prototyping easily leads to backtracking and throwing away of systems: at least it does not lead to a well controlled system development lifecycle (e.g. Hayes-Roth et al., 1983).

System building tools
A complicating factor in prototyping is that in commercial practice the set of potential solutions is reduced to what a particular shell has to offer, so that the chances become even higher that wrong, inefficient, or opaque structures are imposed on the data. Rapid prototyping in knowledge engineering becomes easily driven by implementation formalisms (see Hayes-Roth et al., 1983; Bratko, this volume). The awareness that EMYCIN-like shells are an insufficient answer to the large varieties of 'architectures' of expertise has lead to more advanced, less rigid implementation tools. Knowledge engineering environments

---

*) In AI research, the aims may be far more diverse. AI systems hardly ever solve domain problems, but are used for the construction and/or verification of generic solutions to generic problems.

like KEE, ART, LOOPS, GOLDWORKS, Knowledge Craft (Kahn et al., this volume), KREME (Abrett & Burstein, 1987), BABYLON or KRS (van Marcke, 1988) offer a variation of ready made implementation formalisms that also allow the constructing of special purpose methods by escaping to lower levels (Lisp, Prolog). Another approach in this area is the development of a coherent set of high level "logics" (SOCRATES, Reichgelt & van Harmelen, 1986). For more detailed overviews see Alty (this volume) and Rothenberg (this volume). However, these powerful tools make the knowledge acquisition problem only more urgent. There is an *embarras de choix* among solution methods, and they require from the knowledge engineer far more insight into the AI background of these tools than the simple minded shells do.

Induction tools: statistics and machine learning
Bottom up methods of abstracting structures from data on expertise which have hardly any commitment to implementation formalisms are inductive techniques. In machine learning these techniques are often qualitative ones (e.g. Dieterich & Michalski, 1983; Mitchel et al., 1986; Hart, 1987). Structures in quantitative data can be induced by using statistical, multivariate techniques (see above: repertory grid; Cooke & McDonald, 1987). Disadvantages of these techniques are that they only generate classifications, and that the results are highly dependent on the way the data have been obtained. Particularly sorting and rating tasks are very sensitive to instruction, because the points of view are manifold and can change during the process. To put it simple, the structures that are induced are only relevant for problem solving, if the expert has been put into a problem solving gear. However, that is often not possible, because he can perform only one task at a time. In machine learning this problem is less urgent. The inductive machinery is fed with problem solving examples: not with theoretical concepts in the domain. Multivariate analysis provides hierarchies of objects that can be used for classification, but only if the data are collected with the same purpose in mind. That is one of the reason why repertory grid, multidimensional scaling, etc., but also many inductive machine learning techniques have a limited scope. These limitations can probably be removed to some extent by combining various learning techniques (e.g. DISCIPLE, Kodratoff & Tecuci, 1987; INDE, Terpstra & van Someren, 1988).

Another useful, but specific application of induction techniques is for semi-automatic refinement of the knowledge base. The KE specifies some initial structures and the knowledge acquisition system induces further refinements, e.g. by consulting a database of solved cases (e.g. SEEK2, Ginsburg et al., 1988; BLIP. Morik, 1987). Despite their limited scope, the advantage of inductive methods is evident: data can be abstracted in a more or less automated way.

Knowledge editing tools
Less powerful, but more generally applicable tools for bottom up knowledge acquisition are the various knowledge editing tools which have been developed to support the information management during the analysis of the data. Tools like (direct manipulation) protocol editors, graphical editors and browsers for knowledge and reasoning structures, and linking of analysis objects have proven to be indispensable support for the analysis process (e.g. KEATS; Eisenstadt & Motta, this volume, KRITON; Diederich & Linster, this volume; METAKREK, Solvberg 1987; KADS Power Tools, Anjewierden, 1987; BLIP, Morik, 1987). This functionality -which is similar to or even based on hypertext notions- may be combined with other tools. The most obvious combination is with implementation tools (see above), but other combinations are also very interesting. For instance in BLIP knowledge editing can be combined with inductive methods. In KADS the Powertools are combined with modelling tools (see further), and a development methodology.

1.2.2. Conceptual Modelling

We have discussed two points of departure to bridge the gap between data and artifact in a purely bottom-up way: the data or the artefact. In practical knowledge engineering one wants to avoid these bottom-up situations, because there is no way to predict, let alone control, whether the two ends will meet. The aim in current research is to find constraints and even top-down refinement models to guide the process of development.

Single model acquisition tools

As in the bottom up approaches one can start at one of both ends. In knowledge engineering, the prevailing end to start from is the artifact, or what is called the design space in the KADS methodology (the right half of Figure 1). The development strategy is somewhat similar to that of "shellification", i.e. abstracting domain independent structures from an existing KBS, so that the remaining architecture can be filled with new domain knowledge. The assumption is of course that at the level of abstraction of the architecture the new domain has the same structure as the original domain. This is how MYCIN has lead to EMYCIN (van Melle, 1980). This means that EMYCIN is only to be used when the system to be built should reason in a similar way as MYCIN does, i.e. the kind of reasoning as is used in heuristic classification tasks (Clancey, 1985).

Shellification by itself does not make a knowledge acquisition tool. What is needed is also a front end that bridges the analysis and design space, i.e. a front end that allows a knowledge base specification by interacting with a KE or domain expert. In principle, the front end is often intended to make the KE superfluous by directly interacting with a domain expert. The dialogue is in semi-natural language or is part of a constrained editing environment. The dialogue is controlled by the system, and is aimed at knowledge base refinement. Figure 2 shows part of a dialogue between an expert and ROGET (Bennet, 1985). ROGET is one of the first of this type of knowledge acquisition systems, and uses EMYCIN as its shell.

```
ROGET (19): What are THE OBSERVATIONS FROM A MICROBIOLOGICAL CULTURES test
** THE LABORATORY-REPORTED IDENTITY OF THE ORGANISM FOUND IN THE CULTURE
 .....
ROGET (21): What is the list of expected values for THE LABORATORY-REPORTED
  IDENTITY OF THE ORGANISM FOUND IN THE CULTURE? Please enter each term
  or phrase on a separate line and finish with a blank line or DONE
** E.COLI
** PROTEUS-MIRABILIS
** PSEUDOMONAS
**
ROGET (22): What KIND of values will you expect for THE GRAM STAIN OF THE
  ORGANISM
** TERMS        $$indicates an expected list of terms
ROGET (23): What is the list of expected values for THE GRAM STAIN OF THE
  ORGANISM
** POSITIVE
** NEGATIVE
**
```

Figure 2: Excerpt from a dialogue between ROGET and expert (Bennet, 1985)

The data are automatically transformed in implementation formalisms. In other words, the knowledge acquisition process is *model driven*: the model consists of the shell's architecture and it's conceptual translation in the intelligent front end knowledge. For instance, ROGET has a very explicit "conceptual structure" which forms the intermediate model to translate dialogue data in implementation formalisms. This combination provides both the abstraction and transformation of data in code.

Currently, the number of these knowledge acquisition shells is rapidly growing. Most are rather prototypes and not in commercial use. A serious limitation to their use is that they have (or imply) a *single* conceptual model, i.e. can only cover a small set of domains.

> "MOLE the knowledge acquisition tool gets its power from its knowledge of the problem solving method of MOLE the performance system.. MOLE's problem solving method is a variant of heuristic classification." (Eshelman et al., 1987).

The bottleneck in this 'automatisation of knowledge acquisition by shellification' approach is probably the conceptual model of the reasoning and domain structures. Semi-automated knowledge acquisition systems are mainly developed for varieties of classification tasks (e.g. MOLE, (diagnosis) Eshelman et al., 1987; KNACK (design evaluation) Klinker et al., 1987; TKAW (diagnosis of equipment failure) Kahn et al., 1987; MORE (diagnosis) Kahn et al., 1985; STUDENT (data analysis), Gale, 1987; Yaka (diagnosis), Lambert et al., 1988), but also for simple configuration tasks (SALT, Marcus, 1987). A special type of these semi-automated knowledge acquisition systems are maintenance front-ends for existing systems: examples are TEIREISIAS (Davis, 1979; for MYCIN-like systems) and OPAL (Musen et al., 1987; for ONCOCIN). The latter uses a conceptual model of domain knowledge to drive the interaction.

The work of Chandrasekaran and his collaborators fit somewhere between this shellification approach and the conceptual modelling as is presented in the next section (for an overview see: Chandrasekaran, 1987). The various shells contain highly specific combinations of implementation formalisms, which are called 'languages'. In the KADS terminology they would be called architectures. In these shells the reasoning strategy is fixed, and the constraints for the knowledge base allow only a specific range of domains to fit. There is no conceptual model front end, but in the literature very detailed 'conceptual' descriptions of the reasoning strategies ("generic tasks") are available.

Modelling languages

Another approach is directly aimed at the development of conceptual models which function as a bridge between the data and the artefact. A conceptual model should reflect the understanding of the KE of the expertise in terms that easily map onto implementation elements (Norman, 1983). Traditional software development can be supported by conceptual modelling (e.g. Moran, 1981), but here in general the functional specifications ("data") are directly translated into some design language. In KBS development conceptual modelling languages are applied because understanding the structure of the task and domain knowledge is far more difficult here than in traditional software engineering.

A modelling language provides a vocabulary in which the expertise can be expressed in a coherent way. If all is well, this coherence is derived from a theory on how expertise works; whether human or artificial. This theory forms the basis of the semantics of the vocabulary. It can be derived from studying what KBS are supposed to accomplish. A good example is Clancey's (1985) analysis of heuristic classification tasks. In Figure 1 the bridging function of conceptual models is symbolised by the positions between the points M1 and M2. Some of these modelling languages have a rather direct relation with implementation formalisms (e.g. CSRL; Bylander & Mittal, 1986), and can be situated in the design space, rather than in the analysis space of Figure 1. Other modelling languages are very explicit in stating that they are independent of implementation formalisms (e.g. Expertise Specifications, Johnson et al., 1987; Systemic Grammar Networks, Keravnou & Johnson, 1986; SUPE-SPOONS, Alexander et al, 1987. GLIB, Freiling et al., 1985; KADS, Wielinga & Breuker, 1986; Breuker et al., 1987).

Implementation independence has the advantage that issues about effective design of the system can be postponed until the KE has acquired an explicit understanding of what constitutes the domain expertise. For instance, in the KADS methodology these concerns are handled separately (Hayward, 1987). First, in an analysis stage, the KE develops an abstract model of the expertise from the data. M1 in Figure 1 denotes this conceptual model. This model is transformed into an architecture of the KBS: the design model (M2). The vocabulary of this model consists of terms for implementation formalisms (Schreiber et al. 1987; 1988).

A modelling language can be a very helpful tool to identify domain objects and processes, but it still works mainly bottom up. Knowledge acquisition can become really model driven if also recurrent, generic patterns in expertise can be identified and made available in tools to support initial stages of knowledge acquisition. Both in KADS and CSRL these patterns are sought in the structure of reasoning that is used in various tasks: both call these tasks 'generic tasks' (Chandrasekaran, 1985; 1987; Bylander & Chandrasekaran, 1987). A generic tasks is a prototypical task, which uses a particular method of reasoning. For instance, diagnosis by heuristic classification can be viewed as a generic task (Clancey, 1985; Bylander & Chandrasekaran, 1987; Breuker et al., 1987). Another generic diagnostic task is systematic diagnosis, which is based upon a decomposition of functions and/or components of a device (e.g. Lambert et al., 1988; see also Figure 9). In analysing an expert task, the decomposition of this task can be accomplished in terms of one or more generic tasks. In (conceptual) model driven knowledge acquisition for each generic task an initial, or *interpretation* model is available that provides a macro-structure of the reasoning methods. If the task identification is correct, knowledge acquisition is mainly a refinement process as far as the reasoning strategies are concerned. Independently of providing models for reasoning strategies of generic tasks, like diagnosis, planning, design, classification etc. (see 4.3.), models can be developed that allow top down refinement of the knowledge base, as for instance in OPAL (Mussen et al., 1987). However, it appears that generalising over domain knowledge structures is less evident than over tasks: there are not many domain-knowledge models (or "domain theories") that support are sufficiently generic for knowledge base refinement in a variety of domains. Research in qualitative reasoning and in machine learning (explanation based learning) may provide elements for describing such structures.

2. Overview of KADS

In this section only a global overview of the major ingredients of the KADS methodology is presented. For a methodology to be comprehensive there should be available: a description of activities (task decomposition); concepts for describing the objects in the methodology (e.g. a modelling language), and tools and techniques. The development and evaluation of a methodology is in general a long term affair in which practice, theory and reflection alternate. After 5 years of research and development the KADS methodology is still subject to changes and shows some important gaps. However, the major outline appears to be stable and can be summarised as follows:

Life Cycle Model

A life cycle model, i.e. a task decomposition or division of labour, has been developed, in particular on the basis of software development methodologies (Edin et al., 1987; Hayward, 1987). An important principle is the fact that a full analysis of the data should precede the design and implementation of the KBS (M1 preceding M2 in Figure 1). In this respect, the KADS methodology differs from rapid prototyping or incremental approaches, and is more in accordance with traditional software development practice. However, the Analysis phase in KADS is far more complex than corresponding activities in software engineering. There is an "external stream" of activities, aimed at the specification of external requirements of the KBS: comparable with functional specifications. However, the internal stream which consists of modelling of expertise and communication with the user has no corresponding activity in traditional software engineering. The results of the Analysis phase -external requirements, conceptual model, static domain knowledge- are input for the Desing phase in which these objects are transformed in the specification of the architecture of the KBS.

Modelling Languages and Frameworks
For describing and specifying the various objects modelling languages and frameworks have been developed. The modelling framework for the Conceptual Model (M1 in Figure 1) will be presented in the next section. Other major modelling frameworks are the Design framework (Schreiber et al., 1987; 1988a; 1988b), and the Modality framework (De Greef et al., 1988). Modality is the specification of cooperation and communication of the KBS with the user or other systems. The Design framework describes how the conceptual model and external requirements can be translated into an architecture consisting of (AI-)techniques and implementation formalisms.

Techniques and tools
In KADS a number of techniques for collecting data (elicitation techniques) and bottom-up analysis of data are specified with their conditions for use (KADS-Handbook (Edin et al., 1987); see also: Wielinga et al., 1988). The analysis techniques, and the documentation of the Analysis and Design stages are supported by tools: the KADS Power Tools (Anjewierden, 1987). A next generation of these tools and further support is currently under development as SHELLEY (Anjewierden, 1988). SHELLEY is written in PCE/Prolog *) and consists of an integrated set of direct manipulation editors for analysing data (protocol editor), constructing a conceptual model, building structures of static domain knowledge, etc (see Anjewierden, 1987; 1988). The integrating is accomplished by the use of hypertext-like objects, which are created and maintained through all activities with SHELLEY.

3. KADS Conceptual Modelling Language

The KADS Conceptual Modelling Language (KCML) is derived from a theory about (re)flexible expert problem solving: the four layer theory (Wielinga & Breuker, 1986; Hayward et al, 1987; Breuker et al., 1987; Wielinga et al., 1988). Section 3.1. contains a short description of this theory with a slightly different interpretation than in previous publications. This section is followed by a detailed description of the elements of KCML. The last sections show how a taxonomy of generic tasks and KCML has lead to the development of interpretation models, and how these interpretation models are used in the KADS methodology. KCML is used for a comprehensive description of how expertise works in a particular domain without committment to a particular implementation formalism. KCML is designed for convenient high level conceptualisation of domain expertise in terms that lend themselves also for efficient design decisions for building a KBS.

3.1. Types and roles of knowledge in expert problem solving

The four layer theory which constitutes rather a view on expert problem solving than a fully elaborated and evaluated theory is based upon two premises. The first one holds that it is possible and useful to distinguish between several generic types of knowledge;

*) PCE is an object oriented programming system that allows high level user interface programming in the form of Prolog predicates (or Lisp functions). PCE is written in C and can be interfaced with various Prologs and Lisps. Currently PCE is only to be used with SUNViews as the interface at the other end.

the second, that these types of knowledge can be organised in layers, which have limited interactions. In AI, but also in cognitive psychology distinctions between object- and meta level knowledge and reasoning is useful (e.g. Davis, 1980; Clancey, 1983; Maes & Nardi, 1987) and plausible (e.g. Brown, 1980; Flavel, 1981; Glaser, 1978). Meta knowledge and reasoning provides a far more flexible control regime than plain conditional statements would allow. Psychological plausibility of metalevels can be derived from human reflexive capabilities, and the fact that we are able to monitor (e.g. Brown, 1980) our problem solving, or repair impasses in this process (Brown & De Kleer, 1979; Jansweijer et al., 1986). In KADS we distinguish more than 2 layers. As will become apparent at the end of this section each layer is not necessarily a metalayer of the previous one.

Four layers of Expertise

Domain layer

The knowledge at the lowest, domain level contains concepts and relations which form structures that represent generic facts and models (e.g. of processes or devices). The knowledge in this layer is task-neutral in the sense that there are no means to control its use. This assumption is clearly in contradiction with Chandrasekaran's (1987) interaction hypothesis. The interaction hypothesis states that knowledge must be tuned to its use. However, it seems that neither our assumption of task-neutral knowledge nor the interaction hypothesis is tennable in an extreme form. We are able to use "old" knowledge for new purposes. If we cannot solve a problem one way, we can change strategy and solve it in another way, using the available knowledge. This is why novices are perfectly capable of solving problems (Jansweijer et al., 1986); However, it is also obvious that the flexibility of (even "deep") knowledge has its limitations. This difference in view on the dependence of knowledge and reasoning strategy is also reflected in the tools: the shells developed by Chandrasekaran and his collaborators perform a task with a single, fixed task structure, while in KADS more flexibility within a generic task is identified (see also: task & strategy layer below). The domain layer has an 'axiomatic' structure, because it contains all the generic facts on which the reasoning is based. Solving a particular problem does not add axioms: t can be viewed as a transition (instantiation) of a generic model of a system in a situation specific one (Clancey, 1988).

Inference layer

The inference layer is typical for KADS: what comes closest to this layer in the literature is Clancey's (1985) description of the inference structure of heuristic classification. In this layer the abstract competence of making inferences at the domain level is described: the inference layer contains meta-knowledge about the domain layer. This competence can be viewed as a set of inference making functions, like abstraction, specification, assembly etc. These functions are called *knowledge sources*. Here the term knowledge source has a different meaning than as elements in blackboard architectures, like in HEARSAY (Lesser & Erman, 1977). The arguments of these functions are called *meta-classes*, standing for domain concepts/structures that can fill these roles. Meta-classes have preferrably the name of a role in the problem solving process, as not to confuse them with domain concepts.

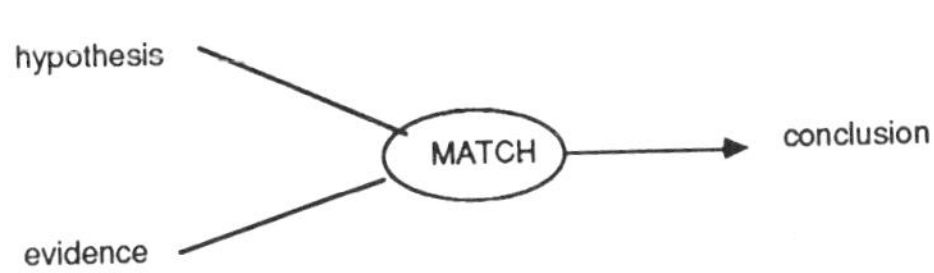

Figure 2a: Meta-classes and a knowledge source in hypothesis testing

A meta-class indicates how a specific set of domain concepts can be used. For instance, in medical diagnosis diseases or organisms can play the role of hypothesis: and in the end also the role of solution. Solution and hypothesis are meta-classes. For instance in testing a hypothesis and evidence can be an input argument for a 'match' knowledge source (KS), resulting in a conclusion (Figure 2a). The hypothesis may be a particular fault; the evidence of identified values for parameters in a working device; the conclusion consist of a true/false value for the particular fault. Note that we have shifted attention from isolated functions and arguments to roles in a wider scope: problem solving. By combining knowledge sources (KS) via input/output arguments (meta classes) an *inference structure* can be constructed that reflects the required inference competence to accomplish a problem solving task. Inference structures can be drawn as graphs. The convention is that labeled ovals stand for KS, and labeled arrows stand for the dependencies that result from connecting the input/output arguments (meta-classes). For instance, a simple inference structure for a very simple hypothesis generation and verification task can look as follows:

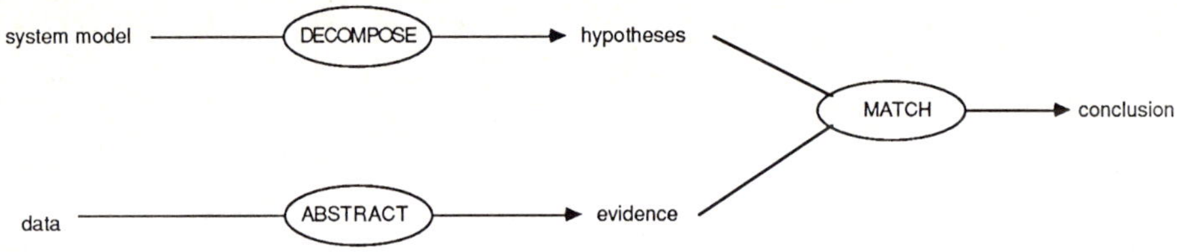

Figure 2b: Inference structure for simple hypothesis generation and - testing

An inference structure describes what inferences can be made, but not how or when they are made. The 'how' will be discussed in the next section; the 'when', i.e. the control, is part of the next layers.

Task layer

In the task layer knowledge about the task decomposition that is used to control the inferences is made explicit. The basic objects here are tasks and goals. Goals can be decomposed in subgoals; these are intended states in the problem solving process. Meta-classes are examples of such states, and can therefore be used to link the task layer and the inference layer. The task layer specifies when inferences are to be made, according to the plan that is created in the next layer:

Strategic layer

In flexible problem solving, goals should be adapted to circumstances -e.g. the type of problem; external (re)sources like availability of data and client/user intentions; internal resources, in particular the (inference) competence in the domain. This should not only result in a plan how to solve the problem, satisfy the client etc., but also implies the capability to monitor the progress in the problem solving process; keeping track of the communication with the external world; finding diagnoses and remedies for failures and impasses; design new plans when remedies do not work, etc. In short, at the strategic level full blown reasoning components are required that are capable of planning, monitoring and diagnosing the problem solving process. This is only a part of the capabilities which we assume to be available in the strategic layer of human problem solving and thinking. At least an additional requirement is that at this level knowledge about problem types, user types etc. should be acquired. In short, this is also the level where the (non-automatic) learning of problem solving in a new domain should be based (Jansweijer et al., 1986). It is obvious that these capacities are not required for building a knowledge based system for a particular domain. However, some of these capacities are needed to be able to operate in a flexible and controlled way to handle variations in problem types, and to "degrade" gracefully when problems get difficult. The latter is important, because it will prevent a system from presenting false solutions to problems beyond its capacities. False solutions can be far more costly than no solution.

How do the layers work together ?

The answer to this question is not obvious from what we have stated above. One view is to conceive these layers as cascades of interpreters. A summary table of the four layers which is also presented in (Wielinga & Breuker, 1986) suggests this (see figure 3):

level	relation	objects	organization
strategic level		plans, meta-rules, repairs, impasses	process structure
	controls		
task level		goals, tasks	task structure
	applies		
inference level		meta-classes, knowledge sources	inference structure
	describes		
domain level		concepts, relations and structures	axiomatic structure

Figure 3. Layers of description of expert knowledge

Each layer has an interpretion at the next layer, so that actions at the domain level, in particular making inferences, are described and controlled at the next levels. Every layer can be considered as a further constraint to what can happen at the domain level. This makes this succession of layers also very useful as an analysis framework, as will become more clear in the next section. Instead of a descriptive framework for successive specifications, one can take these layers as executable, i.e. as interpreters, or executable KBS, interfacing one another by meta descriptions and links. It also means that these layers can be part of an actual implementation of a(n inefficient) KBS. Indeed, a number of systems have been developed with the KADS methodology in which at least 3 of the four layers are identifiable. The strategic layer is only rudimentary specified. There is also work in progress to develop an executable four layer model that can function more or less as a shell for prototyping conceptual models.

Another interpretation of these layers as a model of executable expertise rather than as a framework for analysing expertise is the following. There are only two executable layers: the domain layer and the strategic layer. The two other layers are interfaces -knowledge structures- between these two. The strategic layer is the meta-layer of the domain layer. In order to know what the competences are in a particular domain, i.e. to know what one potentially can know, the strategic layer abstracts the competences of the domain layer. This abstract identification of competence is the inference structure. Given a type of domain problem, the strategic layer can plan on the basis of this inference structure a strategy to solve the particular problem. This strategy is the task structure which will do the job if all inferences about the competence and type of problem have been performed in a realistic and correct way. Figure 4 presents a summary of this view.

This interpretation corresponds with most current ideas on the use of meta-knowledge, in which only two levels are distinguished, or domain knowledge and strategic knowledge are separated (e.g. Clancey, 1985). Although in this view the layers do not have the same 'order' (the task structure is at the same level as the inference structure), and there are only two processing layers, the order of constraining the problem solving process is still in accordance with the successive interpreters view. The task structure is here also a further specification of the inference structure. In specifying a KBS we do not really intend to have task structures being generated by a problem solving strategy planner continuously. It is exactly in the nature of expertise that for all run of the mill problems this task structure is the same, so it can be more or less fixed. However, for complications, large variations in types of problems, potential impasses, etc. we need to specify also further actions at the strategic level. In this sense we can conceive of the strategy layer as a further specification of actions if the task structure does not fit the current problem.

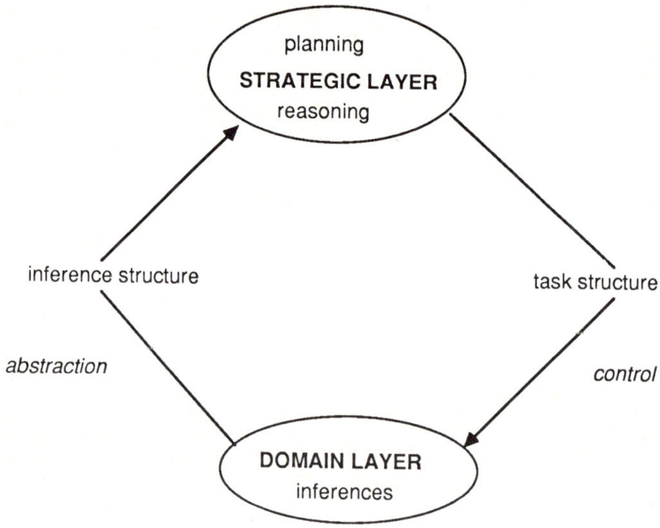

Figure 4: An executable four layer model of expert problem solving

3.2. KCML Descriptive Vocabulary

In this section the structures, types and terms of the elements of KCML are presented. KCML is a further specification, and operationalisation of the four layer theory. For instance, it describes structure and types of knowledge sources, types of task statements, etc. In KADS, KCML is a standard for constructing a conceptual model. *) To some extent, KCML is also a simplification of the four layer theory. For instance, as explained at the end of the previous section, no specific formalisms are developed to model the strategic layer. In actual practice this layer may be almost absent if the range of problems can be solved by using one particular strategy (fixed task structure), and if the control between communication tasks and problem solving tasks is very simple (De Greef et al., 1988b).

Also for the domain layer KCML will not have specific terms, because the KE should be free to use any available and suitable knowledge representation formalism to model the domain knowledge and inference mechanisms. In the KADS Analysis phase, the Static Knowledge activity can be viewed as aimed at a partial specification of the domain layer in which major (is-a; part-of; causal) structures of domain concepts are identified. However, there is no real commitment to formalisms or inference mechanisms (Wielinga et al. 1988;

*) The KCML standard as currently developed for SHELLEY may contain some small deviations from the vocabulary presented here.

Edin et al., 1987, III.2). The emphasis is on the inference structure, because in this respect KADS is new.

3.2.1. Inference Structure

As already described in the previous section (3.1., inference layer) the elements of an inference structure are knowledge sources and metaclasses. A knowledge source represents an inference making function, which has at least one input parameter, and one output parameter. These are metaclasses. In an inference structure KSs depend upon each other because the metaclass of a KS can be a required input of another KS (flow of data). In its graphical form these dependencies are presented as arrows, labeled by a metaclass (see Figure 2).

Knowledge Sources

A knowledge source (KS) is a functional description of an inference making process. A function only specifies what happens to its arguments. What output is produced on the basis of what input; not how this happens. The relation between input and output is described in action-terms and is the *type* of a KS. For instance, the 'abstract' KS indicates that the output parameter is more abstract, i.e. contains fewer attributes, than the input parameter. The current typology of KS is presented below. However, in specifying a KS in a particular domain, we have to link the inference level description with the domain layer. The specification of how in a particular domain this abstract inference function is accomplished consists of a *method* and a *reference* to the domain knowledge which enables this type of inference. A large variety of inference methods may perform the same type of inference. Strictly speaking, the type of a KS belongs to the inference layer; the method and reference indicate which domain elements can be mapped onto the KS. In this sense, an inference structure is an abstraction which can be applied to types of domains and tasks. For a particular domain, the method and reference slots have to be filled in to arrive at a sufficiently accurate description of a KS for designing a KBS. In summary: for a particular domain a KS has the following specification slots:

KS - type (e.g. abstract)
- method (e.g. classification)
- reference (e.g. taxonomy_of_bacteria)

The typology of KS is based upon a characterisation of the relation -difference- between the input and output parameters. These parameters -in fact: metaclasses (see further)- represent knowledge structures. Because there are many ways to represent knowledge, there is no unique way to develop a typology of KS. For instance, the input and output parameters can be viewed as predicates over variables. In this format, only three major types of inferences exist: a variable can be bound to a constant, or a predicate can lead to another predicate, or a predicate -in particular 'true' and 'false'- can be assigned as an argument to another predicate. *) This schema is rather poor, and particularly for the transition between a predicate and another predicate it is difficult to find further meaningful refinements. In KADS the input and output of inferences are currently conceived of as *concepts* in a KL-ONE like sense. The practical advantage of using concepts rather than predicates as principal elements is that it is easier to think in terms of domain concepts than in terms of predicates that define the domain knowledge. Domain terms index concepts. Moreover we arrive at a more refined typology. Before we go into more detail which types of elements we need, it should be noted that commitment to a particular view on what constitutes knowledge is here rather pragmatic and does not imply any commitment to some representation formalism at the domain level. To obtain a the type of KS in a bottom up way, the specific inferences as indicated in the data are translated

---

*) Another typology of inferences consists of induction, deduction and abduction (Charniak & McDermott, 1985). However, these are not functional types, but characterise inferences according to their method.

in terms of actions on concepts. In other words, there is a mapping between the inferences as they occur at the domain level and how these can be classified at the inference level, but it does not mean that the domain should consist of such elements. This mapping is a mental event in the mind of the KE, who can see an inference as an abstraction, a decomposition, a generalisation, etc.

The elements on which inferences can be projected are: (see Figure 5).

structure (of concepts)
  concept
    attribute
    value-restriction
      value
  relation
set (of instances)
  instance

Figure 5. Part-of hierarchy of KS parameter elements

As a structure of concepts can be a concept as well, the major distinction is between concepts and instances. Instances can be quantified. A number of instances forms a set, while concepts are assembled into structures, holding various types of relations. Relations themselves are special kinds of concepts. We assume that there is a distinction in making inferences in a world of instances and the world of descriptions (Brachman et al., 1985; Costa et al., 1988; Sahti et al., 1985). Some types of inferences -e.g. generalisation- form a link between the world of instances and that of descriptions. In KBS instances are important, because each case, problem etc. is an instance of generic structures (cf. Clancey's, (1987) view on generic and situation specific models in KBS knowledge). Inferences can be characterised by the following three major categories of relations between input and output concepts (or instances).

a concept can change, i.e. its values can change

a concept can generate a new, related concept

two concepts can generate a concept (relation)

Because there are special types of inferences required in manipulating structures we will also discuss structure manipulating types of KS, although it may be debatable whether they refer to 'single step', primitive types of inferences, or that they may be in fact composites of primitive KS.

Change Concept: assigning values to attributes

These knowledge sources manipulate a value of an attribute of a concept.

assign_value

concept with attribute --> concept with attribute with value

Knowledge sources of this type derive values for attributes of concepts and assign them to those attributes. An example is the use of default values.

compute

structure --> concept (in structure) gets value assigned to attribute

On the basis of some structure of concepts and their instances the value of some dependent factor is calculated. This structure can be a formula or constraint. It involves any form of value assignment on the basis of interdependencies of concepts.

Generating new concepts, structures or instances

instantiate

concept --> instance

This type of knowledge source creates an instance of a generic concept. Instantiation involves assignment of values. In fact, in an instance all attributes should have values. These values may be given as data, inferred, or default ones.

classify

instance --> concept

Classify is the inverse of instantiate. Another term may be: *identify*, because this KS may easily confounded with the classification task. Classify involves matching the attributes (and structure of these) of an instance with a concept. Classify associates instances with descriptions.

generalise

set of instances --> concept

In generalisation one focuses on common features in the set of instances and tries either to map these on an existing concept, or to develop a new concept. The former resembles classify, and classification methods may be part of the method description. The latter is generally known as *induction*.

abstract #)

concept --> (new) concept

Formally, in abstraction the relation between the input concept and the output concept is that the latter contains fewer attributes than the former one: 'irrelevant' attributes are abstracted (hidden; deleted). For instance, if one infers that a body temperature over 36 C means that the patient has fever, this is called abstraction (see Clancey, 1985, who distinguishes some subclasses of abstraction on the basis of methods). What is relevant and what is irrelevant depends on a *point of view*. Points of view may be prewired in the knowledge base (domain layer). For instance, many structures of static relations (is_a, consists_of) have fixed points of view, and enable abstraction inferences.

specify

concept --> concept

Specification is the inverse of abstraction. A specification KS produces a concept which has at least one more specific attribute than the input concept. A good example of specification is descending some taxonomy of concepts. Specification is the same as *refinement*, although the latter term is often used to denote some complex trajectory of inferences that involve specifications. A 'degraded' form of specify is called: *select*, in which a specific concept is singled out.

Two concepts and their relation

These types of KS produce a concept that expresses what is common or what is different between two concepts. The output is some difference. These KSs are often used to infer whether goals are obtained in reasoning, i.e for control purposes. Match and compare knowledge sources may connect various lines of inference.

#) In the literature the term generalisation is often used for both of what is here described as abstract and as generalise. Generalisation is performed over sets of instances; abstraction over concepts.

compare

value of X, value of Y --> concept with difference_value

The values of (the attributes of) concepts are compared. The concepts are input for the knowledge sources. The output is a class (equal, not equal) or a difference value.

match

structure of X, structure of Y --> concept with difference_structure

In its basic form a match knowledge source has two structures as its input. These structures are compared. The output is a description in which respects the two structures are different. Like *compare*, the function of match in many inference structures is to provide feed-back, or other forms of content dependent control. The description of the difference can be used to focus in a task on particular issues.

Structure Manipulation

These knowledge sources manipulate structures by changing them into some other structure. In principle there can be as many structure manipulation KS as types of structures can be distinguished. Here we will present only some frequently recurring ones:

assemble

set of instances (components) --> part_of structure

All assemble inferences take as their input a number of elements and produces a part_of structure. Assemble is an important KS in synthesis tasks (planning, design, etc. see 3.3.), but is only part of it. The methods for assemble (constraint satisfaction) may be very complex, and in fact consist of many other, more primitive KS.

decompose

part_of structure --> set of instances

Decompose is the inverse of assemble. The input is some composite structure and the output is a set of components.

transform

structure1 --> structure2

Transform converts an input structure into another structure. Essentially, there are two types of transform. The first type leaves the structural elements identical, but simply reorders elements within a structure (e.g. sorting procedures). Another, more interesting type of transformation is where new structural descriptions are assigned to the elements. For instance, a sequence of elements can be transformed into a part-of structure (parsing). Transformation KS may in often hide compounds of other KS, and appear in conceptual models only at very high levels of description.

This typology is not exhaustive. In actual practice a particular KS may in fact consist of an inference structure composed of various types of KS and metaclasses. In this way inference structures can be refined. This refinement may go as deep as to assign for each inference step at the domain level. In this way the borderline between domain and inference layer is a pragmatic one, dependent on the grain size of the analysis (Billault, 1988). In figure 6 the typology of knowledge sources is summarised.

Metaclasses

Knowledge sources can be viewed as functions in the problem solving process; the metaclasses are the arguments or *roles* in this process. A metaclass has therefore no structure; it is a slot that can be filled with a domain concept (i.e. its actual reference

```
knowledge_source
|   change concept
|   |   assign_value
|   |   compute
|   generate concept
|   |   instantiate
|   |   classify (identify)
|   |   generalise
|   |   abstract
|   |   specify (refine)
|   differentiate between concepts
|   |   compare
|   |   match
|   structure manipulation
|   |   assemble
|   |   decompose
|   |   transform
```

Figure 6. Typology of Knowledge Sources

to the domain layer). Because roles are dependent on the stage in the problem solving process a typology of metaclasses is difficult to construct, because the structure of the problem solving process (e.g. inference structure and task structure) varies. Therefore, we have only used a very crude leading principle in viewing the problem solving process

```
metaclass
|   problem
|   |   question
|   data
|   |   data_structure
|   |   |   case description
|   |   |   system description
|   |   individual_data
|   |   |   constraint
|   |   |   variable
|   |   |   symptom
|   |   |   |   complaint
|   intermediary role of data/problem
|   |   parameter
|   |   factor
|   |   finding
|   |   |   evidence
|   intermediary role of domain knowledge
|   |   system_model
|   |   hypothesis
|   |   norm
|   |   term
|   solution
|   |   diagnosis
|   |   decision_class
|   |   plan
|   |   design
```

Figure 7: Some types of metaclasses.

in a pseudo temporal/causal way. In this view, there is some input (problem), some domain specific knowledge (system model), some intermediary stages of data, some intermediary stages of solutions, and solutions. These will be the major classifiers of metaclasses. A provisional is_a hierarchy of metaclasses, based upon the experiences in constructing the interpretation models is presented below. It is to be expected that this structure can be further refined. An important reason the typing of metaclasses has caused us much problems is that the vocabulary in our natural languages contain only few terms to denote roles in reasoning. Therefore, many metaclasses have a newspeak flavour as a consequence of a lack of a well structured naive cognitive psychology. In figure 7 this provisional typology of metaclasses is presented.

3.2.2. Task Structure

For describing task structures we use two types of terms: *goal and control statements*. Goal statements are specified as an action term and an object, e.g. 'obtain (data)'. Because the task structure specifies when elements in the inference structure are used, the most *primitive goal statements* refer to knowledge sources and metaclasses. For all practical purposes we can therefore use the same terms, i.e. a primitive goal statement consists of a KS and the output metaclass, or its type of domain object. Examples of primitive goal statements look like: abstract (evidence), specify (hypothesis), specify (norm), compute (parameter), etc. This use of KS as primitive goal statements has another descriptional advantage. A full task description should contain a goal and a method. The methods that should be specified for primitive goal statements are in fact the inference methods.

Primitive goal statements may be combined by non-primitive, or: *compound goal statements*. Their function is to assemble a sequence or structure of primitive goal statements. Examples of compound goal statements are: generate (hypothesis), test (differential), select (canonical description), etc. Because compound goal statements rather have the function of a label in a task structure, a typology is not really required. On the other hand, a good typology may reveal major structures in problem solving tasks. However, given the flexibility of human problem solving it will take quite a major research effort to come to grips with this problem.

A special type of compound goal statements is: *modality goal statement*. A modality goal statement is rather a slot in the task structure that specifies when the problem solving process should be, or can be interrupted (by the user) in order to communicate objects to or from the environment. The way to specify the cooperation and communication between user (or: environment) and KBS is part of the Modality Framework in KADS (De Greef et al., 1988) and will not be discussed here.

So far, the task structure is a simple AND-tree. However, we also need some ORs, or more specific control. Currently the control statements in the task structure are of two types: *if <state> then <goal statement>*, and *while <state> then <goal statement>*. The former controls branching, the latter controls iteration. As a summary Figure 8 shows the elements of a task structure.

task_structure
| compound goal statement
| | primitive goal statement
| modality goal statement
| control statement
| | if_statement
| | while_statement

Figure 8. Elements of a task structure for KCML

3.2.3. Examples of inference- and task structures

Figure 9a presents the inference structure (at a very high level) of systematic diagnosis. Systematic diagnosis is characterised by a hypothesis generation by decomposing a system, e.g. audio-equipment (Lambert et al, 1988). There are two, closely related versions which occur frequently, and often both in the same KBS. The decomposition can proceed via components, i.e. the structure of the system: this is called localisation. And/or it may proceed via decomposition of a network of functional paths: "causal tracing" (for more details, see Breuker et al., 1987, 7.1.1.1.). The test-part is very simplified, and essentially consists of a compare KS which compares observed with expected values. The task structure (9b) presents a hypothesis driven view of the diagnosis. This is a minimally complicated version. In actual practice parts of the process can be test-driven (e.g. if there are important differences in costs and availability of test-data).

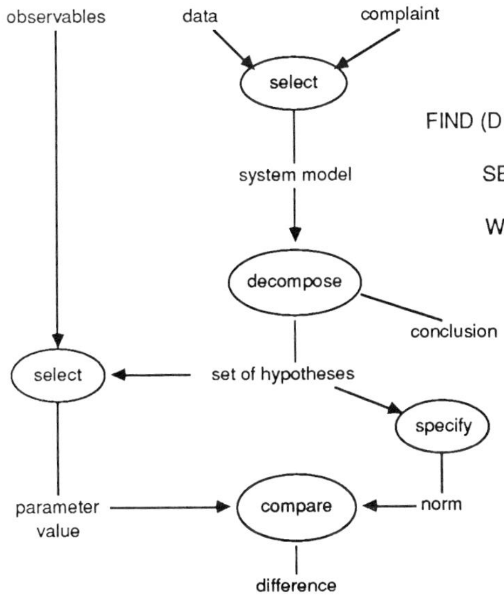


```
FIND (DIAGNOSIS)
  SELECT (SYSTEM MODEL)
  WHILE (~ CONCLUSION)
    DECOMPOSE (SYSTEM MODEL)
    WHILE (# HYPOTHESES > 1)
      SELECT (PARAMETER VALUE)
      SPECIFY (NORM)
      COMPARE (PARAMETER VALUE, NORM)
```

Figure 9a/9b: Inference- and Task structure for systematic diagnosis.

4. Interpretation models and generic tasks

In the KADS methodology various models are used. The most important result of the analysis stage is the conceptual model (M1 in figure 1). The conceptual model is a specification in KCML of the expertise in a domain (e.g. De Greef et al., 1988; Hayward, 1987; Billault, 1988). This model is an input for the Design phase, where it is transformed, in combination with external requirements, to the design model, or architecture of the KBS (M2) (Schreiber et al., 1987; 1988). This model can be further refined into a detailed design (M3).

In the beginning of the analysis stage the KE may find in the library of interpretation models in SHELLEY (see also Breuker et al., 1987, ch7 & 8) a model that may fit the description of the task(s) in the domain. An *interpretation model* is a high level model in KCML that is used as an initial model to guide the analysis of the data. The systematic diagnosis example of the previous section is a summarised instance of an interpretation model (fig. 9a/b). Because an interpretation model is task-, not domain specific, an interpretation model does not contain links to a domain layer. This layer in particular has to be filled in during the analysis process. An interpretation model contains an abstract KCML description of invariant aspects of recurring types of tasks. Therefore, it is not only of importance that the interpretation models are correct, but also that the types of tasks are generic or elementary, so that they can be used as building blocks for the real life tasks in a particular domain. Real life tasks can be viewed as (dynamic) composites of generic tasks. For instance, in troubleshooting audio equipment heuristic diagnosis may precede or alternate with systematic diagnosis. As psychometric studies of problem solving show, most problem solving tasks are composed of more elementary tasks (Guilford, 1967). Below we present a classification of generic tasks. Although a generic task can be further decomposed -as the task structure may show-, it is primitive in the sense that it produces an explicit solution to a problem, and not some intermediary meta-class.

The nature of the solutions is the leading principle in this taxonomy of generic tasks (cf. Guilford, 1967; Sternberg, 1982). The first, major distinction is whether the solution is a pre-existing element (concept, class), or is an assembly of elements. In other words, whether it can be identified or has to be constructed. According to Clancey (1985) the former are *system analysis*, the latter *system synthesis* tasks. *)

```
system_analysis
|   identify
|   |   classify
|   |   |   simple_classify
|   |   |   diagnosis
|   |   |   |   single_fault_diagnosis
|   |   |   |   |   heuristic_classification
|   |   |   |   |   systematic_diagnosis
|   |   |   |   |   |   causal_tracing
|   |   |   |   |   |   localisation
|   |   |   |   multiple_fault_diagnosis
|   |   |   assessment
|   |   monitor
|   predict
|   |   prediction_of_behaviour
|   |   prediction_of_values
system_modification
|   repair
|   remedy
|   control
|   |   maintain
system_synthesis
|   transformation
|   design
|   |   transformational_design
|   |   refinement_design
|   |   |   single_stream_refinement_design
|   |   |   multiple_stream_refinement_design
|   |   configuration
|   planning
|   modelling
```

Figure 10: Taxonomy of Generic Tasks

Analytic tasks have as their solution the identification of unknown properties or behaviour of a system. An unknown property may be a defective component of a device; unknown

*) We use here the term "system" in Clancey's (1985, 1988) sense: a KBS is a model of a system in the world.

behaviour may be the prediction of the state of a system, given a set of initial values for parameters. Analytic tasks leave the structure of a system invariant. Typical analytic tasks are diagnosis and assessment.

Synthetic tasks have as their goal to find a structural description of a system in terms of some given set of elements (vocabulary), formalisms or partial structures. Synthetic tasks may contain initially an analytic flavour, because often the specifications (problem statement) has to be identified in terms of the formalisms or elements. Typical synthetic tasks are design and planning.

The transition between these tasks is not all or none. The higher the level of the elements -partial structures- the more synthetic tasks may turn into analytic tasks: construction becomes selection of systems. In fact, the 'phylogenetic' development of a domain may be described as starting at the synthetic end and moving towards the analytic spectrum, when the solution space has become completely determined. A good example are 'skeletal planners' (Friedland & Iwasaki, 1985). These planners start as classifiers: finding a ready made plan for a stereotypical situation. If this fails, the plan has to be constructed. On this analytic-synthetic dimension one may assume a transition area, where part of a system is modified, but the integrity of the structure of a system is maintained. We call this: system *modification* tasks. Figure 10 shows a taxonomy of generic tasks, which we will further explain in the next sections.

4.1. Analysis Tasks

The major subdivision within the Analysis tasks is whether the solution consists of the identification of a current property of the system, or the 'prediction' of the state of a system. Prediction should not be taken literally: it is the identification of a currently not observable state of the system. Therefore, the major distinction is in the object: the identification of a structural property vs. the identification of a state.

Identification tasks can be further refined into various classification tasks. The most well known group of tasks in this family are diagnostic tasks. Diagnostic tasks differ from other classification tasks, because the solutions consist of finding a fault in a system. A fault is the negation of a correct function or component, and because the universe of 'negations' is much larger than correct system descriptions the fault finding process is often based upon experience that lends priority to frequently occurring malfunctions. This type of knowledge is often of a heuristic nature, and as pointed out by Clancey (1985) diagnosis by heuristic classification is the most typical model found -implicitly- in current diagnostic KBS. Systematic diagnosis may be performed if the system can be decomposed into components whose functioning can be investigated (localisation), or if a causal model of the effects of processes within a system is available (causal tracing; e.g. Steels and Van der Velde, 1986).

Another type of classification task is assessment. In assessment a case description is classified according to the terms of some system model, e.g. law. In monitoring data are checked whether they satisfy norms, and if not the discrepancy is identified.

There are two types of prediction tasks. Prediction of values is the derivation or computation of the value of some attribute when the values of related attributes are given, as for instance in physics problem solving and many other tasks used in educational training. The underlying model of the system is often a formal, quantitative model. Prediction of behaviour corresponds with tasks that answer questions like: "what will/would happen if/when". These are the tasks typically studied under qualitative reasoning: for a more detailed model see Bredeweg & Wielinga, 1988.

4.2. Modification Tasks

In many real life tasks modification tasks are contingent on analytic tasks and in particular on diagnosis. These contingencies are the result of the fact that many analytic tasks identify malfunctions, which call for modifications to restore the system to 'normal' functioning. These contingencies can be summarised as follows:

heuristic classification diagnosis	->	*remedy, repair*
causal tracing diagnosis	->	*remedy, repair*
localisation diagnosis	->	*repair*
monitor	->	*control, maintain*

Because in real life, system modification tasks are often very trivial, or very complex, they are hard to capture as generic tasks. For example, in medical diagnosis the remedy (a medicine, treatment, etc) is often almost directly associated with some disease, i.e. with the outcome of the diagnosis. However, if there is no specific medicine or treatment available, the remedy may range from experimental approaches (even: finding new medicines) to eliminating side effects of the disease (e.g. pain, and specific other symptoms).

In repair a defective component is replaced. It involves disassembling and inserting a new component. In remedy a process or malfunction is counteracted by initiating another process. Repairs are superior to remedies, in the sense that the effect of a remedy may only be the temporary suppression of the effects of a malfunction, while in a repair the full integrity of the original system is reinstated. The simplest form of control is when a discrepancy is observed (monitoring) and the discrepant value is straightforwardly changed by some immediate feedback. If the temperature gets too high, a cooler is used; indiscriminately of the cause of the rise in temperature. Again, this is a form of system modification that can only exist in very simple worlds (e.g. very simple physical process control). In 'generic control' the integrity of the full process is taken into account before a (counter)action is applied.

4.3. Synthesis Tasks

The top-level classification of synthesis tasks is based on the type of input and output the task has. Design tasks are concerned with inputs such as functional specifications, requirements, analogical descriptions of the desired goal, etc., the output is in general a detailed description of an artifact in terms of its components and structure.

Planning task are quite similar to design tasks: the difference being that in plans the elements consist of activities instead of (physical) components. Activities have to be laied out in time, and therefore plans describe temporal structures between activities, while designs describe spatial and structural relations between components.

Modelling tasks are also similar to design tasks, but in this case the input does not simply consists of constraints or requirements i.e. a functional view, but also of a set of data. An extra 'constraint' in modelling is that the solution should be some abstraction of this set of data, and that the mapping between data and model should be explicitly maintained Like in design, the elements of a model may be given in advance, but in many completely bottom up modelling tasks no specific elements are given, but have to be identified (abstracted) from the data and some high level modelling requirements (e.g. that the model should be a numerical model). If from this overview of tasks it appears that modelling is the most "difficult" one, it also makes plausible why knowledge acquisition (in a bottom up way) is a bottleneck (Littman, 1987). For most of the generic tasks interpretation models have been developed (Breuker et al., 1987). These models consist of an inference structure (figure 9a), one or more simple task structures (figure 9b) and verbal descriptions of task characteristics and possible strategic issues. The library of interpretation models is also part of the current KADS Power Tools (KPT) and the new KADS knowledge acquisition environment (SHELLEY-Workbench) which is under development (Anjewierden, 1987; 1988). Guidelines for selecting and combining interpretation models are presented in the KADS-Handbook (Edin et al., 1987 and in Breuker et al., 1987).

The function of interpretation models is to provide a high level initial structure for a conceptual model. The conceptual model itself is constructed by combining interpretation models, by further decomposition of KS and by constructing new lines of inference in a bottom up way by analysing the data in terms of KCLM. This is only a partial specification of the expertise required for a KBS. We have not discussed the specification of the knowledge at the domain level. This is a separate activity in the KADS life cycle: the Static Knowledge specification. The reference and method slots of the KS in the inference structure of the Conceptual Model are used to link this static knowledge. In actual practice there is a strong interaction between the specification of the static knowledge and the construction of the conceptual model. For instance, a KS may suggest a particular organisation of the static knowledge, while a articulate knowledge structure (and associated inferences as observed in the data) can indicate the presence of a particular KS.

5. Experiences & Conclusions

Interpretation models have been used in various studies within the KADS project: e.g. statistical consultancy (De Greef & Breuker, 1985; De Greef et al., 1987; 1988a); underwriting export guarantees (Davoodi in: Hayward, 1987); data network monitoring (Krickhahn et al., 1988); selling chemical equipment (Schachter-Radig & Wemser, 1988); mixer configuration (Billault, 1988); commercial loans assessment (Breuker et al., 1987); mould configuration (Barthelemy et al., 1988); commercial wine making (Wielinga & Breuker, 1984). KADS, including KCLM has been used in other projects as well: mushroom classification (Karbach et al., 1988); software project management (de Jong et al., 1988); social security benefit assessment (de Hoog, 1988); process control (Schrijnen & Wagenaar, 1988); diagnosis in physiotherapy (Achthoven, 1980). Interpretation models have also been applied in commercial practice outside the KADS project. A number of major knowledge engineering companies in the Netherlands have adopted and adapted KADS for their standard practice (e.g. van Lith, 1987). Here we can only summarise some of the major findings.

Although we have no well controlled studies in which the same data are analysed with or without interpretation models, there is invariably the subjective impression that interpretation models support analysis of data at the initial stage. A number of the KE involved in these studies have also experience using other approaches (e.g. prototyping), and some (company management) claim that analysis effort is cut to one third. Another finding is that novice KE have little problems in using models. Finally, it turns out that if initially selected models are not the appropriate ones (see below), a "wrong model is better than no model" (De Greef et al., 1987). This may be explained by the fact that the inappropriate model has probably a strong family resemblance with a fitting one. Lacking hard empirical evidence, a conservative conclusion is that the KE feels far more comfortable with an initial model, than trying to analyse the large amounts of data in a bottom up way.

The conceptual models which are developed from interpretation models consist most often of combinations of models for generic tasks (see also Breuker et al., 1987, ch8). This coincides with our assumption that a real life task is often a composition of several generic tasks (Guilford, 1967). For instance, in medical diagnosis testing hypothesis may involve the planning of obtaining lab-data. The conceptual model then consists of a diagnostic task, which has as one of its subtasks a planning task. Project management consists of alternating planning, monitoring, diagnostic and remedying tasks (de Jong et al., 1988).

Besides important refinements, the conceptual models contain extensions, and sometimes modifications, of the interpretation models. In some cases (e.g. Billault, 1988) the refinements are so detailed that the specification of the domain knowledge and inference methods is almost trivial. In other cases (e.g. statistical consultancy (De Greef et al, 1988a) it appears that the structure of the domain knowledge is so powerful that an abstract description in KCLM does not add any coherence to the analysis.

When a wrong model is selected, this appears to be due to an initial overestimation of the complexity of the task. What looks like a complex design task may degrade to a simple configuration task (Billault, 1988), or even a classification task. There are at least two reasons for this. For practical purposes the number of solutions may be reduced to simple variations of standard or canonical solutions (cf. MOLGEN-1 of Stefik, 1983 vs MOLGEN-2 of Friedland & Iwasaki, 1985). The second reason is that a generative theory -domain model- may exist, which defines all potential solutions. This is for instance the case in the statistical consultancy domain, where an apparent combination of planning and design tasks is reduced to classification and association because there is an underlying, uniform theory (De Greef et al., 1988a).

In using KCML to develop the conceptual model -either from scratch or from interpretation models- it appears that the vocabulary for meta-classes is soon exhausted and replaced by domain terms. Besides the fact that we may not have enough terms for roles in problem solving, the domain terms have the advantage that links between the domain layer and the inference structure become explicit from early on. This also facilitates the following tendency. The set of KS types seems appropriate, but it appears that there is no limit in the decomposition of KS. Each inference method can be viewed as a composite of KSs and meta-classes, so that an inference structure more and more grows into the domain layer (e.g. Billault, 1988). This may seem as a refutation that the inference layer is an ontologically different layer from the domain layer, but it has not been intended this way. The inference layer is an abstraction of the domain layer, and it depends on the level of abstraction where the boundary is situated. It is the old problem: when we specify a function, we may want to specify as well how that function is achieved. In specifying this method, new functions may appear, which may even be of the same type as the original function. There is nothing mysterious about this. However, if we conceive of this framework as a theory of human problem solving, the boundary between domain and inference structure may be less relative, and dependent on the grain size of the abstraction process (cf. Minsky, 1985).

The interpretation models provide support for developing the inference and task layers, but far less support exists for domain structures. However, this reflects also the state of the art in AI, where formalisms are developed for knowledge representation, but there is little insight in what good representations (models) are for objects and actions in a domain. This appears to be an art, and for most students a puzzling trick. Current research in AI towards models for time, space, substance, processes, etc. may in the near future become very valuable for analysing domains and constructing robust domain knowledge bases. These models or domain theories can be developed into tools that provide initial structures for major domain concepts.

Another recurrent finding in these studies is that the strategic layer is absent or only rudimentarily specified. This means that not much control knowledge seems to be required, and that a semi-fixed regime (task structure) may do the job. In other words, there appears to be little need for flexibility at the top, except for dialogue management purposes (see De Greef et al,. 1988b). This may be due to the fact that in practice less variations in problem types annex problem solving strategies occur than we expected on the basis of psychological studies on problem solving. Another reason may be that in none of the studies one is concerned with the range of problems that have to be solved by the KBS. In other words, most analyses are based upon general descriptions and a few probably very typical cases. If the first explanation is true, it seems that the need for meta-layers in KBS is not so much demanded for required flexibility, (Wielinga & Breuker, 1986), but for a meaningfully and transparently organised KBS (Davis & Buchanan, 1977).

So far we have discussed experiences with KCLM and interpretation models. However, the role of a conceptual model is that it is the input for the Design phase. An important assumption in KADS is that the Analysis phase and Design phase can be strictly separated. In a number of early studies -before the KADS Design phase (and language) was developed-, implementation directly follows the analysis, and the conceptual model is used more or less as an architecture of the system. In most of the recent studies, a Design phase follows. No revisiting of the analysis phase from the design or implementation phase is reported, although some amount of knowledge acquisition may still occur for refining the knowledge base. *) In a number of the studies mentioned above (e.g. De Greef et al, 1988a; Krickhahn et al., 1988; Billault, 1988) the separation between these two phases was almost physical in the sense that the system was designed or implemented by other KE than those who performed the analysis. Design or implementation occurred on the basis of only the KADS documentation of the analysis stage.

The majority of these studies indicate that KCLM as a bridge between data and the design of the KBS is useful. The studies also indicate that KCLM and the interpretation models within KADS are not completely stable and fully developed. Examples are the relative underdevelopment of the domain and strategic layers. However, also current (and future) work on formalising and implementing the tools for SHELLEY shows that many ambiguities in the nature of the inference and task layer have to be resolved. It seems that in KADS the practical problems are less drastic than the theoretical ones in funding the conceptualisations on sound experiences respectively formalisms.

Acknowledgement

We like to acknowledge the contributions of the work reported here from: Guus Schreiber, Bert Bredeweg, Maarten van Someren, Robert de Hoog, Paul de Greef, Jan Wielemaker, Massoud Davoodi (STC), Simon Hayward (STC). Maarten van Someren provided useful comments to earlier versions of this article.

References

Abbret, G. and Burstein, M. (1986), The KREME Knowledge Editing Environment *International Journal of Man Machine Studies* 26 24-35

Achthoven, A et al., (1988) Module didacticus rapport, project IIV, Bolesian Systems, Helmond NL

Alexander, J.H., Freiling, M.J. Shulman, S.J.,Rehfuss, S. and Messick, S.L. (1986) Ontological Analysis: An Ongoing Experiment, *International Journal of Man Machine Studies*, 473-486

Anjewierden, A. (1987) Knowledge acquisition tools, AI Communications, vol.1 p.29-39.

Anjewierden, A. (1988) An outline of the Shelley workbench, Memo, University of Amsterdam

Bennett, J. (1985) ROGET: a knowledge-based system for acquiring the conceptual structure of a diagnostic expert system, *Journal of Automated Reasoning*, vol.1, 49-74.

Billault, J.P. (1988) A KADS analysis of a configuration task, Thesis, University of Amsterdam

Boose J.H. (1986) *Expertise transfer for expert system design*, New York, Elsevier

Brachman, R.J. (1979) On the Epistemological status of semantic networks. (1978) In: N.V. Findler (Ed.) *Associative Networks* New York: Academic Press.

---

*) The major part of knowledge acquisition in KADS is in the analysis phase, but the conceptual model contains not all knowledge in fine detail. The analysis phase is not intended to deliver a complete system description on paper, but only the major structures. Therefore, during design and implementation knowledge base refinement is supposed to occur.

Brachman, R.J. and Schmolze, J.G. (1985), An overview of the KL-ONE Knowledge Representation System, *Cognitive Science*, vol. 9, p.171-216.

Bobrow D.G. (ed.), (1984), *Qualitative Reasoning about Physical Systems*, Elseviers Science Publishers B.V., Amsterdam.

Bredeweg, B & Wielinga, B., (1988) Integrating Qualitative Reasoning Approaches, *Proceeding of ECAI-88*, London, Pitman

Breuker, J. A. (1981) *Availability of knowledge*, PhD Thesis, COWO 81-JB. Amsterdam: University of Amsterdam.

Breuker, J.A. & Wielinga, B.J. (1987), Use of models in the interpretation of verbal data In A. Kidd, (ed) *Knowledge acquisition for expert systems: a practical handbook*, Plenum Press, New York.

Breuker, J.A. (ed), Wielinga, B, Schreiber, G, de Greef, P. de Hoog. R., van Someren, M., Wielemaker, J. Billault, J. P., Davoodi, M, Hayward, S. (1987) Model Driven Knowledge Acquisition: Interpretation Models, Del A1, ESPRIT P1098, University of Amsterdam

Brown, A.L. Metacognitive development and reading. In R.J. Spiro, B.C. Bruce & W. Brewer (eds) *Theoretical issues in reading comprehension*, Hillsdale NJ, Erlbaum

Brown, J.S. & van Lehn, K, (1980) Repair Theory: a generative theory of bugs in procedural skills *Cognitive Science* 4

Burton, M. Shadbolt, N., Hedgecock, A. & Rugg, G. (1987). A formal eveluation of knowledge elicitation techniques for expert systems: domain1. In D. Moralee (ed) Research and development in expert systems IV, Cambridge, Cambridge University Press

Bylander, T. and Chandrasekaran, B. (1986) Generic Tasks in Knowledge-Based Reasoning: The 'Right' Level of Abstraction for Knowledge Acquisition *International Journal of Man Machine Studies* 26 231-230

Bylander, T. and Mittal, S. (1986) CRSL: A Language for Classificatory Problem Solving and Uncertainty Handling, *AI Magazine*, vol. 7.

Chandrasekaran, B. (1982) Towards a taxonomy for problem solving *AI Magazine* 4 9-17

Chandrasekaran, B. (1987) Towards a functional architecture for intelligence based on generic information processing tasks, *Proceedings of the 10th IJCAI*, Los Altos, Kaufman

Charniak, E & McDermott, D *Introduction in Artificial Intelligence*, New York, Addison-Wesley

Clancey, W. J. (1985) Heuristic classification. *Artificial Intelligence*, *27*, 215-251.

Clancey, W.J. (1988) The role of qualitative models in instruction. In J.Self (ed) *Artificial Intelligence and human learning*, London, Chapman & Hall

Clancey, W.J., & Letsinger, R. (1981) NEOMYCIN: reconfiguring a rule based expert system for application to teaching *Proceedings 7th IJCAI-81*, Los Altos, CA, Kaufman

Cook , N. M & McDonald, J. E. (1987) The application of psychological sclaing techniques to knowledge elicitation for knowledge based systems, *International Journal of Man Machine Studies* 26, 533-550

Costa, M., Frixione, S., Gaglio, G., Spinelli, G., Traversa, M. & Zolezzi, M. (1988) Was king Arthur a king by definition? ", *AI-Communications*, 1, 32-41

Davis, R (1979) Interactive transfer of expertise *Arificial Intelligence*, 12, 121-157

Davis, R. (1980) Meta-rules: reasoning about control. *Artificial Intelligence*, 15, 179-222.

Davis, R. & Buchanan, B.G. (1977) Meta-level knowledge: overview and applications *Proceedings of the 5th IJCAI*, Los Altos, Kaufman Dieterich, T.G & Michalski R.S. (1983) A comparative review of selected methods for learning from examples In: Michalski, R.S., Carbonell, J. and Mitchell, T.M. (eds) Machine learning: an AI approach, Palo Alto, Tioga Press.

Diederick, J., Ruhmann, I. and May, M. (1986) KRITON: A Knowledge Acquisition Tool for Expert Systems, *International Journal of Man Machine Studies* 26

Dreyfus, H & Dreyfus, S (1986) *Mind over Machine*, Oxford, Blackwell

Edin, G., Rooke, P., Hayes, F. & Breuker, J. (1987) *The KADS Handbook*, ESPRIT P1098, Paris, CSI-J1-HB-001

Eshelman, L., Ehret, D., McDermott, J. Tan, M. (1987) MOLE: A Tenacious Knowledge

Acquisition Tool, *International Journal of Man Machine Studies* 26

Ericsson, K. A., and Simon, H. A.,(1984) *Protocol Analysis: Verbal reports as data.* Cambridge, Mass., MIT Press

Ericsson, K. A., and Simon, H. A.,(1979) Verbal reports as data, *Psychological Review*, 1980, 87, 215-251.

Feigenbaum, E.A. & McCorduck, P. (1983) *The Fifth Generation*, Pan Books, London.

Flavell, J.H. (1981) Cognitive monitoring In W.P. Dickson (ed) *Children's oral communication skills* New York, Academic Press

Freiling, M.J., Alexander, J., Messick, S.L., Rehfuss, S & Shulman, S. (1985) Starting a knowledge engineering project: a step by step approach, *AI-Magazine*, 6, 3-8

Friedland, P.E. and Iwasaki, Y. (1985) The concept and implementation of skeletal plans, *Journal of Automated Reasoning*, vol.1, 161-208.

Gale, W.A. (1987) Knowledge Based Knowledge Acquisition for a Statistical Consulting System, *International Journal of Man Machine Studies* 26

Gammack, J.G. (1987) Different techniques and different aspects on declarative knowledge, In Kidd A. (ed) *Knowledge Acquisition for Expert Systems* New York, Plenum

Ginsberg, A., Weiss, S, and Politakis ,P. (1988) Automatic knowledge base refinement for classification systems. *Artificial Intelligence*, 35,

Glaser, R. (1978) Advances in instructional psycholgy, Hillsdale NJ, Erlbaum

de Greef. P. & Breuker, J. (1985) A case study in structured knowledge acquisition. *Proceedings of the 9th IJCAI* Los Altos, Kaufman

de Greef, P. Breuker, J. Schreiber, G. & Wielemaker, J. (1988a) StatCons: Knowledge Acquisition in a complex domain, *Proceedings of the ECAI-88*, London, Pitman, 100-105

de Greef, P., J. Breuker & T. de Jong (1988b) Modality: an analysis of functions, user control and communication in knowledge based systems. Esprit P1098, Deliverable D4, University of Amsterdam.

Groot, A.D. de (1966) Perception and memory versus thought, In Kleinmutz, B. (ed) *Problem solving: research, method and theory*, New York: Wiley.

Guilford, J. P. *The nature of human intelligence.* New York: Academic Press, 1967.

Hart, A (1987) Role of induction in knowledge elicitation. In A. Kidd (ed) *Knowledge Acquisition for Expert Systems* New York, Plenum

Hayes-Roth, F., Waterman, D. A., and Lenat, D. B. (Eds.) *Building expert systems.* Reading, MA: Addison-Wesley, 1983.

Hayward, S.A. (1987) How to build expert systems: techniques, tools and case studies. *ESPRIT87, Achievements and Impacts*, Vol1., Amsterdam, North Holland

Hayward, S.A., Wielinga, B.J. & Breuker, J.A. (1987) Structured Analysis of Knowledge *International Journal of Man-Machine Studies*, Vol.26, 487-498.

De Hoog, R (1988) Bijstand voor bijstandverlening: een expert systeem *Informatie en Informatiebeleid* 4

Jansweyer, W, Elshout, J. J & Wielinga, B. (1986) The expertise of novice problem solvers, In: B. du Boulay, D. Hoggs & L. Steels (eds), *Advances in Artificial Intelligence*, Amsterdam, North-Holland

Johnson, P, Zaulkerman, I & Garber, S (1986) Specification of Expertise *International Journal of Man Machine Studies* 26, 161-182

de Jong, T., de Hoog, R & Schreiber, G (1988) Knowledge Acquisition for an integrated project management system *Information Processing & Management*, 24, 4

Kelly, G.A. (1955) *The Psychology of Personal Constructs* (2 volumes), New York, W.W. Norton

Keravnou, E.T. & Johnson, L. (1986) *Competent expert systems: a case study in fault giagnosis* London, Kogan Page

Kahn, G, Nowlan, S & McDermott, J. (1985) MORE, an intelligent knowledge acquisition tool *Proceedings of the 9th IJCAI*, Los Altos, Kaufman

Khan, G.S., Breaux, E.H. Joseph, R.L. and Del Clerk ,P. (1986) An intelligent Mixed-Initiative Workbench for Knowledge Acquisition, *Proceedings of the Knowledge Acquisition for KBS Workshop*, Banff, Canada

Kidd A. (1987) (ed) *Knowledge Acquisition for Expert Systems* New York, Plenum

Kitto, C.M. & Boose, J.H. (1987) Heuristics for expertise transfer: an implementation of a dialog manager for knowledge acquisition. *International Journal of Man Machine Studies* 26, 183-202

de Kleer, J. (1985) Review of "Building expert Systems" (Hayes-Roth et al., 1983) *Artificial Intelligence*

Klinker, G., Bentolila, J., Genetet ,S., Grimes, M. and McDermott, J. (1986) KNACK - Report Driven Knowledge Acquisition, *International Journal of Man Machine Studies*

Kodratoff, Y. and Tecuci, G. (1987) Techniques of design and DISCIPLE learning apprentice, *International Journal of Expert Systems*, vol.1, p.39-66.

Krickhahn, R., Nobis, A., Mahlmann, A. & Schachter-Radig, M. (1988) Applying the KADS methodology to develop a knowledge based system. *Proceedings of the ECAI-88* London, Pitman

Lambert, H., Eshelman, S & Iwasaki, Y (1988) Acquiring and complementing the model for diagnostic tasks *Proceedings of the ECAI-88*, London, Pitman

Lesser, V.R. & Erman, L.D. (1977) A retrospective view of HEARSAY-II, *Proceedings of the 5th IJCAI*, 790-800

van Lith, P. (1986) Experiences with knowledge engineering, *Proceedings of the AI & Advanced Computer Technology Conference*, Wiesbaden, FGR, part 4, pp 1-8

Littman, D. (1987) Modelling human expertise in knowledge engineering: some preliminary observations. *International Journal of Man Machine Studies* 26, 81-92

Maes, P. & Nardi, D. (eds) (1988) *Metalevel architectures and reflection*, Amsterdam, North Holland

Maibaum, T.S.E. (1986) Role of Abstraction in Program Development, in: H.-J. Kugler (ed): *Information Processing 86*, Elsevier.

Marcus, S. (1987) Taking Backtracking with a Grain of SALT *International Journal of Man Machine Studies* 26, 383-398

van Marcke, K. (1988) *The use and implementation of the knowledge representation system KRS*, Doctoral Dissertation, VUB-AI Lab, Brussels

van Melle, W. *System aids in constructing consultation programs*. Ann Arbor, Michigan: UMI Research Press, 1980.

Minsky, M. (1985) *Society of Mind*, New York, Basic Books

Mitchel, T.M., Keller, R. & Kedar-Cabelli (1986) Explanation based generalisation: a unifying view *Machine Learning* 1, 47-80

Moran, T. P. (1981) The Command Language Grammar: a represenation for the user interface of interactive computer systems, *International Journal of Man Machine Studies* 15, 3-49

Morik, K. (1986) Acquiring Domain Models *International Journal of Man Machine Studies* 26, 213-230

Musen, M., Fagan, L.M. Combs D.M. and Shortliffe, E.H. (1987) Using a Domain Model to Drive an Interactive Knowledge Editing Tool *International Journal of Man Machine Studies* 26, 105-121

Neale, I.M. (1987) Knowledge acquisition for expert systems: a review and case study, Master Thesis, Loughborough University of Technology

Nisbett, R.E. and Wilson T.D. (1977) Telling more than we know: verbal reports on mental processes. *Psychological Review*, 84, 231-259.

Norman, D.A. (1983) Some observations on mental models. In D. Gentner & A. Stevens (eds) *Mental Models*, Hillsdale, Erlbaum

Reichgelt, H. & van Harmelen, F. (1986) Criteria for choosing representation languages and control regimes for expert systems, *Knowledge Engineering Review* 1, 2-17

Sahti, A., Fox, M. and Greenberg, M. (1985) Representation of activity knowledge for project management, *IEEE Transactions on Pattern Analysis and Machine Intelligence*, vol. PAMI-7, 531-552.

Schachter-Radig M. & Wemser, D. (1988) A sales assistant for chemical measurement equipment *Proceedings of the ECAI-88* London, Pitman

Schreiber, G. Bredeweg, B., Davoodi, M. Wielinga, B,J., (1987) Towards a design methodology for KBS, Del. D8, ESPRIT P1098, University of Amsterdam

Schreiber, G., Breuker, J., Bredeweg, B & Wielinga, B. (1988) Modelling languages in the KADS methodology *Proceedings of 6th International Conference on Expert Systems*, Avignon, june 1988

Schrijnen, L.M. & Wagenaar, G. (1988) Autopes, de ontwikkeling van een expert systeem ten behoeve van procesbeheersing, *Proceedings NAIC-88* Amsterdam, University of Amsterdam

Shaw, M.L.G. and Gaines, B.R. (1986) Techniques for Knowledge Acquisition and Transfer, *Proceedings of the Knowledge Acquisition for KBS Workshop*, Banff, Canada

Solvberg, I (1987) METAKREK, Technical Report SINTEF/RUNIT Knowledge Technology Laboratory, Trondheim, Norway

Steels, L. (1987) Second generation expert systems, In M. Bramer (ed) *Research and development in expert systems III*, Cambridge, Cambridge university Press

Steels, L. (1988) Steps towards common sense *Proceedings of the ECAI-88*, London, Pitman

Steels, L. and Velde, W. v.d. (1985) Learning in second generation expert systems, in: Kowalik (1985).

Stefik, M. (1981) Planning with constraints *Artificial Intelligence* 16, 111-114

Sternberg, R.J. (ed) (1982) *Handbook of human intelligence*, Cambridge: Cambridge University Press.

Swartout, W.R. (1983) XPLAIN: a system for creating and explaining expert consulting programs, *Artificial Intelligence*, 21,

Terpstra, P. P. & van Someren, M. (1988) INDE: Learning by Induction and deduction *Proceedings ECAI-88*, London, Pitman

Tong, X, Karbach, A & Voss, A. (1988) Filling the knowledge acquisition gap: via KADS models of expertise to Zdest-2's expert systems *Proceedings of the European Knowledge Acquisition Workshop*, GMD, Bonn, GMD-Studien 143

van der Velde, W. (1986) Explainable knowledge production In B. du Boulay, D. Hoggs & L. Steels, *Advances in Artificial Intelligence*, Amsterdam, North-Holland

van der Velde, W. (1988) Learning from experience, PhD Thesis, VU Brussels.

Wielinga, B.J. and Breuker, J.A. (1984) Interpretation of verbal data for knowledge acquisition, Report 1.4 Esprit project 12, University of Amsterdam.

Wielinga, B.J. & Breuker, J.A. (1984) Interpretation models for knowledge acquisition. T. O'Shea (ed): *Advances in Artificial Intelligence*, (ECAI, Pisa), Amsterdam: North-Holland.

Wielinga, B.J. and Breuker, J.A. (1986) Models of expertise, In: B. du Boulay, D. Hoggs & L. Steels, *Advances in Artificial Intelligence*, Amsterdam, North-Holland

Wielinga, B., Bredeweg, B & Breuker, J. (1988) Knowledge acquisition for expert systems, In R. Nossum (ed) *Proceedings of the ACAI'87*, Berlin, Springer

Winograd, T., & Flores, E., (1986) *Understanding computers* Reading, MA, Addison-Wesley

Topics in Expert System Design
G. Guida and C. Tasso (Editors)

A METHODOLOGY AND TOOL FOR KNOWLEDGE ACQUISITION IN KEATS-2

Enrico MOTTA, Tim RAJAN, and Marc EISENSTADT

Human Cognition Research Laboratory
The Open University
Milton Keynes, United Kingdom

1. THE PROBLEM OF KNOWLEDGE ACQUISITION

The most popular principle in knowledge based systems states that the performance of an expert system critically depends on the amount of knowledge embedded in the system [1]. Therefore the knowledge engineer usually spends a great deal of time eliciting knowledge from domain experts and even more trying to make sense of the data acquired. This combined activity of eliciting, interpreting and organizing the knowledge acquired from the expert is called 'knowledge acquisition', and is often described as a lengthy and painful process. A number of factors related to the problem being tackled, the techniques used for knowledge elicitation and the personality of the domain expert can make this process extremely difficult, although clearly this is not *inherently* so, as illustrated by the non-problematic cases itemized in Figure 1.

- There is a well established knowledge elicitation technique that suits the current task. For instance, the Repertory Grid method works very well for tackling problems of simple data classification.
- The knowledge engineer already has a model of the task that can drive the knowledge elicitation sessions.
- The structure of the domain and the problem solving strategies are trivial. This is true for a number of mundane domains, for which expert systems are nowadays being built.

Figure 1. Knowledge acquisition is *not* a problem when any of these conditions prevails.

Nevertheless, problems can arise, due to the complexity of the domain and to possible mismatches between the knowledge elicitation technique and the structure of the problem (e.g. techniques such as protocol analysis work very badly for domains which are best represented declaratively). Moreover, recent empirical studies have shown that the efficacy of a particular knowledge elicitation technique can also be affected by the personality traits of the domain expert [2].

Much research has tackled the problem of devising tools [3] and techniques [4] that could support, speed up and eventually automate the knowledge acquisition process. Although all of these proposals attempt to tackle the same problem, they vary a great deal depending on the approaches, functionalities, underlying models and assumptions. In this paper we address some of the issues concerning knowledge acquisition, trying to clarify the nature of the knowledge acquistion process, and to point to the kind of software support the knowledge engineer can be provided with.

The rest of the paper is organized as follows. In section 2 we outline a functional model of knowledge engineering that will provide both the basis for clarifying the typology of the knowledge acquisition task and the theoretical framework for devising a knowledge acquisition tool. In section 3, we describe how these considerations led to the implementation of data analysis and data conceptualization tools in the original KEATS system [5], hereafter referred to as KEATS-1. The strengths and weaknesses of KEATS-1 have in turn led us to the development of a new system, Acquist, that is the kernel of the knowledge acquisition facilities being provided as part of our ongoing KEATS-2 project. Section 4 describes Acquist's structure, and its support for bottom-up and top-down approaches to knowledge acquisition. Finally, section 5 provides conclusions and a restatement of our current view of the state of knowledge acquisition.

2. A STAGE-ORIENTED MODEL OF KNOWLEDGE ACQUISITION

2.1 Critical stages

Figure 2 sketches a functional model of knowledge engineering where the ovals represent activities and the rectangular boxes inputs and outputs. The first three ovals, starting from the top, Knowledge Elicitation, Data Analysis and Domain Conceptualization, are the activities that define the knowledge acquisition stage. Hence, consistently with other descriptions [6], our model represents knowledge engineering as consisting of the acquisition, representation, implementation and debugging of (a model of) the expert reasoning and phenomenology for a chosen target domain. Knowledge acquisition is in turn defined as a composite activity that includes both the elicitation and the interpretation of the data. We want to stress this last point, as knowledge acquisition and knowledge elicitation are often confused. For instance, the paper by Olson and Reuter claims to provide a survey of knowledge acquisition techniques, while almost all of the mentioned techniques only address the *elicitation* level of the task.

The bold arrows represent the ordering relations between the different subtasks. For instance, knowledge elicitation is meant to produce the 'raw data' that are the input for the data analysis task. As the interactions between the various tasks can be fairly unpredictable, the knowledge engineer can be forced to backtrack to a previous activity to gather new knowledge, modify existing data, or detect errors and misconceptions. The right-angled arrows emanating from the left hand side of each oval indicate the iterative nature of (and inherent interdependencies among) all of these activities.

We could, of course, further characterize this model, by opening up the boxes and the ovals and analyzing the subtasks that exist at a more detailed level. We have only hinted at this by drawing a dotted line down the centre of every rectangle in order to indicate potentially divergent foci of interest. The two most obvious foci are (a) what the expert does (left hand side of each rectangle), and (b) how objects in the domain behave (right hand side of each rectangle). Another possible source of expertise is the end-user, who can provide the knowledge engineer with knowledge about the expected *modality* of the system [7]. The two large braces encompassing the top and bottom half of the diagram, respectively, indicate a concomitant emphasis (by the knowledge engineer) on (a) *overt behaviour*, as typified by 'what happens' phenomenologically to objects within the domain as well as by the expert's performance within it, and (b) *internal representations* sufficient to perform the desired task to the satisfaction of the knowledge engineer, domain expert, and end user.

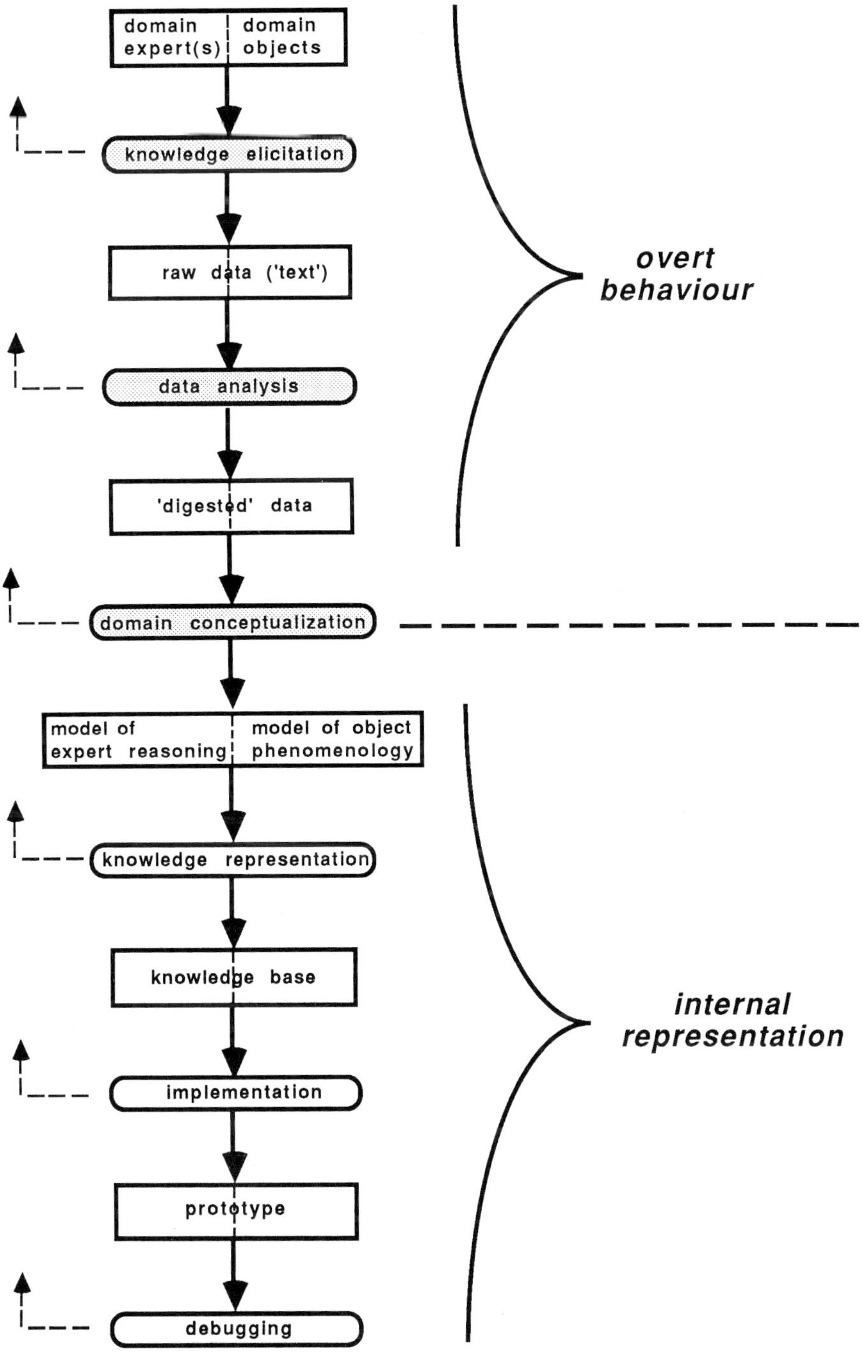

Figure 2. Functional view of the 'stages' involved in knowledge engineering. The shaded ovals define the knowledge acquisition phases.

Finally, the reader should bear in mind that, although the model is complete in representing the sequence starting with the knowledge elicitation sessions and ending with the system's implementation, there are a number of tasks that the knowledge engineer has to perform which are not covered here. These tasks include some preliminary activities, such as domain and problem assessment, and post-mortem activities such as system maintenance. As these problems are tangential to the problem of knowledge acquisition, they will not be included in our discussion. We note, however, that domain assessment, typically regarded as a 'feasibility' exercise, is itself similar to the activities shown in Figure 2 up to and including domain conceptualization, and therefore follows a comparable course.

The functional characterization of knowledge engineering provides a methodological basis for understanding and driving the work of the knowledge engineer. Moreover, on the practical side, we can use the task decomposition sketched above as a guideline for designing tools that could support the knowledge engineer in building expert systems. This idea has led to the development of the first and the second version of the KEATS system, which will be described in sections 3 and 4. In the remainder of this section we concentrate upon describing the stages that make up knowledge acquisition.

2.2 Stages of knowledge acquisition

The preliminary phase of extracting knowledge from the expert usually produces an unstructured and uninterpreted set of data that are often messy, noisy and unreliable, depending on the particular technique being used. Typically, the more general the technique (such as interviews), the more unstructured and noisy are the elicited data, referred to here as 'raw data'. Figure 3 provides an example of the sort of raw text one usually gets from preliminary interviews with the expert. The figure illustrates part of a transcript obtained from interviewing an expert in a neurobiological domain.

> Mike: Because, I mean, the main thing that I'm interested in doing is to look at the, well, to do 2 things: one is to look at the cells which are changing when the animals are learning something new, to ask questions about how the patterns of dendritic connections are varying when the animal learns, to see how the spatial dimensions of the dendritic processes are changing, to see how their orientation, their field (which is this whole sort of area that they're growing in) to see how that changes, and to look at the connections that occur between the dendritic processes of one cell and the axons of another cell, or it may even be the dendrites of another cell...

Figure 3. Portion of a transcript of a knowledge elicitation session in the domain of neurobiology. This transcript is 'raw data'.

Figure 4 shows an excerpt from a journal article which serves as part of the knowledge engineer's 'homework'. We call this 'homework' because the knowledge engineer needs to gain some familiarity with the domain (exactly how much is an open research question), and therefore the study of background literature is an integral part of knowledge engineering. Other researchers, e.g. [7], describe comparable 'homework' activities as forming an important part of the 'preliminary interview' phase.

The most important aspect at the knowledge elicitation level is clearly the technique being used. In particular, there are trade-offs concerning the use of formal vs informal approaches, direct vs indirect methods [4] and between weak (domain independent) and strong (domain dependent) techniques. Typically, knowledge engineers tend to use informal, direct methods, such as interviews. This style of elicitation has some advantages, as it suits industrial environments and it allows the expert to express a large amount of knowledge, as s/he is not constrained by a particular technique or representational encoding. On the other hand, the result of an unconstrained interview is usually a very unstructured set of data ('raw data'), that can require a major effort from the knowledge engineer to be analysed and conceptualized. Another problem, well analyzed in [2], is that the personality traits of the expert, for instance whether s/he is an introvert or an extrovert, also affect the elicitation of knowledge by interviews. Therefore, formal techniques, usually based on psychological principles, are also being used, in order to put knowledge elicitation on a firmer basis and to avoid getting unstructured and hence messy data. These techniques include: multidimensional scaling [9], repertory grid [10] and hierarchical clustering [11]. Although the assumptions and the methods are different for the the various techniques, all of them attempt to produce a precise representation of the way the expert organizes his/her knowledge. For instance, multidimensional scaling produces n-dimensional diagrams that give an account of the similarities and the differences between concepts according to different relations. The main problem with these techniques is that they don't really allow a knowledge engineer to build an expert system. Techniques such as multidimensional scaling or repertory grid only elicit declarative knowledge. Analogously, think aloud protocols [12] primarily aim at eliciting procedural knowledge. Besides, the elicitation procedures for some of these techniques can actually be quite boring and can easily create problems with an expert who may be glad to talk about his/her job, but not so happy to carry out psychological experiments.

> Presentation of a bright bead to day-old chicks (*Gallus domesticus*: Ross 1 Chunky Chicks) elicits spontaneous pecking. If the bead is coated with an aversive substance (e.g. methylanthranilate), they will avoid similar beads subsequently; if it is coated with water, they peck avidly on re-presentation. Formation of a memory for this one-trial passive avoidance task is unaffected by subconvulvie transcranial electoshock when applied 10 min. after training in 60% of birds, whereas "immediate" post-training electroshock renders 63% of chicks amnesic. Memory formation and retention is associated with a large bilateral enhancement in trained over control chicks (320 and 350% in left and right hemispheres, respectively; $p < 0.001$) of a particular spontaneous multi-unit firing pattern, that is, short-duration (15-40 ms) bursts of large-amplitude ($\geq$ 200 μV. 450 μV max p-p), high-frequency (400-450 Hz) spiking in anesthetized chicks.

Figure 4. Portion of relevant journal article [8] in the domain of neurobiology. This article also serves as 'raw data', and constitutes part of the knowledge engineer's 'homework'.

An important practical implementation of a formal knowledge elicitation technique is ETS [10], that uses the repertory grid technique. ETS asks the user to enter a list of domain *elements* first, and then to structure them, by differentiating triads of elements in terms of a trait that is true only for two of them. For instance, if the domain is a list of databases, a possible trait can be 'Run on Vax' or 'Hierarchical'. The combination of a trait and its opposite is referred to as a *construct.* Once a number of constructs have been elicited, the system asks the user to rate each element against each construct, therefore producing a rating grid. Finally, the system produces an entailment graph, that shows the implications between halves of constructs. These implications are then transformed into rules that, together with those generated from the rating grid, produce the final rulebase. ETS has the advantage of providing very fast prototyping (two hours) and of making the construction of the prototype completely automated. On the other hand, its technique seems suitable only for classificatory problem solving.

Finally, as the above mentioned techniques don't reflect the structure of a particular task, they are said to be *weak* . Researchers have found it useful to use strong models of knowledge elicitation, based on the structure of the domain and/or of the task. KNACK [13] has knowledge about the design of electromechanical systems and uses such knowledge to make sense of the data it elicits from written reports and from interviews with the domain expert. A more interesting approach is found in MOLE [14], where a heuristic classification model [15] is used to elicit and interpret the data.

The above approach is based on the idea that the architecture of an expert system should rely on a more principled framework than a mere collection of frames and rules. For instance, heuristic classification models perform their reasoning in terms of general concepts such as 'data', 'solutions', 'abstraction' and 'heuristic step'. *Generic task models*, as advocated in [16] are also based on a similar approach. Modelling problem solving in terms of generic tasks has a number of advantages.

These models provide principled explanations [17], based on the generic control structure of the problem, and they are more flexible and general. Generic task models can also be applied to knowledge acquisition [7] to support top-down approaches. In section 4.3 we shall return to this point to discuss top-down support in Acquist.

Once a set of data has been elicited, the knowledge engineer attends to the data analysis activity with the aim of removing the noise and the unnecessary material from the raw data, by identifying and extracting atomic 'chunks' of knowledge in the form of concepts, statements, definitions or relations. The way data analysis is carried out heavily depends on the knowledge elicitation technique. Hence, it is relatively straightforward, when formal techniques are used, but it can be problematic if the raw data are particularly unstructured.

```
Objects
        Axons
        Cells
        - Type of cells
        - Activity of a cell
        Dendrites
        Transmitter
        Synapse
Change
        - analyzed statistically
Changes in the membrane
        -very rapid
Changes in the transmitters
        - very rapid
Changes in the patterns of dendritic connections
Changes following passive avoidance learning
Changes of binding of substances to the transmitters
        - Time dimensions
        - Space dimensions
Changes due to relocation from one region to another; from one dendrite to
another
...
```

Figure 5. Atomic 'chunks' forming part of the so-called 'digested data'.

Data analysis is characterised by the emphasis placed upon the linguistic aspect of the data. For instance, preliminary data analysis of a report is carried out in KNACK by identifying and isolating keywords and concepts in the text, and in KRITON [18], by means of a statistical text analysis. A similar approach is also expressed by Breuker and Wielinga [19], where the authors discuss a linguistic level, characterised by the process of knowledge identification. At this level "The representation is superficial and has not been integrated into a conceptual framework. The same knowledge of different experts may have to be represented differently, because they use different terminology, or because their knowledge is structured differently" [19]. Hence, a typical outcome of the data analysis stage is the production of glossaries and loose categorizations, such as the one showed in Figure 5, forming what we refer to as 'digested data'.

The categorizations produced at this stage do not need to be concerned only with the level of domain concepts. Figure 6 shows an attempt at a categorization of generic meta-level concepts, which can be used to account for the expert's behaviour in a neurobiology example. The purpose of this generic categorization is to pull out the concepts needed to build abstract models of scientific reasoning.

It is worth stressing the fact that the so called 'digested data' produced by this analysis only exhibit a local meaning, as they are not bound together by a comprehensive model of the domain and the task. In fact, they express isolated chunks of knowledge that the expert can recognize, while not yet providing a model of the problem. This data analysis activity is useful for helping the knowledge engineer to home in on important aspects of the problem.

The production of glossaries and loose categorization is only a part of the data analysis activity. More generally, as the aim of the linguistic analysis is to impose a structure upon a piece of a text, the outcome of this process should be the production of a linguistic model, characterized by a web of linguistic relations between textual entities. In sections 3 and 4, we shall describe what kind of support is provided in CREF and Acquist to produce linguistic models.

- research goals
  - ...
- observations
  - goals
  - rationale
  - space
    - structural
      - macro
      - individual
      - micro
    - temporal
      - pre-post
      - longitudinal
    - spatial/here-there
  - type
    - who-which
    - what
    - where
    - when
    - how
    - why
  - method
    - technique
    - apparatus
    - variables
  - outcome
- hypotheses
  - type
  - ...
- paradigms
  - dogmas
    - e.g. synaptic neurotransimitters,
    - e.g. 2 pathways = an 'association'
  - classic results
    - e.g. Pervis
  - data sources
- models
  - inputs
  - outputs
  - functions
  - flows
  - objects
  - relations
  - ...
- ...

Figure 6 Generic concept groupings

At the domain conceptualization stage, the knowledge engineer attempts to impose a structure upon the data collected so far in order to produce an abstract model of the problem in terms of taxonomic hierarchies, causal networks, tables, flow diagrams, or whatever organization s/he finds convenient for modelling the domain and the problem solving structure of the problem. The important element that differentiates this level from the knowledge representation one is that the representation at this level doesn't need to be runnable, but is meant to be a semi-formal characterization of the structure of the task. For example, Figure 7 shows a fine-grained characterization of 'event sequences', based upon the journal article excerpted in Figure 4. The representation is pseudo-code, i.e. it is not intended to be runnable as shown, but is intended to map directly onto a runnable representation.

```
event-class peck1, ; CHICK PECKS AT BRIGHT BEAD
        types: [bead(X), exp(E), chick(C)]
        salient-relations: [ ]
        sequence: [present(E,X,C)-1, peck(C,X)-2]
        replicability: good
        prior-events: [necessary: [] excluded: [] ] .

event-class avoid1, ;CHICK AVOIDS POISON BEAD
        types: [bead(X), exp(E), chick(C), aversive(Chem)]
        salient-relations: [coated(X,Chem)]
        sequence: [present(E,X,C)-1, avoid(C,X)-2]
        replicability: good
        prior-events: [necessary: [disgust1] excluded: [] ].

event-class shock10, ;10 MIN SHOCK HAS NO EFFECT
        types: [bead(X),electroshock(S), exp(E), chick(C)]
        salient-relations: [coated(X,Chem), delay-before-zap(10)]
        sequence: [prior-events-1/5, zap(E,S,C)-15,
                present(E,X,C)-16, avoid(C,X)-17]
        replicability: .6
        prior-events: [necessary: [peck1,disgust1,avoid1] excluded: [] ].

account a7
        type-of-account: all-simple-diffs
        comparing: peck1 vs avoid1
        basis-for-comparison: sequence
        query-of-interest: why
        args-of-interest: peck vs avoid
        relevant-diffs: [ ] vs [aversive(Chem), coated(X, Chem)].

...
```

Figure 7. More domain conceptualization, this time at a finer grain of detail, based upon an analysis of the journal article excerpted in Figure 4.

An example of conceptual structures is found in the interpretation models used in KADS [19] and in ROGET [20], that represent the strategic layer of the task. Indeed, there is no reason for conceptual models to be characterized only at the meta-level. In fact, in domains that exhibit complex device behaviour, such as electronic fault diagnosis, most of the action actually lies at the domain level, i.e. in understanding the functionality and phenomenology of the devices, while the strategic layer is often much less complex. We have underlined this aspect in Figure 2 by splitting the outcome of the domain conceptualization stage into two ports, dealing with the strategic level ('model of expert reasoning') and the phenomenology of the objects in the domain.

Domain conceptualization is a very complex and delicate stage of the knowledge engineering process, as it is at this level that inconsistencies and holes appear in the knowledge base, although, given the semi-formal nature of the models, they can't automatically be spotted. Another problem concerning top-down approaches is that when conceptual models are used to drive the acquisition of knowledge, it may be the case that the model and the domain don't match. This is especially true for systems that implement automated knowledge acquisition (see for instance MOLE [14]), as they can only map the domain dependent data into the prestored model and provide little help when such a mapping is not feasible. To make things more complex, the expert may not be fully aware of his/her assumptions and problem solving strategies. Therefore, it may be up to the knowledge engineer to uncover and make explicit the rationale supporting the elicited data. For instance, in [5] we showed some examples of common-sense based strategies used in fault diagnosis. These strategies were inferred inductively by the knowledge engineer after an analysis of the rules describing the behaviour and the diagnostic choices of the expert.

2.3 Knowledge acquisition as the production of conceptual models

According to the 'stage' model in Figure 2 the goal of knowledge acquisition is to produce an abstract model of the problem that can then be implemented and refined. Thus, knowledge acquisition can be characterized as an independent enterprise and not necessarily as an ancillary activity of knowledge engineering.

In fact, the separation of acquisition from implementation leads to a view of knowledge acquisition as the production of an abstract architecture that is distinct from the implementation of the system. This view has some advantages that include the factorization of the tasks and the possibility of examining the strengths and weaknesses of the model before implementing it [7]. On the other hand, this characterization is also problematic, as it seems to clash with the problem of devising methods for checking whether knowledge has been acquired and whether the abstract architecture is a real model of the problem. In fact, the only way we know of testing an expert systems application is to run it. Only then is it possible to check whether the appropriate knowledge has been operationally acquired. Therefore, even if it is methodologically useful to characterize knowledge acquisition as an activity whose aim is to produce a conceptual model, we believe that in practice the boundaries between acquisition and implementation can actually be very fuzzy. Clearly, this is due to the lack of an appropriate formalism and of primitives for conceptual structures. Whether such primitives can be found, is an open problem.

A number of researchers have advocated the separation of knowledge acquisition from implementation and they all share the problem of providing a formalism for representing such 'abstract architectures'. This seems true for the KADS system [7], whose aim is to produce, at the end of the knowledge acquisition process, a document describing the structure of the problem. A potentially attractive approach is found in KRITON [18] which uses an intermediate level representation based on frames and propositional calculus. However, KRITON thereby commits itself and the knowledge engineer to a particular representational choice. Another possible alternative could be the use of logic as the 'lingua franca' for describing abstract models. This has been suggested in different contexts [21], but it has both theoretical and practical difficulties. On the one hand it is not simple to represent things like defaults, qualitative processes and time-based processes, and on the other it is often the case that the amount of time needed to produce a formal model of the problem is comparable to the time needed to implement the system. A different, more pragmatic approach is suggested by KEATS, which uses a graphical interface to store the architecture of the problem. Although in the earlier KEATS-1 implementation such an interface has some expressive limitations, it provides a representation that is disjoint from a particular knowledge representation formalism, while at the same time being formal enough to be mapped into a running implementation. Moreover, it also provides the user with a practical environment for inputting and analyzing the conceptual structure.

The choice of a formalism to represent abstract models of the target task is not the only problem related to this functional view of knowledge acquisition. Another issue concerns the nature of the model specification. As mentioned before, we agree with the view expressed in [7] where the authors advocate the use of models at the 'epistemological' level, based on the 'generic tasks' paradigm, both to drive and to characterize the outcome of the knowledge acquisition process.

2.4 Supporting the knowledge engineer

Most commercially available AI toolkits only support the knowledge engineer during the phases of implementing and debugging the system. No support is normally provided at the knowledge acquisition stage. On the other hand, a number of efforts have been made toward the direction of automating the knowledge acquisition process [26] [10] [20] [14]. For better or worse, automated knowledge acquisition hasn't yet reached the point of making the knowledge engineer redundant, and, for most applications, it is still necessary for the knowledge engineer to tackle all of the activities described in our model. To understand why this is the case, consider an analogy between knowledge engineers and traditional programmers. In the case of programmers, although life can

aforementioned 'continuity' requirement is fundamental for supporting the smooth progression and the incremental refinement of models implied by Figure 2.

For instance, a typical operation that a knowledge engineer performs upon a piece of text is that of isolating a rule, fact or concept. A knowledge acquisition support tool should then allow the specification of links from the newly created objects to the original piece of text. This allows such a structure to be used for generating automatic documentation/explanation, which records the rationale underlying the definition of such an object, or alternatively to be used for the sake of bookkeeping. A simple operation such as the one described here is possible in CREF/GIS only if the knowledge engineer specifies this link indirectly, which requires a number of steps to duplicate structures across the two systems. As a result, the KEATS-1 user often resorted to tackling data analysis and domain conceptualization as two discrete, separate processes, or to avoiding the CREF component altogether.

The problems experienced in the use of CREF and GIS have caused the KEATS-1 knowledge acquisition module to be re-evaluated and have led to the design and development of Acquist, a knowledge acquisition tool to be embedded in 'KEATS-2'. KEATS-2 is itself an evolving software research environment, intended to take the lessons learned from KEATS-1 and provide support tools suitable for scaling up to the size of problems faced by teams of (possibly disparate) knowledge engineers working in an industrial context. Acquist tries to bridge the gap between those phases in Figure 2 concerned with overt behaviour and the knowledge engineer's primary concern with internal representation. To achieve this, Acquist is expected to assist the knowledge engineer in both 'bottom-up' and 'top-down' activities. In the former the knowledge engineer 'feels his/her way' around a domain for the first time, and in the latter the knowledge engineer tries to verify or instantiate or 'flesh out' the skeleton of pre-existing schemas by observing the expert in action or discussing the domain in detail with the expert.

We encourage a mixture of styles, depending on the problem at hand and the user's own preferences. Purely top-down regimes can be uncomfortable for some users, in that they appear to 'steamroll' the user into a pre-determined style of representation. Purely bottom-up regimes can be too *adhoc* for some users. KEATS-2 aims to allow the user to build up an account of expert behaviour in a domain in a bottom-up fashion, then to apply that account top-down to further examples of (the same or related) behaviour, or to freely intermix the two styles. The next section describes out latest efforts in this area.

4. ACQUIST

4.1 Introduction

Acquist is a hypertext based facility [24] [25] that allows the knowledge engineer to carry out knowledge acquisition through the process of abstracting and structuring the knowledge contained in 'raw text' (typically transcripts). Units of knowledge are isolated from the raw text through a process of defining chunks of text called 'fragments' (data analysis). Structuring of the knowledge contained in fragments occurs at three different levels. Firstly, fragments are collected around 'concepts'. A concept can be thought of as the abstract label for the notion that the fragments in that collection define, or concretize. Secondly, concepts can be factored into 'groups', and 'groups' into 'Meta-groups', which split the concepts into higher order categories. The third and most flexible means of structuring the knowledge is a means of defining links and applying these links between 'items' (i.e. fragments, concepts or groups) either across the same level of abstraction, or, as is the case with the 'documentation' link, across different levels (domain conceptualization). A collection of fragments, concepts, groups and links constitutes a model or theory of the knowledge for a given domain, and can be saved by the user as a 'theory'.

In addition to its focus on text, Acquist also provides a generic graphical layout facility which we refer to as 'maps'. Maps provide a graphical representation of the emerging structure which is being imposed on the text, and equips the knowledge engineer both with a high level view of the knowledge extracted, and a means of navigating through the transcript. Maps also provide a graphical interface to the acquisition process, allowing the knowledge engineer to carry out all but the fragment generation operation via a graphics rather than text based interface. More importantly, the graphical layout produces an intermediate level of representation, bridging the gap between knowledge acquisition and the implementation of the system.

While the CREF/GIS modules in KEATS-1 were only able to (partially) support bottom-up approaches to knowledge acquisition, Acquist aims also to provide top-down support, by means of a mechanism for on-line creation and completion of 'coding sheets'. These are templates for driving the knowledge acquisition process, and will be discussed in section 4.3.

Acquist aims to integrate both the philosophy and the functionality of the two original KEATS-1 facilities, CREF and GIS, in order to produce a more natural and more efficient progression from the transcript, through data analysis, to domain conceptualization, and finally, to the formalization of the knowledge into a machine readable form. Acquist builds upon the lessons learned in the implementation and use of CREF, and like CREF, its design aims to support the tasks that knowledge engineers have been observed carrying out when analysing transcripts. These tasks include, editing/revising the transcript to filter out uninteresting and irrelevant parts of the transcript; segmentation of the transcript into logical units of information (fragments); indexing of fragments; highlighting of particularly important information; annotation of the fragments; construction of diagrams; generation of models from the information held in the transcript.

However, Acquist differs from CREF in that the emphasis is placed upon creating conceptual models based upon the fragments of text that the knowledge engineer deems to be important. Thus, the processes of data analysis and domain conceptualization are not kept separate but rather become intertwined, allowing the knowledge engineer to work at both levels at will, by chunking the transcript into meaningful pieces of knowledge, asserting links between them, and at the same time generating concepts and relations in the domain. This activity leads to the construction of an abstract architecture of the domain that is *tied to* and *supported by* the fragments of text from the transcript. Moreover, from the abstract architecture, the user can automatically generate a frame-based representation, which can then be used as the kernel of the prototype system. This is precisely the 'bridge' between overt behaviour and internal representation emphasized in our discussion of Figure 2 earlier.

We now turn to a more detailed discussion of the structure and facilities provided by Acquist.

4.2 Providing support for bottom-up approaches

4.2.1 Transcripts

Acquist deals first and foremost with raw text obtained either from interviews with domain experts or from relevant domain literature. The transcript is read into Acquist using the command 'Read Transcript' (Figure 8 - top right) which provides the knowledge engineer with access to a read-only version of the text. This ensures that any future analysis of the transcript, by the same or other knowledge engineers, is based on exactly the same text.

4.2.2 Fragments

The basic textual unit manipulated by Acquist is called a 'fragment', which is an arbitrarily chosen chunk of text taken from the raw text base. A fragment can be any size from a letter or a sentence to a whole transcript. It is left to the knowledge engineer to decide which parts of the transcript are important, and what the boundaries of this information should be. It is possible to create fragments that overlap, i.e. have common pieces of text, and also for fragments wholly to contain text used in other fragments.

Fragments are created when the user selects a region of text from the transcript, and assigns it to a concept by mousing on the relevant concept name in one of the two concept scroll menus. Figure 8 shows a screen snapshot of Acquist in action. On the far left, a transcript which is being analysed is displayed in a specialized text editor. A fragment chosen by the knowledge engineer can be seen highlighted in inverse video. Also shown in Figure 8 is a pop-up window displaying the contents of the fragments clustered under the concept 'amnesia'. This was achieved via a pop-up menu which resulted from the user selecting the concept 'amnesia' from the scrolling concepts menu. A mouse-click on any of the fragments allows the user to apply a number of fragment-specific operations, such as scrolling the transcript directly to the chosen fragment.

Fragments are created by selecting a chunk of text with the mouse and then clicking on the concept which categorizes that fragment. That fragment then becomes part of a collection of fragments which together embody the meaning of that concept. In Figure 8, a list of defined concepts reside in two scrolling menus at the bottom right of the display.

4.2.3 Concepts

A 'concept' can be thought of as a label representing a class of items, in this case fragments of knowledge, that contribute to a concrete description of that concept. Concepts can be used in two ways, top-down and bottom-up. In the former case (top-down) the knowledge engineer starts off with a particular concept and searches through the transcript to find fragments which are members of the class described by the concept. In the latter case (bottom-up) the knowledge engineer finds an interesting fragment and thinks up an appropriate concept which classifies it. Concepts can be generated by hand or from an automated lexical analysis of the transcript, as described in section 4.2.4.

When concepts are created, it is possible, at the same time, to create a frame to provide an internal representation of that concept, so that the user can work at different levels at the same time. When there is a 1:1 mapping between concepts, icons and frames, an operation at each of the editing, graphical or implementational levels affects the environment at the two other levels. This is especially important in order to give the user a correct view of the knowledge base, as changes at the frame level automatically update the graphical interface.

4.2.4 Lexical analysis of the transcript

As an easy entry point into knowledge acquisition in a new domain, and as a means of identifying important domain concepts, Acquist provides a first pass lexical analysis of the transcript(s). The knowledge engineer chooses a transcript or set of transcripts and can use them to create a new lexicon, or add to the existing one. This lexical analysis produces a list of all the different words that are used in the transcript. However, because many of the words will be uninteresting and irrelevant, the knowledge engineer can also create a filter to extract these uninteresting words from the lexicon. The filter is created or added to by reading in an ordinary text file of the words that the knowledge engineer is not interested in. Sets of filter files will be available for knowledge engineers to produce a concise lexicon. Such a set might include, adjectives, determiners, names, numbers, verbs, and possibly domain specific words.

When the lexical analysis has been carried out, all the words generated are placed into the group 'lexicon', which then acts as a pool of concepts. The knowledge engineer can then peruse this list and factor into 'groups' those concepts that might be of interest. S/he can also kill those uninteresting words that were not extracted by the filter. Concepts can then be used as keywords with which to access the transcript, i.e. the knowledge engineer can visit each place in the transcript where that concept or word occurs, possibly creating fragments as s/he proceeds.

4.2.5 Groups

A 'group' can be thought of as a higher order concept that provides an abstract rationale for a number of concepts. For example where a concept is a class, a group is a meta-class labeling that class of concepts. In practice groups are used in the same way as concepts, so there is no reason why groups cannot contain other groups as well as concepts. The main use of groups is in factoring

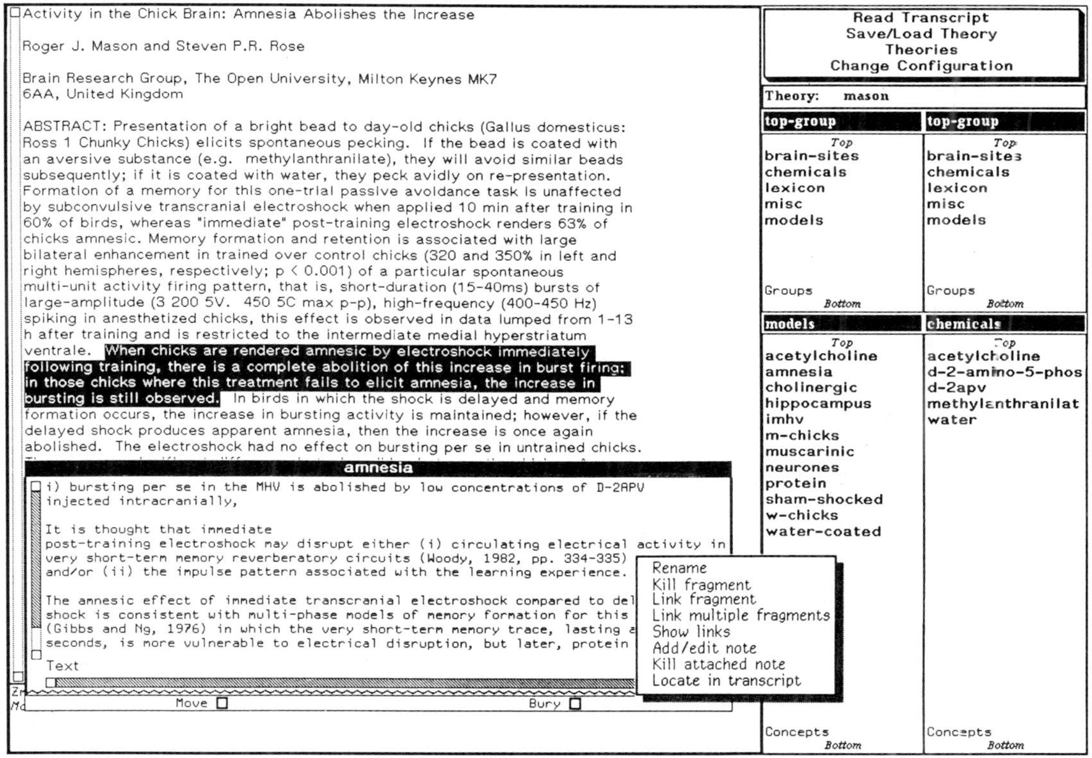

Figure 8. Acquist in its 'main configuration'. The top right hand corner of the display contains a command menu, which provides the knowledge engineer with the means of reading in a new transcript, loading and saving theories (the work done during acquisition) and changing the Acquist configuration. Notice the pair of 'concept' and 'group' menus on the right hand side. These are discussed in sections 4.2.3 and 4.2.5.

concepts into meaningful categories, making the acquisition of knowledge from large domains easier to handle. This process can be taken as far as the knowledge engineer wishes, as groups can also be factored into higher order groups. Two group menus can be seen directly above the concept menus in Figure 8. The name of the group whose contents is on display can be seen at the top of the corresponding group menu.

When the knowledge engineer selects a group from either group menu with the mouse, the concepts in that group get displayed in the concept menu directly beneath, and the name of the selected group becomes the title of that concept menu. In order to change the group whose contents is being displayed in both the group and concept menus, the knowledge engineer must click the mouse on the group title. S/he is then presented with a menu of either that group's parents, or all its superior groups. The groups and concepts of the selected group are then displayed in the appropriate menus. The reason for having two concept and group menus is to facilitate the linking and movement of concepts. Since Acquist depends heavily on the use of easily-expressed binary relations, the provision of two concept and group menus is more expedient than just one.

There are three system defined groups, 'top-group', 'lexicon' and 'misc'. The lexicon is used to store the words generated by the automated lexical analysis, while the misc group is provided as a scratch pad to place concepts for which the knowledge engineer has not yet found a home. The top-group is the highest level group, ie the most superior group.

4.2.6 Relational Links

Acquist allows the user to link items (i.e. fragments, concepts, groups) in several different ways. These links allow the creation of linguistic models based on relations between textual objects and to link textual objects to other non-textual objects. Besides, the user can impose a particular structural organization by defining new types of links. These facilities provide the Acquist user with a flexible means of abstracting and structuring the knowledge contained in the transcript(s). The following set of domain independent links, based on our own experience in analyzing documents, is provided for linking items together:

- NOTES can be attached to items so that the knowledge engineer can make some comment about the item in question. The note may be a summary, a reminder to ask the expert a question, or extra information about the topic contained in the item. The way in which notes are used is left up to the user. The 'secondary' Acquist configuration, illustrated in Figure 9, has a scroll window adjacent to the menu containing the names of concepts/groups which shows at a glance whether a concept /group has a note attached or not.

- SPECIAL-CASE links relate one fragment to another that contains a more general restatement of a concept, a class of a relation.

- JUSTIFIES links are used to link some statement in the text to a fragment that provides a justification for it.

- EXPLAINS links relate a piece of text to a fragment, that clarifies or gives the rationale for it.

- REINFORCES links relate an assertion to a fragment that contains some information strengthening the assertion.

- WEAKENS links relate an assertion to a fragment that contains information weakening the assertion.

- INCONSISTENT-WITH relates two mutually inconsistent fragments.

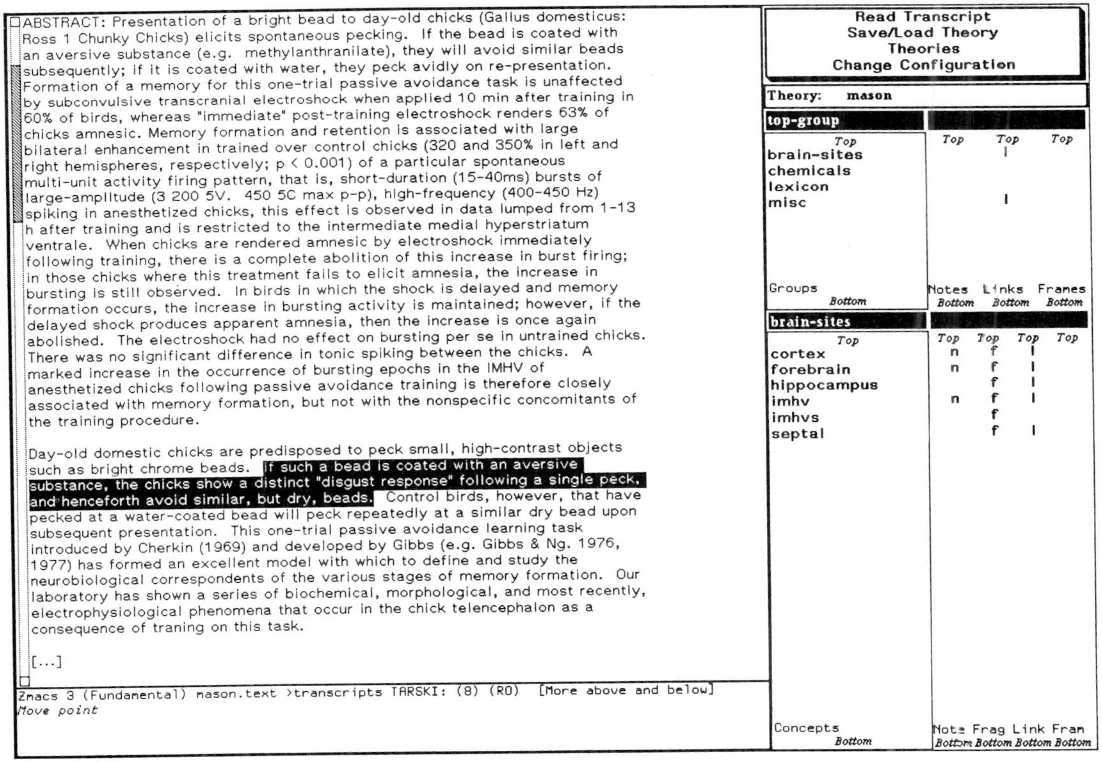

Figure 9. The secondary Acquist configuration, obtained by selecting the 'Change Configuration' option, given the snapshot depicted earlier in Figure 8. The right-hand group and concept menus have been replaced with menus that display whether the groups and concepts on their left have a note attached, link(s) to other groups or concepts, or a corresponding frame. In addition the concept menu has an attached scroll menu which shows whether concepts are defined by a collection of fragments. An 'f' denotes a concept defined by such fragments.

- DOCUMENTATION links allow fragments to be used to document a concept. If this has a frame attached, the fragment can be used as the documentation for the frame as well.

The user can also define links to allow a wider range of relationships to be made between items. The knowledge engineer is thus not restricted in the way s/he is able to represent the knowledge contained in the transcript. User defined links consist of a forward and a backward component. The forward component is the name of the link from item 'A' to item 'B', whilst the backward component is the name of the link from 'B' to 'A'. If either of the link components is left out then the link becomes unidirectional, while if both components are the same it becomes symmetric. In maps (see below) these links are represented by arrows between the graphical representations of the items. As with 'notes' there is a scroll window which shows whether an item has links attached to it. These 'notes' and 'links' menus are tied to their respective group and concept menus and move with them when they are scrolled. A mouse click provides a more detailed breakdown of the details of which links are used and which items are linked by them. A similar menu can be called up for fragments.

4.2.7 Maps

A 'map' is a graphical representation showing the topology of a set of concepts, groups or fragments. The relationships or links between items are shown by arrows between the graphical objects. These links can be specified by hand in Acquist or by means of the graphical interface. Maps do away with the intermediate linear view of collections used in CREF and provide the knowledge engineer with an immediate high level view of the structure that s/he is building. For example if the knowledge engineer wants to view the collection of fragments that define a concept whilst viewing a map, s/he just mouses on the concept, chooses the relevant menu option, and a pop-up window displays the fragments. Figure 10 displays an example of a map showing the relationship between a set of concepts. The 'F' in the menu to the right of the concept menu shows whether concepts are represented by a frame.

The knowledge engineer can manipulate items through mouse and menu driven operations from either the graphical interface or the Acquist display. Maps are a very important part of the process of analysing transcripts, because they are a vehicle for producing conceptual models. One problem with transcript analysis is the huge amount of information generated. Maps provide a means of organizing that information. Once a map has been constructed, or is in a state of construction, it provides the knowledge engineer with a simple means of navigating through the mass of text contained in one or more transcripts. Moreover, the knowledge engineer is in charge of the decisions concerning the layout, and a number of facilities are provided for working on the displayed representations. These facilities are similar to those provided by GIS in KEATS-1 and include means for working with multiple but consistent diagrams, defining graphical links, moving groups of icons and links, duplicating graphical structures, and selecting long-distance and close-up views.

As mentioned above, maps provide the means for a smooth progression from the generation of an abstract description of the knowledge contained in transcript(s) to the generation of a frame based representation and ultimately an implemented knowledge based system. In this case, the 'overt behaviour'/'internal representation' gap (Figure 2) is effectively bridged. It remains for the knowledge engineer to specify an interpreter which can 'walk over' a given representation and behave correctly. In the most problematic (and interesting) cases, maps allow the specification of 'coarse-grained' descriptions, that can then be iteratively refined to produce more fine-grained ones. For instance, in [5] we show how different levels of descriptions can be integrated to account for the phenomenology of the domain both at a coarse-grained level (black-box devices) and at a fine-grained one (component circuit diagram).

4.2.8 Theories

Theories are the means that Acquist provides for saving collections of fragments, concepts, groups and links, which constitute some form of text based model of the domain. This is carried out with the 'Save/Load Theories' menu command. Acquist allows multiple theories to be loaded at the same

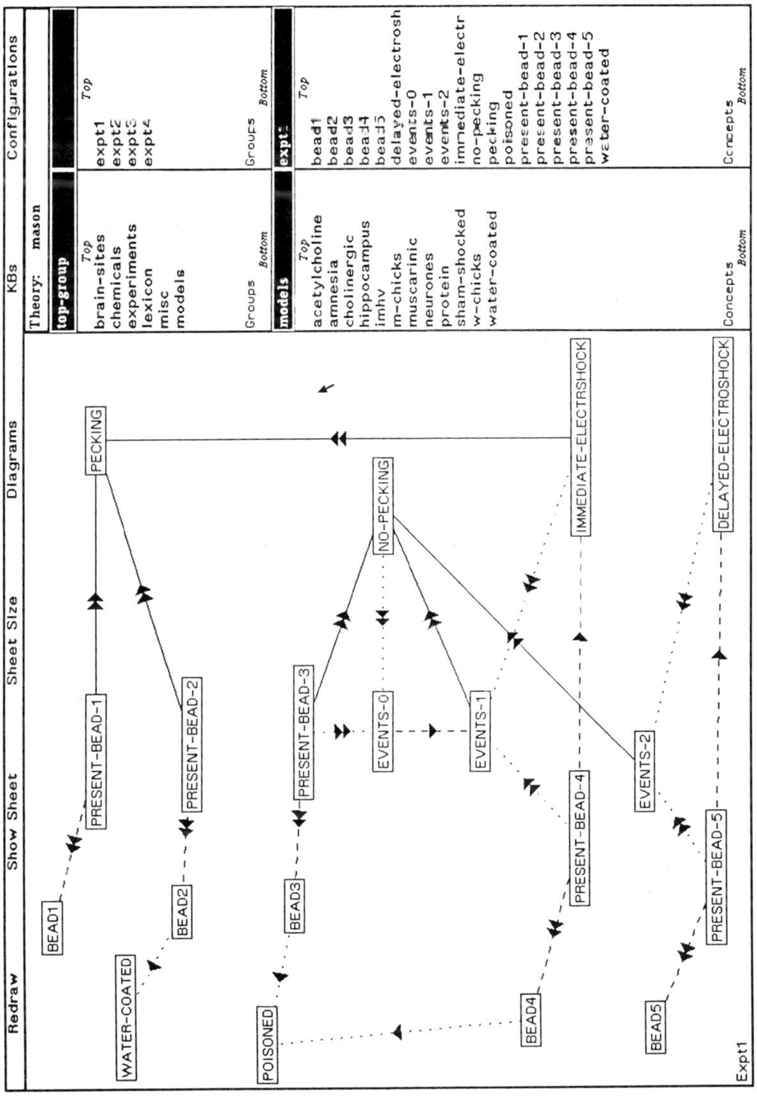

Figure 10. An Acquist 'map', showing the interrelation of selected concepts.

time, so that the knowledge engineer can switch between theories at will. This facility also allows different knowledge engineers to work on the same set of transcripts, building independent models of the domain. Acquist also provides a means of merging 'theories' should this be necessary. The name of the current theory is shown just under the main command menu, in this case 'mason'.

A parallel feature, called knowledge bases, is provided by the frame based system. A combined text and frame based model can be saved and loaded as a 'model'.

4.2.9 Implementation Details

Acquist is written in a combination of Common Lisp and Flavors and runs on the Symbolics™ 3600 family of computers under release 7.2.

The system is built around an enhanced version of Zmacs (the normal Symbolics text and code editor) using an object oriented methodology where fragments, concepts and groups are all implemented as objects.

Figure 11 shows an example of the internal structure of a 'fragment' (the items inside angle brackets are Lisp objects).

```
#<FRAGMENT 40106727>, an object of flavor FRAGMENT, has instance variable values:
START-BP:     ("ventrale.  When chicks are rendered amnesic by electroshock
              immediateley" 11 : MOVES #<FILE-BUFFER "mason.text >transcripts
              TARSKI:" 16500471>)
END-BP:       ("bursting is still observed.  In birds in which the shock is delayed and
              memory" 26 :MOVES #<FILE-BUFFER  "mason.text >transcripts TARSKI:"
              16500471>)
TEXT:         "When chicks are rendered amnesic by electroshock immediately following
              training, there is a complete abolition of this increase in burst firing; in those
              chicks where this treatment fails to elicit amnesia, the increase in bursting is
              still observed."
NAME:         "amnesia-f374"
CONCEPTS:      (#<CONCEPT 274662033>)
NOTE:         "Ask the expert about the nature of this bursting"
FILE:         "TARSKI:>transcripts>mason.text"
BUFFER:       #<FILE-BUFFER "mason.text >transcripts TARSKI:" 16500471>
USER-DEFINED-LINKS:  #<HASH-TABLE40264772>
FRAME-P       NIL
```

Figure 11. The internal structure of a fragment

A brief description of each of the instance variables will provide some insight into the implementation of Acquist.

The first two instance variables 'START-BP' and 'END-BP' are pointers into the Zmacs buffer which contains the text from the transcript, and denote the start and end points of the fragment. Together with the 'BUFFER' and 'FILE' instance variables these pointers allow the efficient location of the fragment in the editor at any time.

The 'TEXT' variable contains the body of text from the fragment in the form of a string. This is used both as a means of storing the fragment (the buffer pointers are dynamic and can only be used at run-time) and displaying the text of fragments to the user.

The 'NAME' of the fragment, a string, is actually redundant information as all the fragments are stored in a hash table, hashed under the name of the fragment. However, it is useful to have it as a slot in the object.

The value of the 'CONCEPTS' variable is a list of instances of concepts which contain that fragment. All fragments, concepts and groups are referenced by their internal instance name so that renaming of the objects can be carried out efficiently. All that is necessary in renaming is to hash the item under a different name, and alter the name slot of that object. The instance name remains the same, and so none of the references to that object need to be altered, as they would if objects were referenced by their real names.

'NOTE' is a string which contains a note from the knowledge engineer which is attached to this fragment. This is used as an anchor point for thoughts, reminders or messages.

The 'FILE' and 'BUFFER' variables hold, respectively, the values of the file and buffer which contain the transcript from which the fragment is taken. The 'buffer' is used at run-time to access the buffer in locating a fragment, while the 'file' is used to locate the fragment when the transcript has not yet been loaded into a buffer.

Lastly, the variable 'FRAME-P' is a flag denoting whether the fragment has a corresponding frame or not. The value is either 'T' or 'NIL'.

Concepts, and groups are implemented similarly, using objects whose instance variables are mainly pointers to other instances of concepts or groups. Concepts and groups are stored in hash tables in the same manner as fragments.

4.3. Providing support for top-down approaches: 'Coding sheets'

So far we have shown how Acquist can lead to the development of a knowledge base, through the analysis of text and the development of a conceptual description of the domain. We have observed that in some cases the knowledge engineer may already have a predefined abstract model of the task and/or the domain that can be used to drive the knowledge acquisition process. In this section we introduce and describe the notion of 'coding sheet' and we show how it can be used to drive knowledge acquisition in a top-down fashion.

A coding sheet is a form on which to record a caricature of the observed behaviour of the domain expert. Knowledge acquisition systems base their behaviour upon weak or strong models of the problem, which are used to drive the knowledge elicitation session and to understand the data elicited. As the mapping between the problem and the preexisting model can be fairly loose, the acquired knowledge base (and the eventual system) automatically built may not be a faithful representation of the problem. However, as experience shows, the use of preexisting models (even inadequate ones) can lead to dramatic improvements in the time required for performing knowledge acquisition and building a prototypical system.

We have found in practice that a carefully constructed coding sheet for a task such as electronic fault diagnosis has enabled a pair of knowledge engineers to conduct very rapid 'knowledge acquisition raids' on a domain expert. In our case, one knowledge engineer conducted the bulk of the interview while the other filled out the coding sheet in real time throughout the length of the six-hour session. The coding sheet form itself reflects the coarse-grained activities which occur during straightforward electronic fault diagnosis. Early versions of the form simply used paper and pencil variations, but we are now experimenting with 'rapid cross-indexing' versions, using the hypertext facilities of Acquist, as well as those of independent software tools such as HyperCard [27]. Any given coding sheet comprises a set of individual 'cards'. Figure 12 shows a single card from a coding sheet used for a fault diagnosis interview session.

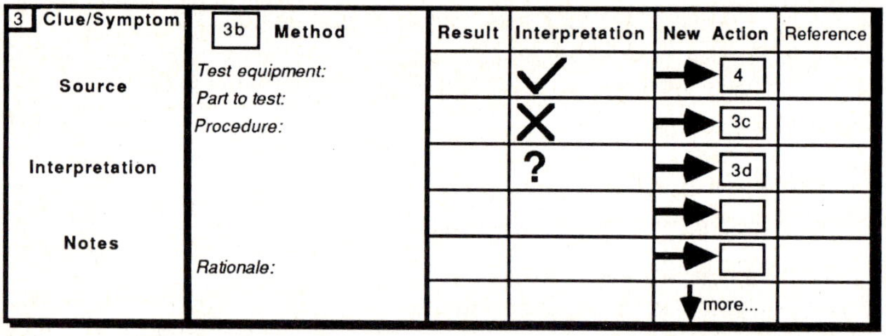

Figure 12. Coding sheet used for real-time encoding of expert behaviour on a fault diagnosis task. Sheet can either be paper-and-pencil variety, or true hypertext style with mouse-sensitive arrows for branching to new sheets.

The left-hand column of Figure 12 is a place for noting the current symptom and where it comes from (e.g. 'fault docket'). We use the word 'clue' to indicate that diagnosis is not just symptom-based, but may be based on the outcome of previous intermediate results. Indeed, in our hypertext implementation, the 'source' entry includes an automatic (mouse-sensitive) link back to the coding sheet result which led us here in the first place. The second column can be used to indicate the particular diagnostic technique. In the case of a hypertext implementation, such techniques can be carried on (pasted) from one coding sheet to the next to avoid tedious reduplication. The last four columns provide a means for recording any of six possible outcomes of a test, with the possibility of 'extending' the sheet by pointing off to 'more' results. Three standard interpretations are catered for ('win', 'lose', and 'don't know'), although these can be specified in more detail by the knowledge engineer. The new action is typically just a pointer off to more coding sheets, wherein the diagnostician follows through the initial interpretations.

In Acquist, each coding sheet is represented as a group, and each card is represented as a concept belonging to that group. The individual cell entries can be concepts, fragments, or links thereto. When the coding sheets are used in real time for knowledge elicitation, Acquist takes care of generating (a) new cards with links to previous ones, (b) the appropriate internal structures (i.e. concepts and fragments) for the cell entries keyed in by the knowledge engineer, and (c) links corresponding to specific coding sheet labels (e.g. 'Notes' and 'Source').

Another important use of the coding sheet is for retrospective detailed analysis of the transcript. Consider, for example, the case when the domain expert explains the interpretation of the 'lose' outcome of a particular test in great detail. The knowledge engineer can simply highlight the text of the entire explanation in the transcript, and mouse-click on the relevant cell in the 'Reference' column on the right hand side of the coding sheet. The result of this action is to leave a fragment symbol ('f') in the Reference column, which itself may be selected for performing fragment-specific operations.

The coding sheet shown in Figure 12 is at first glance nothing more than a way of encoding very large decision trees or discrimination nets without having to fill up enormous wall-charts. This in itself is not such a bad thing, as it concisely encapsulates a wide range of diagnostic behaviour. On second glance, however, it is much more flexible than an ordinary decision tree, because (like the production rule architectures which inspired it) there may be numerous entry points/paths into a particular node, which can be cumbersome to represent in the form of a tree. The main point we wish to make here is that a concise encoding of the knowledge elicited during an interview can facilitate later analysis, because it may be possible to encode at least a coarse-grained variant of the entire session in real time.

Coding sheets are mainly intended as an aid to yielding an analyzable set of 'digested data', as in Figure 2, although they may be useful in their own right if the entries are precise enough to be converted directly into an internal representation. Our own experience with the use of the coding sheet depicted in Figure 12 has shown that it proved effective in encoding most of the diagnostic behaviour of the expert and led to the rapid implementation of a prototype. However, the type of system so generated, organized around a decision tree diagnostic structure, was a 'shallow' one and, as such, of limited power. A much more powerful and principled implementation, as described in [5] could only be devised after developing functional and formal models of the domain and after an in-depth analysis of the expert's cognitive behaviour. Nevertheless, this experience convinced us of the advantages, in terms of the quality of the elicited data, provided by the use of strong (domain-dependent) techniques for knowledge elicitation.

4.4 Acquist, KADS and KRITON

Two other knowledge acquisition systems place the same importance on analysing transcripts in order to extract expert knowledge: KADS and KRITON. KADS supports both a bottom-up and top-down approach to knowledge acquistion, while KRITON only supports a bottom-up style.

KADS [3] supports data analysis and domain conceptualization with two separate tools called PED and CE. PED is a hypertext based protocol editor, which provides facilities for fragmenting a transcript, creating links between fragments, grouping fragments together, attaching notes, and assigning fragments to concepts. The Concept Editor allows the knowledge engineer to create concept hierarchies with user defined links. Concepts can be given a list of attributes which can be inherited down through 'isa' links. Both the concept hierarchy and the fragment network can be viewed graphically to show the topology of the structure.

Top-down knowledge acquistion is supported through the provision of a library of interpretation models. An interpretation model consists of a set of inference structures describing the meta-level structure of a generic task. The knowledge engineer then chooses which interpretation model best fits the current domain, and applies it to that domain. Although the precise way in which these libraries are used by the user is unclear, the basic idea is that the product of the knowledge acquisition process is an interpretation model, that can be either constructed or selected from the preexisting library.

Hence, there are a number of similarities between KADS and Acquist, that include the emphasis on supporting the user at different levels, provisions for both top-down and bottom-up support, and the use of hypertext metaphors and graphical interfaces. From a general point of view, the main difference is that while KADS emphasizes the production of a 'documentation handbook' and the development of semi-runnable conceptual models, KEATS is meant to be an environment for actually building the end product and therefore it provides facilities at the knowledge representation and debugging level as well. Hence, we feel that the different levels are more tightly integrated in KEATS, and therefore the iterative refinement of models is better supported. KEATS also provides a richer set of predefined links at the linguistic level, while KADS only predefines 'groups' and 'annotations' links.

The approach taken by KRITON is slightly different from that offered by Acquist and KADS. KRITON aims to make knowledge acquisition fully automated, by eliciting, analyzing and representing knowledge. A number of knowledge elicitation techniques are prestored: interviews, incremental text analysis and protocol analysis. Interviews are carried out through the use of the repertory grid technique and aim to pull out declarative knowledge. Protocol analysis produces the goal structure of the domain, and text analysis provides the knowledge engineer with statistical information about the text. Such declarative and procedural knowledge is encoded in an intermediate knowledge representation formalism, that uses a propositional calculus and a language for describing devices. This intermediate representation is semi-automatically translated into a machine runnable representation, with the goal structure becoming a rule set, and the content structure a frame base. Other processes act on the knowledge base, by propagating constraints and checking for inconsistencies.

As KRITON also supports different levels of analysis, including the linguistic one, much of the philosophy of the system is similar to KADS and KEATS. The main difference between these approaches concern the fact that while KRITON aims to make the knowledge acquisition process fully automated, KADS and KEATS provide tools that support a more comprehensive and principled methodology for knowledge engineering. This can be seen by comparing the notion of 'intermediate level' in KRITON with that of domain conceptualization in KEATS. The former seems only instrumental to the way the system works, the latter is a fundamental part of knowledge engineering.

5. CONCLUSIONS

We began with a description of a 'stage' account of knowledge engineering. This account emphasized the progression from knowledge elicitation through data analysis and domain conceptualization. We then took a look at KEATS-1, which provided a range of knowledge acquisition facilities, but found that they were not as closely integrated as they could have been. Moreover, they were only aimed at supporting bottom-up approaches. These considerations have led to the development of Acquist, a hypertext-style tool, with the provision of facilities to integrate a bottom-up style of textual analysis with a top-down (model-driven) approach. Acquist incorporates a graphical 'map' facility which helps to bridge the gap between a sketched-out account of overt behaviour and a true (runnable) internal representation thereof. We feel strongly that this gap-bridging is important if knowledge acquisition is to remain firmly in the AI tradition of providing testable (executable) theories. The KEATS-2 project as a whole aims to address some of the 'front line' problems of knowledge engineering. In particular, the sorts of problems which interest us are as follows:

- Very large knowledge bases. How can enormous knowledge bases (consisting of, say, tens of thousands of production rules using current technology) be implemented and maintained by a team of knowledge engineers in a clear and consistent manner, using knowledge derived from disparate sources? We are beginning to tackle such problems by developing an interlingua for teams of knowledge engineers.

- Learning. How can a knowledge base be acquired by experience? Our current research indicates that the acquisition of expertise by humans is an intensive process requiring the refinement of both declarative and procedural knowledge over a period of years. One recent study in our lab [28] showed that the learning of recursive programming techniques is greatly facilitated by the inclusion of analogies in which the analogical mapping relation is made explicit in the course text (something mysteriously missing from most texts on programming!). We are interested in pursuing research on analogical reasoning in the context of the acquisition of expertise.

- Common sense reasoning. Our current work distinguishes among textbook knowledge, empirical associations, and common sense reasoning. In our work on the behaviour of faulty devices, for example, we have found that many fault diagnosis techniques can be broken down into a phase of preliminary hypotheses (driven by empirical associations gained through years of experience), followed by a phase of structural isolation (which is a common sense divide-and-conquer strategy), merged with specialized instances of device-specific reasoning (frequently exhibiting standard textbook knowledge such as algebraic formulas). Common sense reasoning is still elusive, and is a characteristic of much expert behaviour. Expert systems builders are warned to stay away from domains in which common sense is required. We regard such a warning as a challenge to be addressed by the 'next phase' of knowledge engineering.

- Environments. In line with our broader objective of providing 'life-cycle' support for knowledge engineers, we are also engaged in activities aimed at improving the knowledge representation and debugging stages. In particular, we have implemented a new frame language and new tools for rule tracing [29] and for knowledge base checking.

Tackling these problems will require a fruitful combination of empirical research, top-down methodologies and supporting environments. Work on Acquist and KEATS-2 as a whole continues in this spirit, and we eagerly await future results.

Acknowledgement: This research is supported by a grant from British Telecommunications, plc. John Domingue participated in the discussions which led to this paper. Steven Rose and Mike Stewart of the Open University's Brain Research Group provided valuable domain expertise.

REFERENCES

[1] Feigenbaum, E. A. The Art of Artificial Intelligence: Themes and case studies of knowledge engineering. *Proceedings IJCAI 77*, Cambridge MA, 1977.

[2] Burton, A. M., Shadbolt, N. R., Hedgecock, A. P., and Rugg, G. A. formal evaluation of knowledge elicitation techniques for expert systems: domain 1. In D. S. Moralee(ed), *Research and Development in Expert Systems 4*, Cambridge University Press, 1987.

[3] Anjewierden, A., Knowledge Acquisition Tools. *AI Communications*, Vol 0 No. 1, pp 29-38, 1987.

[4] Olson, J. R. and Reuter, H. H. Extracting expertise from experts: Methods for Knowledge Acquisition, *Expert Systems* 4(3), August 1987.

[5] Motta, E., Eisenstadt, M., Pitman, K., and West, M. Knowledge Acquisition in KEATS: The Knowledge Engineer's Assistant. *Expert Systems,* 5(2), 1988 (Also available as Technical Report No. 30, Human Cognition Research Laboratory, The Open University, Milton Keynes, U.K., 1988.)

[6] Hayes-Roth, F., Waterman, D. A., and Lenat, D. B. *Building expert systems*, Reading, Massachussetts: Addison-Wesley 1983.

[7] Wielinga, B. J., and Breuker, J. A. Models of expertise. *Proceedings ECAI 86*, Brighton, U.K., 1986.

[8] Mason, R. J., and Rose, S. P. R. Passive avoidance learning produces focal elevation of bursting activity in the chick brain: amnesia abolishes the increase. *Behavioural and neural biology*, 1988.

[9] Shepard, R. N., Romney, A. K., and Nerlove, S. B. Multidimensional Scaling: Theory and Applications in the Behavioural Sciences, Volume 1, Seminar Press, New York, 1972.

[10] Boose, J. A Knowledge Acquisition Program for Expert Systems Based on Personal Construct Psychology. *Int. J. Man-Machine Studies*, 23, 1985.

[11] Johnson, S. C., Hierarchical clustering schemes. Psychometrika, 32, 1967.

[12] Ericsson, K. A., Simon, H. A. Protocol Analysis. Verbal reports as data. Cambridge, MA, 1984.

[13] Klinker, G., Boyd, C., Genetet, G., and McDermott, J. A KNACK for Knowledge Acquisition. *Proceedings AAAI 87*, Seattle, WA, 1987.

[14] Eshelman, L., McDermott, J. MOLE: A Knowledge Acquisition Tool That Uses Its Head. *Proceedings AAAI 86*, Philadelphia, PA, 1986.

[15] Clancey, W. J. Heuristic Classification. *Artificial Intelligence* 27, 1985.

[16] Chandrasekaran, B. Towards a Functional Architecture for Intelligence Based on Generic Information Processing Tasks. Proceedings IJCAI 87, Milan, 1987.

[17] Clancey, W. J. The Epistemology of a Rule-Based Expert System - a Framework for Explanation. Artificial Intelligence 20, 1983.

[18] Diederich, J., Ruhmann I., and May, M. KRITON: a knowledge-acquisition tool for expert systems. *Int. J. Man-Machine Studies*, 26, 1987.

[19] Breuker, J., and Wielinga, B. KADS: Structured Knowledge Acquisition for Expert Systems. Proceedings of Expert Systems and their Applications, Avignon, 1985.

[20] Bennet, J.S. ROGET: A knowledge-based consultant for acquiring the conceptual structure of an expert system. Stanford Heuristic Programming Project, Memo HPP-83-24, Stanford University, October 1983.

[21] Hayes, P. J. In defence of Logic, *Proceedings IJCAI 77*. Los Angeles: Morgan Kaufmann, 1977.

[22] Pitman, K. CREF: An Editing Facility for Managing Structured Text. Technical Report No. 14, Human Cognition Research Laboratory, The Open University, Milton Keynes, UK. 1985.

[23] Stallman, R.M. EMACS - The Extensible, Customizable, Self Documenting Display Editor, Memo No. 519, Artificial Intelligence Laboratory, MIT, Cambridge massachusetts, June 1979.

[24] Nelson, T. Replacing the Printed Word: A Complete Literary System. IFIP Proceedings, Information Processing. North-Holland pp 1013-1023, 1980.

[25] Conklin, J., Hypertext: An Introduction and Survey. *IEEE Computer Magazine*, pp 17-41, September 1987.

[26] Davis, R., Lenat, D. *Knowledge-Based Systems in Artificial Intelligence*. McGraw-Hill, 1982.

[27] Goodman,.D. The Complete HyperCard Handbook, Bantom Books, 1987.

[28] Conway, M. A., and Kahney, H. Transfer of learning in inference problems: learning to program recursive functions. In J. Hallam and C.S. Mellish (Eds.), Advances in Artificial Intelligence. New York: J. Wiley and Sons, pp. 239-250, 1987.

[29] Domingue, J. TRI: The Transparent Rule Interpreter. Technical Report No. 35, Human Cognition Research Laboratory, The Open University, Milton Keynes, U.K., 1988.

Topics in Expert System Design
G. Guida and C. Tasso (Editors)

KNOWLEDGE-BASED KNOWLEDGE ELICITATION

Joachim DIEDERICH (°) **and Marc LINSTER** (°°)

International Computer Science Institute (°)
Berkley, CA, USA

Institute for Applied Information Technology (°°)
German Research Institute for Mathematics and Data Processing
Sankt Augustin, Federal Republic of Germany

1. INTRODUCTION

The efficient and wide-spread use of expert-systems seems, among other reasons, to be restrained by the lack of methods and theories on knowledge acquisition. The knowledge acquisition bottleneck is a good metaphor describing the current state of the art in knowledge acquisition, even though many tools have been described in the literature (for an overview of 26 tools see [1]) and the first results and experiences are being summed up to provide the framework for the second generation of knowledge acquisition systems as proposed by Gaines [2].

In the expert system group's research project KRITON at the GMD we view knowledge engineering as an incremental process consisting of many phases as shown in figure 1 [3].

The actual state of KRITON focuses on the elicitation phase. Research questions addressed are :

- Which elicitation methods should be parts of KRITON ?
- Which method serves best which purpose ?
- How can we integrate the results of the methods ?

- Is their domain-independent meta-knowledge that can be used to guide the acquisition process ?

- What can be done in the elicitation phase to guarantee a sound expert system life cycle ?

The questions mentioned above and our view of the knowledge engineering process leads to a tool that consists of different elicitation methods, founded on techniques from cognitive science and specialized in different acquisition tasks (see figure 2). The methods currently realized are :

- interview

- protocol analysis

- text analysis

They have been implemented as independent software-modules integrated in a blackboard architecture.

In the next section of our paper we will give a description of the methods in KRITON and of their theoretical background. Section 3 is concerned with the internal knowledge representation used in KRITON. Sections 4, 5 and 6 describe the potential use of meta-knowledge in knowledge elicitation, section 7 describes KRITON´s architecture and its advantages. An illustration of the techniques is given in section 9. In section 10 we compare KRITON to other tools. In the last section we sum up the points and show up where KRITON heads

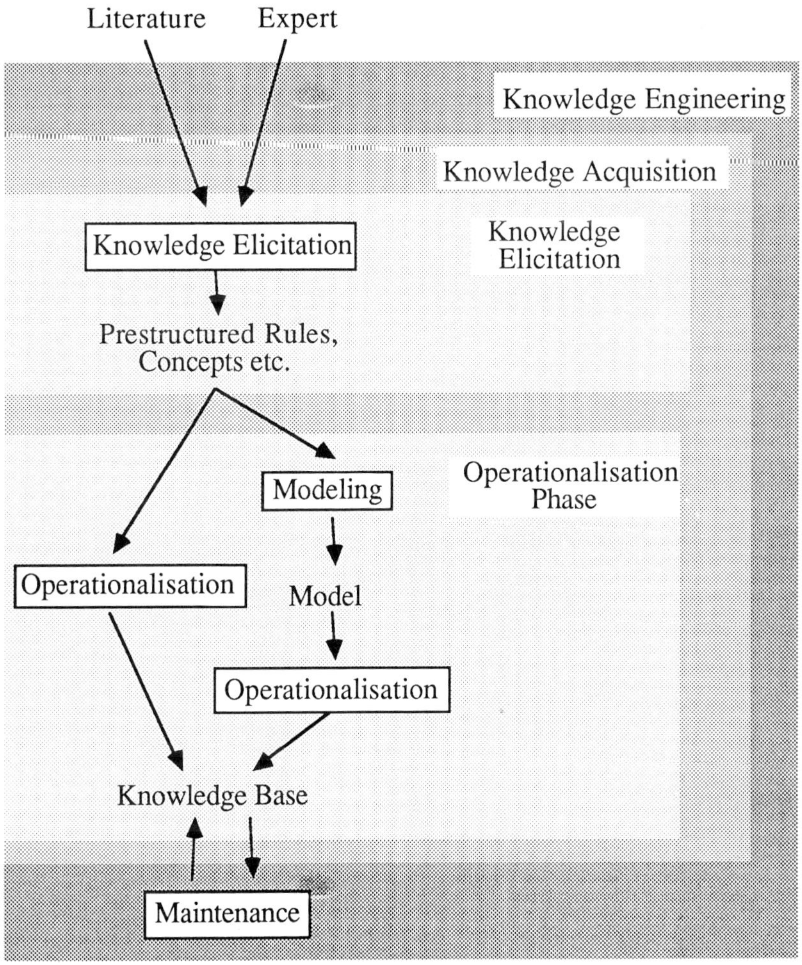

Figure 1 Phases of the knowledge engineering process

2. METHODS FOR KNOWLEDGE ELICITATION

We describe general elicitation methods and those used in KRITON, their theoretical background and their limits.

2.1. Interview

One of the most important strategies of knowledge engineering is the interview. Grover [4] distinguishes four different interview techniques for knowledge acquisition:

Forward scenario simulation

An application situation within a problem domain is selected and investigated under laboratory conditions. The expert reports on the relevant terms and concepts and describes the steps in problem solving, i.e. his or her own reasoning to achieve a goal.

Goal decomposition

The knowledge engineer divides the problem into subgoals and asks the expert to describe ways to achieve these subgoals.

Procedural simulation

Grover uses this term for what we refer to as protocol analysis. In his opinion controling interventions by the knowledge engineer are absolutely necessary.

Pure reclassification

In a dialogue between expert and knowledge engineer the expert´s statements are further differentiated and classified into specific objects and relations between objects. As a result of this interview, object-relations may be reclassified and eventually new taxonomic relations discovered.

Laddering

Laddering is an interview technique not mentioned in Grover's classification. The expert is asked to name important concepts of the problem domain. These concepts are then used as basis for the interview to follow. Especially supertypes and instances of generic concepts are inquired about, allowing the derivation of a taxonomic structure.

Repertory grid

This technique, first mentioned by Kelly [5] is used in personal construct theory to elicit a set of personal constructs given a set of concepts of a certain domain. The concepts of the domain are arranged in triplets. During an interrogation the expert is asked to state a property that two of the concepts share and that differentiates them from the third. The purpose of this questioning technique is the elicitation of very personal constructs that the expert uses to describe concepts of the domain. A version of this interview technique is implemented in AQUINAS [6] [7] and KSS0 [8].

2.1.1 Interview Methods in KRITON

In the KRITON system, interview techniques are completely automated, i.e. the expert interacts directly with the system. A combination of the repertory grid technique and laddering is used to explore the relevant concepts of a problem domain. The top level technique is the repertory grid approach: triplets of semantically related concepts are presented and the expert is asked for attributes that two of these concepts share distinguishing them from the third. If the expert is not able to name discriminating attributes, the system switches into a laddering mode to explore taxonomic relations between the concepts.

The expert may answer these questions with attribute-value pairs, thus defining an attribute that all the concepts in the question share and that differentiates the concepts with the values they have with regard to the attribute.

The interview produces structured objects at the intermediate knowledge representation level. These objects incorporate the explored taxonomic relations and attributes.

2.1.2 Limits of the Interview Methods in KRITON

The automated repertory grid and laddering techniques are limited to the building of taxonomies, and describe the elements of these taxonomies through attribute-value pairs. The power of these techniques cannot be compared to other manual interview methods, e.g. the knowledge-acquisition-grid [9], involving cross-references, examples, generalizations, multiple questions for different aspects, etc.

Another important problem specific to repertory-grid techniques is the relevance of the context. This context can or be defined by the elements of the question or by other previous information. A question like "What do a rug and a refrigerator have in common that an empty bottle does not have?" seems senseless. If however the user is told that the context of this question is fire-insurance policies, then a meaningful answer (e.g. "rug and refrigerator are covered by the insurance, the empty bottle is not") can be given.

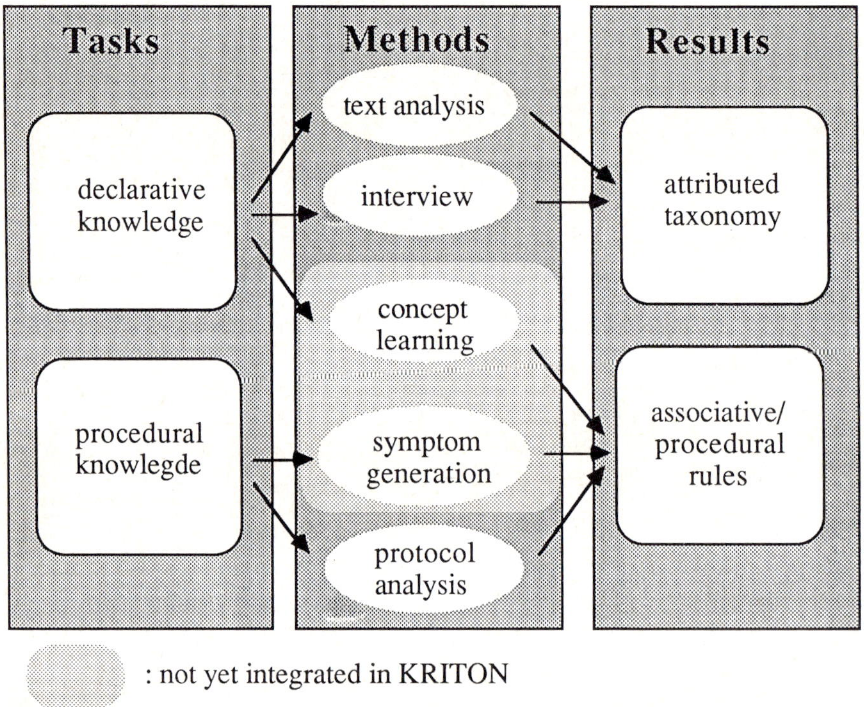

Figure 2 Knowledge acquisition tasks and their corresponding methods in KRITON.

2.2 Protocol Analysis

Protocol analysis refers to the automated or semi-automated analysis of thinking-aloud protocols, i.e. tape-recorded utterances of an expert during a problem solving episode. The result of the protocol analysis can be considered as a path through successive knowledge states representing the sequence of the problem solving events. If an expert system uses this sequence of knowledge states in a problem solving process a surface modeling of the human problem solving process takes place. Although automatic protocol analysis has been suggested as an adequate method for knowledge acquisition in expert systems for some time now, fully developed systems are rare. A consistent approach to protocol analysis is described by Kuipers and Kassirer [10] [11], their approach aiming at both, a structural description of the problem domain and a qualitative simulation of the transitions between knowledge states during the problem solving process.

The power of protocol analysis depends quite decisively on the quality of the protocol recording. Only if the protocol is actually one of thinking-aloud during a problem solving process and only if this protocol has been correctly transcribed, automatic analysis may be successful. The success of any protocol analysis depends on the quality of the recorded information. Therefore detailed and adequate instructions concerning the verbal utterances during the problem solving process are of great importance. In any case, it requires psychologically trained manpower to achieve a constant cognitive load of the thinking-aloud expert. For a comprehensive review on problems with verbal data see [12].

Granularity of expert knowledge has turned out to be a serious and difficult problem. Even the most careful employment of protocol analysis will not avoid the acquisition of problem-irrelevant data. As soon as not directly problem-relevant concepts are uttered by the expert, they are included in the verbal material and hence are fed into the analysis. This may be the case when the expert starts commenting, explaining or evaluating his thoughts or actions. The other extreme, however, is an expert communicating his *compiled knowledge* to the system, i.e. that during his extended learning process the expert has combined inference steps, so that the verbal report on the problem solving process is incomplete. The expert skips, more or less small, but essential inference steps. Even if this does not necessarily affect the efficacy of the future expert system, it will reduce the explainability of the problem solving process.

2.2.1 Protocol Analysis in the KRITON System

Protocol analysis is used as a knowledge elicitation method in the KRITON system to get hold of procedural aspects of human knowledge. Knowledge elicited in the interview is observed *in action* during the protocol recording. The procedural and associative aspects of the protocol are encoded as rules, and stored in an intermediate representation. This transformation process takes place in four steps, some of them fully automated and some of them relying on the experts decisions.

These steps are :

- the division of the transcribed protocol into segments using the expert´s pauses of speech as segment limits
- the syntactic analysis of the segments, transforming the segments into operator-argument structures.
- the presentation of the selected operator-argument structures for post-editing or acknowledgement
- the arranging of the propositions into rules according to their appearance in the natural language protocol.

2.2.2 Limits of the Protocol Analysis in KRITON

The automated parts of the protocol analysis have to be limited to those phases not requiring interpretation of the data. Thus the first two steps can be automated, even if the expert has to confirm or post-edit the results. The last step of combining operator-argument structures into rules can only be supported through appropriate editing facilities.

Even within these limits, the techniques seem valuable as they provide facilities to speed up the process and document the transformation from protocols into rules, thus providing a natural-language justification for the rules introduced into the knowledge base.

2.3 Text Analysis

Knowledge engineering phase models recommend the knowledge engineer to start off with studying manuals and documents on the problem domain. This can be very time consuming, particularly if the knowledge engineer is supposed to become an expert on the topic before beginning his or her actual work. For about forty years content analysis has been concerned with analyzing texts. Since the fifties, programs for automatic content analysis are available [13]. The use of these methods for constructing knowledge-based systems has best been outlined in the published literature. Nishida, Kosaka and Doshita [14], for example, analyze hardware manuals by means of action-event models. Frey, Reyle and Rohrer [15] use discourse representation structure as *intermediate level* between the natural language text and a data basis.

2.3.1 Text Analysis in KRITON

The text analysis in KRITON is limited to editing facilities allowing the expert to pick concepts out of the text and organize them graphically into a conceptual framework, which serves as a basis for the interview. This is to make sure that the expert is being confronted with as many aspects of the domain as possible and to reach a pre-structuring of these concepts.

2.3.2 Limits of the Text Analysis in KRITON

The limits of such a procedure are evident. The effort required is only justified if the text is available on some electronic medium or if it can be scanned. Improvement seems possible though. Statistical methods comparing the use of words in the text to be analyzed with the average use in scientific texts, or graphical methods representing the contexts of important concepts used in the text seem promising [16].

The most important problem with automated text analysis, namely the fact that the computer cannot read between the lines and find second meanings, will however not be overcome by these methods either.

2.4 Symptom Generation

This chapter describes a feature not yet introduced in KRITON, but that could help to specialize KRITON in the acquisition task in the domain of diagnosis.

Protocol analysis is used to acquire procedural knowledge. Real situations in the experts environment or artificial laboratory situations are the starting points for protocol analysis.

Symptom generation would allow systematic completion of a knowledge base for a diagnosis expert system. During a diagnosis the expert has to recognize and process situations. Symptoms are the characteristics of diagnosis. If it were possible to generate all the symptoms a knowledge-based system might encounter and rate them by their relevance and probability, then protocol analysis could be used to systematically scan the needed procedural knowledge for diagnoses purposes.

This would allow statements about the completeness of an expert system with regard to a domain, the domain being the static representation in the system, not the domain outside the machine.

2.4.1 Symptom Generation in KRITON

We define symptoms as logical combinations of attributes, functions and malfunctions. As it is known whether two functions can be active at the same time, and as we can give a rating of the probability that a malfunction happens, it seems possible to systematically generate symptoms. The technique we propose is domain independent, and because it is not yet based upon a deep model, every required information has to be acquired from the user.

Four kinds of questions are asked:

- *Can <function-1> and <function-2> be active at the same time ?,*
- *<function-1>, what will you do ?*, to trigger reactions to simple situations,
- *Do you expect new relevant information from the combination of <function-1> and <function-2> ?*, both functions describing subgraphs, whose members could be combined to form complex symptoms,
- *<function-1> and <function-2>, what will you do ?*, triggering reactions to more complex situations.

The most important aspect of the symptom generation is its capability to systematically scan the field of probable situations that the expert system may be up against. As long as it is not based upon a deep model the symptom generation cannot be complete, nor can it be efficient. But at least it forces the expert to deal with a wide range of possible cases. For an extensive presentation of symptom generation see [17].

2.5 Concept Learning

The aim of this feature is the integration of machine learning with psychological elicitation methods.

There are several ways to integrate machine learning with cognitive science methods. First, learning mechanisms can be used as knowledge elicitation methods, together with interview techniques, text analysis and protocol analysis. Second, learning mechanisms can operate on structured objects at the intermediate knowledge representation level to find similarities between them and recommend a certain organization of the structured objects (e.g. if an analogy is discovered). Third, the learning component can observe user activities on line, support the user with feedback about regularities in his use of the system and display related items in the form of rules. This last possibility will be adopted in KRITON.

The KRITON architecture supports such an integration. The intermediate knowledge representation system allows the storage of knowledge together with references to the sources of a particular entry. This facility avoids a major disadvantage of learning systems. In KRITON, the step back from generated rules to the original facts and sources is always possible by special markers at the intermediate knowledge representation level.

In addition, the above described application of learning mechanisms supports the knowledge-based knowledge elicitation process. Because the state of the existing knowledge in the system may always change, additional information about similarities and regularities of parts of the intermediate knowledge representation is necessary.

COLE (COncept LEarner) is a learning-by-example system similar to ACLS [18]. It uses induction mechanisms. The induction-algorithm in COLE is a modification of Quinlan´s ID3 [19]. From an input of classes and their attributes COLE induces concepts of these classes. These concepts allow conclusions from attributes to classes.

COLE does not, like other learning systems, generate a decision tree, but it produces rules in the form of Horn-clauses. The reason for that is the lack of clarity in decision-trees when they reach a certain size and complexity. Rules in the form of Horn-clauses are not only much more compact, but are the representation-form used in many expert systems. In KRITON, COLE will translate its Horn-clauses into BABYLON-Format [20], but rules can be generated for any other expert system shell as well.

2.5.1 Concept Learning in KRITON

The presently implemented version concentrates on the use of COLE as an acquisition method. Currently COLE has not yet been integrated into the KRITON software-system. Just like the other methods in KRITON, COLE will allow the user to make the input in a non-formal, simple, and natural language-like syntax. Attributes, their values and the classes they characterize are analyzed through a keyword-recognition mechanism.

When the user has finished his input, COLE checks all classes whether they were assigned an identical set of attributes and values. If a duplicate is found, COLE asks the user if the reason is due to :

- incorrect input,
- an undetected hierarchical relation, or
- the lack of a discriminatory attribute.

This procedure is repeated until every class of objects is unequivocally defined through a set of attributes and the corresponding values. The rule generation tries to build the simplest rule, i.e. the rule with the shortest if-part. It tries to find unequivocal attribute values for each class of objects. Ranges of values are represented with a disjunction.

Conceptual learning in COLE is to be used as a starting point for the employment of other learning techniques in KRITON. The next step will be the conversion of the input acquired by COLE and by the other acquisition-methods in KRITON into a formal concept lattice. Its advantages are the completeness as well as the clearness of representation and the reduction of computation time, especially with larger data-sets. A formal concept lattice allows also the integration of methods from similarity-based learning.

3. INTERMEDIATE KNOWLEDGE REPRESENTATION LEVEL

Some knowledge acquisition tools include different knowledge representation stages in order to represent intermediate results of the total knowledge acquisition process, e.g. OPAL [21] and KADS [22]. An intermediate knowledge representation level is useful to maintain information closer to the sources, especially if learning methods are integrated in the acquisition process. The step from generated operational knowledge back to the original facts is often necessary to evaluate the results of the acquisition process.

In KRITON all output from the knowledge elicitation techniques (see figure 2) is translated into an intermediate knowledge representation. This representation has two subparts :

- a descriptive language for functional and physical objects, representing the concepts, and
- a procedural notation representing the way these concepts are used in the problem solving process and the causal or associative links established between them by the domain expert.

The description language consists of structured objects, their features and interrelations. It is used to define semantic relations in a domain. The classification of taxonomic relations is similar to that described by Brachman

[23]. This semantic net is the goal language for the interview and text analysis methods.

The second part of the intermediate knowledge representation language is a set of propositions, consisting of primitives to describe the basic relations of concepts discovered by protocol analysis. These primitives are results of the protocol analysis. The set of primitives is domain-dependant.

The intermediate knowledge representation level allows the integration of different knowledge sources and the extension of the tool with elicitation methods currently not available. Moreover, it can be used to generate various knowledge bases for different expert system shells and knowledge representation systems.

From this point of view, an intermediate knowledge representation supports at least these six desirable properties:

- Openness of the system (possible integration of currently unknown elicitation methods).
- Knowledge acquisition for different knowledge representation languages.
- Storage of incomplete and inconsistent knowledge for the ongoing acquisition process.
- Integration and employment of acquisition knowledge bases.
- Maintaining information closer to the sources (e.g. through references to the original expert utterances, protocols etc.).
- Management of knowledge bases with varying degrees of completeness in different knowledge representation languages.

4. USING ALREADY ACQUIRED KNOWLEDGE

A very important aspect of this paper is an introduction to the method of knowledge-based knowledge elicitation.

The employment and use of the already acquired knowledge has major advantages and is an important task for knowledge acquisition tools. General purpose knowledge acquisition systems like KRITON show certain drawbacks compared to domain-specific tools, as as they cannot make a priori assumptions about the knowledge to be acquired and its underlying structure. OPAL [21] is a tool specifically designed for cancer therapy that makes extensive use of the domain properties. The only chance for a general purpose knowledge acquisition tool to achieve a performance comparable to domain- or inference-specific tools is to use as much as possible of the already acquired knowledge to adapt the system to the task.

Another problem arises if different problem solving strategies (e.g. heuristic classification, planning, configuration) are to be supported. In this case meta-knowledge is necessary to realize different strategies of applying the available knowledge.

In KRITON, already captured knowledge can be used in several ways. Existing knowledge is completed by *acquisition knowledge bases* (AKBs) for better guidance of the ongoing elicitation process. These acquisition knowledge bases are viewed as an integral part of the KRITON system. In every stage of the acquisition process, the user can use these knowledge bases in addition to existing knowledge for better employment of the KRITON facilities for knowledge-based knowledge elicitation.

AKBs contain a set of structured objects defining important concepts of the domain. They are predefined declarative models of a domain with the sole purpose of optimizing the ongoing acquisition process. There is no guarantee that the AKBs are complete or consistent : they themselves are the results of acquisition processes and are used only for the purpose of further knowledge elicitation.

Depending on the richness and quality of the existing knowledge, the already acquired knowledge is used in the following ways:

- Subject of further specialization processes.
- Guidance of the acquisition process by discovery of missing components
- Completion of domain-dependent models (AKBs).

5. USING INCOMPLETE KNOWLEDGE FOR REFINEMENT AND SPECIALIZATION

The discovery of incomplete knowledge and the search for hypotheses with best evidence is one important feature of knowledge acquisition tools, e.g. MOLE [24]

In KRITON, the employment of a certain knowledge elicitation method depends not only on decisions of the knowledge engineer but also on requirements the system discovers by analysis of the already acquired knowledge.

A significant role in dealing with incomplete knowledge is played by Watcher, which is a permanently active demon controling the intermediate knowledge representation for missing components.

The user (the knowledge engineer or expert) might have generated several objects during the incremental text analysis without any relation to the taxonomic organization of the objects of the corresponding domain (e.g. no information about the inheritance paths, part-of relations or instance relations was given). These items are known to the system, but should be subject to further investigations. Watcher checks all objects at the intermediate knowledge representation level for missing, but possible or indispensable links (e.g. every object has to be placed in a taxonomic organization), and recommends the employment of an elicitation method to complete the knowledge base.

A simple example. As a part of an AKB, the system has stored at the intermediate knowledge representation level a *part-of* relation between the objects *motor* and *car*. Watcher will discover this relation and will trigger an interview. More precisely, Watcher selects a question from the laddering component to explore the *part-of* relation between *motor* and *car*. First, *physical-part-of* relations are analyzed, next *subset* or *generalization* relations and so on, until the most specialized relation is found.

Watcher is also invoked if an elicitation method starts, informing the user about incomplete parts of the knowledge base. Furthermore, the user can delegate the selection of concepts to be used in an interview to Watcher. This demon then looks for semantically related but incompletely described objects and triggers an interview to complete the knowledge base.

To complete incomplete knowledge bases, and to find *gaps* within them, Watcher would need meta-knowledge, knowledge about knowledge to tell him what acquisition method to trigger next.

The discovery of missing objects and links in a semantic structure is only possible by using knowledge about the required semantic relations for an object. Here knowledge about semantic structuring in KRITON becomes important.

Although Watcher is realized purely procedurally now, the KRITON approach could in the future profit from a knowledge-based organization of Watcher.

The general aim of this approach is to extend the facilities of the knowledge-based Watcher. The purpose of this component is not only to recommend knowledge elicitation methods but also to automatically employ them.

6. RULE-GUIDED EMPLOYMENT OF KNOWLEDGE ELICITATION METHODS THROUGH THE WATCHER

An example illustrates the potential role of a knowledge-based Watcher component in KRITON.

We assume that the meta-knowledge used by the watcher contains indications about the refinement of hierarchical structures, i.e. *physical-part-of* is a refinement of *part-of*; *part-of*, *is-a* and *subset* being refinements of *hierarchical relation*, the indication that every concept must be integrated into the taxonomic structure, the very general information that every concept should be described through attributes and that every concept should appear in rules resulting from protocol analysis.

The example will show how such meta-knowledge could be used in a system like KRITON to direct the acquisition process.

6.1 The Triggering of the Repertory-Grid Component as Part of the Interview

Suppose the concept *gearbox* is part of the taxonomic structure on the intermediate knowledge representation level (declarative structures). This object has three subconcepts : *automatic gearbox, gearbox with gearshift and gearbox with floor shift.* There is no information available concerning the describing attributes or the specialization of the hierarchical relations.

Watcher will discover this particular situation. The Watcher program incorporates a rule which is applicable here and triggers the repertory-grid part of the interview component. The expert is asked wether *gearbox with gearshift and gearbox with floor shift share an attribute or property that automatic gearbox doesn't have*. The user might attribute *hand use* to *gearbox with gearshift* and *gearbox with floor shift* to differentiate them from *automatic gearbox*. The concept *automatic gearbox* gets the attribute *not hand use*.

6.2 The Employment of the Laddering Component as Part of the Interview

Suppose the concept *gearbox* is part of the taxonomic structure of the intermediate knowledge representation system of KRITON. Furthermore, there exists a *part-of* relation between *gearbox* and *floor-shift* and another *part-of* relation between *gearbox* and *gearshift*. No further information is available. Watcher will again discover this particular situation and will employ the laddering component. This interview method is used to explore the *part-of* relations between concepts and tries to specialize this relation. First, a question will be put to the user asking whether a *physical part-of relation* holds between *gearbox* and *gearshift/floor shift*. If this is not true, a question is asked whether there exists a *subset* relation between *gearbox* and *gearshift/floor shift*. If this is not true, a possible generalization relationship between the objects in question is explored.

This examination of possible taxonomic relations is oriented towards Brachman's classification of taxonomic links in semantic networks [25]. This classification seems to be adequate for many domains, but the question arises, whether the user-oriented questions of the laddering component capture the semantics of the links in the resulting taxonomic structure. Therefore, a reexamination of the outcome of the laddering through the knowledge engineer is necessary.

6.3 The Recommendation of a Protocol Analysis through the Watcher

The aim of the *knowledge-based knowledge elicitation* approach of KRITON is not only to select the appropriate questions of the interview component in order to complete the existing taxonomic network, but also to guide the knowledge engineer in his planning of the ongoing knowledge acquisition process. The recommendation of a protocol analysis through the Watcher program would be one first step in this direction.

As mentioned earlier, protocol analysis is an extremely costly procedure. One of the most difficult tasks for the knowledge engineer, who plans the protocol recording, is the selection of appropriate situations where the human expert can realize the thinking aloud technique.

KRITON could give hints for such a selection, using the basic assumption that every well defined concept of the taxonomic-declarative structure should also be included in the procedural part of the knowledge base. Furthermore, concepts that appear during protocol analysis should be defined in the declarative structures before they become a part of the procedural knowledge.

The Watcher program therefore searches the procedural part of the intermediate knowledge representation for an appearance of all objects that are part of the declarative structures. If for example, the object *gearbox* doesn't appear in an argument position of the operator-argument structures (outcome of the protocol analysis; procedural part of the intermediate knowledge representation) the user is asked (in this case the knowledge engineer) whether it is possible and useful to make a protocol analysis that incorporates *gearbox*.

In summary, existing knowledge bases are permanently analyzed for the discovering of parts that could be subject for refinement, specialization and completion. This is not the only criteria for a successful application of a protocol analysis, of course. Nevertheless, it is a first step towards guiding the knowledge engineer in his doing and to develop a methodology for the knowledge engineering process.

7. SUPPORTING KNOWLEDGE ACQUISITION WITH A HYBRID ARCHITECTURE

In the first paragraphs of this paper we have discussed how a variety of methods can be used in different domains.

No single knowledge acquisition method seems strong enough to acquire knowledge for all discourse domains and all problem solving strategies. Interview techniques, like repertory-grid or laddering, are fit for the acquisition of knowledge for classification and differential diagnosis. Protocol analysis acquires knowledge for solely rule-based systems, text analysis is still of very limited use as a stand-alone procedure.

KRITON is not just a merger of these three loosely connected methods, but it strongly tends towards using the advantages of each technique in the domain that the technique is best at. The symbioses of the three techniques is organized as a blackboard model.

Text analysis provides the intermediate knowledge representation (IKR) with concepts and attributes. The interview uses what is present in the IKR to build, complete or modify a semantic network in a dialogue with the expert. This network represents a taxonomic structure describing the declarative aspects of the domain. The protocol analysis feeds rules, concepts and attributes back to the IKR as they occur during the thinking aloud process of the expert. This interaction allows for an incremental process of knowledge acquisition, each method pitching in what it is best at. As there are no conflicts between methods, because their ranges are distinct, we have no need for conflict resolution on this epistemological level.

AKBs can be introduced into the IKR as generic knowledge bases or as skeletons of knowledge bases. If the AKB is the sketch of a taxonomy, the acquisition procedures are directed toward the elicitation of static knowledge, whereas if it is a set of triggering cases, the acquisition of procedural knowledge will be stressed.

The interaction of the techniques is guided by the watcher, who in daemon-like fashion watches the blackboard, and if need is triggers acquisition methods.

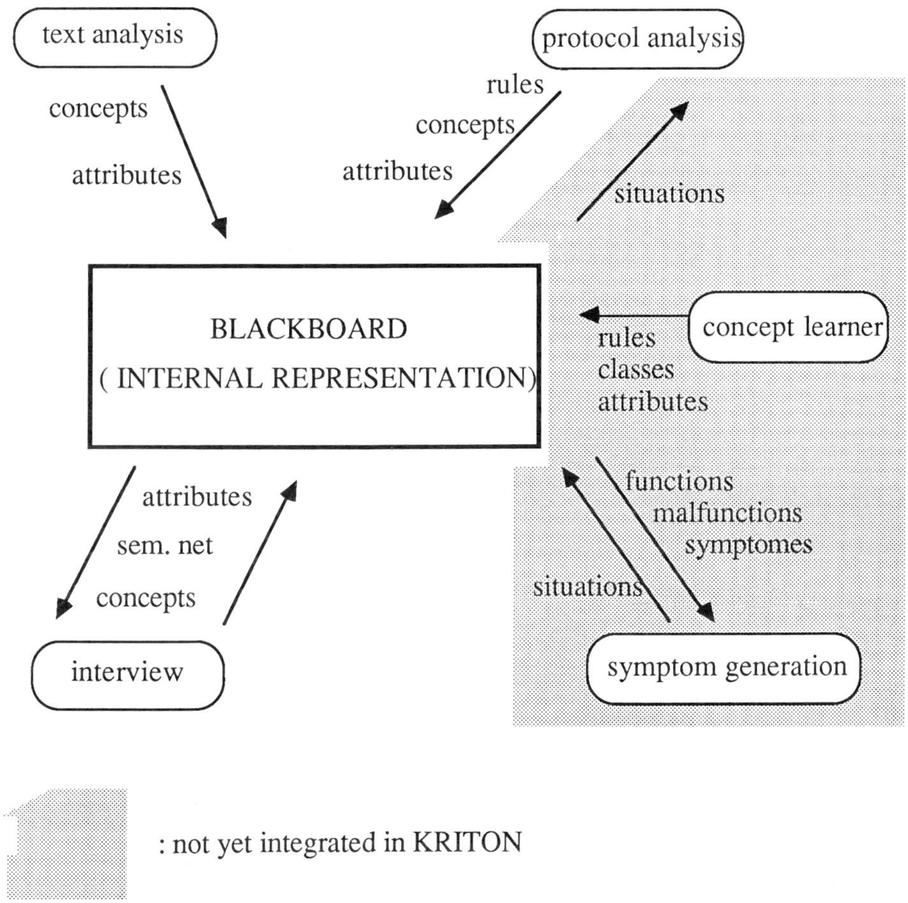

Figure 3 Organization of the acquisition techniques and their interaction.

8. EXAMPLES

A sample knowledge base for motor diagnosis will be partly generated using several knowledge acquisition methods.

The text analysis[1]. of a technical description generates some objects:

engine, carburetor, cylinder, piston, crankshaft etc.

As these objects are not yet integrated into the knowledge base, the watcher triggers an interview. The interview component, as part of the repertory grid technique presents them to the expert as triplets.

INTERVIEW

KRITON : Which property do carburetor and cylinder share, that piston does not have?
Expert : They are containers.

KRITON : Which property do cylinder and engine share, that piston does not have?
Expert : None.

Here KRITON switches from the repertory grid technique to a laddering technique to elicit taxonomic structures.

KRITON : Is piston a part of cylinder or engine?
Expert : Yes.

etc.

This will produce a taxonomy like :

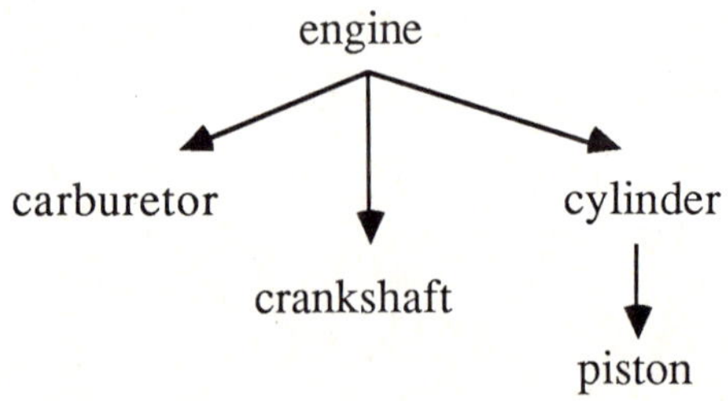

[1]We do not include screen-copies as KRITON is geared towards German language, and it is utterly unable to process non-German protocols or texts.

All vertices in the graph represent *part-of* relations. The watcher triggers refining questions :

KRITON : *Is piston a physical part of cylinder ?*
Expert : *Yes.*

More repertory-grid questions are triggered to provide differentiating attribution:

KRITON : *Which property do crankshaft and piston share that carburetor doesn´t have?*
Expert : *They are moving.*

The result of the repertory grid and laddering techniques is represented as declarative knowledge in a frame-like syntax in the intermediate knowledge representation language.

PROTOCOL ANALYSIS

The protocol analysis, employed for the acquisition of procedural knowledge, is used independently of the interview technique. The transcription of the experts thinking aloud protocol contains markers indicating pauses within the experts speech.

*Expert: ...*I open the gearbox*the fittings are o.k.*the oil is burned and brown ** the clutch and the breakbelts are damaged**...*

This sentence is segmented :

(D1[2] open gearbox)

D2 o.k. fittings)

(D3 the oil is burned and brown)

(D4 the clutch and the breakbelts are damaged)

Further transformation produces :

(open D1 gearbox)

(o.k. D2 fittings)

(burned D3 oil)

---

[2]These reference-markers point to the sub-sentence in the actual protocol, that was used to generate the operator-argument structure. They serve documentation purposes.

(brown D3 oil)

(damaged D4 clutch)

(damaged D4 breakbelts)

One possible rule that can be generated by the expert with the help of the knowledge engineer :

IF	(burned D3 oil)	\$AND	(brown D3 oil)
THEN	(damaged D4 clutch)	\$AND	(damaged D4 breakbelts)

This propositional representation uses domain-dependent primitives which have to be elicited with the interview techniques to assure that the rules KRITON generates are backed up with declarative knowledge. The watcher will trigger an interview to integrate *breakbelts* and *clutch* into the taxonomic structure.

KRITON : *Which property do breakbelt and clutch share, that engine does not have* ?
Expert : *None.*

KRITON : *Are breakbelt or clutch parts-of engine ?*
Expert : *Yes.*
etc.

ACQUISITION KNOWLEDGE BASES

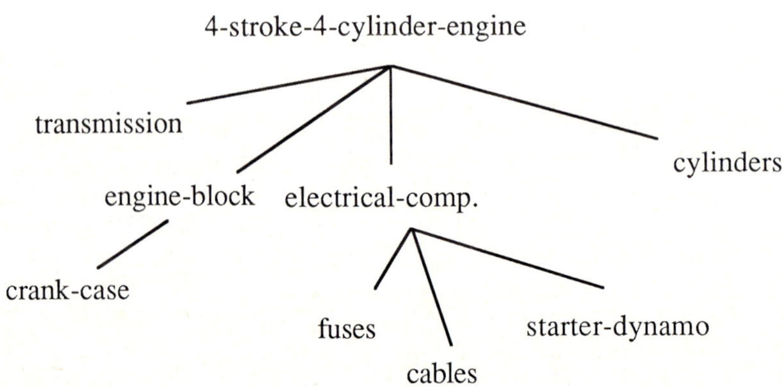

Figure 4 An acquisition knowledge base describing important concepts of an engine.

AKBs can be written onto the blackboard at any time during the acquisition process. They can be used as skeletons, structuring the future knowledge base, which can be very useful if several experts enter their knowledge into the system, or AKBs can be used as generic bases. In the latter case the description of a 4-stroke-4-cylinder engine can be refined into a 1100-cc engine of the same type, and then be made into a special model of some type etc. This makes it possible to re-use already acquired knowledge in other knowledge bases.

CONCEPT LEARNING

The concept learner COLE defines classes through the values they have for sets of attributes.

KRITON : Give the value for the class oil and the attribute color.
Expert : Yellow.
KRITON : Give the value for the class oil and the attribute viscosity.
Expert : Low.
KRITON : Give the value for the class breakfluid and the attribute color.
Expert : Yellow.
KRITON : Give the value for the class breakfluid and the attribute viscosity.
Expert : High.

COLE allows the generation of rules like :

IF color yellow
viscosity high
subclass-of liquids

THEN class is breakfluid.

9. COMPARING KRITON WITH OTHER ACQUISITION TOOLS

We will compare KRITON to some other systems that are, just like KRITON, concerned with the elicitation of knowledge and are not limited to a specific domain or problem solving strategy. Tools considered are : KSS0 [8], KADS-POWER-TOOLS [26], AQUINAS [6] [7]. KADS [22] will not be considered, as it is a comprehensive methodology, offering a general knowledge acquisition frame-work wherein KRITON might be integrated as one component.

KSS0 (Knowledge Support System Zero) is an acquisition tool based on repertory-grid test [5] techniques that graphically represents the results of the repertory-grid after a hierarchical clustering analysis. The clustering distances being computed using the distances the concepts have on the sum of their attributes. KSS0 is limited to one acquisition technique and does not produce directly encodable data. The data acquired is extensively analyzed with the ENTAIL-algorithm [27]. KSS0 is a tool to support the knowledge engineer in the elicitation process.

AQUINAS, an extended version of the Expertise Transfer System (ETS) [28] is a hybrid tool that includes features to elicit distinctions, decompose problems, combine uncertain information, automatic refinement and integration of expertise from different sources. The basic elicitation technique is the repertory-grid test [5]. AQUINAS delivers knowledge-bases suited for rapid prototyping.

The KADS-POWER-TOOLS provide the bottom-up support for the knowledge acquisition with the KADS methodology. The KADS-POWER-TOOLS include a concept-editor, a hyper-text like protocol-editor and the interpretation-model librarian helping to choose an interpretation model in the KADS-interpretation-model library.

Comparing KRITON with KSS0 it becomes obvious that even though KRITON encompasses more elicitation methods, KSS0 makes more extensive use of available analysis methods to present the expert with *what he really said* and with the possible implications and entailments of the bits of knowledge fed into the system. KSS0 does not include any equivalent of KRITON´s protocol analysis though.

When we compare KRITON and AQUINAS we find another system relying heavily on personal construct theory [5] and that does not use protocol analysis. AQUINAS offers better possibilities to manage and organize larger sets of concepts of a domain than KRITON does. The fact that AQUINAS delivers operational knowledge bases implies that rapid-prototyping can be used to validate the acquisition process, a potential that cannot be underestimated. This relies however on the point of view that bits of knowledge, as they result from an elicitation process are an operational knowledge base, and that they do not need previous interpretation and modeling to describe how they are to be used in the problem solving process. This is a point of view we do not share.

Looking at the KADS-POWER-TOOLS we find strong editing, managing and design support to devise conceptual models [22]. Elicitation is limited to hypertext-based text- and protocol-analysis. The protocol-analysis facilities are totally different from those of KRITON. They do not present any automated phases, but are limited to imposing a structure upon the text. This implies however that more kinds of protocols and texts can be analyzed. KRITON is currently limited to analyzing concurrent thinking-aloud protocols.

The overall picture is that KRITON does have some drawbacks :

- lack of tools to analyze the elicited data (KSSO and AQUINAS)
- no rapid prototyping (AQUINAS)
- insufficient editing and managing facilities (AQUINAS and KADS-Power-Tools),

but that it :

- presents a wider range of elicitation techniques for more knowledge-domains then any of the other tools considered,
- represents the elicited knowledge in the experts terminology and formulations. Thus the knowledge bases developed with KRITON can be read and edited by the expert together with the knowledge engineer. This will hopefully reduce the knowledge engineer´s bias that is encountered all too often if the knowledge base can not be verified by the expert,
- delivers the acquired knowledge in a non-operational document thus forcing the knowledge engineer into a modeling and operationalizing phase (see figure 1) before developing an operational knowledge base.

10. CONCLUSION

We presented KRITON, an elicitation tool currently being developed at the GMD´s expert system research group. We showed how such a tool integrating different weak elicitation methods, each specialized in a domain, can help reduce the knowledge acquisition bottleneck. First evaluations of our tool have shown that KRITON cannot be considered the solution to this problem though. At least not yet.

Future work will focus on :

- integration of more elicitation techniques to cover larger areas of the elicitation domain. Potential candidates are networking [16], cluster-analysis [29] and case-based knowledge acquisition [30].

- study of integration aspects, to handle different approaches to the same *bit of knowledge*, and to be able to coerce these different approaches into one consistent piece,
- editing-facilities and knowledge-organizing-facilities, as implemented in KREME [31] or KET [32] to cover the representation aspects of the knowledge engineering process. This will allow to include the prototyping phase into the computer-aided knowledge engineering.

ACKNOWLEDGEMENTS

Thanks to Barbara Becker, Hans-Werner Güsgen and Karin Lagrange whose comments on the paper where of great help. Special thanks to Ulrich Willenbrock who did much of the editing work for this paper.

REFERENCES

[1] Boose, J., A Research Framework for Knowledge Acquisition Techniques and Tools, in: Boose, J., Gaines, B. and Linster, M. (eds.), Proceedings of the European Knowledge Acquisition Workshop 1988 (GMD, St. Augustin 1988)

[2] Gaines, B., Second Generation Knowledge Acquisition Systems, in: Boose, J., Gaines, B. and Linster, M. (eds.), Proceedings of the European Knowledge Acquisition Workshop 1988 (GMD, St. Augustin 1988)

[3[Christaller, T., Güsgen, H.-W., Hertzberg, J., Linster, M., Voß, A., Voß, H., Was ist Expertise und wie bekommt man sie auf den Rechner?, in : GMD-Jahresbericht 1987 (GMD, St. Augustin 1988)

[4] Grover, M.D., A Pragmatic Knowledge Acquisition Methodology, in : Proceedings of IJCAI 1983 (Karlsruhe, 1983)

[5] Kelly, G., The Psychology of Personal Constructs, (Norton, New York, 1955)

[6] Boose, J., Bradshaw, J., Expertise Transfer and Complex Problems, Using AQUINAS as a Knowledge Acquisition Workbench for Expert Systems, in : Boose, J., Gaines, B., (eds), Proceedings of the Knowledge Acquisition for Knowledge-Based Systems Workshop, (Banff, Canada, 1986)

[7] Boose, J., Bradshaw J., AQUINAS, A Knowledge Acquisition Workbench for Knowledge-Based Systems, in : Addis, T., Boose, J., Gaines, B. (eds.), Proceedings of the First European Workshop on Knowledge Acquisition for Knowledge-Based Systems (Reading, U.K., 1987)

[8] Gaines, B., Rapid Prototyping for Expert Systems, (University of Calgary, Canada 1987)
[9] LaFrance, M., The Knowledge Acquisition Grid : A Methodology for Training Knowledge Engineers, in : Boose, J., Gaines, B., (eds), Proceedings of the Knowledge Acquisition for Knowledge-Based Systems Workshop, (Banff, Canada, 1986)
[10] Kuipers, B., Kassirer, B., Causal Reasoning in Medicine : Analysis of a Protocol, Cognitive Science, 8 (1984) 363-385
[11] Kuipers, B., Kassirer, B., How to Discover a Knowledge Representation for Causal Reasoning by Studying an Expert Physician, in : Proceedings of IJCAI 1983 (Karlsruhe 1983)
[12] Ericsson, K., Simon, H., Protocol Analysis, Verbal Reports as Data, (MIT-Press, Cambridge, 1984)
[13] Merten, K., Inhaltsanalyse, (Westdeutscher Verlag, Opladen 1983)
[14] Nishida, T., Kosaka, A., Doshita, S., Towards Acquisition from Natural Language Documents - Automatic Model Construction from Hardware Manuals, in : Proceedings of IJCAI 1983 (Karlsruhe 1983)
[15] Frey, W., Reyle, U., Rohrer, C., Automatic Construction of a Knowledge Base by Analyzing Texts in Natural Language, in : Proceedings of IJCAI 1983, (Karlsruhe 1983)
[16] Bonato, M., Knowledge Elicitation with Structure Formation Techniques, in : Diederich, J., Uthmann, T., (eds.), Knowledge Acquisition for Expert Systems, Arbeitspapier 281 der GMD, (GMD, St. Augustin 1987)
[17] Linster, M., Structuring Knowledge for Incremental Knowledge Acquisition, in : Addis, T., Boose, J., Gaines, B. (eds.), Proceedings of the First European Workshop on Knowledge Acquisition for Knowledge-Based Systems (Reading, U.K., 1987)
[18] Paterson, A, Niblett, T., ACLS User Manual, (ITL, Edinburgh 1982)
[19] Quinlan, J., Discovering Rules by Induction from Large Collections of Examples, in : Mitchie, D. (ed.), Expert Systems in the Micro-Electronic Age (Edinburgh University Press, Edinburgh 1979
[20] DiPrimio, F., Brewka, G., BABYLON : Kernel System for an Integrated environment for expert system development and operation, in : Proceedings of the 5th International Workshop on Expert Systems and Applications (Avignon 1985)
[21] Musen, M., Using a Domain Model to Drive an Interactive Knowledge Editing Tool, in : Boose, J., Gaines, B., (eds), Proceedings of the Knowledge Acquisition for Knowledge-Based Systems Workshop, (Banff, Canada, 1986)
[22] Wielinga, B., Breuker, J., Model Driven Knowledge Acquisition : Interpretation Models, Esprit Project 1098 Report (University of Amsterdam, Amsterdam 1987)
[23] Brachmann, R., What Is-A Is and Isn´t, an analysis of taxonomic links in semantic networks, IEEE-Computer 16 (Special issue : Knowledge Representation) (1983)

[24] Eshelman, L., Ehret, D., McDermott, J., Tan, M., MOLE : A Tenacious Knowledge Acquisition Tool, in : Boose, J., Gaines, B., (eds), Proceedings of the Knowledge Acquisition for Knowledge-Based Systems Workshop, (Banff, Canada, 1986)

[25] Brachmann, R., On the Epistemological Status of Semantic Networks, in : Findler, N. (ed.) : Associative Networks (Academic Press, New York 1979)

[26] Anjewierden, A., The KADS System, in : Addis, T., Boose, J., Gaines, B. (eds.), Proceedings of the First European Workshop on Knowledge Acquisition for Knowledge-Based Systems (Reading, U.K., 1987)

[27] Gaines, B., Shaw, M., New Directions in the Analysis and Interactive Elicitation of Personal Construct Systems, in : Shaw, M. (ed.), Recent Advances in Personal Construct Theory (Academic Press, London 1981)

[28] Boose, J., Expertise Transfer for Expert System Design (Elsevier, New York, 1986)

[29] Cooke, N., McDonald, J., The Application of Psychological Scaling Techniques to Knowledge Elicitation for Expert Systems, in : Boose, J., Gaines, B., (eds), Proceedings of the Knowledge Acquisition for Knowledge-Based Systems Workshop, (Banff, Canada, 1986)

[30] Becker, B., Towards a Case-Oriented Concept for Knowledge Acquisition, in : Boose, J., Gaines, B., Linster, M. (eds.), Proceedings of the European Knowledge Acquisition Workshop 1988 (GMD, St. Augustin 1988)

[31] Abrett, G., Burstein, B., The KREME knowledge editing environment, International Journal of Man-Machine Studies 27 (1987)

[32] Esfahani, L.,Teski, F., KET, a knowledge encoding tool, in : Boose, J., Gaines, B., Linster, M. (eds.), Proceedings of the European Knowledge Acquisition Workshop 1988, (GMD, St. Augustin 1988)

PART 6

Validation and evaluation

Topics in Expert System Design
G. Guida and C. Tasso (Editors)

KNOWLEDGE BASE VERIFICATION

Walton A. PERKINS, Thomas J. LAFFEY,
Deanne PECORA, and Tin A. NGUYEN

Lockheed Artificial Intelligence Center
Menlo Park, CA, USA

1 Introduction

Knowledge-based systems must be debugged and validated just like any other piece of software. Knowledge bases use a declarative style which separates knowledge from control. This style and separation make possible more semantic checking than in conventional software systems, where knowledge and control are mixed together. As advances in hardware and software make it possible to build and run very large rule-based systems, the importance of checking the knowledge base becomes even greater.

As with most software, syntax checking as the knowledge base is read in is useful for avoiding serious problems during execution. The user needs to be informed about the nature and location of these errors. This information is analogous to the compiler error messages resulting from syntax errors in an ordinary programming language.

This work was supported under Lockheed Independent Research and Development funds

A common method of validating any software is to run examples with known results and to compare the performance of the program against the correct answers. This method can also be used with knowledge-based systems, although the number of test cases required may be rather large if the domain is complicated. An automated test case capability can help the knowledge engineer by easing the task of creating, saving, running, and modifying test cases.

One way in which knowledge-based systems differ from other software systems is that many of them depend, at least in part, on the use of rules for the representation of knowledge, and the behavior of the system depends on how the rules interact. If there is a rule missing, the chaining will fail as an ordinary program will fail if a subroutine is missing. However, the fact that the knowledge-based program failed because of a missing rule may not be obvious. There are many other potential problems in rule-based systems, such as contradictory rules or rules which can never fire because they need information which is never obtainable.

The types of checking which can be performed are dependent upon the rule and knowledge base structure. For example, if a frame-based system allows the specification of legal values for a slot, the checker can verify that only permitted values are used in the rules. A rule checker is a tool which addresses the rule-based structure of the system. It analyzes the knowledge base after the rules and frame structures have been read in, determining the relations between the rules and identifying potential problems with rules. It may also create a graph or table showing the relationships among the rules.

In this paper we assume that the expert system shell for which the knowledge base is being developed is a hybrid system containing both *frames* and *rules*. The frame is assumed to be composed of *slots* which hold values. Slots are frequently referred to as *attributes*, because they are used to hold values of attributes of the object represented by the frame. Some shells also allow the specification of *attribute properties* such as whether the user may be asked for the value of the attribute (see Section 3.2 for more information about attribute properties). In addition, we assume that variables are allowed in rules and that both backward and forward chaining are possible. There are several commercial packages that satisfy these conditions.

The work described in this paper is derived from a project to build a rule checker for the Lockheed Expert System (LES) [1], a Lockheed-proprietary knowledge base system development tool (i.e., shell) which has all of the features mentioned in the previous paragraph. CHECK [2] is a program which examines a LES knowledge base for potential problems. The capabilities in Section 3 are present in CHECK, and the other checking features described in Section 4 are built into LES. The algorithms described in this paper are "generic" and could be applied to almost any rule-based system.

2 Background

The TEIRESIAS program [3] was the first attempt to automate the knowledge-base debugging process. Working in the context of the MYCIN [4] infectious disease consultation system, TEIRESIAS examined the "completed" MYCIN rule set and built rule models showing various relationships, including which attributes were used to conclude other attributes. Thus, when a new rule was added to MYCIN, it was compared with the rule model for the attributes found in the IF conditions. The program then proposed missing clauses if some attributes found in the IF part of the model did not appear in the new rule. TEIRESIAS did not check the rules as they were initially entered into the knowledge base. Rather, it assumed the knowledge base was "complete" (or close to it), and the knowledge transfer occurred in the setting of a problem-solving session.

Suwa, Scott, and Shortliffe [5] have written a program for verifying knowledge base completeness and consistency. The program was devised and tested within the context of the ONCOCIN system, a rule-based system for clinical oncology. ONCOCIN's rule checker examines a rule set as it is read into the system. Unlike TEIRESIAS, it was meant to be used as the system is being developed. Knowledge base problems are found by first partitioning the rules into disjoint sets based upon what attribute is assigned a value in the conclusion. It then makes a table displaying all possible combinations of attributes used in the IF conditions and the corresponding values which will be concluded in the THEN part of the rule. The table is then checked for conflicts, redundancy, subsumption, and missing rules. Finally, a table is displayed with a summary of any potential errors that were found. The rule checker assumes that there should be a rule for each possible combination of values of attributes which appear in the antecedent. It hypothesizes missing rules based on this assumption. This may result in the system's hypothesizing rules which have semantically impossible combinations of attribute values. Also, if the number of attributes is large, the system could suggest a very large number of missing rules. Nevertheless, the developers of the ONCOCIN system found it extremely useful in helping them to debug their evolving knowledge base. Although the system checks the rule set used in the ONCOCIN system, its design was general, so that it could be adapted to other rule-based systems.

The CHECK program of Nguyen et. al. is an extension of the rule checking program used in the ONCOCIN project modified for use with LES. CHECK differs from the ONCOCIN checker in that CHECK is applied to the entire set of rules for a goal, not just the subsets which determine the value of each attribute. Because of this more global view of the knowledge base, CHECK includes several new rule checking criteria: unreachable conclusions, deadend IF conditions, deadend goals, unnecessary IF conditions, unreferenced attribute values, and illegal attribute values. Furthermore, CHECK produces dependency charts and detects any circular rule chains.

The development of knowledge base checkers is currently a very active field, and we will only mention a few of the more recent systems. Reubenstein [6], in his MIT Master's thesis, discusses a rule checker for OPS5 called OPMAN, which allows the user to specify knowledge base constraints as a form of meta-knowledge about the rule base. OPMAN has many other features which assist the user in developing and modifying an OPS5 rule base.

A number of expert system shells have incorporated various kinds of rule checkers. For example, TIMM [7], an expert system shell which generates its rules from examples (i.e., induction), has some capability for checking rules, and KES [8] is an expert system shell which has a support tool called INSPECTOR. KEE [9] has a number of graphical and text displays which allow the user to examine the possible rule chains which might be created, watch the actual chaining which occurs, and receive information about knowledge base changes. CLIPS [10], a forward-chaining, rule-based (no frames) shell developed by NASA, has a rule cross-reference program to analyze the relations among the rules.

Stachowitz et. al. [11] are developing EVA, the Expert Systems Validation Associate.

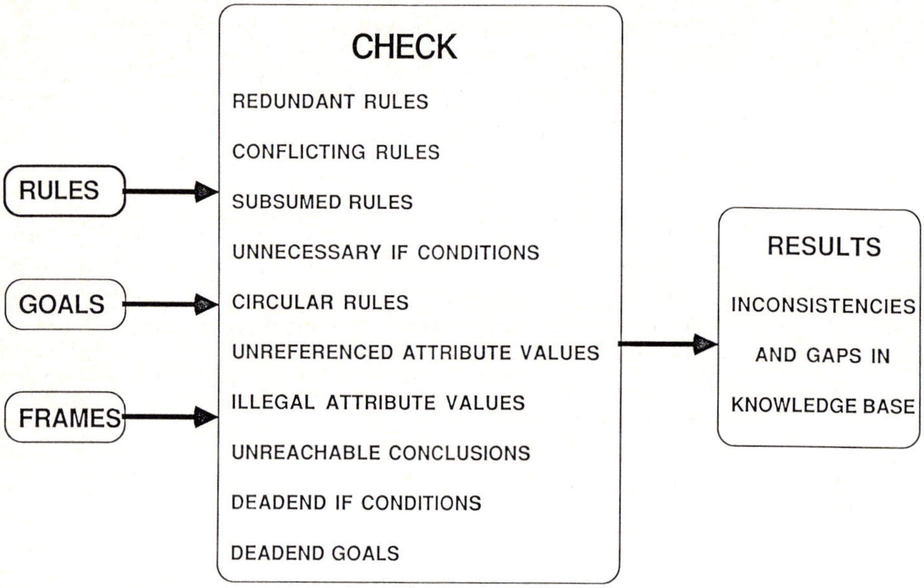

Figure 1: CHECK analyzes a knowledge base reporting inconsistencies and gaps

Their goal is to create a generic tool which can validate applications written in any expert system shell by translating the language of the shell into a declarative metalanguage, which is also used for describing constraints. EVA, which is being implemented in Prolog, will consist of a number of modules, each of which does a specific type of check.

3 Checking for Potential Problems in the Knowledge Base

A static analysis of the rules can detect many potential problems that exist in a knowledge base. (This analysis is unique to rule-based systems, and no good analogy exists in checking ordinary programs.) We will first identify, then give definitions and examples of knowledge base problems which can be detected by performing an analysis of *goal-driven* rules. Later in this paper we will then see how these definitions must be modified for *data-driven* rules.

Knowledge base problems can only be detected if the rule syntax is restrictive enough to allow one to examine two rules and determine whether situations exist in which both can succeed, and whether the results of applying the two rules are the same, conflicting, or unrelated. In rule languages which allow a very unrestricted syntax, it becomes difficult or impossible to implement the algorithms described in this paper.

The CHECK program analyzes rules and goals in a knowledge base and uses attribute properties stored in a frame database. Figure 1 illustrates the different tests that CHECK performs on a knowledge base.

3.1 Checking for Consistency

By statically analyzing the logical semantics of the rules, a rule checker can detect redundant rules, conflicting rules, rules that are subsumed by other rules, unnecessary IF conditions, and circular-rule chains. These five potential problems are defined in the subsections which follow.

3.1.1 Redundant Rules

Two rules are redundant if they succeed in the same situation and have the same conclusions. This means that the IF parts of the two rules are equivalent, and one or more conclusions are also equivalent. The IF parts of two rules can be equivalent only if each part has the same number of conditions and each condition in one part is equivalent to a condition in the other part. Because variables are allowed in rules, two conditions are equivalent if they are unifiable.

More formally, using the notation from predicate calculus, rule "p(x) → q(x)" is equivalent to the rule "p(y) → q(y)", where x and y are variables, and p and q are logical relationships.

For example, consider the two rules which follow:

```
(1) IF   ?X has a hoarse cough, AND
         ?X has difficulty breathing
    THEN type-of-disease of ?X is CROUP

(2) IF   ?Y has difficulty breathing, AND
         ?Y has a hoarse cough
    THEN type-of-disease of ?Y is CROUP
```

"?X" and "?Y" represent variables which will be instantiated to a person in the database. These two rules would be redundant even though they use different variables and their IF conditions are in a different order.

As reported by Suwa, Scott, and Shortliffe [5], redundancy in a knowledge base does not necessarily cause logical problems, although it may affect efficiency. In a system where the first successful rule is the only one to succeed, a problem will arise only if one of two redundant rules is revised or deleted, while the other is left unchanged. Also, if the system uses some type of scoring scheme (e.g., certainty factors), redundancy could cause a problem.

3.1.2 Conflicting Rules

Two rules are conflicting if they succeed in the same situation but with conflicting conclusions. This means that the IF parts of the two rules are equivalent, but one or more conclusions are contradictory.

More formally, using the notation from predicate calculus, the rule "p(x) → not(q(x))" is contradictory to the rule "p(x) → q(x)".

For example, consider the two rules which follow:

```
(1) IF   ?X has a hoarse cough, AND
         ?X has difficulty breathing
    THEN type-of-disease of ?X is CROUP

(2) IF   ?X has a hoarse cough, AND
         ?X has difficulty breathing
    THEN type-of-disease of ?X is BRONCHITIS
```

These two rules are conflicting because given the same information, one rules concludes that the disease is croup, the other concludes bronchitis.

NOTE: It is possible that rules with similar premises might not conflict at all, especially when they are concluding values for a multivalued attribute. (A multivalued attribute may assume multiple values simultaneously. For example, a person may be allergic to many different drugs, or may be infected by numerous organisms.)

3.1.3 Subsumed Rules

One rule is subsumed by another if the two rules have the same conclusions, but one contains additional constraints on the situations in which it will succeed. This means one or more conclusions are equivalent, but the IF part of one rule contains fewer constraints and/or conditions than the IF part of the other rule.

More formally, using the notation from predicate calculus, the rule "(p(x) and q(y)) → r(z)" is subsumed by the rule "p(x) → r(z)". Whenever the more restrictive rule succeeds, the less restrictive rule also succeeds, resulting in redundancy.

For example, consider the two rules which follow:

```
(1) IF   ?X has flat pink spots on his skin, AND
         ?X has a fever
    THEN type-of-disease of ?X is MEASLES

(2) IF   ?X has flat pink spots on his skin
    THEN type-of-disease of ?X is MEASLES
```

In this case we would say that Rule (1) is subsumed by Rule (2) since Rule (2) only needs a single piece of information to conclude **measles**. Whenever Rule (1) succeeds, Rule (2) will also succeed.

3.1.4 Unnecessary IF Conditions

Two rules contain unnecessary IF conditions if the rules have the same conclusions, an IF condition in one rule is in conflict with an IF condition in the other rule, and all other IF conditions in the two rules are equivalent. Using our notation from predicate calculus, if we had two rules, (1) "(p(x) and q(y)) → r(z)", (2) "(p(x) and not(q(y)) → r(z)", the condition involving "q(y)" in each rule is unnecessary. These two rules could be combined into "(p(x) and (q(y) or not(q(y))) → r(z)". The condition "(q(y) or not(q(y)))" resolves to TRUE, thus the rule becomes "p(x) → r(z)". In this case, the unnecessary IF condition actually indicates that only one rule is necessary.

For example, consider the two rules which follow:

```
(1) IF   ?X has flat pink spots on his skin, AND
         ?X has a fever
    THEN type-of-disease of ?X is MEASLES

(2) IF   ?X has flat pink spots on his skin
         ?X does not have a fever
    THEN type-of-disease of ?X is MEASLES
```

In this case, the second IF condition in each rule is unnecessary. Thus the two rules could be collapsed down into one.

A special case occurs when there are two rules with the same conclusion, one rule contains a single IF condition, and it is in conflict with an IF condition of the other rule which has two or more IF conditions. Using our notation from predicate calculus, if we had two rules, (1) "(p(x) and q(y)) → r(z)", (2) "not(q(y)) → r(z)", then the second IF condition in Rule (1) is unnecessary, but both rules are still needed and can be reduced to: (1) "(p(x)) → r(z)", and (2) "not(q(y)) → r(z)".

3.1.5 Circular Rules

A set of rules is circular if the chaining of those rules in the set forms a cycle. Using our notation from predicate calculus, if we had a set of rules as follows: (1) "p(x) → q(x)", (2) "q(x) → r(x)", (3) "r(x) → p(x)", and the goal is r(A), where A is a constant, then the system will enter an infinite chain at run time, unless the system has a special way of handling circular rules. Also, this definition includes the possibility of a single rule forming a circular cycle (e.g., "p(x) → p(x)").

For example, consider the following set of rules:

```
(1) IF   temperature of ?X > 100 (in Fahrenheit)
    THEN ?X has a fever
```

```
(2) IF   ?X has a fever, AND
         ?X has flat pink spots on his skin
    THEN type-of-disease of ?X is MEASLES

(3) IF   type-of-disease of ?X is MEASLES
    THEN temperature of ?X > 100 (in Fahrenheit)
```

Given a goal of

type-of-disease of patient is MEASLES,

this set of rules would go into an infinite chain if one attempted to backward-chain them together as the goal would match the conclusion of Rule (2); the first IF condition of Rule (2) would then match the conclusion of Rule (1); the IF condition of Rule (1) would then match the conclusion of Rule (3); and the IF part of Rule (3) would match the conclusion of Rule (2); thus completing our circular cycle.

3.2 Checking for Completeness

The development of a knowledge-based system is an iterative process in which knowledge is encoded, tested, added, changed, and refined. Knowledge flows from the expert into the knowledge base via a middleman (the knowledge engineer). This iterative process often leaves gaps in the knowledge base which both the knowledge engineer and the expert have overlooked during the knowledge acquisition process. Furthermore, as the number of rules grows large it becomes impossible to check every possible path through the system. Four situations indicative of gaps (i.e., missing rules) in the knowledge base are:

- unreferenced attribute values,
- deadend goals,
- unreachable conclusions, and
- deadend IF conditions.

Any one of these four conditions may indicate that there is a rule missing.

In the ONCOCIN system, the rule checker assumes there should be a rule for each possible combination of values of attributes which appear in the antecedent. In practice, this criterion may cause the system to hypothesize a very large number of missing rules. This problem was not serious in the ONCOCIN project because their checker was tested on only a single application.

One of the features of some expert system shells (e.g., EMYCIN [12], KEE, and LES) which facilitates the detection of gaps is that it allows the knowledge engineer to strongly type the attributes which they define. For each attribute, one can define a set of properties, including whether the user can be queried for the value, and a set of values the attribute can take on (i.e., its *legal values*). It has been recognized for some time in the area of software engineering that this is excellent programming practice. In fact, the newer programming languages (e.g., Pascal and Ada) have type-checking capabilities along these lines.

Attribute properties which are frequently implemented include:

- restriction of acceptable attribute values
- whether the user can be queried for the attribute value
- whether the attribute is single-valued or multivalued.

In the subsections which follow, we describe how one uses these properties to find possible gaps and errors in the knowledge base.

3.2.1 Unreferenced Attribute Values

Unreferenced attribute values occur in situations in which some values in the set of possible values of an object's attribute are not covered by any rule's IF conditions. In other words the legal values in the set are covered only partially or not at all. A partially covered attribute can prohibit the system from attaining a conclusion or cause it to make a wrong conclusion when an uncovered attribute value is encountered at run time. Unreferenced attribute values may also indicate that rules are missing.

For example, suppose we have the attribute TEMPERATURE with the set of legal values {high, normal, low}. If the attribute values "high" and "normal" are used in the IF conditions of rules, but not "low", the rule checker would alert the knowledge engineer that "low" is not used. The knowledge engineer would then have to decide if he is missing a rule or if the value "low" should be removed from the set of legal values.

3.2.2 Illegal Attribute Values

An illegal attribute value occurs when a rule refers to an attribute value which is *not* in the set of legal values. This error is often caused by a spelling mistake. No extra work is required to check for this condition as it is a by-product of checking for unreferenced attribute values.

Suppose we have the attribute TEMPERATURE with the set of legal values {high, normal, low}. If there is a rule which has a condition like

IF temperature of ?X is very high...

or

...THEN temperature of ?X is medium

the rule checker would alert the knowledge engineer that the values "**very high**" and "**medium**" are illegal attribute values for temperature.

3.2.3 Unreachable Conclusions

In a goal-driven production system, a conclusion of a rule should either match a goal or match an IF condition of another rule. If there are no matches for the conclusion, it is said to be unreachable.

For example, suppose we have the rule:

```
(1) IF   temperature of ?X > 100 (in Fahrenheit)
    THEN ?X has a fever
```

If the condition "?X has a fever" does not appear in the IF part of any rule and is not part of the goal, the rule checker would alert the knowledge engineer that this conclusion is unreachable.

It is possible that such a rule is merely extraneous, in which case it may affect efficiency, but not the outcome, since it will never be triggered. It is also possible that the conclusion does not match a goal (or subgoal) because of a terminology error. For example, there may be a rule with an IF condition of the form:

```
IF   ?X has an elevated temperature
THEN ...
```

where "**elevated temperature**" and "**fever**" are synonymous to the expert, but not to the expert system.

3.2.4 Deadend IF Conditions and Deadend Goals

To achieve a goal (or subgoal) in a goal-driven system, it is required that either:

- the truth of the goal can be determined by asking the user
- the goal is matched by a conclusion of one of the rules in the rule sets applying to that goal.

If neither of these requirements is satisfied then the goal cannot be achieved (i.e., it is a "deadend goal"). Similarly, the IF conditions of a rule also must meet one of these two conditions, or they are "deadend IF conditions".

For example, suppose we have the following as a goal (or subgoal):

type-of-disease of patient is MEASLES,

If the attribute "type-of-disease" is not askable and there are no rules that conclude this fact, than this goal would be labeled as "deadend".

3.3 Checking Data-Driven Rules

Up to this point, we have only considered goal-driven rules. Checking a data-driven rule set for consistency and completeness is very similar to checking goal-driven rules. The detection of conflicting rules, redundant rules, subsumed rules, circular rule chains, dead-end IF conditions, unreferenced attribute values, and illegal attribute values is done in the same manner as described earlier.

Detection of unreachable conclusions is not applicable in checking a data-driven rule set since there are no goals to match to the conclusions.

List of Rules

R1: IF A and X then Z
R2: IF B and C then A   R2a: IF A and B and C then A
R3: IF D then C   R3a: IF A and D then C
R4: IF R then X
R5: IF S then X

Goal

GC1: determine Z

Then (columns) / **If** (rows)

	R1	R2	R3	R4	R5
R1		*		*	*
R2		*2	*		
R3		*3			
R4					
R5					
GC1	*				

Figure 2: Rules with associated Dependency Chart

3.4 Dependency Chart and Circular-Rule Chains Detection

As a by-product of the rule checking, the CHECK program developed for LES generates two dependency charts, one showing the interactions among the data-driven rules and the other showing the interactions among the goal-driven rules and the goals. An example of a dependency chart for a small set of rules is shown in Figure 2.

A * indicates that one or more IF conditions or a goal condition (G.C.) matches one or more conclusions of a rule. The dependency chart is very useful when the knowledge engineer deletes, modifies, or adds rules to the rule base, as it gives him a means of immediately seeing the dependencies among the rules.

Note that in Figure 2 the *'s without superscripts indicate the dependencies for the original rule set. For example, the * in row R1, column R2 indicates than an IF clause of rule R1 is concluded by rule R2. Adding a condition to Rule R2 (see rule R2a) caused the ***2** dependency to appear. Note that Rule R2a now references itself (i.e., self-circular rule). The addition of one condition to Rule R3 (see rule R3a) caused the ***3** dependency to appear. This also causes the rule set to be circular, since a condition of Rule R3a is matched by the conclusion of Rule R2, and a condition of Rule R2 matches the conclusion of Rule R3a.

In general, circular rules should be avoided since they can lead to an infinite loop at run time. However, sometimes circular data-driven rules are useful for iterative looping in continuous operations such as monitoring. Usually some IF clause in the rule is used to terminate the looping. Nevertheless, the knowledge engineer will want to know which rules are circular. CHECK uses the dependency chart to generate graphs representing the interactions between rules and uses a cyclic graph detection algorithm to detect circular rule chains.

3.5 How Uncertainty Affects the Checking

The method for handling uncertainty in a knowledge base is a much debated topic. The classical formalism for quantifying uncertainty is probability theory (Bayesian), but other alternatives have been proposed and used. Among these are certainty theory, possibility theory, and the Dempster-Shafer theory of evidence. The earliest work was done by the designers of the MYCIN system. They developed a theory (called Certainty Theory) which is simple and can be implemented efficiently in a rule based system. It has been shown that Certainty Theory is a subset of Bayesian.

Because Certainty Theory is the most widely implemented, we concentrate our analysis on that particular methodology. Assume that certainty factors (CFs) are implemented in the same manner as in the EMYCIN system, with a value of **+1.0** meaning definitely true, **0.0** unknown, and **-1.0** definitely false. Furthermore, assume the certainty theory implementation allows the user to specify a threshold at which the value becomes unknown. (In MYCIN this threshold was set at 0.2.)

Allowing rules to conclude with less than certainty and also allowing data to be entered with an associated certainty factor affects our definitions as follows:

- **CONFLICT**—Two rules which succeed in the same situation but with different conclusions is a common occurrence in rule sets using certainty factors. Often, given the same set of symptoms, the expert may wish to conclude different values with different certainty factors.

- **REDUNDANCY**—Rules which are redundant can lead to serious problems. They may cause the same information to be counted twice, leading to erroneous increases in the weight of their conclusions.

- **SUBSUMPTION**—Subsumption is used quite often in rule sets with certainty factors. The knowledge engineer will frequently write rules so that the more restrictive rules add more weight to the conclusions made by the less restrictive ones.

- **UNNECESSARY IF CONDITIONS**—IF conditions which were labeled as unnecessary when rules conclude with absolute certainty may be necessary when dealing with CFs. The knowledge engineer may wish to conclude a value at different CFs. If the rules conclude with the same CF, then the IF conditions will still be unnecessary.

- **UNREFERENCED ATTRIBUTE VALUES**—Certainty factors do not affect our definition nor the way we detect unreferenced attribute values.

- **ILLEGAL ATTRIBUTE VALUES**—Certainty factors do not affect our definition nor the way we detect illegal attribute values.

- **DEADEND IF CONDITIONS**—Finding deadend IF conditions (or deadend goals) becomes more complex when taking certainty factors with thresholds into consideration. Thus, a deadend goal could occur if there is a THEN clause which concludes with a certainty factor less than the threshold (or a chain of rules, which when combined, produce a certainty factor less than the threshold). For example, suppose there is a linear reasoning path of three rules (R1, R2, and R3) where A is to be asked of the user and D is the initial goal that initiated this line of reasoning:

```
    R1        R2        R3
A -----> B -----> C -----> D
   0.4       0.7       0.7
```

  If A is known with certainty, D would only be known with a CF of $(0.4)(0.7)(0.7) = 0.19$. This is less than the threshold used in MYCIN, and thus D would be a deadend goal. If D were an IF condition, rather than a goal, then it would be a deadend condition if it were not askable and there were no other lines of reasoning to determine it.

- **UNREACHABLE CONCLUSIONS**—Detecting unreachable conclusions in a rule set with certainty factors also becomes much more complex. A conclusion in a rule could be unreachable even though its IF part matches a conclusion in another rule. This may happen if the conclusion which matches one of the IF conditions cannot be determined with a CF above the threshold. For example, suppose we have the following two rules:

```
R1: IF A THEN B (cf=0.1)
R2: IF B THEN C (cf=1.0)
```

  If the only way to determine B was with rule R1, then the conclusion of rule R2 would be unreachable because even if A were known with certainty, C could not be determined with a CF above the threshold of 0.2.

- **CIRCULAR RULE CHAINS**—The detection of circular rule chains is not affected by certainty factors. However, it should be noted that CFs may cause a circular chain of rules to be "broken" if the CFs of a conclusion falls below the threshold.

From this discussion we can see that CFs may result in the knowledge engineer making a different interpretation of the messages produced by the rule checker.

3.6 Implementation of the Rule Checker

If rules are partitioned into rule sets, each set of rules can be checked independently. To check a set of rules the program performs the following steps (note that the term "IF *part* of a rule" means the entire set of antecedent clauses, and "THEN *part* of a rule" means the entire set of conclusions; "IF *clause*" and "THEN *clause*" refer to a single antecedent or conclusion, respectively):

1. Each IF and THEN clause of every rule in the set (and each goal clause) is compared against the IF and THEN clauses of every other rule in the set. The comparison of one clause against another results in a label of "SAME", "DIFFERENT", "CONFLICT", "SUBSET", or "SUPERSET" being stored in a two-dimensional table maintaining the interclause relationships. The comparison operation is not straightforward, since variables and the ordering of clauses must be taken into consideration.

2. Deduce relationships for IF part and THEN part of every rule (and the goal) against the IF and THEN part of every other rule. This is done by using the two-dimensional table of interclause relationships together with the number of clauses in each part in order to determine how an IF or THEN part (or goal) is related to another IF or THEN part. The possible relationships resulting from the deductions are the same as described in step 1.

3. The part relationships of each rule are compared against the part relationships of every other rule to deduce the relationships among the rules. These comparisons are then output to the user with the possible relationships being "SAME" (redundant), "CONFLICT", "SUBSET" (subsumption), "SUPERSET" (subsumption), "UNNECESSARY CLAUSES", or "DIFFERENT".

4. Gaps are checked for using the two-dimensional table of interclause relationships. Unreachable conclusions are identified by finding those THEN clauses which have the "DIFFERENT" relationship for all IF clauses and goals. Deadend goals and IF conditions are identified by the fact that they have the "DIFFERENT" relationship for all conclusions and the attribute they refer to is not askable.

5. The dependency chart is also generated from the two-dimensional table of interclause relationships. A rule is said to be dependent on another rule if any of its IF conditions have the relationship "SAME", "SUBSET", or "SUPERSET" with any of the other rules' conclusions.

The first version of the algorithms used to do the checking was published in Nguyen, et al. [2]. Since the publication of the algorithms, the capability to check for "unnecessary IF conditions" has been added and the definition of missing rules has been revised. The current version of the algorithms is given in the Appendix to this paper. (Circular rules are detected using a cyclic graph detection algorithm which is not shown.)

The following is sample output of CHECK for a small knowledge base (not shown) with many inconsistencies and gaps.

```
LES: I am now checking the knowledge base for goal "DIAGNOSE_LAMP"

*****************************************
*                                       *
* Redundancy, Subsumption, and Conflict *
*                                       *
*****************************************
   (1) Rule DIAGNOSE5 is a superset of rule DIAGNOSE1.
   (2) Rule DIAGNOSE5 is a superset of rule DIAGNOSE2.
   (3) Rule DIAGNOSE5 is in possible conflict with rule DIAGNOSE9.


**************************
*                        *
* Unnecessary IF clauses *
*                        *
**************************
   (1) IF clause #2 of rule DIAGNOSE3.


******************
*                *
* Circular Rules *
*                *
******************
Circular rule path: "R1 -> R7 -> R8 -> R7".
Circular rule path: "R2 -> R7 -> R8 -> R7".
Circular rule path: "R4 -> R7 -> R8 -> R7".
Circular rule path: "R7 -> R8 -> R7".
Circular rule path: "R8 -> R7 -> R8".



*********************************
*                               *
* Unreferenced attribute values *
*                               *
*********************************
NOTE: This may indicate missing rules.
   (1) Attribute value "FALSE" of attribute "WORN_OUT" in
category "LIGHT-BULB".
   (2) Attribute value "TIGHTLY" of attribute "SCREWED_IN" in
category "LIGHT-BULB".
    .
    .
    .
```

```
*************************************************
*                                               *
* Illegal attribute values found in the rules *
*                                               *
*************************************************
   (1) Attribute value "DULL" for attribute "COLOR" in category
"LIGHT-BULB" used in rule DIAGNOSE7.


****************************
*                          *
* Unreachable THEN clauses *
*                          *
****************************
   (1) THEN clause of rule DIAGNOSE6.
   (2) THEN clause of rule DIAGNOSE7.


**********************
*                    *
* Deadend IF clauses *
*                    *
**********************
   (1) IF clause #2 in rule DIAGNOSE2.
   (2) IF clause #1 in rule DIAGNOSE7.


************************
*                      *
* Deadend GOAL clauses *
*                      *
************************
   (1) GOAL clause #1 in goal DIAGNOSE_LAMP.
```

---

4 Other Knowledge Base Checking Tools

This section describes several other tools for checking the input to an expert system shell. The syntax checker and the test case facility are capabilities that are desirable for many types of software, not just for rule-based systems, while the cross referencer, like the rule checker, pertains to rule-based systems.

4.1 Syntax Checking

Building an expert system requires putting knowledge into the format required by the particular tool being used. Depending on the development tool, the format may be more or less rigid, but there are usually some syntax restrictions which must be observed in order for the knowledge to be stored and used correctly. Simple types of syntax errors may include unbalanced parentheses or brackets, missing quotes, and missing or misspelled keywords. More complicated errors, which may be simple misspellings or may be semantic errors, include referring to nonexistent objects or assigning illegal values to attributes.

The types of syntax checking which are appropriate depend on the tool being used and on the facilities provided for creating the knowledge base. If the facts and rules are entered with a general-purpose editor, the user has more opportunity to make errors than if a specialized editor with knowledge of the tool's syntax is used.

A syntax checker should do a thorough syntactical analysis of the knowledge base as it is read in and indicate to the user the type and location of any errors found. Some of the items which should be checked as the knowledge base is read in are:

- Unbalanced delimiters (parentheses, brackets, braces, quotes)
- Duplicate object and rule names
- Use of undeclared attribute and object names
- Correct rule syntax
- Allowable values for attribute properties

The specific items which can or should be checked will depend on the particular shell. Because the syntax checking can slow the loading of the knowledge base, there should be a provision to turn off the checking once the system has been debugged.

4.2 Relations Between Rules and Attributes

The rule checker lets the knowledge engineer see the relations between different rules, but another kind of information is needed to show the relations between rules and attributes. Utilities are needed to show which rules determine the value of an attribute and which rules refer to the value of an attribute.

Information about which rules reference a certain attribute is useful if the knowledge engineer needs to change the meaning of the attribute or change its legal values. It might also be used to verify that the attribute was indeed used. Information about which rules conclude a value for a certain attribute is useful if the knowledge engineer realizes that a problem in his system is caused by an incorrect value for an attribute and needs to determine all of the possible rules that could store a value for the attribute.

To provide information about which rules use a particular attribute, the system needs to search the IF clauses of all of the rules to find those which reference that attribute, while to find which rules determine the value of an attribute, the system must search all of the THEN clauses of all of the rules to identify those which store a value for that attribute.

4.3 Test Case Facility

Although CHECK can be used to identify potential problems, it does not verify that the software performs the desired function. Test cases are needed for this as with any software. Since test cases must be rerun often, the process needs to be automated.

Test cases exercise various features of the shell and the knowledge base. Unanticipated interactions of new and old rules or facts may cause test cases to fail, and the knowledge engineer must modify the system (or the test case) until all of the cases again run correctly. Since modifications to the underlying shell may also cause problems with test cases which at one time ran correctly, it is important to rerun test cases when the shell has been updated.

Since test cases may be long both in the time they take to run and the amount of user input required, a facility for *automatically* generating test cases and running new versions of the system against them can help the knowledge engineer to revalidate his system after making changes. Such a test facility for conventional software has been generated by Chapman [13].

Desirable test case capabilities are

1. creating test cases,
2. running test cases and identifying discrepancies,
3. generating a new test case using an existing case as input, and
4. running an unattended demo using a test case.

The implementation and use of these features are described in the following paragraphs.

Test cases can be created by turning on an input-output logging facility and then running a problem in the usual manner. The test facility records all user input and program output.

After a test case has been created, it can be rerun to evaluate the effect of changes in the knowledge base or in the expert system shell by using the second option. When a test case fails, the system generates a file containing the differences between the present expert system output and its output when the test case was generated.

The third option allows the user to generate a new test case using the same input as for an existing case when changes to the knowledge base or the shell lead to small changes in the results. This option is only valid if the changes are not too drastic–for example, the expected user responses must be the same. This option makes it easier for the user to keep his file of test cases up to date.

With the fourth option, the system takes its input from a test case rather than the user and displays both input and output on the terminal. This option is very useful for observing where and how a test case fails.

5 Conclusions

In this paper we have described several tools and techniques for validating a knowledge base, with emphasis on the rule checker. The other tools, such as the syntax checker and test case manager, also help the knowledge engineer to maintain the correctness of his knowledge base and of the tool he is using.

From our experiences with constructing different knowledge bases, we find that many changes and additions are made during the development and maintenance of a knowledge base. The most frequent problems which CHECK has detected are unreachable and dead-end clauses. These type of errors are difficult to detect with conventional knowledge base debugging aids (e.g., rule stepper or attribute watch facility). We have found that redundant and conflicting rules appeared the least often. Nevertheless, CHECK's automated facilities have saved knowledge engineers many hours of tedious debugging.

As the field of knowledge-based systems matures, large expert systems will be fielded in critical situations. Since it will be impossible to test all paths beforehand, one must have assurance that deadly traps such as circular rules and deadend clauses do not exist in the knowledge base. Thus, verification facilities similar to the ones described in this paper becomes essential.

6 REFERENCES

1. T. J. Laffey, W. A. Perkins, and T. A. Nguyen, "Reasoning about Fault Diagnosis with LES", *IEEE Expert*, Intelligent Systems and their Applications, Volume 1, Number 1, Spring, 1986, pp. 13-20.

2. T. A. Nguyen, W. A. Perkins, T. J. Laffey, and D. Pecora, "Checking an Expert Systems Knowledge Base for Consistency and Completeness", *Proceedings of the 9th International Joint Conference on Artificial Intelligence*, Los Angeles, CA., August 18-24, 1985, pp. 374-378.

3. R. Davis, "Applications of Meta-level Knowledge to the Construction, Maintenance, and Use of Large Knowledge Bases", Doctoral dissertation, Computer Science Department, Stanford University, 1976.

4. E. H. Shortliffe, *Computer-Based Medical Consultations: MYCIN*, Elsevier, New York, NY (1976).

5. M. Suwa, A. C. Scott, and E. H. Shortliffe, "An Approach to Verifying Completeness and Consistency in a Rule-Based Expert System", *The AI Magazine*, Fall 1982, pp. 16-21.

6. H. B. Reubenstein, "OPMAN: An OPS5 Rule Base Editing and Maintenance Package", Master's thesis, M.I.T. Department of Electrical Engineering and Computer Science, June, 1985.

7. *TIMM User's Manual*, General Research Corporation, Santa Barbara, California, pp. 46-49.

8. *KES General Description Manual*, Software Architecture and Engineering, Inc., Arlington, Virginia, November, 1983, p. 33.

9. *IntelliCorp KEE Software Development System Rulesystem3 Reference Manual*, KEE Version 3.0, November 13, 1986.

10. *CLIPS Reference Manual (Version 4.1)*, Artificial Intelligence Section, Johnson Space Center, September 1987.

11. R. A. Stachowitz, C. L. Chang, T. S. Stock, and J. B. Combs, "Building Validation Tools for Knowledge-Based Systems," *First Annual Workshop on Space Operations Automation and Robotics*, NASA Conference Publication 2491, Houston, TX, August 5-7, 1987.

12. W. J. Van Melle, *System Aids in Constructing Consultation Programs*, UMI Research Press, Ann Arbor, MI (1981).

13. D. Chapman, "A Program Testing Assistant," *Communications of the ACM*, Vol. 25, No. 9, September 1982, pp. 625-634.

A CHECKING ALGORITHMS

The following pseudocode outlines the procedures used to compare the rules against the goals and the other rules. N is the number of rules and G is the number of goal clauses.

```
procedure Analyze_KB(Rules, Goal, N, G);
begin
   for i = 1 to N begin
      /* compare rules against each other */
      for j = i to N begin
         for k = first_clause(i) to last_clause(i) begin
            for n = first_clause(j) to last_clause(j) begin
               match_result(k) = Compare_clauses(k, n);
               end; /* n */
            end; /* k */
         end; /* j */
         /* compare goal clauses against rule clauses */
         for g = 1 to G begin
            for k = first_clause(i) to last_clause(i) begin
               match_result(g) = Compare_clauses(g, k);
            end; /* k */
         end; /* g */
         /* collect information on attribute value coverage */
         for p = first_if_clause(i) to last_if_clause(i) begin
            determine attribute referred to by clause p;
            store the attribute's value covered by clause p;
         end; /* p */
    end; /* i */
    /* check for possible problems in rules */
   for i = 1 to N begin
      for k = first_clause(i) to last_clause(i) begin
         matched_rule = Transform(i, k, clause_relations);
         while (matched_rule <> 0) do begin
            Check_problems(i, matched_rule, clause_relations);
            matched_rule = Transform(i, k, clause_relations);
         end;
      end; /* k */
   end; /* i */
   /* check for possible gaps in rules and goals */
   Check_gaps(goal_clauses, rules);
   /* generate the dependency chart */
   Generate_dependency_chart(goal_clauses, rules);
   /* check for possible missing rules */
   for m = first_category to last_category begin
      for n = first_attribute(m) to last_attribute(m) begin
         compare covered values with legal values;
         if not_completely_covered then
            inform user that some rule is missing;
         if illegal_attribute_values then
```

```
            inform user that attribute value is illegal;
      end; /* n */
   end; /* m */
end; /* Analyze_KB */


Procedure Check_gaps(goal_clauses,rules);
begin
   for i = first_then_clause to last_then_clause begin
      if (i not_match any IF clause or GOAL clause) then
         then_result(i) = UNREACHABLE;
   end;
   for i = first_goal_clause to last_goal_clause begin
       if (i not_match any THEN clause \& not askable(i)) then
           goal_result(i) = DEADEND;
   end;
   for i = first_if_clause to last_if_clause begin
      if (i not_match any THEN clause \& not askable(i)) then
         if_result(i) = DEADEND;
   end;
end; /* check_gaps */


procedure Check_problems(Rule_i,Rule_m,clause_relations)
begin
   same_count = 0;
   conflict_count = 0;
   negation_count = 0;
   samep = FALSE;
   differentp = FALSE;
   subsetp = FALSE;
   supersetp = FALSE;
   for ic in get_if_clauses(Rule_i) do
      if clause_relations(ic) = SAME then
         samep = TRUE;
      else if clause_relations(ic) = SUBSET then
         subsetp = TRUE;
      else if clause_relations(ic) = SUPERSET then
         supersetp = TRUE;
      else if clause_relations(ic) = CONFLICT then
         conflict_count = conflict_count + 1;
      else if clause_relations(ic) = NEGATION then
         negation_count = negation_count + 1;
      else
         differentp = TRUE;
      if member(clause_relations(ic), {NEGATION,SAME,SUBSET,SUPERSET})
         then same_count = same_count + 1;
   end; /* ic */

   if ((conflict_count > 1) or (negation_count > 1) or
```

```
        ((conflict_count = 1) and (negation_count = 1)))
   if_if_result = DIFFERENT;
else if ((conflict_count = 1) and (not (subsetp or supersetp)))
   if (differentp or
        (number_conditions(Rule_i) = number_conditions(Rule_m)))
      if_if_result = DIFFERENT;
   else
      if_if_result = CONFLICT;
else if ((negation_count = 1) and (conflict_count = 0))
   if (differentp and (number_conditions(Rule_m) > same_count))
      if_if_result = DIFFERENT;
   else
      if_if_result = NEGATION;
else if (subsetp and supersetp)
   if (differentp or
        (number_conditions(Rule_i) <> number_conditions(Rule_m)))
      if_if_result = DIFFERENT;
   else
      if_if_result = SAME;
else if subsetp
   if (differentp or
        (number_conditions(Rule_i) < number_conditions(Rule_m)))
      if_if_result = DIFFERENT;
   else
      if_if_result = SUBSET;
else if supersetp
   if (differentp or
        (number_conditions(Rule_i) > number_conditions(Rule_m)))
      if_if_result = DIFFERENT;
   else
      if_if_result = SUPERSET;
else if samep
   if (differentp and (number_conditions(Rule_i) > same_count)
       if_if_result = DIFFERENT;
   else if (number_conditions(Rule_i) = number_conditions(Rule_m))
       if_if_result = SAME;
   else if (number_conditions(Rule_i) > number_conditions(Rule_m))
       if_if_result = SUBSET;
   else if (number_conditions(Rule_i) < number_conditions(Rule_m))
       if_if_result = SUPERSET;
else
   if_if_result = DIFFERENT

if (if_if_result = SAME)
    for tc in get_then_clauses(Rule_i) do
        if (clause_relations(tc) = SAME)
           result(Rule_i,Rule_m,tc) = REDUNDANT;
        else if (clause_relations(tc) = CONFLICT)
           result(Rule_i,Rule_m,tc) = CONFLICT;
if (if_if_result = CONFLICT)
```

```
        for tc in get_then_clauses(Rule_i) do
            if (clause_relations(tc) = SAME)
               result(Rule_i,Rule_m,tc) = CONFLICT;
    if (if_if_result = NEGATION)
        for tc in get_then_clauses(Rule_i) do
            if (clause_relations(tc) = SAME)
               result(Rule_i,Rule_m,tc) = UNNECESSARY_CONDITION;
    if (if_if_result = SUBSET)
        for tc in get_then_clauses(Rule_i) do
            if (clause_relations(tc) = SAME or
                clause_relations(tc) = SUBSET)
                result(Rule_i,Rule_m,tc) = SUBSET;
    if (if_if_result = SUPERSET)
        for tc in get_then_clauses(Rule_i) do
            if (clause_relations(tc) = SAME or
                clause_relations(tc) = SUPERSET)
                result(Rule_i,Rule_m,tc) = SUPERSET;
end; /* Check_problems */
```

Topics in Expert System Design
G. Guida and C. Tasso (Editors)

EVALUATION OF EXPERT SYSTEMS

Erik HOLLNAGEL

Advanced Information Processing Division
Computer Resources International
Birkerød, Denmark

1. INTRODUCTION

Evaluations of expert systems are needed for a number of reasons. One of them is the increasing commercial interest in expert systems. The concept of an expert system has now existed for almost a decade, and the number of expert systems that have been developed and put to practical use probably run into the thousands. The increasing application of expert systems in routine tasks, and the consequent gradual automation of knowledge intensive work, has led to a need for some kind of assurance of the quality of the new tool, i.e. a need for evaluating the expert systems. This is particularly so in areas where the consequences of a mistake (on the part of the expert system) may be serious, but also to a lesser extent for systems in other domains. Another reason is that expert systems are moving from being hand-crafted pieces of 'art' to becoming industrial products. They are no longer the output from advanced research laboratories at selected universities or development centers, but rather 'standardised' products from commercial companies. As such they must necessarily be subjected to the more rigorous demands that are common in the field of software products.

This chapter will consider the evaluation of expert systems as a methodological problem within the larger field of quality control. Since a search of the existing literature has shown that the treatment of expert system evaluation still is in its beginning, in the sense that there is a clear lack of a generally recognised methodology, the discussion will be an analysis of the fundamental methodological issues rather than a conventional literature survey. It will be confined to a discussion of the assessment of the quality of the expert system in use, although this clearly is a gross simplification. It must be made clear from the start, that expert system evaluation is not something that can be added as the last step in system development, but rather something which must be considered throughout the entire design and development process.

The simplification is nevertheless made for two reasons. First of all because the evaluation of the system in use highlights the *raison d'être* of expert systems: expert systems are not hidden beneath the system surface, as just another kind of software or algorithm, but are highly conspicuous and enter directly into the interaction with the user. This, at least, has been the predominant feature so far. Practically all expert systems are interactive, i.e. they present their results directly to the user rather than through an intermediary module. As the technology has matured, expert systems are also being used in a different fashion as sophisticated software modules which either engage in a one-way communication with the user (i.e. not allowing interaction or interrogation) or which only indirectly show their results to the user, i.e. the results are mediated through other systems or even used internally in the total system (e.g. as cooperating expert systems, fancy control 'algorithms', self-monitoring diagnostics, self-contained expert systems, etc.) - in other words, used in a closed-loop rather than an open-loop fashion. The output from the expert system must, however, sooner or later be communicated to the user, and it is on this level that one must consider the evaluation. The interaction between user and system, their joint functioning and the way in which the expert system supports the user, is thus in focus.

The second reason for the simplification is that the assessment of the functionality of the system - in a sense, the quality control - as a software system or a joint man-machine system (whichever view one prefers) is very similar, if not identical, to the established procedures for other software engineering projects. This does not mean that it is an easy matter since the development of expert systems may be messier than for other software systems. But from a software engineering point of view there is no reason to consider expert systems to be of a different species. I will therefore, for the sake of the discussion, proceed as if the expert system that is to be evaluated has been completed using the conventional software engineering methods, rather than still being in a state of development.

1.1 Problems in Expert System Application

Expert systems are now being used in a wide range of critical applications as decision aids, including control and safety monitoring of process plants, implementation of financial rules, and economic advice - in addition to the more 'conventional' applications in medicine, chemistry, system configuration, etc. Expert systems are used, among other reasons, because they have the capability to handle loosely structured problems, where uncertainty plays a large role, far better than unaided humans can. A practical advantage is that an expert system permits the expert to spend more time solving demanding problems that truly require his special skills, while the less experienced user can solve problems that before required an expert. These reasons for the use of expert systems must, however, be considered against a number of possible problems, for instance:

- Are there possibilities for traps, false assumptions, side effects, and instabilities in the expert system's reasoning?
- How robust is the expert system regarding misleading or conflicting information?
- Is the expert system capable of handling incomplete or imprecise information?
- Can the expert system do approximate reasoning when time is limited?
- Will the advice provided by an expert system be good?
- Will the advice of the expert system be accepted blindly?
- Will the advice be applied automatically, without the aid of a controlling human judgment?
- What are the limits of application of the expert system?

These are some of the aspects that must be considered before an expert system is released for practical use. Some of them can be clarified through an expert system evaluation while others may require a consideration of the working environment as a whole, including the possible organisational ramifications. In all cases it is, however, important that a thorough analysis of the design specifications is used to produce functional requirements that are stated as explicitly and unambiguously as possible. The quality of the expert system can only be evaluated if the relevant criteria are clearly stated. One problem that soon arises, and which is dealt with in the context of empirical validity described below, is whether one can anticipate, describe and test a representative set of the situations that the expert system will encounter in practical use. The answer is, unfortunately, a **no**. This means that the evaluation of expert systems will meet many of the problems that are found in other types of system evaluation, c.f. Hollnagel (1981). In a sense, expert systems can be considered as highly similar to the man-machine systems that traditionally are used in the field of industrial production and process control. The most significant difference is that expert systems tend to be more complex and less clearly described than other computerised support systems, and that they may function in a deliberately non-deterministic way.

1.2 Expert Systems and Risk

When an expert system is introduced in a work environment for commercial reasons, it is with the clear expectation that the organisational function will be improved in some way by making it either faster, more reliable, safer, more efficient, etc. Since expert systems are applied, in particular, to situations where human judgment otherwise has a predominant role, an obvious motive is to reduce the number of cases with unfavourable consequences (i.e. bad decisions or erroneous actions). Human judgment is a versatile but uncertain 'tool' which has been used because there, so far, have been no alternative solutions. Expert systems have been hailed as a possible replacement for human judgment and decision making, at least for routine applications, but because expert systems often have a high degree of complexity their use necessarily, but unfortunately, introduces several types of risk which may endanger the potential improvements. The risks can be described along a number of dimensions:

- o Expert systems deal with imprecise knowledge. They therefore often apply the known to the unknown - particularly in the way rules may be used, generalised or induced from a number of cases and then applied to others. Hence, the validity of the reasoning of the expert system is unknown, and relying on the outcome may therefore be risky (i.e. uncertain).
- o Although expert systems are quite reliable as reasoning mechanisms, there may be a risk in using them because the validity of their reasoning is not easily assessed. The internal consistency and stability of an expert system is, for instance, not always known. Particularly if the expert system contains

very many rules, e.g. in the order of 500 to thousands, it may be difficult to ensure that it is internally consistent. Rules may also be given as general rather than specific rules, and new rules may be generated automatically.

- Expert systems, as software systems, suffer from the same weaknesses and have the same problems in software validation as other products of software engineering. Expert systems are furthermore, as most other software systems, tested with a limited set of exemplary cases. It is therefore not known with certainty how robust the system is to incorrect or even contradictory input. Quite another problem is the updating of multiple knowledge bases and the propagation of consequences of changes.

- Expert systems often try to make use of experience, e.g. in the formulation of rules. An expert system will, however, consider the history - the previous events - in a very precise way, whereas human beings will consider it more loosely so. Humans are very good at extracting new knowledge from experience while expert systems, at least at present, are more clumsy and cumbersome and may miss the 'obviously' important points.

- Expert systems lack a sense of responsibility, i.e. they carry out their reasoning but are not aware of it, hence cannot consider the consequences of reasoning per se. They further lack knowledge and awareness of subsidiary events, of circumstances in general, of possible side-effects and enabling / disabling conditions. They can only consider what they have been told to consider, and are therefore - in terms of reasoning - myopic. This may be a benefit for the reliability, but a drawback when situations become too complex or when unanticipated circumstances occur.

Most of these risks (and a few more) are, of course, also present in the case of a human decision maker, but they become more conspicuous when expert systems are employed. In many cases an expert system evaluation may provide a proper basis for assessing most of these risks. One consequence of the experience from financial market management problems during 1987 is the clear recognition of the practical problems in the use of expert systems in particular and complex software systems in general. Prominent among those problems is the aspect of risk. The same experience had been made earlier in other fields, e.g. the process industries. Although the problems may be clearly described the theoretical basis for solving them unfortunately does not yet appear to exist. But the practical attempts at solving them have shown that some of the questions that need to be answered are:

- o How can the performance of expert systems be analysed?
- o How can the stability and robustness of the expert system be described?
- o How can decision making traps be detected?
- o On what models of the world are expert systems based?

The use of expert systems has gradually been spreading from technical to financial and administrative applications. But they are unlikely to become an integral part of business and administration, until they emerge as a proven technology. Before this happens they must be shown to be highly reliable, so that they can be safely employed even in sensitive areas. One step towards that is to perform a proper evaluation of the expert system as a system in use (*in vivo*, rather than *in vitro*). The following sections will clarify the problems and methods encountered in that referring, in particular, to the first two of the four questions mentioned above.

1.3 The Need for an Evaluation Methodology

The evaluation of expert systems can be interpreted in two ways. The most obvious is to consider it as the evaluation of the **functionality of the system**, i.e. determining what it does and how it does it, and comparing it with some kind of standard or criterion to decide whether the expert system functions satisfactorily. The second interpretation is to consider the problem of the **evaluation methodology** as such. On closer inspection, this is an implicit condition for the first interpretation. If one does not have a trustworthy evaluation method, then, clearly, it is impossible to make any kind of evaluation or measurement. Although one may say that the evaluation concerns, e.g. whether the expert system reasons correctly, the problem really boils down to specifying a method which can be used to determine just that. The default method may be to rely on the judgment of a human expert, but in the long run this is not satisfactory. As expert systems are moving into the world of industrially applied systems, the demands to an objective evaluation of their performance grow. Consequently, the demands to a proper methodology for carrying out the evaluation also grow. The topics of this chapter are precisely the problem of the evaluation methodology, which, in a sense, is not fundamentally different from many other types of performance evaluation. The steps on the way are to specify the aspects of expert systems that are important for the evaluation, to specify the criteria that are relevant for each aspect, and to specify the methodology that can reasonably be used in each case. The conclusion from a study of the available literature is that the methodology problem is not always seriously considered in its constituent parts, but rather treated on a wholesale basis. This makes it difficult to compare different approaches, as well as to carry out the expert system evaluation in a proper manner.

The problem of the adequacy of the methodology arises because the expert system that is evaluated never is the same as the expert system that is used (i.e. the target system). The two main concerns of the methodology are:

- o Whether it can be used to get reliable results, and
- o whether the results are representative for the target system.

This distinction is not always clearly recognised. One reason for that can be that expert systems until recently never were brought into actual use as target systems. The evaluated system, the model system or the prototype, was therefore identical to the target system. There was consequently no reason to develop an elaborate evaluation methodology, such as one can find in other scientific fields. The developments over the last couple of years have, however, led to an increasing number of expert systems being produced on an industrial basis for application in real-life systems and tasks. The need for conducting a proper evaluation has therefore slowly been recognised, although there as yet are no established solutions.

This change in the status of expert systems also means that the difference between the model system or prototype and the target system has become real. Customers and clients are paying for specific expert systems developed according to their needs, and it is the responsibility of the producers to make sure that the systems have the expected functionality. To a certain extent this is a problem for software engineering, as stated above. But the unique functionality of an expert system cannot be properly evaluated in this way. It is therefore necessary seriously to consider the methodological aspects of expert system evaluation, particularly the problems that arise from the differences between the tested and the target systems. It is this problem which is the focus of this chapter.

2. EVALUATION CRITERIA

2.1 Fundamental Concepts

When talking about expert systems there are a number of key terms that must be defined such as validity, efficiency, operability, reliability, usability, etc. Precise definitions of the terms may be found in several fields, e.g. software engineering and behavioural sciences, but the definitions have been made for different purposes and may not always be in agreement with each other. In the case of expert system evaluation there does not even seem to be any generally recognised definition of the what the term 'evaluation' means. For instance, Gaschnig et al. (1983) distinguish between evaluation of accuracy and evaluation of utility, while Liebowitz (1985, 1986) distinguish between evaluation and validation. Pearce (1987) makes a distinction between automatic validation, acceptance by users and achievement. In another context I have argued for recognising the difference between performance analysis and performance evaluation (Hollnagel, 1986). For the purpose of this discussion it is reasonable to make a distinction between the following terms as shown in Figure 1a.

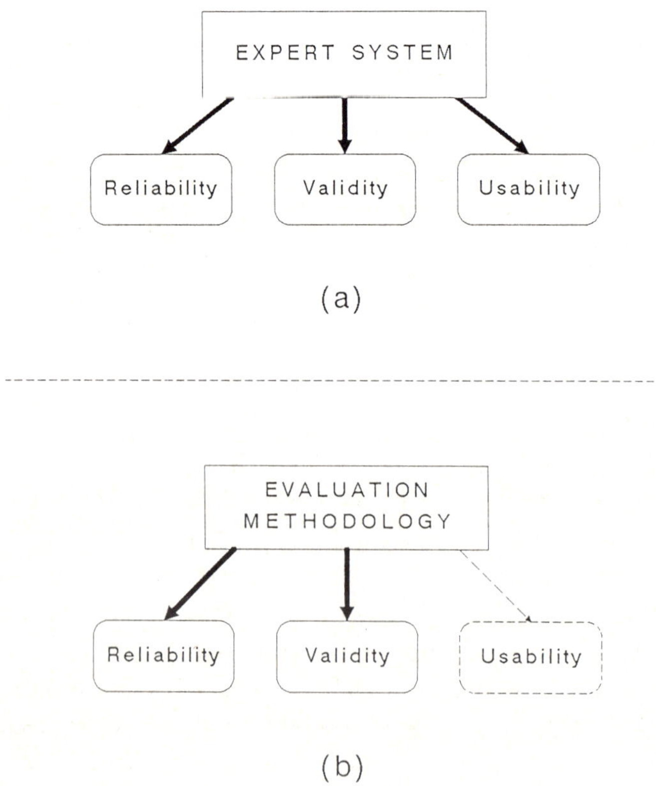

Figure 1: Fundamental Concepts in Expert System Evaluation.

The above distinction reflects the goal of the evaluation as being the interaction between the user and the expert system - or the role of the expert system as a support for the user in carrying out a task. Accordingly, an expert system evaluation can be seen as comprising three different aspects of the expert system. The first is its reliability; the second is its validity (or more precisely, the empirical validity); and the third is its usability. Aspects such as verification, in the software engineering sense, are not considered as a part of the evaluation but rather seen as a different and complementary aspect of system development.

It is important to realise that a similar distinction can be made with regard to the evaluation methodology. One may thus consider both the reliability and the validity of the evaluation method. (From a practical point of view one may also consider its usability, but I shall not be concerned with that in this chapter.) This provides the relations shown in Figure 1b. The following sections will discuss the more precise meaning of these terms seen with regard to both the evaluation methodology and the expert system as such.

2.2 Reliability

2.2.1 Method Reliability

Reliability is perhaps the easiest term to define. In relation to expert system evaluation, the reliability of the method refers to the degree of unexplained variance in the results. Imagine that an evaluation is carried out on the same expert system at different times (or, more likely, on two very similar expert systems). Assuming that the same methodology is used, one would expect to get the same results, i.e. there should be little variance in the outcome. Furthermore, if there is some variance (i.e. if the results differ), one should be able to explain why that is so by referring to factors that might be different in the two situations, for instance, different input. If the variance is low, or if the observed variance can be systematically accounted for (i.e. avoiding the use of *ad hoc* explanations), then the reliability of the method is high. Conversely, if the results vary a lot and this variation cannot be attributed to recognisable situational differences, then the method is said to be unreliable, i.e. to have a low reliability.

A sufficiently high degree of reliability is obviously a condition for an evaluation method if it is going to be of any practical value and become accepted for general use. If the method is unreliable, then one cannot trust the results and it would be extremely difficult to distinguish between the reliability of the method and the reliability of the expert system. The determination of the reliability of an evaluation method is, however, not a problem that I will consider here. There are a several well-established techniques for that in the literature on experimental design and statistics (cf. Campbell & Stanley, 1963).

2.2.2 System Reliability

In addition to the reliability of the evaluation method one may also consider the reliability of the expert system as such. Reliability in technological or 'mechanical' systems is normally jeopardized by the breakdown of components or random fluctuations in performance brought about by unexpected disturbances. In the case of expert systems one would normally assume that the computer hardware is sufficiently reliable to be used without questioning. Furthermore, the reliability of the software is also assumed to be acceptable, although this assumption often is made implicitly. To ensure the proper reliability of the software as such is, however, a problem for software engineering rather than something which is specific for expert systems. On the whole expert systems should be more reliable than human experts, just as 'mechanical' systems generally are more reliable than human beings. An expert system, by virtue of following predefined rules in a predefined manner must necessarily be reliable in the sense that given the same input it will produce the same output. This will certainly be the case for the many rule-based advisory and diagnostic systems that have been developed for off-line applications. There are, nevertheless, problems of reliability which are unique to expert systems. Such problems may occur in expert systems that are part of on-line applications and which are able to modify their knowledge base or their rules. In both cases the problem of maintaining consistency may be a threat to the reliability.

2.3 Validity

2.3.1 Method Validity

In addition to making the distinction between method and system validity, it may also be necessary to make a distinction between several types of method validity.

One obvious problem is whether the evaluation method or test focuses on the relevant aspects of the expert system's performance, i.e. whether the method has **content validity**. This refers, in other words, to whether the evaluation of the (final) prototype system addresses the basic functionality it is intended to measure. A traditional example is that a test for arithmetic performance should consist of arithmetic tasks rather than e.g. reading problems. This is so simple an example that content validity is obvious, hence easy to establish. However, it becomes less obvious when the performance is more diffuse as it well may be in the case of an expert system evaluation, cf. the lack of agreement over what expertise, as such, is. For instance, evaluating user satisfaction or 'favourite' test cases will probably not address the fundamental features of the expert system. Still, content validity is usually taken for granted although that assumption may be unjustified.

The problem of content validity is quite often resolved by pointing to the **face validity**, i.e. the apparent similarity of the test situation with the expected actual use (which, interestingly enough, falls back on an 'expert' observer's judgment). The problem can be refined and partly resolved by relating it to **construct validity**. The construct here denotes the aspect of performance that one wants to study or which the expert system is expected to affect. If, for instance, we are concerned with decision making then we must be able to specify precisely which types of behaviour represent decision making, and which do not. Next, we must find some suitable measure of the extent to which each test item or part of the test, as well as the test as a whole, corresponds to or correlates with the construct. This measure is then an expression of the construct validity of the evaluation method. This is, clearly, preferable to relying on the more vaguely defined face validity.

2.3.2 System Validity

System validity is a more difficult concept to deal with than system reliability, and it is in particular far more difficult to operationalise. First of all, validity and validation must be clearly distinguished from **verification**. Verification is basically a test of whether the expert system matches the design ideas, i.e. whether it matches the technical requirements and expectations. In the terminology of expert systems, the design can be verified through the use of a (rapid) prototype. This test may be repeated during the system's design and development and the number of details gradually be increased, but the verification basically is addressing the testing of the system design with hypothetical cases, which often are derived from the design principles themselves.

Validation, on the other hand, refers to whether the expert system in practical use provides the results it should. Verification and validation are thus identical only if the system being evaluated is the same in the two cases, i.e. if the test system is identical in all respects to the target system, and if the conditions (cases, problems) also are identical. Since this practically never is the case, the difference between the verification and validation is real. Put differently, verification concerns the expert system while it is still in the hands of the developer, while validation concerns the expert system when it is actually used in the field. (For expert systems one may sometimes wonder how often this is the case - due to the immaturity of the field - although there is little doubt that the number of cases is growing.)

When performing an expert system evaluation one should bear in mind that the evaluation always is made with a sample of the system, i.e. a specific version which differs from the system in use (among other things because the evaluation must also be part of the system development, hence take place before the final system is delivered). The system validity is therefore basically a question of the **empirical validity**. This is, as the name indicates, the degree to which the results of the evaluation corresponds to the results from the real-life application of the expert system. In other words, to what extent the expert system does what it is supposed to do (design verification) and to what extent what it did during the evaluation actually corresponds to what it does in real life, i.e. in practical use with practical users. Empirical validity is often stated as a specific relation between two sets of measurements, hence a statistical or quantitative type of validity, e.g. the extent to which the results of the evaluation corresponds to the empirical facts. It thus corresponds closely to the commonly used meaning of validity. The relation between validity and verification can be shown as in Figure 2, which also tries to clarify the difference between method validity and system or empirical validity.

The distinction between system reliability and validity is important. The reason is that the issues easily become confused if one only refers to evaluation in a loose sense. Thus assessing whether the expert system does what it should do (empirical validity) is different from assessing how it does it (which may be more related to reliability or, in a sense, the content validity of the system). The advantage of making a clear distinction between the different aspects of evaluation is that the methods to be used will be different, and furthermore that in some cases there may already be established methods. This is the case, for instance, for reliability measures.

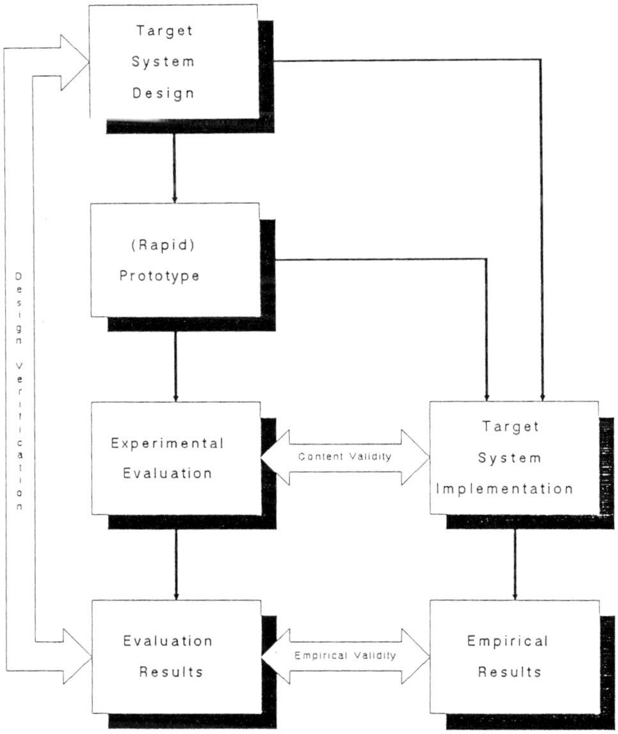

Figure 2: The Steps in System Evaluation.

2.4 Usability

The term usability may be used in a number of ways. Clearly, it is not as easily defined as either reliability or validity were. In a way it appears to belong together with terms such as 'user-friendliness' or 'understanding' which, although they are good common sense terms that are inherently meaningful, remain somewhat ambiguous and vague when the time comes to operationalise them.

Usability must be distinguished from the correctness (veridity) and empirical validity of the expert system. Usability rather refers to the ease with which the user can apply the system according to its purpose, irrespective of the level of experience and proficiency of the user. Usability thus has many aspects, such as a good ergonomic design, a reasonable sense of transparency or comprehensibility, a flexible and powerful dialogue structure, a good (intelligent) help facility, a high level of forgivingness for mistakes in the use, etc. Many of these aspects can be further specified and operationalised. Thus Kidd & Cooper (1985) evaluated the man-machine interface in terms of knowledge acquisition, knowledge representation, and communication adequacy. Usability, however, mostly refers to something which is general for man-machine systems rather than specific for expert systems. I shall therefore not consider it further in this chapter, but instead refer the reader to one of the many excellent books that are written about this topic, e.g. Norman & Draper (1986) or Pfaff (1985).

2.5 Specific Evaluation Criteria

The preceding sections have described the different ways in which one may use the term evaluation. Another important matter is the choice of **evaluation criteria**, in a sense the further specification of the components of expert system reliability, validity, and usability. The evaluation criteria naturally depend on what the purpose of the evaluation is. If the emphasis is on the software engineering aspects, the following set of criteria have been suggested by Boehm (1978):

- Portability (device independence),
- reliability (completeness, accuracy, consistency),
- efficiency (device efficiency, accessibility),
- human engineering (communicativeness),
- testability (structuredness),
- understandability (self-descriptiveness conciseness, legibility), and
- modifiability (augmentability).

These criteria are clearly aimed at the software engineering side of the expert system, and aspects such as portability, efficiency, testability, and modifiability are of little concern for the evaluation of the usefulness of expert systems as defined here. A more directly useful set of criteria have been defined by Gaschnig et al. (1983), as follows:

- o Quality of the system's decision and advice,
- o correctness of the reasoning techniques used,
- o quality of the human-computer interaction (both its content and the mechanical issues involved),
- o the system's efficiency, and
- o the cost-effectiveness.

These criteria obviously concern the aspects of usefulness far more than the software engineering side, i.e. the validity and usability of the target system. Along the same lines Assemat & Bonnet (1986) have suggested the following criteria:

- o Correctness of the final decision,
- o accuracy of the final decision,
- o sensitivity, i.e. the minimum variation in input needed to change the decision,
- o robustness, i.e. the ability to absorb and compensate for non-standard input (noise, disturbances, incompleteness, contradictions, etc.), and
- o correctness of the reasoning.

There is clearly a substantial overlap between the criteria suggested by Gaschnig et al. and Assemat & Bonnet. The intersection of these sets seem to capture the crucial aspects of human-computer interaction and decision / reasoning support. I will consequently suggest the following set of criteria as being a reasonable basis for expert system evaluation:

- o **Correctness of the final decision**, i.e. whether the output from the expert system (the chosen alternative, the advice or recommendation given) is consistent with the needs of the situation and the criteria for a good solution. Put differently, it is the question of whether the output from the expert system is valid in the given context. One problem is, of course, that this may only become clear at a later stage when the recommendation has been fully implemented and the consequences have become known. The correctness can, however, not be determined with the final outcome of the decision as the only criterion. One must also take into account the information that was available for the expert system when the decision was made. Clearly, if the information was incomplete, uncertain, or incorrect one must reduce the demands to correctness of the advice. Yet this is not an easy matter to settle, particularly not in real use.

- The **accuracy of the final decision**, i.e. the extent to which the consequences of the alternative were satisfactory. Clearly, even if the decision was correct in recommending the right kind of solution (e.g. reducing the temperature of a vessel rather than increasing the inventory or level), it may have been inaccurate in specifying the magnitude of the change. Again, the final determination of the accuracy can only be made after all the consequences of the alternative have become known. This may be easier to attain in a test situation than in real use, but it may present a significant problem even there.

Together the two first criteria (and partly the third as well) are relevant for assessing the empirical validity of the expert system. They can thus be used as a basis for defining the aspects of the expert system's performance that the evaluation methods must address. In the terminology of Gaschnig et al. these criteria refer to the quality of the system's decisions and advice. But splitting 'quality' into 'correctness' and 'accuracy' makes it much easier to define the operational measures through which the system's quality can be determined.

While the first two criteria refer to the outcome or result of using the expert system, the following criteria refer to the way in which the expert system works, i.e. its internal mechanisms. One must here avoid the obvious trap of only investigating the mechanisms when something goes wrong, as in the 'black box' approach. It is just as important to analyse the inner workings of the expert system when it apparently functions correctly, cf. Hollnagel (1986).

- **Correctness of the reasoning techniques**, i.e. whether the internal logic of the expert system was consistent with the design. This can be a question of whether the inference engine of the expert system works as supposed, whether the control over the reasoning is adequate (backwards-forwards chaining, pruning, truth maintenance, etc.), or whether the more intricate mechanisms (such as a possible worlds concept or non-monotonic reasoning) function correctly. The problem of the correctness thus refers both to the rules that the system designer explicitly has described and the default logic mechanisms of the system. They can both be a serious problem, cf. below. Determining the correctness of the reasoning techniques will depend on how transparent the expert system is, as well as on how easy it was for the expert system designer to comprehend the problem. On one level the reasoning mechanisms will be correctly executed because the expert system is highly reliable as a computing machine. (An exception may, of course, occur in the case of non-monotonic reasoning or other peculiarities of real-time KBSs.) But comprehending the internal functioning of the system may not be an easy matter.

Evaluating the correctness of the reasoning techniques is obviously made easier if the expert system is well designed (internally), i.e. if it is a good piece of software engineering with clean rules and code, rather than a mess of kludges. Evaluating the correctness of the reasoning technique can, of course, also be supported by first performing a Knowledge Base Verification or by checking the integrity of the knowledge and rules of the system (Pearce, 1987).

- **Sensitivity**, i.e. the minimum variation in input needed to change the outcome of the decision. This is important both in the case of oversensitivity (hair-trigger control) and in the case of reduced sensitivity (or growing insensitivity) - which must not be confused with robustness, cf. below. The sensitivity is, in fact, closely related to the efficiency of the expert system. It should react to the changes in the input that are real, but disregard those that are spurious or insignificant. This is very similar to how a good process control system should function and to how a good human expert functions. Determining the sensitivity very much depends on the selection of test cases. But it is also a relative issue in the sense that the sensitivity is something that may have to be adjusted after the system has been in use for some time - just as one may have to adjust a controller or a regulator in a process control system. In this sense an evaluation can serve to fine tune the performance of the expert system (Duda et al., 1979). The ease with which this can be done depends very much on how the expert system has been designed and implemented. A little foresight may save a lot of trouble later on. Among other things there should be a good operational measure to assess the sensitivity and predict the consequences of changes. One can easily imagine that the sensitivity of an expert system used in the stock market may be a highly critical issue. Knowing what the sensitivity is and how it may be controlled is therefore a very important part of the evaluation.

  Sensitivity can be seen as analogous to a semantic filtering of the input, i.e.

something which takes the context and the meaning of the input into account. In contrast to that robustness can be seen as analogous to a syntactical filtering.

o **Robustness** refers to the ability to absorb and compensate for non-standard input (noise, disturbances, incompleteness, contradictions, etc.). Robustness can be seen as a selective kind of sensitivity. The expert system should be sensitive to certain types of input and insensitive to the rest. This is again a very controversial issue, and one that depends very much on the definitions of the conditions for the test. It poses a particular problem for the evaluation because it may be next to impossible to imagine or anticipate the types of non-standard input that can occur. One simple test would be to provide the expert system with nonsense input. This is, in fact, a good test for any software system. If the system cannot survive that the robustness is clearly inadequate. Robustness of the system is thus a way of defeating the fundamental law of 'garbage in, garbage out.' This, unfortunately, is still true of many conventional software systems, which blindly will process any input given to them. But in a good expert system 'garbage in' should result in 'nothing out' rather than 'garbage out', i.e. the expert system should recognise the garbage and disregard it. This can also be seen as defining the lower end of the expert system's expertise. It can determine what is clearly irrelevant. A much more difficult problem is to define the higher limit for its expertise, i.e. the level when it is incapable of producing reasonable results. Here the input can also be seen as a kind of garbage or nonsense, in the sense that the expert system is unable to handle it adequately. In other words, its competence has been transgressed. But it is not an easy matter to determine that.

Taken together the three criteria of correctness of reasoning, sensitivity, and robustness are all relevant for assessing the system's reliability (with the first of these also being partly relevant for assessing the validity as well as for system design verification). The system's reliability may, of course, be assessed in a more direct way by simply comparing results from two or more sessions. (Here the evaluation method would be quite simple, hence very reliable.) In the case of a discrepancy a more sophisticated method will nevertheless be valuable to identify more precisely why system reliability may be low, hence which measures one should take to improve it.

The two final criteria cover the expert system's usability and its efficiency.

- The **quality of the human-computer interaction** is paramount for its usability. Much of this has already been addressed in the many studies of human-machine interaction, interface design, ergonomics / human factors, and cognitive engineering that have been carried out in relation to man-machine systems in general. Since the problems, with the possible exception of explanation mechanisms and comprehension of knowledge representation, are not essentially different in the two fields, I shall refrain from going further into it here. Evaluating the adequacy of the human-computer interaction is, in many ways, in itself as difficult as evaluating an expert system.

- The **cost-effectiveness** refers to the gains from using the expert system compared with the direct and indirect costs in developing and implementing it. This is a rather delicate matter which is not easy to resolve. In many cases the decision to use the expert system has already been made when the design process is started, and the cost-effectiveness is not considered seriously after that. But with the increasing commercialisation of the field the issue cannot always be ignored. It is, of course, not something which directly can be addressed through an expert system evaluation although some of the results from that can be pertinent for calculating the effectiveness. But the problem of cost-effectiveness may be important as the final step in deciding whether or not to build the system, hence be heavily influenced by whether one can describe precisely what the strong and the weak points of the system are. It thus provides part of the rationale for carrying out the evaluation in the first place, hence gives a direction for the issues that should be emphasised.

To summarise, I have in this section considered the more precise meaning of the term 'evaluation'. A distinction has been made between the evaluation method and the evaluation of the system, as well as between the aspects of reliability, validity, and usability. In the following sections the details of various evaluation methodologies will be discussed, referring to the classification presented here.

3. PROBLEMS IN EXPERT SYSTEM EVALUATION

The preceding sections have discussed the several aspects of the expert system evaluation that must be considered before an evaluation method is chosen or designed. A number of problems have been identified with regard to the methods and the evaluation criteria, and the most important of these are discussed in greater detail in this section.

3.1 Correctness of Test Cases

The functioning of a computer system is normally tested by means of a number of selected cases. Proving that a program is correct is a very complicated matter, particularly for realistic domains, and empirical testing is normally the preferred way. This, however, has obvious shortcomings, the main being that the specification of test cases becomes crucial. The problem is central to software engineering in general and to the development of expert systems in particular.

The problem of specifying an appropriate set of test cases can be interpreted in two different ways. The first is whether the test cases are relevant for the expert system vis-a-vis its design specifications, and this is discussed below. The second is whether the test cases are representative for the situations that the expert system is likely to encounter in practical use. This is discussed in the following section.

Using the terminology introduced in this chapter, the issue in the first case is really whether the test cases are adequate for the verification of the expert system. One recommended procedure is to generate the test cases as a part of the system specification or the design process (Littman & Soloway, 1987). According to this the cases are normally generated with regard to specific goals, which can occur on four different levels:

- On the problem level the test cases should refer to the problems the expert system is intended to solve - or to assist in solving. The evaluation should focus on the problem to be solved, rather than on the specific implementation of the expert system.

- On the decomposition level the test cases should refer to the finer structure of the problems, i.e. the sub-problems that they may be broken into and the problem solving strategies that are employed.

- On the plan level the test cases should refer to the specific techniques (plans, knowledge representation, control structures) that are used to solve the problems - the larger problems as well as the sub-problems.

- Finally, on the composition level, the test cases should refer to how the plans are being put together. This could, for instance, be done by verifying the knowledge bases or checking the integrity of the rules.

If this procedure is followed it should be relatively easy to provide a verification of the system (cf. Figure 2). The generation of test cases on multiple levels must, however, be done systematically and is therefore only feasible if it has been anticipated in the overall planning of the project. The alternative is that the verification is made on a more ad hoc basis, e.g. by testing or evaluating the line of reasoning by comparing it with that of an expert. This assumes, of course, that the expert is able to reason correctly, which brings back the quagmire of knowledge elicitation.

3.2 The Representativeness of Test Cases

While verifying the function of the expert system is a necessary part of the evaluation, it must be complemented by an assessment of the validity of the expert system. To do so requires that the test cases are representative for the situations that the expert system is likely to encounter in practical use.

The completeness of the knowledge and rules in the expert system is crucial for its performance. Expert systems are similar to many other technological system by being required to function in a wide range of circumstances; in particular, one must expect that the system will encounter circumstances that have not been completely anticipated or specified in advance. In the world of process control it is common to talk of the design basis, hence also to have events that go beyond the design basis. The same may happen for expert systems. This obviously makes it difficult to test the completeness of the expert system's knowledge and rules, hence to assess its validity.

One problem is the **representativeness** of the test cases. Ideally, one should be able to prove that the test cases were complete. That, however, is only possible for small, closed domains where the test cases can be generated and enumerated. In all other cases it will be impossible to generate an exhaustive set of test cases or even to produce an exhaustive description of them. It is therefore necessary to ensure that the test cases which actually are used are representative for the situations that may possibly occur. This can be done in a number of ways using techniques ranging from statistics to qualitative / quantitative simulation. The methodology for that is highly developed e.g. in reliability engineering and risk analysis.

Another problem is that it may be difficult to determine the **completeness** of knowledge even within the design basis. Since the domains in most cases are not designed but rather taken as subsets of the 'natural' domains that people normally handle, the completeness depends on a pragmatic rather than a formal classification, hence cannot easily be determined. To account for the completeness of the knowledge requires a good description of the design base, i.e. the normal and expected range of functions, as well as a description of how the tasks are carried out in real life.

A final, and potentially very serious, problem is that one cannot be sure that the expert system will break down when it encounters unusual or 'illegal' cases. It may instead go through its rules as usual and produce blatant nonsense as output. The danger is that this may not be detected by the user and therefore cause problems that only are realised later. Some checks may be included in the expert system, but it is - by definition - impossible to anticipate all possible combinations. The problem is closely related to that of responsibility, which is particularly prevalent in the case of decision support systems (cf. Hollnagel, 1988).

3.3 Correctness of Reasoning

Assessing the correctness of reasoning is important for both system reliability and system validity. It plays a crucial role because the reasoning is the way in which the expert system derives or produces its results, i.e. it is the process of the expert system. From another point of view the reasoning as perceived by the user is also important. The reasoning may be formally correct, but it may not be understandable to the user of the system. Since, however, an important part of the expert system's functioning is the interaction with the user - and since furthermore the trust of the user is essential for the effectiveness of the expert system - the comprehensibility of the reasoning is important. The general comprehensibility of the reasoning as provided by the explanations of the expert system must, however, not be confused with the expert system's efficiency as a teaching system. While there may be a considerable teaching effect of using the system, this is only incidental and should not be the main basis for judging its performance. The primary function of an expert system is to give advice (to solve problems, to make decisions even), not to teach.

The purpose of an expert system is to improve the quality of information available to the user. This information is often generated rather than retrieved, and makes use of logic and reasoning of various types. The processes that generate the information and the reasoning mechanisms are obviously crucial for the proper functioning of the expert system. This is in quite similar to problems that are met in other uses of computers, e.g. in process control and calculation. Users often rely blindly on the programs they use, e.g large statistical packages, and faults in these programs therefore have potentially serious consequences.

The correctness of the reasoning is probably the most difficult aspect to evaluate. It may, of course, be assumed that the reasoning mechanisms of an expert system are correct. If the reasoning was restricted to elementary logic, such as Boolean algebra, this assumption might be warranted. After all, the mechanisation of this type of logic is a trivial matter and the very foundation for digital computers. The experience from other software systems nevertheless suggests that errors may occur and remain undetected for long periods of time even in fundamental logical or arithmetic functions. Moving on to other and more sophisticated types of logic and reasoning, or even just using more complex combinations of the elementary operations, will almost certainly introduce failures - simply because the programs are written by fallible humans.

An expert system basically carries out some kind of reasoning or processing of information, following a set of rules or procedures. The underlying logic of the reasoning is, however, difficult to externalise, hence to validate. One problem is that it may be difficult to establish test cases where one can define what the right reasoning is. Evaluating decision alternatives is different from logical deduction and syllogistic reasoning. It is no solution to have a qualified person scrutinize the reasoning mechanism. This may be done for each rule in isolation, but not when they interact. As many psychological experiments have demonstrated, people are very bad at reasoning in a consistent way if the problem is even moderately complex (Wason & Johnson-Laird, 1972). That goes for syllogistic reasoning and certainly also for understanding how a reasoning mechanism works.

We thus seem to be trapped in an impasse: reasoning mechanisms are introduced to compensate for the shortcomings of human reasoning, but these very shortcomings make it extremely difficult to determine whether the reasoning mechanisms work correctly.

When we try to prove the correctness (or even functionality) of artificial reasoning systems we run into the following problems:

o Dealing with simple individual rules, a proof of correctness is possible.

- o Dealing with combinations of rules for simple objects, proof is again possible. At least one can become convinced of the correctness.
- o Interactions between objects is beyond the reach of human cognition - particularly when time-dependent reasoning is required.
- o Interactions between rules - such as chaining and inheritance - is again very difficult to deal with, partly for the same reasons
- o Interpretation of rules (the resolution mechanisms) are normally completely hidden in the software, and rather taken for granted by the user. Hence they are not subject to inspection or verification.

The problem of proving and evaluating the correctness of reasoning obviously gets worse the more difficult it is for the user to understand the functioning of the system i.e. the less transparent the expert system is. It also poses the very practical problem of who, eventually, is responsible for making the (right) decision, although that goes beyond the scope of the evaluation.

3.4 Component vs. High-level Specifications

Assessing the correctness of the reasoning may also be influenced by the level on which the reasoning is described. Expert systems are expressed in terms of rules and the accompanying knowledge. Even though this is a great advantage from having to evaluate the minute code that goes into the rules, much as one would have to do with a system using a procedural language, it is still - in the world of expert systems - to work on the level of components. The problem is that this quickly becomes unmanageable in the sense that the system evaluator (to say nothing of the system designer, the system manager or the user) looses the overview. A good case of that is XCON where around 50% of the 6000 rules were changed each year. Evaluating it in the first place would have been difficult enough. Maintaining the system became a major job in itself, and clearly there were few who could keep an overview to say nothing about following its reasoning.

The solution to this problem may be to go one step higher and include a description of the rules and the way they are structured in the system itself - i.e. a kind of meta-rule or meta-knowledge. Many of the available high level tools appear to provide such a facility. This is, however, not really so. They do offer a well-defined scheme for organising rules and for expressing rules and knowledge, but this is independent of the application. What is needed is instead a meta-level rule description which is application specific. That could then be consulted whenever changes were made, much as the 'elemental' rules reflect the changes in the raw data through consistency checking by backwards and forwards propagation. In a sense, what is advocated is a truth maintenance system for the expert system rather than for the domain knowledge. This would go a long way towards establishing the correctness of the reasoning.

3.5 The Cost of an Expert System Evaluation

The evaluation of an expert systems is something which takes time and costs money, and the need for it may therefore be seriously questioned. This is a fate that it shares with all other types of specialised system evaluation, e.g. ergonomic, human factors, risk, reliability, etc. Whereas some of these have now been accepted as necessary - sometimes as a consequence of spectacular, and costly, accidents - they are still considered by system managers as something that one would rather dispense with if possible, or at least only pay lip service to.

It is difficult to provide guidelines for how much the evaluation of an expert system will cost, partly because it has not yet become an established practice. An indirect estimate can be given by considering the cost of incorrect decisions following the advice of an expert system. That may range from minor nuisances to the loss of lives or a major disaster. The possibility of such negative consequences become more important as the application of expert systems is spreading to new and more complex domains. Examples are expert systems in finance and banking, on-line monitoring of processes or traffic systems, tax assessment and control - to say nothing of military and aerospace. Errors can obviously be very costly, and it may be worthwhile to prevent them as far as possible.

An outstanding problem is the definition and development of a good model for cost-benefit analysis of evaluation of expert systems (and for that matter for other systems as well). If the experience from evaluation of man-machine systems from other fields is anything to go by, the evaluation of an expert system may easily consume 10% of the total system cost. The costs of doing an expert system evaluation must, however, be weighted against the risks of doing it incorrectly or incompletely - even though the quantification may be difficult. It can, however, safely be said that expert system evaluation will require considerable resources in the form of time and money (for man-power). The evaluation cannot be made automatically, e.g. as a measurement, but must involve behavioural assessments of some kind as well as other methods to test software quality. The problems are that there is yet insufficient experience to define clearly the criteria that are valid, nor the methodology.

Here we must once more undo the simplification made in the introduction, i.e. that expert system evaluation is considered separately from the evaluations that are an integrated part of system development. In fact, a warning must be given against the use of expert system evaluations as the finishing touch. If the evaluation is going to have any effect at all - apart from a reassessment of the risks - it must happen early enough to be allowed an impact on system development. In other words, it must not be the last thing that is done. Several authors have pointed to the need for clear and unambiguous evaluation results to overcome the inertia (or resistance) against changes that characterise any system of reasonable size - particularly if it is difficult to overview. In summary, it must be possible to relate the evaluation to the design process.

4. EVALUATION METHODOLOGY

Software engineering and software development has over the years produced a number of well-described methods for system requirement specification, development, and documentation. They range from formal (mathematical) specification methods, over various national and international standards, to project management principles and guidelines. It is, however, still an open question to what extent they can be applied to the development of expert systems or whether that requires development of a separate set of methods. Even if the established methods from software engineering can be applied to expert system development, it is doubtful whether the traditional software verification and validation methods can be used in expert system evaluation because they do not address the issues that are essential for expert systems, i.e. the interaction between user and system, their joint functioning and the way in which the expert system supports the user.

At present there is no standardised repertoire of evaluation methods that can be applied to expert systems. There are, to be sure, a few approaches which are commonly used and which will be characterised in the following. I shall, however, argue that they are insufficient, basically because they do not clearly recognise what the important aspects of an expert system evaluation are. But before I begin discussing the various methods, it is necessary to consider the role of the expert system evaluation in the overall system design and development process.

4.1 Single vs. Continuous Evaluation

This is the question of whether the evaluation should be carried out on the finished system or as an integrated part of the development. Even though I began by making the simplifying assumption that expert system evaluation concerns the system in use, hence a system that is functionally mature, it is still necessary to consider whether the evaluation is a single event or rather several evaluations in progression. By making clear that the simplifying assumption was an assumption, it has already been indicated that expert system evaluation should take place on a continuous basis rather than as the final step in system development. Expert system evaluation should, in fact, be seen as an integral part of expert system development. One should, however, recognise that evaluating the usability of the individual components or modules of an expert system, or the separate functional aspects, do not guarantee the functionality of the expert system as a whole. Therefore, even though the separate modules may be evaluated as they are produced and completed, a further evaluation which takes their interaction into account is also needed. A test of the functionality must necessarily take place after the system is finished but before it is delivered.

The practical problem with having this final test when the development has been completed is that the possibilities of influencing or changing the design of the system are much reduced, and the costs consequently much increased. Not only may the practical problems in making a modification be greater, because of the larger number of interactions in the system and the possible spread of effects to other modules, but they may also be less welcome from the project management's side. Quite often the development of the expert system is delayed and the time which is available from the evaluation takes place to delivery must occur is reduced. There is accordingly a strong incentive to minimise the consequences of the evaluation if they point towards major modifications, often justifying this attitude with the part evaluations that have taken place during the development. Expert systems are furthermore not unique in this respect, but rather suffer from the same conditions that can be experienced in other types of system development. The lesson to be learned from this is, of course, to account for the evaluation in the planning of the system development, and to be realistic in assessing the resources needed both for the evaluation and the possible (and probably inevitable) changes that may follow. Although this is not directly part of the evaluation methodology, it is nevertheless important in establishing the proper conditions for the evaluation. If, in fact, an expert system evaluation can have no effect for the expert system but only is carried out as a formal exercise (perhaps because it is required by customers or authorities), then one might better avoid it altogether.

4.2 Turing's Test

Turning towards the commonly used evaluation methods, the classical way of evaluating AI systems and expert systems is to use Turing's test (Turing, 1945). This was originally proposed by Allan Turing as a method to determine whether one could say that a machine can think (and he did that tongue in cheek, I assume). Despite that, the test has been used in many cases, including such celebrated systems as MYCIN and INTERNIST (cf. Alty & Coombs, 1984; Yu et al., 1979). The basic principle of Turing's test is that an expert judge compares the functionality of a system (or rather: the output from a system) with that of another system. If the expert judge cannot distinguish between the two systems then they are said to be functionally equivalent, hence to possess the same qualities. (This crude comparison in the originally proposed test may, of course, be refined by using statistical criteria or other elaborations (Colby & Hilf, 1974), although this does not change the basic principle.) In Turing's case one system was a human being and the other either a computer or a human, the point being that if the expert judge could not distinguish the output of the computer from that of the human then it might reasonably be said that the computer could think (at least as well as the human!). In case of expert system evaluation the test has been used to see whether an expert judge could distinguish between the output from an expert system and the output from a human expert in the field, e.g. in the form of diagnoses.

Put more formally, the basis for Turing's test is the indistinguishability between the performance of two systems. Performance data are collected from the system to be evaluated as well as from a suitable reference system - often being the human experts in the domain. The data are transformed to a common format to eliminate obvious cues and the performance records are evaluated 'blindly' by a group of experts, using suitable reliable methods. The results are then used to determine whether the expert system meets the specified criteria.

Turing's test is obviously not a very good method for expert system evaluation. The weak point is that it only considers the validity of the system. In the terminology used here it considers a mixture of the correctness and the accuracy of the final decision, and ignores the rest, cf. Table 1. Furthermore, this evaluation is made by a method which is completely uncontrolled, hence must be assumed to have a very low reliability and validity. The method, being based on human expert judgment is completely opaque and one cannot known how it is done - unless it becomes possible to bootstrap the expert judgment onto a machine (in which case the test, by definition, would have become obsolete). Turing's test, while it has a common sense appeal, is thus quite useless for expert system evaluation. Allan Turing, I am sure, would agree wholeheartedly with this.

4.3 Expert Assessment

There are several ways in which Turing's test can be improved, although none of them will remove its basic flaw - that it relies on an unknown process called human judgment. One improvement is to have the output from the expert system assessed by an expert judge in an absolute way rather than based on a comparison with another system. This could, for instance, focus on a specific aspect such as the 'hit' rate of a diagnosis, the soundness of an investment advice, the efficiency of a proposed action, etc. Thus Mozetic et al. (1984) evaluated a system for ECG interpretation by having cardiologists assess the performance on the system, using the performance of internists as a reference. Another case was the development of a prototype expert system for credit evaluation (Ben & Sterling, 1985), where the performance was evaluated by subject matter experts. The same approach may, of course, also be used if the evaluation concerns the reasoning mechanisms of the expert system rather than the overall performance (Hart, 1985).

Another improvement is to define clearly the criteria used in the assessment, and possibly even provide a set of 'standards' as references. This will replace the general criterion of indistinguishability, which is at the heart of Turing's test, with a more objective standard of performance. This is an option used by many evaluation studies. Thus Yu et al. (1984) used the performance of clinicians to evaluate the performance of MYCIN; Hudson & Cohen (1984) used retrospective patient data to evaluate the effectiveness of the EMERGE system, which analysed chest pains; and Gaschnig (1979) used target values supplied by the model designer to evaluate the performance of PROSPECTOR.

Both type of improvements will enhance the reliability of the evaluation method. In the first case it is done simply by reducing the variability among the judging experts, by restricting the sample and increasing the level of skill and experience. In the second case it is done by using a reference criterion which, at least in principle, can be replicated by other evaluations. But the validity of the method can only be improved to the extent that the expert's assessment can be specified in the number of steps that make up the assessment. Furthermore,this type of evaluation still concentrates on the validity of the system, rather than the reliability.

One variant of Turing's test is the **black box** approach. As the name implies the basic principle is that the expert system that is being evaluated is considered as a black box, i.e. the internal mechanisms are assumed to be unknown and the evaluation is restricted to a comparison of input-output sets. For instance, given certain symptoms (the input) the expert produces a certain diagnosis (the output). The expert system is given the same inputs, and the output is compared with the expert's diagnosis. Although Turing's test was an orthodox black box approach, because Turing was not interested in the processes that lay behind the performance, the black box approach is on the whole unsuitable for the evaluation of expert systems. The method can achieve a high reliability if the number of input-output sets is large enough (cf. below), but it concentrates on the face validity of the expert system and is therefore unable to provide information about the functional details. It is, in particular, unable to provide any kind of explanation of why the expert system may fail in some situations and succeed in others, even though this often is the most interesting question to get answered.

4.4 Statistical Sampling

Another way of improving the basic Turing's test is to base the comparison on representative samples and to use a statistically based test. The advantage of this is that one does not rely on a - possibly flawed - selection by (and of) experts but can use data sets that are known to be representative. The main drawback is that it may take a lot longer to do, unless the data is already available.

The data sets may either be derived from empirical performance data (Hudson & Cohen, 1984; Yu et al., 1984) or specified by the designer or the model (Duda, Gaschnig & Hart, 1979; Gaschnig, 1979). One obvious advantage of this is that it may be possible to use the same data set as reference for different expert system evaluations. If, for instance, several systems were made to diagnose faults in a power plant, using the same sets of data as a reference would enable not only an evaluation of each system in turn, but also a comparison between different versions of the same system (cf. Pearce, 1988), e.g. in performance tuning, or even between completely different systems. At present expert systems can, at best, be compared with regard to speed, number of rules, etc. But if the present development continues it is conceivable that a demand will arise not only to have better evaluation methods but also to have a more objective standard for different kinds of expert systems.

Statistical sampling can be used to improve the reliability of the evaluation method. It can be seen as a 'mechanisation' of the expert assessment method, since the expert judge is replaced by a recognised statistical method. This, furthermore, makes it possible to determine the validity of the evaluation method, since it now is clear how the evaluation is performed. Although statistical sampling does not automatically increase the validity of the evaluation method it does provide a reasonable gross measure of the validity of the expert system and thus helps to establish the lower boundary for its functionality. It can be used to assess specific aspects such as correctness of the final decision, accuracy of the final decision, sensitivity, robustness, and - to a certain extent - the cost-effectiveness of the expert system. Statistical sampling is also much better suited to assess the reliability of the system because it can be used together with conventional experimental methods. The main drawback with statistical sampling is that it must be done consistently after the expert system has been taken into use, and probably for rather a long time. That requires a close collaboration between the producer and the customer / user. It also adds a burden on the user as well as an additional (although probably rather small) cost. This may nevertheless be prohibitive, particularly if it has not been included in the system development plan or anticipated by the user.

4.5 Summative and Formative Evaluation

Summative and formative evaluation are terms proposed by Littman & Soloway (1987). Although they do not refer to a distinct methodology, but rather use a variant of Turing's test, they are of interest here because they are proposed as a way of capturing the basic principles of expert system evaluation.

Summative evaluation is defined as being concerned with the quality control of the expert system and answering the '**what**' questions, i.e. whether the expert system does what it should do. **Formative evaluation** provides developmental guidance and answers the '**why**' and '**how**' questions, i.e. about the functionality and 'mechanisms' of the expert system. This is exemplified as questions of whether the expert system should do something else, and how the expert system does what it does. In addition to summative and formative evaluation the concepts of **external evaluation** and **internal evaluation** are also introduced. These refer to whether the evaluation considers the results or output from the expert system (external evaluation) or rather concentrates on the inner 'mechanisms' of the expert system (internal evaluation).

Littman & Soloway (op. cit.) uses these terms to consider a number of well-known expert systems such as MYCIN, INTERNIST, PROSPECTOR, Proust, and R1. The conclusion is that both summative / external and formative / internal evaluations are needed. If we try to consider what the terms mean in relation to the classification used here, this conclusion is not really surprising. To take the simpler terms first, external evaluation refers to the validity of the expert system, while internal evaluation refers to its reliability. Obviously both of these are necessary for a proper expert system evaluation. Summative evaluation, exemplified by the 'what' question, corresponds to the validity of the expert system. Formative evaluation can either correspond to system verification (the 'whether' question) or to system reliability (the 'how' question). Again, both types are needed for an expert system evaluation.

What is missing from these terms is first of all a more precise way of assessing the system's reliability and validity, e.g. evaluation criteria such as correctness, accuracy, sensitivity, etc. In addition, the terms fail to consider the problems of the reliability and validity of the evaluation method itself. This is probably because the evaluations in most cases are made by human experts, thus basically employing a variation of Turing's test or the expert assessment, hence subject to the same strengths and weaknesses. Littman & Soloway also argue for a unified methodology which considers software engineering and expert system evaluation together (at least implicitly, cf. the emphasis on quality control in the summative evaluation). It may, however, be better to keep them separate, because they look at two completely independent sides of expert system functionality. By this I mean that an expert system may score very high on the software engineering dimension but still be miserable in terms of man-machine functionality and usability. And the reverse is, perhaps, even more frequently the case - for instance demonstrated by all the early 'hand-crafted' expert systems (MYCIN, INTERNIST, PROSPECTOR, etc.). Altogether summative and formative evaluation do not completely cover the aspects that must be considered in an expert system evaluation, and should therefore be used with caution.

4.6 Analytic Hierarchy Process

The Analytic Hierarchy Process, developed by Saaty (1980), has been proposed for expert system evaluation by Liebowitz (1985, 1986) and the use of it for a specific case has been reported in Liebowitz (1985). The Analytic Hierarchy Process is basically a method which helps the user to decompose the problem into its constituent parts and, based on a simple pair-wise comparison which may be qualitative as well as quantitative, to calculate the priorities of the subproblems. It thus focuses on the problem rather than on the system, but does, of course, illustrate how the system solves a specific problem. The advantage of this method, which has been implemented in a software system, is that it helps the user to maintain the overview of the evaluation process by keeping track of the lower level comparisons and carrying out the statistical calculations. It is, however, only really useful if clear evaluation criteria can be defined and if the problem is amenable to a hierarchical decomposition (although the pair-wise comparisons probably can be replaced by another estimation method).

In relation to the classification proposed here the Analytic Hierarchy Process is an example of a method with high reliability (due to the computerisation) but probably low validity. It can probably address both the reliability and validity (as well as usability) of the system, provided a hierarchical decomposition can be made and the appropriate criteria defined. It is, however, rather doubtful whether this is possible for the majority of expert systems that need to be evaluated and the general applicability of the method is therefore limited. The Analytic Hierarchy Process instead seems suited to provide a measure of the expert system's effectiveness, thus supporting the assessment of the cost-effectiveness.

Other methods exist, both as formal metrication studies (e.g. Moffat et al., 1986) and as more informal evaluation principles. One way of improving both Expert Assessment and Statistical Sampling is to employ properly described benchmarks. These may be exemplary test cases, significant real cases or even a complete alternative expert system! The latter approach has been described by Pearce (1988). Here an expert system, which was built by using the traditional knowledge engineering approach, was compared with an expert system which was constructed using induction on a knowledge base automatically synthesised from a qualitative model of the application (in this case a Satellite Power Subsystem). Although the procedure was highly successful for this particular system, it is not generally applicable. Firstly, it requires that a qualitative simulation of the application is available. This is rarely the case, except for domains within the engineering field. And secondly, it still leaves the problem of ensuring that the qualitative simulation is accurate and valid. That may be a formidable problem, particularly when one goes to the limits of the design knowledge, i.e. to the slightly abnormal cases. But the method does emphasise the value in having proper benchmarks available for the evaluation. Depending on the generality of the expert system in question this might be facilitated by establishing proper libraries of case studies.

When it comes to the evaluation of usability or user acceptance, a number of methods have been tried, e.g. interviews, questionnaires, subjective ratings, as well as specific performance measurements (response times, visual clutter, errors, mistakes, etc.). In the evaluation of usability there is, of course, a considerable overlap with the methods and issues of the evaluation of human computer interaction as a whole. In the evaluation of expert systems one may also consider less precise characteristics such as system transparency and system comprehensibility - in particular the adequacy of explanations, since this often has been hailed as a unique aspect of expert systems. Other criteria that have been included in the evaluation of usability are knowledge engineering attributes such as knowledge representation and the communications interface (Kidd & Cooper, 1985), or ease of debugging and system extension (Sticklen et al., 1984).

4.7 Summary

If we consider the different approaches to expert system evaluation described above, the advantages of each can be compared by referring to the criteria established previously. The result of that is shown in Table 1. In addition to the seven aspects of expert system functioning, which together constitute the validity and reliability of the system (cf. below), the table also considers the validity and reliability of each method. One conclusions which can be drawn from this table is that there is no method which is the overall best. Two methods stand out as being better all around than the others: Statistical sampling and the Analytic Hierarchy Process. Both, however, have disadvantages. Statistical sampling requires a prolonged evaluation period and a strong commitment from the user. The Analytic

Hierarchy Process requires that a hierarchical decomposition can be made and the appropriate criteria defined.

	Correctness of decision	Accuracy of decision	Correctness of reasoning	Sensitivity	Robustness	Quality of HCI	Cost – effectiveness	Method Validity	Method Reliability
Turing's test	x	x						L	L
Expert Assessment	x	x	(x)					L	M
Statistical Sampling	x	x		x	x		x	M	H
Summative & Formative Evaluation	x	x				(x)		L	M
Analytical Hierarchy Process	(x)	(x)		x	x		x	L	H

Table 1: Comparison between five Evaluation Methods.

A different problem with expert system evaluations, which they share with most other types of system evaluation, is the tendency to focus on the cases where the system does not function as expected. These instances are considered as highly significant and are accordingly analysed in detail. It stands to reason that something may be wrong if the expert system fails to perform as it was supposed to do. But, because a correct answer does not imply a correct process, one should not neglect to consider the cases where the expert system performs as expected. If the expert system evaluation is based on a detailed study of individual cases, this should include cases which provide the right answer as well as cases which provide a wrong one. The limiting factor is, of course, the time and resources required for this kind of analysis which in practice may reduce the number of cases to only a few. This emphasises the need for a careful planning of the evaluation as an integral part of system development.

5. CONCLUSIONS

In this chapter I have discussed some of the essential aspects of expert system evaluation. The basis was the increasing use of expert systems in real applications, hence the growing need to evaluate their functionality as a natural extension to the software engineering aspects of the design and development process. The chapter started by making a clear distinction between the evaluation methodology and the system evaluation. Either could be characterised with regard to their reliability and validity, although the detailed criteria were different. The reliability of an evaluation method can be established using techniques commonly known in other fields, whereas the validity of the method required more thorough considerations of the content validity and the construct validity. The reliabllity and validity of an expert system were discussed using a number of basic evaluation criteria, and have been summarised in Table 2.

METHOD EVALUATION	SYSTEM EVALUATION	EVALUATION CRITERIA
Reliability	Reliability	Correctness of Reasoning Techniques Sensitivity Robustness
Validity	Validity	Correctness of Final Decision Accuracy of Final Decision (Correctness of Reasoning Techniques)
(Usability)	Usability	Quality of HCI

Table 2: Components of Method and System Evaluation

Each of these criteria were described in more detail. It was pointed out that whereas the validity can be reasonably well assessed by looking only at the results or output from the expert system, assessing the reliability also requires that the 'mechanisms' of the system are studied in some detail. This should be done not only for the cases where something goes wrong (i.e. as part of a diagnosis) but also for normal conditions. Following that a number of frequently used evaluation methods were discussed using the classification established above. The methods include Turing's test, expert assessment, and statistical sampling, as well as some more specialised approaches. It was concluded that none of these methods address all the important problems, and that most of them neglect to consider the reliability and validity of the evaluation method as such. This is probably due to the lack of a firm tradition for expert system evaluation. Finally, a number of remaining problems in expert system evaluation were discussed. These include determining the correctness and adequacy of the test cases, the correctness of the reasoning, the use of meta-level descriptions, and the estimation of the cost of an expert system evaluation.

The conclusion is that there is yet a shortage of consolidated experience in expert system evaluations, hence a lack of a proven methodology and generally accepted criteria. Although expert system evaluations are becoming more frequent, they are still too few to support the specification of a solid methodological repertoire. A contributing factor may be the lack of a concerted or centralised effort to bring the various experiences together. Until that happens, the growing needs of expert system customers will be answered in an *ad hoc* fashion, because there will be too little time to develop thorough solutions in the individual cases.

REFERENCES

Alty, J. L. & Coombs, M. J. (1984). **Expert systems. Concepts and examples.** NCC Publications.

Assemat, C. & Bonnet, A. (1986). **Conceptualisation, coherence et validation des bases de connaisances.** The 6th International Workshop on Expert Systems & Their Applications, Avignon, France, 28-30 April.

Ben, D. A. & Sterling, L. (1985). **A prototype expert system for credit evaluation.** Rehovot: Weizmann Institute of Science, Dept. of Applied Mathematics.

Boehm, B., Brown, J. R., Kaspar, H., Lipow, M., MacLeod, G. J. & Merrit, M. J. (1978). **Characteristics of software quality.** North-Holland.

Campbell, D. T. & Stanley, J. C. (1963). Experimental and quasi-experimental designs for research. Chicago: Rand-McNally.

Colby, K. M. & Hilf, F. D. (1974). Multidimensional evaluation of a simulation of paranoid thought processes. In L. W. Gregg (Ed.), **Knowledge and cognition**. Lawrence Erlbaum.

Duda, R., Gaschnig, J. & Hart, P. (1979). Model design in the Prospector consultant system for mineral exploration. In D. Michie, (Ed.), **Expert systems in the micro-electronic age**. Edinburgh: Edinburgh University Press.

Gaschnig, J. (1979). **Preliminary performance analysis of the Prospector consultant system for mineral exploration.** Proceedings of IJCAI-79, vol. I, 308-310.

Gaschnig, J., Klahr, P., Pople, H., Shortliffe, E. & Terry, A. (1983). Evaluation of expert systems: Issues and case studies. In F. Hayes-Roth, D. A. Waterman & D. B. Lenat (Eds.), **Building expert** systems. Addison-Wesley.

Hart, A. E. (1985). Experience in the use of an inductive system in knowledge engineering. In M. A. Bramer (Ed.), **Research and development in expert systems**. Cambridge: Cambridge University Press.

Hollnagel, E. (1981). **The methodology of man-machine systems: Problems of verification and validation** (Risø-M-2313). Roskilde, Denmark. Risø National Laboratory.

Hollnagel, E. (1986). Cognitive system performance analysis. In E. Hollnagel, G. Mancini & D. D. Woods (Eds.), **Intelligent decision support in process environments**. Heidelberg, F. R. Germany: Springer Verlag.

Hollnagel, E. (1988). **Responsibility issues in intelligent decision support systems.** Conference on 'Human and Organisational Issues of Expert Systems', Stratford-upon-Avon, 4th - 6th May, 1988.

Hudson, D. L. & Cohen, M. E. (1984). **EMERGE, a rule-based clinical decision making aid**. IEEE Computer Society First Conference on Artificial Intelligence Applications, Denver, 5th - th7 September, 1984.

Kidd, A. L. & Cooper, M. B. (1985). Man-machine interface issues in the construction and use of an expert system. **International Journal of Man-Machine Studies, 22**, 91-102.

Liebowitz, J. (1985). **Evaluation of expert systems: An approach and case study.** IEEE Computer Society Second Conference on Artificial Intelligence Applications, Miami Beach, Florida, 11th - 13th December, 1985.

Liebowitz, J. (1986). Useful approach for evaluating expert systems. **Expert Systems**, 3(2), 86-96.

Littman, D. & Soloway, E. (1987). **Evaluation of expert systems: Examples and principles.** Tutorial given at IJCAI 1987, Milano, Italy.

Moffat, B. et al. (1986). **Identification of metrication aspects** (P857-KUL-WP22-009). Leuven, Belgium: Catholic University.

Mozetic, I., Bratko, I. & Lavrac, N. (1984). **The derivation of medical knowledge from a qualitative model of the heart.** Ljubljana: Jozef Stefan Institute.

Norman, D. A. & Draper, S. W. (1986). **User centered system design.** Lawrence Erlbaum.

Pearce, D. (1987). **KIC: A knowledge integrity checker.** Glasgow, Scotland: The Turing Institute.

Pearce, D. (1988). **The induction of fault diagnosis systems from quantitative models.** Glasgow, Scotland: The Turing Institute.

Pfaff, G. E. (Ed.) (1985). **User interface management systems.** Springer verlag.

Saaty, T. L. (1980). **The analytic hierarchy process.** McGraw-Hill.

Sticklen, J., Chandrasekaran, B. Smith, J. W. & Svirely, J. (1984). **A comparison of the diagnostic subsystems of MDX and MYCIN.** Proceedings of IEEE Workshop on Principles of Knowledge-Based Systems, Denver, 3rd - 4th December, 1984.

Turing, A. M. (1950). Computing machinery and intelligence, **Mind**, 1950, 433-460.

Wason, P. C. & Johnson-Laird, P. N. (1972). **Psychology of reasoning.** B. T. Batsford, Ltd.

Yu, V. L., Fagan, L. M., Bennett, S. W., Clancey, W. J.., Scott, A. C., Hannigan, J. F., Buchanan, B. G. & Cohen, S. N. (1984, org. 1979). An evaluation of MYCIN's advice. In B. G. Buchanan & E. H. Shortliffe (Eds.), **Rule-based expert systems: The MYCIN experiments of the Stanford Heuristic Programming Project**. Addison-Wesley.

PART 7

Further reading

Topics in Expert System Design
G. Guida and C. Tasso (Editors)

BUILDING EXPERT SYSTEMS: A STRUCTURED BIBLIOGRAPHY

Giovanni GUIDA and Carlo TASSO

Department of Mathematics and Computer Science
University of Udine
Udine, Italy

Introduction

This paper presents a structured bibliography on the topic of building expert systems. The purpose of this bibliography is twofold: offering a comprehensive source of references in an important field of expert system technology, and serving as a searching referral aid for accessing literature materials. Moreover, it also contains the proposal of an original taxonomy of the field of expert system design and construction, which can be used as a scheme for topic classification.

The bibliographic research reported in this paper has been supported by several motivations. Among others, we mention:
- literature in the field of building expert systems is very rich but rather poorly organized, and, moreover, it includes a large number of materials of different types and qualitative levels;
- the professional need to access references on the topics covered by this bibliography is very common and usually very urgent;
- in front of a specific information need, it is often difficult to identify relevant literature materials and to reach them;
- no other comprehensive and structured bibliography in this field is available to interested readers, as far as we know.

This bibliography has a quite broad scope. It covers a large set of topics related to the construction of expert systems, focusing on methodologies and tools for building expert systems in the large, and including, in particular the following issues: development methodology and life cycle, choice of the domain and preliminary analysis, development techniques, development tools, knowledge acquisition, validation and evaluation, project management, technology transfer. More technical topics, such as knowledge representation, reasoning mechanisms, system architectures, interfaces, etc., fall outside the coverage of this bibliography as they are dealt with in a systematic way in several other publications.

The compilation of this bibliography has been based on a very wide and as far as possible exhaustive bibliographic research, carried out both through direct library investigation and through online search in the major data banks on the field. However, the fundamental criterion adopted for including references in the bibliography has not been exhaustivity but usefulness. Only those materials which have been considered reliable and important have been included, trying as much as possible to avoid unnecessary redundancy. In particular, the following criteria have been adopted for deciding about inclusion of a literature item in the bibliography:

- intrinsic technical level;
- accessibility of the source: international journals and books have been preferred to conference proceedings and technical reports;
- publication date: recent publications have been preferred to old ones;
- coverage: items with a broad coverage and a sound organization (possibly including a tutorial or survey part) have been preferred to very specific and narrow-scope references;
- distribution of references: while in fields where literature is scarce (e.g., development tools, project management, and technology transfer) citations have been rather exhaustive, in the fields where literature is very large and often redundant (e.g., knowledge acquisition, validation and evaluation) citations have been strictly controlled and accurately pruned;
- controlled redundancy: for each approach or author or research project only the most meaningful publications have been mentioned.

Of course, possible deviations from the above criteria, omissions and mistakes are unwanted faults of the authors.

The bibliography has been structured into sections, each one devoted to an individual topic. The topic is defined by an heading, specified through a set of keywords, and briefly illustrated at the beginning of each section. References inside a section are alphabetically ordered. The taxonomy adopted for topic classification is reported in Table 1.

The intended users of this bibliography are professionals in the area of expert system technology, including system designers, project managers, potential users, researchers and scholars. The bibliography may be used both as a reference for information search and as a guide to selected readings.

A. Development methodology and life cycle	
	development methodology in general
	life cycle
B. Choice of the domain and preliminary analysis	
	domain evaluation
	appropriateness of technology
	technical feasibility
	organizational impact
	cost/benefit analysis
C. Development techniques	
	requirement analysis
	specification
	prototyping
	technical choices
	knowledge base construction, refinement, and extension
	maintenance
	documentation
D. Development tools	
	classification
	evaluation
	choice
E. Knowledge acquisition	
	knowledge elicitation and transfer of expertise
	knowledge analysis and modeling
	knowledge editing
	knowledge acquisition tools
F. Validation and evaluation	
	knowledge base verification and validation
	system performance evaluation
	user acceptance
	organizational and economic assessment
G. Project management	
	project start-up
	project planning
	project monitoring
	project team organization
H. Technology transfer	
	management involvement
	user familiarization
	education and training
	continuous education
	research and development

Table 1 - Expert system design and construction: a taxonomy of topics.

A. Development methodology and life cycle

keywords: development methodology in general - life cycle.

This section includes references in the area of methodologies for building expert systems, focusing on expert system life cycle. More precisely, the section contains:

- articles focusing on general topics in the area of expert system design and construction;
- papers covering, under a unitary approach, several specific aspects of expert system life cycle;
- materials discussing case studies and practical experience with exemplary expert system projects.

As literature in the area of development methodology and life cycle is not very rich, available materials have been taken into account rather extensively in the compilation of this section. Some references present case studies related to specific projects.

Badiru, A.B. 1988. Expert systems and industrial engineers: A practical guide to a successful partnership. Computers Ind. Engng. 14(1), 1-13.

Bobrow, D.G., S. Mittal, and M.J. Stefik. 1986. Expert systems: Perils and promise. Comm. of the ACM 29(9), 880-894.

Breuker, J.A., B.J. Wielinga, and S.A. Hayward. 1986. Structuring of knowledge based systems development. In The Commission of the European Communities (Ed.), ESPRIT '85: Status Report of Continuing Work, North-Holland, Amsterdam, NL, 771-784.

Brooking, A.G. 1985. Towards a methodology for the design of knowledge based systems. In J. Roukens, J.F. Renuart (Eds.), ESPRIT '84: Status Report of Ongoing Work, North-Holland, Amsterdam, NL, 147-158.

Buchanan, B.G., D. Barstow, R. Bechtel, J. Bennett, W. Clancey, C. Kulikowski, T. Mitchell, and D.A. Waterman. 1983. Constructing an expert system. In F. Hayes-Roth, D.A. Waterman, and D.B. Lenat. (Eds.) Building Expert Systems. Addison-Wesley, Reading, MA, 127-166.

Citrenbaum, R., and J. Geissman. 1987. A cost-conscious expert system development methodology. Proc. Artificial Intelligence and Advanced Computer Technology Conf., Long Beach, CA.

Curtis, G.A. 1987. Should you try to build your own? Information Center 3(3), 42-46.

De Salvo, D.A., A.E. Glamm, and J. Liebowitz. 1987. Structured design of an expert system prototype at the National Archives. In B.G. Silverman (Ed.), Expert Systems for Business, Addison-Wesley, Reading, MA, 40-77.

Ebrahimi, M. 1987. A structured approach to expert system design. Proc. WESTEX-87 Conf. on Expert Systems, Anaheim, CA, 18-24.

ESA, European Space Agency. 1986. Life-cycle for an expert system. TMS/86-091/MG/md, ESA, estec, Noordwijk, NL.

Freiling, M., J.H. Alexander, S.L. Messick, S. Rehfuss, and S.J. Shulman. 1985. Starting a knowledge engineering project: A step-by-step approach. AI Magazine 6(3), 150-164.

Gudes, E., A. Shafrir, and S. Gerlitz. 1986. Software and knowledge engineering methods in building expert systems. Proc. 2nd Int. Expert Systems Conference, London, UK, 237-245.

Guida, G. and C. Tasso. 1989. Building expert systems: From life cycle to development methodology. In G. Guida and C. Tasso (Eds.), Topics in Expert System Design - Methodologies and Tools, North-Holland, Amsterdam, NL, 3-24.

Harmon, P. and D. King. 1985. Expert Systems - Artificial Intelligence in Business. John Wiley & Sons, New York, NY. (Chapters 11 and 12)

Hu, D. 1987. Programmer's Reference Guide to Expert Systems. Howard W. Sams & Co., Indianapolis, IN. (Chapters 3 and 9)

Maguire, B. 1988. An incremental approach to expert systems development. Proc. 8th Int. Workshop Expert Systems & their Applications, Avignon, F, Vol. 1, 249-259.

Maney, T. and I. Reid. 1986. A Management Guide to Artificial Intelligence. Gower, Aldershot, UK. (Chapters 3, 4, 5, 6, and 7)

McDermott, J. 1981. R1: The formative years. AI Magazine 2(2), 21-29.

Odette, L.L. 1987. Expert systems: when to make them, when to buy them. Proc. Expert Systems in Business '87, New York, NY, 175-181.

Prerau, D., A. Gunderson, R. Reineke, and S. Goyal. 1985. The COMPASS expert system: Verification, technology transfer, and expansion. Proc. 2nd IEEE Conf. on Artificial Intelligence Applications, Miami, FL, 597-602.

Rauch-Hindin, W.R. 1986. Artificial Intelligence in Business, Science, and Industry - Vol. I: Fundamentals. Prentice-Hall, Englewood Cliffs, NJ. (Chapter 10)

Walters, J.R. and N.R. Nielsen. 1988. Crafting Knowledge-Based Systems. John Wiley & Sins, New York, NY.

Waterman, D.A. 1986. A Guide to Expert Systems. Addison-Wesley, Reading, MA. (Chapters 12 and 19)

B. Choice of the domain and preliminary analysis

keywords: domain evaluation - appropriateness of technology - technical feasibility - organizational impact - cost/benefit analysis.

This section focuses on a crucial problem arising in the application of expert system technology, namely: choice of the domain and preliminary study. This topic is specially critical in developing expert system applications for several reasons:

- first of all, while expert system technology can fit a variety of application domains, it is definitely inappropriate for others;
- moreover, technical feasibility and cost/benefit analysis are often based upon a few empirical rules derived from limited practical experience;
- finally, the implications of expert system applications on the organization are generally deep and need to be adequately analyzed and planned.

Literature items in this area are not very numerous, and, therefore, available materials have been taken into account rather extensively in the compilation of the section.

Butler Cox Foundation. 1987. Expert systems in business. Research report 60, London, UK. (Chapters 2, 3, and 4)

Gregory, D. 1986. Delimiting expert systems. IEEE Trans. on Systems, Man, Cybernetics SMC-16(6), 834-843.

Hayes-Roth, F., P. Klahr, and D.J. Mostow. 1986. Knowledge acquistion, knowledge programming, and knowledge refinement. In P. Klahr and D.A. Waterman (Eds.), Expert Systems - Techniques, Tools and Applications, Addison-Wesley, Reading, MA, 310-349.

Johnson, T. 1984. The Commercial Application of Expert Systems Technology. Ovum, London, UK. (Part D)

Prerau, D.S. 1985. Selection of an appropriate domain for an expert system. AI Magazine 6(2), 26-30.

Rauch-Hindin, W.R. 1986. Artificial Intelligence in Business, Science, and Industry - Vol. I: Fundamentals. Prentice-Hall, Englewood Cliffs, NJ. (Chapter 4)

Slow, R., S. Lunn, and P. Slatter. 1986. How to identify business applications of expert systems. Proc. 2nd Int. Expert Systems Conference, London, UK, 327-338.

Teknowledge Inc. 1983. Evaluating knowledge engineering applications. Palo Alto, CA.

Walters, J. 1987. Determining the feasibility of knowledge-based system applications. Proc. 1st Annual ESD/SMI Expert Systems Conf. and Exposition for Advanced Manufacturing Technology, Dearborn, MI, 209-222.

Waterman, D.A. 1986. A Guide to Expert Systems. Addison-Wesley, Reading, MA. (Chapter 11)

Zack, B.A. 1987. Selecting an application for knowledge-based system development. Proc. 3rd Int. Expert Systems Conference, London, UK, 257-269.

C. Development techniques

keywords: requirement analysis - specification - prototyping - technical choices knowledge base construction, refinement, and extension - maintenance - documentation.

This section focuses on two aspects:
- decision making aspects related to the techniques for building expert systems, covering works aimed at identifying criteria for supporting the expert system designer in the choice of appropriate paradigms for the development of an expert system;
- general techniques, such as requirement analysis, specification, prototyping, maintenance, and documentation, specifically tailored to expert system technology.

The presentation of specific expert system techniques, such as knowledge representation, reasoning mechnaisms, etc., and the discussion of their use is beyond the scope of this section. Specific literature in this area is not very rich, and, therefore, relevant materials have been taken into account rather extensively.

Alexander, J.H., J. Freiling, S.J. Shulman, J.L. Staley, S. Rehfuss, and S.L. Messik.1986. Knowledge level engineering: Ontological analysis. Proc. 5th Nat. Conf. on Artificial Intelligence, Philadelphia, PA, 963-968.

Alvey, P.L., C.D. Myers, and M.F. Greaves. 1985. An analysis of the problems of augmenting a small expert system. In M.A. Bramer (Ed.), Research and Development in Expert Systems, Cambridge University Press, Cambridge, UK, 61-72.

Carlsen, S. and G. Stokke. 1987. Conceptual modeling + prototyping = functional specification. Proc. 3rd Int. Expert Systems Conference, London, UK, 49-60

Chandrasekaran, B. 1984. Expert systems: Matching techniques to tasks. In W. Reitman (Ed.), AI Applications for Business, Ablex, Norwood, NJ, 116-132.

Chandrasekaran, B. 1986. Generic tasks in knowledge-based reasoning: High-level building blocks for expert system design. IEEE Expert 1(3), 23-30.

Clancey, W.J. 1985. Heuristic classification. Artificial Intelligence 27, 289-350.

Clancey, W.J. 1985. Software tools for developing expert systems. In I. De Lotto, M. Stefanelli (Eds.), Artificial Intelligence in Medicine, North-Holland, Amsterdam, NL, 155-178.

Freiling, M.J., J.H. Alexander, S.L. Messick, S. Rehfuss, and S.J. Shulman 1985. Steps toward automating expert system development. IEEE 1985 Proc. Int Conf. on Cybernetics and Society, Tucson, AZ, 988-93.

Friedman, J.Y. and A. Jain. 1986. Framework for prototyping expert systems for financial applications. Proc. 5th Nat. Conf. on Artificial Intelligence, Philadelphia, PA, 969-975.

Ginsberg, A., S. Weiss, and P. Politakis. 1985. SEEK-2: A generalized approach to automatic knowledge base refinement. Proc. 9th Int. Joint Conf. on Artificial Intelligence, Los Angeles, CA, 367-374.

Gruber, T. and P. Cohen. 1987. Design for acquisition: Principles of knowledge system design to facilitate knowledge acquisition. Int. Journal of Man-Machine Studies 26(2), 143-159.

Gruber, T. and P. Cohen. 1987. Knowledge engineering tools at the architecture level. Proc. 10th Int. Joint Conf. on Artificial Intelligence, Milano, Italy, 100-103.

Kahn, G.S. and M. Bauer. 1989. Prototyping: Tools and motivations. In G. Guida and C. Tasso (Eds.), Topics in Expert System Design - Methodologies and Tools, North-Holland, Amsterdam, NL, 47-68.

Kline, P.J. and S.B. Dolins. 1986. Problem features that influence the design of expert systems. Proc. 5th Nat. Conf. on Artificial Intelligence, Philadelphia, PA, 956-961.

Kulikowski, C.A. 1989. Knowledge base design and construction: From prototyping to refinement. In G. Guida and C. Tasso (Eds.), Topics in Expert System Design - Methodologies and Tools, North-Holland, Amsterdam, NL, 145-178.

Kunz, J.C., M.J.Stelzner, and M.D. Williams. 1989. From classic expert systems to models: Introduction to a methodology for building model-based systems. In G. Guida and C. Tasso (Eds.), Topics in Expert System Design - Methodologies and Tools, North-Holland, Amsterdam, NL, 87-110.

McGraw, K.L. 1986. Guidelines for producing documentation for expert systems. IEEE Trans. on Professional Communications PC-29(4), 42-47.

Moll, R.G. 1986. A method for analysing requirements for possible expert system implementations. Proc. 2th Int. Expert Systems Conference, London, UK, 339-349.

Neches, R., W.R. Swartout, and J.D. Moore. 1985. Enhanced maintenance and explanation of expert systems through explicit models of their development. IEEE Trans. on Software Engineering SE-11 (11), 1337-1351.

Oliver, A.E.M. 1986. Control of rapid prototyping in expert systems development. Proc. 2nd Int. Expert Systems Conference, Oxford, UK, 247-252.

Oliver, A.E.M. 1987. How to make rapid prototyping effective when developing expert systems. Proc. 3nd Int. Expert Systems Conference, Oxford, UK, 45-48.

Politakis, P.G. and S. Weiss. 1984. Using empirical analysis to refine expert system knowledge bases. Artificial Intelligence 22, 23-48.

Politakis, P.G. 1985. Empirical analysis of expert systems. Pittman, Boston, MA.

Schatz, H., R. Strahs, and L. Campbell. 1987. ExperTAX: The issue of long-term maintenance. Proc. 3rd Int. Expert Systems Conference, Oxford, UK, 291-299.

Shaw, M.L.G., J.M. Bradshaw, B.R. Gaines, and J.H. Boose. 1988. Rapid prototyping techniques for expert systems. Proc. 4th IEEE Conf. on Artificial Intelligence Applications, San Diego, CA, 34-39.

Stefik, M., J. Aikins, R. Balzer, J. Benoit, L. Birnbaum, F. Hayes-Roth, and E. Sacerdoti. 1982. The organization of expert systems: A tutorial. Artificial Intelligence 18, 135-173.

Vesoul, P. 1988. A specification and documentation approach to expert systems. Proc. 8th International Workshop Expert Systems & their Applications , Avignon, F, Vol. 1, 297-316. (in French)

D. Development tools

keywords: classification - evaluation - choice.

This section deals with the problems related to classification, evaluation, and choice of expert system building tools. It does not present detailed descriptions of specific tools nor experience with their use, but it focuses on general analysis and evaluation criteria. It also includes some surveys of commercial tools, organized according to different classification paradigms. The issue of selection of the most appropriate tool in front of a specific application is also addressed. Since literature in this area is very specific and limited, the section tends to present a rather exhaustive collection of the relevant materials.

Alty, J.L. 1989. Expert system building tools. In G. Guida and C. Tasso (Eds.), Topics in Expert System Design - Methodologies and Tools, North-Holland, Amsterdam, NL, 181-204.

Barstow, D.R., N. Aiello, R.O. Duda, L.D. Erman, C.L. Forgy, D. Gorlin, R.D. Grenier, D.B. Lenat, P.E. London, J. McDermott, H.P. Nii, P.G. Politakis, R. Reboh, S. Rosenschein, C. Scott, W. van Melle, and S.M. Weiss. 1983. Languages and tools for knowledge engineering. In D.A. Waterman, R. Hayes-Roth, and D. Lenat (Eds.), Building Expert Systems, Addison-Wesley, Reading, MA, 283-345.

Expert Systems Strategies. 1985. Overview of small expert systems-building tools. 1(1), 1-10.

Expert Systems Strategies. 1986. Expert systems-building tools. 2(8), 17-24.

Expert Systems Strategies. 1987. Currently available expert systems-building tools. 3(6), 11-18.

Expert Systems Strategies. 1988. Currently available expert systems-building tools. 4(7), 3-15.

Gevarter, W.B. 1987. The nature and evaluation of commercial expert system building tools. Computer 20(5), 24-41.

Grigoriou, M.M. and P.C.T. Willey. 1987. Multi-criteria method for selecting an expert system shell. Proc. 3th Int. Expert Systems Conference, London, UK, 277-289.

Harmon, P. and D. King. 1985. Expert Systems - Artificial Intelligence in Business. John Wiley & Sons, New York, NY. (Chapters 7 and 8)

Richer, M.H. 1986. An evaluation of expert system development tools. Expert Systems 3(3), 166-183.

Rothenberg, J. 1989. Expert system tool evaluation. In G. Guida and C. Tasso (Eds.), Topics in Expert System Design - Methodologies and Tools, North-Holland, Amsterdam, NL, 205-229.

van Koppen, J. 1986. A survey of expert system development tools. Proc. 2th Int. Expert Systems Conference, London, UK, 157-173.

Walker, T.C. and R.K. Miller. 1986. Expert systems 1986. SEAI Technical Publications, Madison, GA. (Chapter 3)

Waterman, D.A. 1986. A Guide to Expert Systems. Addison-Wesley, Reading, MA. (Chapters 8, 9, 10, 13, 27, 28, and 29)

Waterman, D.A. and F. Hayes-Roth. 1983. An investigation of tools for building expert systems. In F. Hayes-Roth, D.A. Waterman, and D.B. Lenat. (Eds.) Building Expert Systems. Addison-Wesley, Reading, 169-215.

E. Knowledge acquisition

keywords: knowledge elicitation and transfer of expertise - knowledge analysis and modeling - knowledge editing - knowledge acquisition tools.

This section focuses on a core and very important topic in the field of expert system development, namely: knowledge acquisition. This area spans over several topics, ranging from elicitation and transfer of expertise to knowledge modeling and editing. Themes more directly related to the construction and refinement of the knowledge base as a step of the development process are however beyond the scope of this section (they have been included in section C). Also the topics of automatic acquisition and synthesis of knowledge (such as rule induction, knowledge compilation, etc.) are not considered here since they are more directly related to the specific technical issue of machine learning. Since literature materials in this area are very numerous, in order to confine the growth of this section within reasonable limits, we have applied very strictly the selection criteria mentioned in the Introduction. Therefore, we have preferred broad spectrum, introductory materials and we have discarded several publications which, although relevant to this area and of very good quality, have been considered too specific.

Abrett, G. and M.H. Burstein. 1987. The KREME knowledge editing environment. Int. Journal of Man-Machine Studies 27(2), 103-127.

Anjewierden, A. 1987. Knowledge acquisition tools. AI Communications 0(1), 29-38.

Bennett, J.S. 1985. ROGET: A knowledge-based system for acquiring the conceptual structure of a diagnostic expert system. Journal of Automated Reasoning 1, 49-74.

Boose, J.H. 1985. A knowledge acquisition program for expert systems based on personal construct psychology. Int. Journal of Man-Machine Studies 23, 495-525.

Boose, J.H. 1986. Expertise Transfer for Expert System Design. Elsevier, New York, NY.

Boose, J.H. and J.M. Bradshaw. 1987. Expertise transfer and complex problems: Using AQUINAS as a knowledge-acquisition workbench for knowledge-based systems. Int. Journal of Man-Machine Studies 26(1), 3-28.

Boose, J. and B. Gaines (Eds.). 1987. Special Issue: Knowledge Acquisition for Knowledge-based Systems. Int. Journal of Man-Machine Studies, Part 1: 26(1), Part 2: 26(2), Part 3: 26(4), Part 4: 27(2), Part 5: 27(3).

Breuker, J. and B.Wielinga. 1987. Use of models in the interpretation of verbal data. In A.L. Kidd (Ed.), Knowledge Acquisition for Expert Systems. A Practical Handbook, Plenum Press, New York, NY, 17-44.

Breuker, J.A. and B.J. Wielinga. 1989. Models of expertise in knowledge acquisition. In G. Guida and C. Tasso (Eds.), Topics in Expert System Design - Methodologies and Tools, North-Holland, Amsterdam, NL, 265-295.

d'Agapeyeff, A. 1988. Practical elicitation for business applications. Proc. 8th International Workshop Expert Systems & their Applications, Avignon, F, Vol. 1, 625-642.

Davies, M. and S. Hakiel. 1988. Knowledge harvesting: A practical guide to interviewing. Expert Systems 5(1), 42-50.

Diederich, J., I. Ruhmann, and M. May. 1987. KRITON: A knowledge-acquisition tool for expert systems. Int. Journal of Man-Machine Studies 26(1), 29-40.

Diederich, J. and M. Linster. 1989. Knowledge-based knowledge elicitation. In G. Guida and C. Tasso (Eds.), Topics in Expert System Design - Methodologies and Tools, North-Holland, Amsterdam, NL, 323-350.

Dym, C.L. and S. Mittal. 1985. Knowledge acquisition from multiple experts. AI Magazine 7(2), 32-36.

Ericsson, K.A. and H.A. Simon. 1984. Protocol Analysis: Verbal Reports as Data. MIT Press, Cambridge, MA.

Eshelman, L., D. Ehret, J. McDermott, and M. Tan. 1987. MOLE: A tenacious knowledge-acquisition tool. Int. Journal of Man-Machine Studies 26(1), 41-54.

Gaines, B.R. 1987. An overview of knowledge-acquisition and transfer. Int. Journal of Man-Machine Studies 26(4), 453-472.

Gammack, J.G. and R.M. Young. 1985. Psychological techniques for eliciting expert knowledge. In M.A. Bramer (Ed.), Research and Development in Expert Systems, Cambridge University Press, Cambridge, UK, 105-112.

Gammack, J.G. 1987. Different techniques and different aspects on declarative knowledge. In A.L. Kidd (Ed.), Knowledge Acquisition for Expert Systems. A Practical Handbook, Plenum Press, New York, NY, 137-163.

Hoffman, R.R. 1987. The problem of extracting the knowledge of experts from the perspective of experimental psychology. AI Magazine 8(2), 53-67.

Johnson, L. and N.E. Johnson. 1987. Knowledge elicitation involving teachback interviewing. In A.L. Kidd (Ed.), Knowledge Acquisition for Expert Systems. A Practical Handbook, Plenum Press, New York, NY, 91-108.

Kahn, G.S., E.H. Breaux, P. De Klerk, and R.L. Joseph. 1987. A mixed-initiative workbench for knowledge acquisition. Int. Journal of Man-Machine Studies 27(2), 167-179.

Kahn, G., S. Nowlan, and J. McDermott. 1985. Strategies for knowledge acquisition. IEEE Trans. on Pattern Analysis and Machine Intelligence PAMI-7(5), 511-522.

Kidd, A.L. (Ed.). 1987. Knowledge Acquisition for Expert Systems. A Practical Handbook. Plenum, New York, NY.

Kidd, A.L. 19887. Knowledge acquisition - An introductory framework. In A.L. Kidd (Ed.), Knowledge Acquisition for Expert Systems. A Practical Handbook, Plenum Press, New York, NY, 1-16.

Krickhahn, R., R. Nobis, A. Maehlmann, and M.-J. Schachter-Radig. 1988. Applying the KADS methodology to develop a knowledge based system - Nethandler. ECAI 88 - Proc. of the 8th European Conference on Artificial Intelligence, Munich, FRG, 11-17.

Kitto, C.M. and J.H. Boose. 1987. Heuristics for expertise transfer: An implementation of a dialog manager for knowledge acquisition. Int. Journal of Man-Machine Studies 26(2), 183-202.

Klinker, G., J. Bentolila, S. Genetet, M. Grimes, and J. McDermott. 1987. KNACK - Report-driven knowledge acquisition. Int. Journal of Man-Machine Studies 26(1), 65-79.

Kuwaguchi, A., R. Mizoguchi, T. Yamaguchi, O. Kakusho. 1987. SIS: A shell for interview systems. Proc. 10th Int. Joint Conf. on Artificial Intelligence, Milan, I, 359-361.

Marcus, S. 1987. Taking backtracking with a grain of SALT. Int. Journal of Man-Machine Studies 26(4), 383-398.

Motta, E., T. Rajan, and M. Eisenstadt. 1989. A methodology and tool for knowledge acquisition in KEATS-2. In G. Guida and C. Tasso (Eds.), Topics in Expert System Design - Methodologies and Tools, North-Holland, Amsterdam, NL, 297-322.

Musen, M.A., L.A. Fagan, D.M. Combs, and E.H. Shortliffe. 1987. Use of a domain model to drive an interactive knowledge-editing tool. Int. Journal of Man-Machine Studies 26(1), 105-121.

Olson, J.S., H.H. Reuter. 1987. Extracting expertise from experts: Methods for knowledge acquisition. Expert Systems 4(3), 152-168.

Prerau, D.S. 1987. Knowledge acquisition in the development of a large expert system. AI Magazine 8(2), 43-51.

Roth, E.M. and D.D. Woods. 1989. Cognitive task analysis: an approach to knowledge acquisition for intelligent system design. In G. Guida and C. Tasso (Eds.), Topics in Expert System Design - Methodologies and Tools, North-Holland, Amsterdam, NL, 233-264.

Schreiber, G., J. Breuker, B. Bredeweg, and B.J. Wielinga. 1988. Modeling in KBS development. Proc. 8th International Workshop Expert Systems & their Applications, Avignon, F, Vol. 1, 283-296.

Shaw, M.L.G. and B.R. Gaines. 1987. An interactive knowledge-elicitation technique using personal construct technology. In A.L. Kidd (Ed.), Knowledge Acquisition for Expert Systems. A Practical Handbook, Plenum Press, New York, NY, 109-136.

Shaw, M.L. and B.R. Gaines. 1987. KITTEN: Knowledge initiation and transfer tools for experts and novices. Int. Journal of Man-Machine Studies 27(3), 251-280.

Waterman, D.A. and A. Newell. 1971. Protocol analysis as a task for artificial intelligence. Artificial Intelligence 2, 285-318.

Waterman, D.A. 1986. A Guide to Expert Systems. Addison-Wesley, Reading, MA. (Chapters 14 and 18)

Wright, G. and P. Ayton. 1987. Eliciting and modelling expert knowledge. Decision Support Systems 3(1), 13-26.

F. Validation and evaluation

keywords: knowledge base verification and validation - system performance evaluation - user acceptance - organizational and economic assessment.

This section deals with a topic of increasing interest in expert system technology, namely the validation and evaluation of expert system applications. This is a rather new area, but, nevertheless, it has been developing very fast in recent years and available materials are numerous.

Most of them are however only research proposals which still need assessment through experimental activity and professional practice. In this section literature items have been selected according to quite restrictive criteria, trying to discard both too specific works and too preliminary proposals.

Bachant, J. and J. McDermott. 1984. R1 Revisited: Four Years in the Trenches. AI Magazine 5(3), 21-32.

Chandrasekaran, B. 1983. On evaluating AI systems for medical diagnosis. AI Magazine 4(2), 34-37, 48.

Gaschnig, J., P. Klahr, P. Pople, H. Shortliffe and A. Terry. 1983. Evaluation of expert systems: Issues and case studies. In D.A. Waterman, R. Hayes-Roth, and D. Lenat (Eds.), Building Expert Systems, Addison-Wesley, Reading, MA, 241-280.

Geissman, J.R. and R.D. Schultz. 1988. Verification and validation of expert systems. AI Expert 3(2), 26-33.

Green, C.J.R. and M.M. Keyes. 1987. Verification and validation of expert systems. Proc. WESTEX-87 Conf. on Expert Systems, Anaheim, CA, 38-43.

Hollnagel, E. 1989. Evaluation of expert systems. In G. Guida and C. Tasso (Eds.), Topics in Expert System Design - Methodologies and Tools, North-Holland, Amsterdam, NL, 377-416.

St. Johanser, J.T. and R.M. Harbridge. 1986. Validating expert systems: Problems & solutions in practice. Knowledge Based Systems, Proc. of the Int. Conf., Online Publications, London, UK, 215-229.

Liebowitz, J. 1986. Useful approach for evaluating expert systems. Expert systems 3(2), 86-96.

Marcot, B. 1987. Testing your knowledge base. AI Expert 2(8), 42-47.

Nguyen, T.A., W.A. Perkins, T.J. Laffey, and D. Pecora. 1987. Knowledge base verification. AI Magazine 8(2), 69-75.

O'Keefe, R.M., O. Balci, and E.P. Smith. 1987. Validating expert system performance. IEEE Expert 2(4), 81-90.

Oliver, A.E.M. 1987. Techniques for expert system testing and validation. Proc. 3rd Int. Expert Systems Conf., London, UK, 271-276.

Perkins, W.A., T.J. Laffey, D. Pecora, and T.A. Nguyen. 1989. Knowledge base verification. In G. Guida and C. Tasso (Eds.), Topics in Expert System Design - Methodologies and Tools, North-Holland, Amsterdam, NL, 353-376.

Pipard, E. 1988. Detecting inconsistencies and incompleteness in rule-bases: The INDE system. Proc. 8th International Workshop Expert Systems & their Applications, Avignon, F, Vol. 3, 13-35. (in French)

Suwa, M., A.C. Scott, and E.H. Shortliffe. 1982. An approach to verifying completeness and consistency in a rule-based expert system. AI Magazine 3(4), 16-21.

Yu, V.L., L.M. Fagan, S.W. Bennett, W.J. Clancey, A.C. Scott, J.F. Hannigan, B.G. Buchanan, and S.N. Cohen. 1984. An evaluation of MYCIN's advice. In B.G. Buchanan and E.H. Shortliffe (Eds.), Rule-based expert systems: The MYCIN Experiments at the Stanford Heuristic Programming Project, Addison-Wesley, Reading, MA, 589-596.

G. Project management

keywords: project start-up - project planning - project monitoring - project team organization.

This section deals with the management of an expert system project. It focuses on specific aspects of project management related to the development of expert system applications such as how to start a new project, how to plan a project and to prepare a reasonable budget, how to control project advancements, how to organize the project team, etc. More classical topics related to project management in general are beyond the scope of this section. As literature in this area is very poor, all types of materials related (even indirectly) to this topic has been taken into account. Some references present case studies related to specific projects.

Clanon, J. 1985. Guide to knowledge engineer selection. Artificial Intelligence Guide Series, Intelligent Systems Technologies Group, Digital Equipment Corporation, Merrimack, NH.

Cook, S.B. and G.H. Warfel. 1984. Breaking the knowledge engineering logjam: The use of domain expertise in a structured team approach. Financial Industries Center Report, SRI International, Menlo Park, CA.

Coward, I. and L. Moore. 1987. Managing knowledge based system developments. Proc. Australian Computer Conf. Melbourne, Vic., Australia, 631-648.

Cupello, J.M. and D.J. Mishelevich. 1988. Managing prototype knowledge/expert system projects. Comm. of the ACM 31(5), 534-541.

Gray, M. 1988. Getting expert systems into use. Proc. 4th Int. Expert Systems Conference, London, UK, 123-128.

Kelly, B. 1988. Knowledge management: The organisational perspective. Proc. 4th Int. Expert Systems Conference, London, UK, 77-84.

Lange, R., L. Hearn, and F.W. Kearney. 1986. The use of knowledge engineering teams as a method for the development of expert systems. In D.Sriram, R. Adey (Eds.) Applications of Artificial

Intelligence in Engineering Problems, Springer-Verlag, Berlin, FRG, 45-53.

Mumford, E. 1988. Participative design for expert systems. Proc. 4th Int. Expert Systems Conference, London, UK, 1-7.

O'Farrell, P., J. Pingry. 1988. Expert system in manufacturing. Proc. 8th International Workshop Expert Systems & their Applications, Avignon, F, Vol. 1, 463-476.

Sargeant, R.A.E. and A. Jardine. 1987. Expert systems project management. Proc. Offshore Computer Conference, Aberdeen, UK, 1500-1520.

Waterman, D.A. 1986. A Guide to Expert Systems. Addison-Wesley, Reading, MA. (Chapters 16 and 17)

Wilkerson, W.S. 1985. Guide to expert systems program management. Artificial Intelligence Guide Series, Intelligent Systems Technologies Group, Digital Equipment Corporation, Merrimack, NH.

H. Technology transfer

keywords: management involvement - user familiarization - education and training - continuous education - research and development.

This section covers the important topic of technology transfer, which is typical of a young emerging field such as expert systems. However, although a large professional practice exists in this area, only little has been written about it. Literature is scarce and, therefore, this section has been compiled with rather comprehensive criteria.

Butler Cox Foundation. 1987. Expert systems in business. Research report 60, London, UK. (Chapter 5).

Kaplan, S.J. 1984. The industrialization of artificial intelligence: From by-line to bottom line. AI Magazine 5(2), 51-57.

Hazeltine, N. 1987. Knowledge systems technology transfer. Proc. Annual Artificial Intelligence and Advanced Computer Technology Conf., Long Beach, CA, USA, April 22-24, 271-272.

Hägglund, S. 1988. The Linköping approach to technology transfer in knowledge engineering. The Knowledge Engineering Review 2(3).

Marchand, H. 1986. On commercial expert systems projects. Future Generations Computer Systems 2(4), 213-216.

Polit, S. 1985. R1 and beyond: AI technology transfer at DEC. AI Magazine 5(4), 76-78.

Rauch-Hindin, W.R. 1986. Artificial Intelligence in Business, Science, and Industry - Vol. I: Fundamentals. Prentice-Hall, Englewood Cliffs, NJ. (Chapter 3)

Schutzer, D. 1987. Artificial intelligence and end user computing. Proc. Expert Systems in Business '87, New York, NY, 209-217.

Shri, K., D.S. Prerau, A.V. Lemmon, A.S. Gunderson, and R.E. Reinke. 1985. COMPASS: An expert system for telephone switch maintenance. Expert systems 2(3), 112-126.

Smith, R.G. 1984. On the development of commercial expert systems. AI Magazine 5(3), 61-73.

Taylor, E.C. 1985. Developing a knowledge engineering capability in the TRW Defense Systems Group. AI Magazine 6(2), 58-63.

LIST OF CONTRIBUTORS

Alty J.L.	The Turing Institute George House 36 North Hanover Street GLASGOW G1 2AD - United Kingdom
Baskin A.B.	Department of Computer Science University of Illinois 1304 West Springfield URBANA, IL 61801 - USA
Bauer M.	Carnegie Group Inc. 5 PPG Place PITTSBURGH, PA 15222 - USA
Bratko I.	Institut "Jozef Stefan" Jamova, 39 61111 LJUBLJANA - Yugoslavia
Breuker J.	Vakgroep Sociaal-Wetenschappelijke Informatica I.O. Universiteit van Amsterdam Herengracht, 196 1016 BS AMSTERDAM - The Netherlands
Diederich J.	International Computer Science Institute BERKLEY, CA 94720 - USA
Eisenstadt M.	Human Cognition Research Laboratory The Open University MILTON KEYNES MK7 6AA - United Kingdom
Guida G.	Dipartimento di Matematica e Informatica Università di Udine Via Zanon, 6 33100 UDINE - Italy
Hollnagel E.	Computer Resources International Bregnerødvej, 144 3460 BIRKERØD - Denmark
Kahn G.S.	Carnegie Group Inc. 5 PPG Place PITTSBURGH, PA 15222 - USA

Kulikowski C.A.
Department of Computer Science
Hill Center for the Mathematical Sciences
Rutgers University
Busch Campus
NEW BRUNSWICK, NJ 08903 - USA

Kunz J.C.
IntelliCorp
1975 El Camino Real West
MOUNTAIN VIEW, CA 94040 - USA

Laffey T.J.
Lockheed Artificial Intelligence Center
2710 Sand Hill Road
MENLO PARK, CA 94025 - USA

Linster M.
Gesellschaft für Mathematik und Datenverarbaitung mbH
Schloss Birlinghoven
Postfach 1240
5205 SANKT AUGUSTIN 1 - Federal Republic of Germany

Michalski R.S.
Department of Computer Sciences
George Mason University
FAIRFAX, VA 22030 - USA

Motta E.
Human Cognition Research Laboratory
The Open University
MILTON KEYNES MK7 6AA - United Kingdom

Nguyen T.A.
Lockheed Artificial Intelligence Center
2710 Sand Hill Road
MENLO PARK, CA 94025 - USA

Pecora D.
Lockheed Artificial Intelligence Center
2710 Sand Hill Road
MENLO PARK, CA 94025 - USA

Perkins W.A.
Lockheed Artificial Intelligence Center
2710 Sand Hill Road
MENLO PARK, CA 94025 - USA

Prerau D.S.
Computer and Intelligent Systems Laboratory
GTE Laboratories Inc.
40 Sylvan Road
WALTHAM, MA 02254 - USA

Rajan T.	Human Cognition Research Laboratory The Open University MILTON KEYNES MK7 6AA - United Kingdom
Rothenberg J.	The RAND Corporation 1700 Main Street SANTA MONICA, CA 90406 - USA
Roth E.M.	Department of Engineering and Public Policy Carnegie-Mellon University 5000 Forbes Avenue PITTSBURGH, PA 15213 - USA
Stelzner M.J.	IntelliCorp 1975 El Camino Real West MOUNTAIN VIEW, CA 94040 - USA
Tasso C.	Dipartimento di Matematica e Informatica Università di Udine Via Zanon, 6 33100 UDINE - Italy
Wielinga B.	Vakgroep Sociaal-Wetenschappelijke Informatica I.O. Universiteit van Amsterdam Herengracht, 196 1016 BS AMSTERDAM - The Netherlands
Williams M.D.	IntelliCorp 1975 El Camino Real West MOUNTAIN VIEW, CA 94040 - USA
Woods D.D.	Department of Industrial and Systems Engineering The Ohio State University 290 Baker Hall 1971 Neil Avenue COLUMBUS, OH 43210 - USA

AUTHOR INDEX